F. SCOTT FITZGERALD

F. SCOTT FITZGERALD

The Last Laocoön

ROBERT SKLAR

NEW YORK
OXFORD UNIVERSITY PRESS
1967

For my mother and father

CONTENTS

F. SCOTT FITZGERALD

CHAPTER ONE

Of important American novelists, F. Scott Fitzgerald was the last to grow up believing in the genteel romantic ideals that pervaded late nineteenth-century American culture. Santayana said of the brothers William and Henry James that one, the novelist, overcame the genteel tradition in the classic way, by understanding it, the other, the philosopher, overcame it in the romantic way, by continuing it into its opposite. Overcoming the genteel tradition was also, in Fitzgerald's case, the prerequisite for creating lasting art. The genteel tradition was a mode of order; by criticizing the genteel tradition, adapting it, and finally transforming its values, Fitzgerald more than any other American novelist of the present century attained in his fiction the power to create an alternative vision of order, an Apollonian vision of moral order and measured beauty.

In Virgil's *Aeneid*, Laocoön, a priest of Apollo, thrust his spear into the wooden horse to warn his Trojan countrymen against Greek treachery. The Trojans failed to heed him. Then two serpents at Athena's call came up from the sea and destroyed him with his sons. The English writer Malcolm Lowry, recognizing the Apollonian qualities of Fitzgerald's fiction, made the story of Laocoön into a metaphor for Fitzgerald's career. In his novella *Through the Panama*, playing on the title of Fitzgerald's unfinished final novel, he named Fitzgerald the Last Laocoön. "To my mind," said Lowry's character,

3

who had been reading *The Crack-Up*, "[Fitzgerald's] latter work represents essentially best qualities of chivalry and decency now too often lacking in the English themselves. This quality true essentially of soul of America. Can this be expressed without obsequiousness?" [1]

When *The Crack-Up* appeared in 1945, five years after Fitzgerald's death, many others read it with a similar feeling. Fitzgerald's fiction, set free from the frustrations and weaknesses of his life, rose in critical and public regard to rank with the work of the greatest and most exemplary American writers; with Cooper, Hawthorne, Melville, and James, whose fiction portrays, among whatever else, the bravest and strongest and most gracious values in the nation's life. But how can F. Scott Fitzgerald be so praised without obsequiousness? Few American writers have been as ruthlessly honest as he in documenting the record of his failures and ignominies. For a long time he was respected so little that few critics bothered to treat him with dignity; later, compensating for neglect, critics and biographers threw away critical standards in their efforts to be more than fair. Now his reputation is high, and almost all is known about his life and writing that can possibly be known. Yet his artistry has not been fully appreciated, the measure of his significance not yet taken.

The record of Fitzgerald's development seems to stand more open than most, for he used his own life as material for his fiction and wrote a number of revealing autobiographical essays as well. Nothing has encouraged distorted interpretations of Fitzgerald's life and art more than the temptation this full record affords to treat his art and life as if they could be interchanged. One capacity has still been withheld from Fitzgerald, the power, lacking which, no novelist's style and moral could ever find a lasting voice—the quality of critical and creative intelligence. In his effort to master the genteel tradition, Fitzgerald came to grips, both consciously and unconsciously, and in a sense more fully than any other novelist of his generation, with modern movements in Western culture and philosophy. Fitzgerald's novels cannot be taken, then, as if they comprised a multi-volume autobiography; and his autobiographical essays, properly understood in relation to his career, must be regarded not as source material but as further aspects of his artistry. To reconstruct the development of Fitzgerald's intelligence is the way to confront, most completely, the meaning and the achievement of his autonomous, created works of art.

As a youth Fitzgerald had already begun to think of himself as an artist. His first opportunity to display his talents came in theatricals. In St. Paul, Minnesota, where he was born in 1896, and where his parents settled permanently when he was eleven, he organized the ceremonies of his boyhood club. He excelled in playlets and debating at the St. Paul Academy, and developed into a versatile playwright, director, and actor for the Elizabethan Dramatic Club; in his teenage years he wrote and produced five plays for the club, the last after his freshman year at Princeton. "I imagined he would become an actor of the variety type," his prep school English teacher later recalled.[2] Thomas Mann's Tonio Kröger discovered in his youth that the creative temperament must be forever severed from the active temperaments of his peers. But Fitzgerald's dramatic imagination led him as a youth more fully than ever into active life. For in his own person he was acting out the role of the genteel tradition's romantic hero.

The romantic aspect of the genteel tradition in America was only one of its many facets, and was largely confined to its popular literature. In nearly all of its aspects the genteel tradition was a conservative force against change; and its spokesmen, knowing precisely what they wished to preserve, were usually more hortatory than descriptive. The ethical standards of genteel heroism are described by James Thompson Bixby in *The Crisis in Morals,* published in 1890; but for a rounded picture of the genteel hero one must turn to fiction.[3]

Tom Sawyer is the archetype in literature for this hero, in all respects but one: he is too much a boy to portray a young lover. Americans today have so far abandoned the ideal he represented that readers can hardly be patient with Tom's antics in *Huckleberry Finn.* The romantic hero of the genteel tradition was a young man who knew his English classics well and would nobly sacrifice himself for womanhood or honor. The infinite possibilities of life were open, in theory, to his will; but if he sometimes opposed his will, in practice, to the dictates of social order, he never questioned their essential justness. More likely his will moved only in harness with his romantic imagination. The true foundation for his heroism lay in his ability to devise fanciful ways to reach the goals others drove toward more prosaically. He would be his own man; but only playfulness should prove it. Imagination could build a setting where one might exercise his independent will, give pleasure to other imaginations, and attract the admiration of the timid and the disapproval of the dull—yet never run the risk of stepping beyond social convention. When the clever games were over, the romantic hero won the girl, the money, and the social prestige, because his entertainment invariably led to the victory of true over false morality. This was his rite of passage to maturity. Thereafter his prestige and social position guaranteed him unobstructed use of his will, for his status both recognized and insured his sense of social responsibility. In later life imagination would serve to honor women with romantic dreams of love.

Readers who want to see the genteel hero as a mature man will find a classic portrait in Robert Acton of Henry James's *The Europeans,* which appeared only two years after *Tom Sawyer.* But James was a subtle critic of genteel ideals, and Acton is a rigid, weak, loveless, and slightly comic figure. It is difficult to see how an uncritical portrait of the genteel hero could be possible in a serious work of fiction; and that makes it even more important to recognize how deeply the heroes of Fitzgerald's mature novels—Jay Gatsby of *The Great Gatsby,* Dick Diver of *Tender Is the Night,* and Monroe Stahr of *The Last Tycoon*—have the roots of their characters implanted in the nature of the genteel hero, the creator of romantic dreams.

The romantic hero of genteel literature was linked to Fitzgerald's youthful writing by the novels and stories of Booth Tarkington. Tarkington was the only American writer in whom Fitzgerald took any sustained interest during his college years, and thus he established the first connection for Fitzgerald with an American literary tradition. Moreover, his own career may have formed the model for Fitzgerald's earliest literary aspirations. By the time Fitzgerald was a schoolboy Tarkington had published almost a dozen novels and had begun a successful career as a Broadway playwright. In 1913, Fitzgerald's last year in preparatory school, Tarkington was the only well-known American writer who had gone to Princeton; of other Princeton graduates, David Graham Phillips was recently dead and Ernest Poole had not yet become prominent, and their fiction was

6

not so congenial to Fitzgerald's youthful interests as was Tarkington's. As a member of the Princeton class of 1893 Tarkington had edited the literary and humor magazines, sung in the glee club, orated, and written and acted in dramatics. He told the author of a promotional biography—published in 1914 during Fitzgerald's freshman year at Princeton, and later included in the Grosset and Dunlap reprint edition of *Penrod*—that Princeton gave him "Some happy years and recollections—an uninterrupted affection for and interest in classmates and friends. Princeton becomes part of the life of her sons. Also I have no doubt that I imbibed some education there. Though it seems to me that I *tried* to avoid *that* as much as possible." [4] The words might equally describe Fitzgerald's undergraduate career.

Tarkington earned a permanent place in Princeton history by founding the Triangle Club, the university's touring musical comedy organization, and writing its first production. Twenty years later, in Fitzgerald's youth, Triangle presented its annual show at Christmastime in a dozen Eastern and Midwestern cities. Over the years it has started a number of Princeton men toward stage and motion picture careers. With his youthful interest in writing for the theater Fitzgerald was drawn to Princeton—whatever more romantic reasons he occasionally gave—primarily by the Triangle Club. "Near the end of my last year at school," he wrote in 1920 in an autobiographical essay for *The Saturday Evening Post,* "I came across a new musical-comedy score lying on top of the piano. It was a show called His Honor the Sultan, and the title page furnished the information that it had been presented by the Triangle Club of Princeton University. That was enough for me. From then on the university question was settled. I was bound for Princeton." [5] Of Fitzgerald's Triangle experience Christian Gauss was later to write, "Some of the incidents of that Triangle trip of 1915-16 make even the Golden Nineties pale their ineffectual fires. The *Princetonian,* reviewing the trip on January 7, 1916, reports that 'At the Chicago performance of "The Evil Eye" three hundred young ladies occupied the front rows of the house and following the show, gave the Princeton locomotive and tossed their bouquets at the cast and chorus.' This is the very ecstasy of admiration. I am not sure whether Bunny [Edmund Wilson] was present at this performance. I am quite certain Scott Fitzgerald was.

It is not forcing the probabilities to assume that when under this hail of corsages he heard that Princeton locomotive issue from debutante throats his prophetic soul foresaw that age of the flapper whose chronicler he was to become." [6]

From his own Triangle Club experience, in the Golden Nineties that were to pale before the ardor of Fitzgerald's generation, Tarkington had gone on to become one of the most popular chroniclers of the age of the genteel romantic hero. In Penrod Schofield he created the most famous twentieth-century version of these boy heroes. Fitzgerald was so interested in the genre he wrote his first review—printed in the *Nassau Literary Magazine* for January 1917— on a book of stories in the Penrod series. If Penrod was not modeled directly on the figure of Tom Sawyer, certainly he was intended to be a successor to Tom's romantic style. In "an appreciation" written for a new edition of *Tom Sawyer,* Tarkington gave Mark Twain credit for writing the "first story of a boy in which the hero was recognized *as a boy* throughout the whole narrative." [7]

Tarkington in the Penrod series succeeds as an entertainer of children, but as a novelist he cannot sustain the interest of adult readers as does Twain. His style in the Penrod books is sentimental and literary. He assumes a tone of detached superiority, but his self-amusement lacks the compassion Twain could show for his characters. And Tarkington's stories contain none of the implicit social criticism in *Tom Sawyer* which Twain developed and made the foundation for the tone and structure of *Huckleberry Finn.* What Tarkington achieved in the Penrod stories was an honesty that enabled him to portray pre-adolescent genteel manners in a comic and sympathetic way. Fitzgerald praised this in his review of *Penrod and Sam* when he wrote, "Mr. Tarkington has done what so many authors of juvenile books fail to do: he has admitted the unequalled snobbishness of boyhood and has traced the neighborhood social system which, with Penrod and Sam at the top, makes possible more than half the stories." [8] Fitzgerald expressed even greater admiration for Tarkington's *Seventeen* when it appeared during his junior year in college. He listed it with *The Varmint* by Owen Johnson and *Youth's Encounter* by Compton Mackenzie as one of the finest novels of youth of the period. And it is in *Seventeen,* where the romantic hero has passed the age of puberty, that the problems of the genteel formula emerge most clearly.

William Sylvanus Baxter, the young man of *Seventeen,* aspires to be a romantic hero, but fate and an uncomprehending family seem to conspire eternally against him. At their hands he suffers a series of embarrassing indignities that he knows must make him look like a fool in the eyes of Miss Lola Pratt, the baby-talking visitor with whom William has fallen in love, along with all the other boys in town. William Baxter is presented to the reader rather as a victim than as a hero, and Tarkington takes pains early in the book to editorialize about the cause: "For in the elder teens adolescence may be completed, but not by experience, and these years know their own tragedies. It is the time of life when one finds it unendurable not to seem perfect in all outward matters: in worldly position, in the equipments of wealth, in family, and in the grace, elegance, and dignity of all appearances in public. And yet the youth is continually betrayed by the child still intermittently insistent within him, and by the child which undiplomatic people too often assume him to be ... what injured his sensibilities was the disposition on the part of people—especially his parents, and frequently his aunts and uncles— to regard him as a little boy." [9] This is the kind of injustice, of course, which causes boys like Tom Sawyer and Penrod to begin their careers of willful imaginative revolt, leading eventually to re-acceptance and reward. But William Baxter possesses neither will nor imagination; his little sister Jane, who is Tom Sawyer and Penrod's age, possesses all the imagination and willfulness in the Baxter family, and William is the helpless sport of his social environment. This turnabout of expectations creates the basic comic situation of the novel. But it also points to a deeper problem genteel writers faced when their young heroes were ready to leap into manhood. William thinks he loves Miss Lola Pratt, and he thinks he wants to marry her. Yet marriage to William is nothing more than an inexpressibly vague state of bliss, and the only desire William feels for Miss Lola Pratt is to be in her presence or dance with her—he doesn't even dream about a kiss.

This lack of candor about youthful desires came under attack from the critics in the different literary atmosphere of the 1920's, though with readers *Seventeen* remained as popular as ever. The columnist

9

Heywood Broun accused Tarkington of ignoring the torment of sexual awakening, and Tarkington answered: "I don't see it. I never knew a youth who had that sense of torment under the circumstances depicted in 'Seventeen.' William didn't recognize anything." [10] With his acute awareness of social mores, Fitzgerald was later to set the date for the beginning of "petting" among young people in 1915, the very year *Seventeen* was appearing serially in a magazine; but he added, "petting in its more audacious manifestations was confined to the wealthier classes—among other young people the old standards prevailed until after the war." [11] Tarkington thus may have been telling the truth about the small-town boy. But if he had justification in social fact for depriving William of sexual consciousness, he had also to deprive William of will and imagination for connected reasons of literary taste. "We are not necessarily ignorant of what we ignore in art," he was later to say in his reply to Broun.[12] Both Tarkington and his readers, one must assume, were aware in 1915 that no young man of seventeen, who possessed will and imagination, could be so ignorant of sex. If for reasons of taste and sentiment Tarkington felt it necessary to deprive William of a particular awareness, he had also to deprive him of particular capacities. William then is a failure as a romantic hero. Much of the comedy derives from the unstated absence of those qualities which could make him a success—and we laugh at William, not with the sympathy and support which underlies our laughter at Penrod, but because he is weak and foolish. Unlike *Penrod*, *Seventeen* is a situation comedy in which character plays no role at all. So long as genteel restrictions prohibited the honesty that Tarkington displayed in *Penrod*, the genteel romantic hero could not be portrayed as a young man between the years of pre-adolescence and worldly maturity. It was the smashing of these restrictions in the aftermath of the First World War—to look ahead for a moment—that enabled young novelists like Fitzgerald to write about romantic youth and thus prolong momentarily the life of the genteel romantic hero.

Fitzgerald also drew in his youth on the intellectual tradition arising out of his Roman Catholic religion. From a present-day perspective one might assume that Roman Catholicism and the genteel American tradition stood in polar hostility to each other, re-enacting the old opposition between "Romanism" and nativist Protestantism that dated back in America to colonial times. But the culture of the genteel tradition had begun to flourish only after strict Calvinist constraints had fallen away. By the end of the nineteenth century genteel American Protestants were struggling to build a culture which Roman Catholic intellectuals attained almost by birthright. In genteel eyes the Catholic intellectual culture lived in unself-conscious familiarity with the great art and literature of the past. It conducted its daily observances with ritual and beauty, and seemed to possess a natural sense of social decorum and order and ease. Unoppressed by the passage of time, it lived happily with a feeling for continuity and tradition. The young Catholic like Fitzgerald, whose secular ambitions were directed into the dominant Protestant social life, might find that his intellectual background fitted him as well as any to express the aspirations of genteel American culture.

Fitzgerald's first significant encounter with Catholic intellectual tradition came at a time when he was already beginning to feel that his Church stood in the way of his literary aspirations. For the last two years before entering Princeton he attended the Newman School, a Catholic preparatory school near Hackensack, New Jersey. There he became friends with Father Sigourney Webster Fay, a wealthy convert to Catholicism who introduced Fitzgerald to the sophisticated social and intellectual life of upper-class Eastern Catholics. Fay in turn brought Fitzgerald together with Shane Leslie, a visiting young Catholic writer from England, a member of the Irish landholding aristocracy who was only a few years out of Eton and King's College, Cambridge. In their conversations Leslie made Fitzgerald familiar with the obscure English Catholic writers whose names crop up in Fitzgerald's early letters and reviews. From his later recollections it is apparent that Leslie, with all the confidence of his own youth and success and social standing, found the schoolboy Fitzgerald callow and ignorant, and humored his literary ambitions in the spirit of a lark. "The Monsignor and perhaps myself had induced Fitzgerald to believe he was the future Catholic novelist for the United States, a parallel to Mgr. Hugh Benson in this country," Leslie wrote in *The Times Literary Supplement*. "We encouraged him to believe that he would write the unwritten great Catholic novel . . . of the United States." [13] Robert Hugh Benson was the son of the Archbishop of Canterbury, a convert to Catholicism who entered the priesthood, whom Leslie had known at King's. Of Benson's novels George N. Shuster wrote in *The Catholic Spirit in Modern English Literature,* "His work...was prompted by peculiar and special interests which may be summed up here as curiosity in the borderlands of life and an appetite for magnificence.... [A] ghost could have aroused him at any moment. The details of an apparition left him in a state of eager excitement.... Philosophically, Benson was an egoist who did not consider sufficiently, perhaps, the nature and value of environment." [14] In writers like Benson, Fitzgerald no doubt found his precedent for the episode of the Devil that has so bothered later readers of *This Side of Paradise;* there was an even more elaborate ghost scene in the unpublished early manuscript, based on a story Fitzgerald heard from Father Fay. The romantic egoist of English Catholic literature cut, so it seems, a slightly more independent figure than his cousin, the romantic hero of genteel American fiction.

In later life Fitzgerald never fulfilled the ambition which Father Fay and Leslie had harbored for him. During his college years his adherence to his faith was apparently already wavering. Later he was, nominally at least, to leave the Church, and after his death his body was refused burial in a Catholic cemetery. The Catholic intellectual background he absorbed from Father Fay and Leslie rarely shows up explicitly in his fiction. But when he was closest to Father Fay, Fitzgerald did write one story on a Catholic theme—"The Ordeal," his first printed undergraduate fiction. It is not the most interesting of his college stories, but in many ways it is the most polished. "The Ordeal" is set at a seminary in Maryland, where Fitzgerald had once visited a distant relative who was entering the Jesuit order. The young man in Fitzgerald's story is about to take his vows and enter his novitiate. He has already overcome his desire for success in the world, his family's objections—"They told him he was ruining a promising young life because of a sentimental notion of self-sacrifice, a boyish dream"—overcome even his desire for a selfhood outside his faith. He knew "his individuality, his physical ego would be effaced." Still, as he stands alone in the late afternoon sunshine, memories and doubts assail him. He recalls a girl. "Then as in a crystal he seemed to hear Huxley, Nietzsche, Zola, Kant cry, 'I will not'—he saw Voltaire and Shaw wild with cold passion. The voices pleaded 'why?' and the girl's sad eyes gazed at him with infinite longing." Without difficulty he turns back this improbable combination of anti-Christs and enters the chapel. There a far more dangerous power confronts him. His eye is drawn to a burning candle. "He realized only that the forces around him were of hell and . . . the single candle contained the essence of evil. He felt himself alone pitted against an infinity of temptation. . . . He must look at the candle and look and look until the power that filled it and forced him into this plane died forever for him." He pits his faith against the evil power in the flame. "Then suddenly he became aware of a new presence. . . . It was the stained window of St. Francis Xavier. He gripped at it spiritually, clung to it and with aching heart called silently for God." [15] The service ends, the flame goes out, he takes his vows.

Like all of Fitzgerald's college fiction, "The Ordeal" is no more than a good undergraduate story, of little interest except that its author was to become a novelist of importance; it demonstrates a youthful capacity to create a dramatic and evocative prose style accompanied by a corresponding crudity in the effects and feelings evoked. "The Ordeal" is unusual in that its supernatural element is well controlled by the symbols created in natural description and action. The emphasis on the afternoon sun and its effects on the seminary in the opening sentences leads through the young man's first response to the light within the chapel to the moment when the stained glass window, illuminated by the afternoon sun, seems to body forth his faith. Moreover, the movement of the young man's spiritual crisis in step with the outward forms of the service heightens the symbolic expiration of the flame, for the candle must go out at the proper moment in the ceremony. The quality of symbolism is undercut by the inability of Fitzgerald at this point to create a fictional conception, except in vague or crudely theological terms, of the evil which mystically lives in the flame. When he rewrote this story four years later after his first novel had been accepted—it was printed as "Benediction" in *The Smart Set* and included in Fitzgerald's first book of stories, *Flappers and Philosophers*—the theological implications of the symbolism were to lead a young girl, sister of a novice, almost to hold back from entering a love affair; but not quite.

Yet there were other aspects of Leslie's Anglo-Irish point of view which Fitzgerald responded to deeply, and absorbed into his own intellectual outlook. In 1916 and 1917, before the United States entered the war, Leslie brought out for American readers two books on English culture, *The End of a Chapter* and *The Celt and the World*. But they hardly resemble the patriotic appeals from the mother civilization to her infant that crossed the Atlantic in those months. Leslie's tone was surprisingly dispassionate. His Catholicism and his Irish ancestry enabled him to detach himself from blindly uncritical loyalty to the English cause. No matter how strong his love and admiration for English life, his world-historical attitude forced him to view the crisis in a philosophical and, on the whole, pessimistic way. He distinguished between two major races in Aryan civilization, the Celt and the Teuton, the one mystical in nature, the other material. And he viewed the world war as a struggle between two Teutonic nations, with the Celts—primarily the Irish—tragically divided and yet drawn into a conflict in which they could expect only further loss. From the point of view of Irish faith and Irish dignity, first England, then Europe, were judged and found wanting. And if Europe and England do not avail, where is civilization to turn? The last chapter of the second book ends with a veiled prophecy: "It will be a long time before the West and the East, the Republic of the Stars and the Empire of the Rising Sun meet in conflict over the bones of the old Kings of the Sea." [16]

The Celt and the World brought out Fitzgerald's Irish self-consciousness. Reviewing the book for the *Nassau Lit,* he wholeheartedly took up Leslie's Celtic point of view. "To an Irishman the whole book is fascinating," he wrote, and he called the book a "bible of Irish Patriotism." [17] For a time thereafter he signed off his letters to Edmund Wilson "Celtically" and "Gaelically yours"; and in a letter of June 10, 1917, to his cousin Mrs. Richard Taylor he brought his hopes and his adopted attitudes strikingly together:

> Had I met Shane Leslie when I last saw you? Well, I've seen a lot more of him—He's an author and a perfect knockout—On the whole I'm having a fairly good time—but it looks as if the youth of me and my generation ends some time during the present year, rather summarily —If we ever get back, and I don't particularly care, we'll be rather aged—in the worst way. After all, life hasn't much to offer except

youth and I suppose for older people the love of youth in others. I agree perfectly with Rupert Brooke's men of Grantchester

"Who when they get to feeling old
They up and shoot themselves I'm told."

Every man I've met who's been to war—that is, this war, seems to have lost youth and faith in man unless they're wine-bibbers of patriotism which, of course, I think is the biggest rot in the world.

Updike of Oxford or Harvard says "I die for England" or "I die for America"—not me. I'm too Irish for that—I may get killed for America —but I'm going to die for myself. . . .

Do read *The End of a Chapter* and *The Celt and the World* by Shane Leslie—you'd enjoy them both immensely.[18]

In his review Fitzgerald quoted from memory—and thus slightly misquoted—a phrase from Leslie's preface to *The End of a Chapter:* "I had witnessed the suicide of the civilization called Christian and the travail of a new era to which no gods have been as yet rash enough to give their name." [19] Leslie's books were the earliest sources for the historical perspectives, and a persistent philosophical pessimism, which form an important, and neglected, aspect of Fitzgerald's artistry.

How little Fitzgerald took from the academic side of his Princeton years is well known. What Princeton provided for Fitzgerald's intellect is more difficult to say, and leads in turn to an even more problematic question, that of what one should expect from the encounter between a modern university and a young man of creative talent. Fitzgerald has always been one of the chief targets of those critics who have found the generation of the twenties wanting in the capacity to handle general ideas. "It is in this department of fiction," Irving Howe wrote in his study on Faulkner, ". . . that so many gifted American novelists conspicuously fail, particularly those 'natural talents' of Faulkner's generation who are unstained by the imprint of literary tradition or training." [20] But the young writer at Princeton fifty years ago could have had nothing imprinted on his intellect from his studies in the humanities—particularly his studies in English literature—if not formal literary tradition and training. The issue is more complex than one of simply acquiring a literary tradition. Tradition is valuable when it deepens the writer's historical and philosophical perspective on his style and his aims and his contemporary situation. The young men of Princeton before the First World War were burdened with a formal literary tradition which was absolutely hostile to the living arts and culture of their day. The English Department set up its barricades against the present on a line running —on its most exposed front—from *A Tale of Two Cities* through *Silas Marner* and Robert Browning's poetry to the criticism of Matthew Arnold. For them the choice truly lay between their culture, in Arnold's phrase, and anarchy. Christian Gauss made a daring choice in 1914 when he gave the last lecture in his French romanticism course on Anatole France, who had celebrated his seventieth birthday that year, and thus may have qualified because he was past his allotted three-score-and-ten. Moreover, Gauss lectured to his students on a literary movement he defined as "a movement to obtain freedom from tradition and conventions which were beginning to be felt as constraining, a movement toward freedom for modern artists to choose their own subjects and to treat them in their own way." [21] Young writers at Princeton found no such impetus to freedom in the English curriculum. "Princeton is stupid...," Fitzgerald wrote to Edmund Wilson in the fall of 1917, just before he left to take up a commission in the Army. "I'm rather bored here but I see Shane Leslie occasionally and read Wells and Rousseau." [22] One cannot condemn Fitzgerald out of hand for turning his back on the classroom and learning what he could of contemporary literature on his own and in company with other undergraduate writers.

Outside the lecture hall Princeton did confront Fitzgerald and his fellow writers with living traditions—with the eating clubs, with athletics, with wealth and cultivation and power in the old aristocratic names among their friends, with the values and habits of Princeton's old Presbyterian small-college past as it moved into the twentieth century. In *This Side of Paradise* Fitzgerald tried to convey in lyric prose the emotions evoked out of the beauty of the Princeton campus and the customs and tenor of college life. Later he and Wilson and John Peale Bishop, the three writers who went through Princeton together, each gave in essays his memories and interpretations of university life. The atmosphere of Princeton obviously worked itself deeply into Fitzgerald's intellectual outlook, but no one can say objectively what effect it was eventually to have upon his art; each time he drew on it for his fiction, or in his essays, he was to re-create it and shape it for his own immediate artistic purposes. After both Bishop and Fitzgerald were dead, Wilson, in a letter to Christian Gauss, made the most penetrating attempt to judge the significance of their Princeton experience for their later careers as writers; it is also the least known. When Gauss published in 1944 his memoir of Wilson's undergraduate days, Wilson wrote to him:

> I have been thinking about the whole group and I believe that, in certain ways, Princeton did not serve them very well. I said this to Mary [McCarthy, then Wilson's wife], who has had considerable opportunity to observe the men from the various colleges, and she said: "Yes, Princeton didn't give them quite moral principle enough to be writers." Instead, it gave us too much respect for money and country house social prestige. Both Scott and John in their respective ways, I think, fell victims to this.—I don't want to be pharisaical about them: I was more fortunate than either of them, not in gifts, but in the opportunity to survive, because I had enough money for study and travel in the years when those things are most valuable, but not so much that . . . I didn't have to think about earning some.—One's only consolation is that Princeton did give us other things that were good—a sort of eighteenth-century humanism that probably itself was not unconnected with the rich-patron relationship of the University to somebody like M. T. Pyne. And then, if we had gone to Yale, though we should probably all have survived in the flesh, we might never have survived in whatever it is that inspires people not to take too seriously the ideal of the successful man.[23]

Fitzgerald's indifference, as an undergraduate, to success in the classroom led directly to his failure to realize his theatrical ambitions at Princeton, and brought about the first major shift in the movement of his artistic career. Though he wrote the lyrics for three consecutive Triangle shows, he was declared ineligible, because of low grades, to participate in any of them. In the fall of his junior year he fell ill, quite possibly because he overworked himself in Triangle rehearsals, and subsequently was asked to leave college for the remainder of the year. When he returned in the following September the prestige and the power of the Triangle presidency, which he had expected to gain, were closed off to him; though he still worked hard for Triangle, he was ready to give most of his time to literature. He

17

had already contributed two stories and a poem to the *Nassau Lit* and a great deal of humor and light verse to *The Tiger.* Over the next two years he was to publish six stories and more than a dozen poems, sketches, and reviews in the literary magazine. At the same time he began to read fiction and poetry in a consciously literary context, for discussion with other writers and as impetus and example toward composition.

Too many students of Fitzgerald have taken for granted that the quality of this reading was poor, that it directed Fitzgerald's interests toward inferior or dying movements in the arts, delaying and ultimately stunting his full development as a modern artist. They have seized on Wilson's youthful admonition to Fitzgerald—"do read something other than contemporary British novelists" [24]—and his later recollection, "I remember Scott Fitzgerald's saying to me, not long after we had got out of college: 'I want to be one of the greatest writers who have ever lived, don't you?' I had not myself really quite entertained this fantasy because I had been reading Plato and Dante. Scott had been reading Booth Tarkington, Compton Mackenzie, H. G. Wells and Swinburne. . . ." [25] It is difficult to re-establish the consciousness of young writers before the First World War, groping to discover what was original and innovating in modern literature in an atmosphere of confusion and hostility; not everyone was as brilliant as T. S. Eliot at Harvard, or as fortunate in coming upon Jules Laforgue. Wilson himself, in his letter of 1944 to Christian Gauss, recalled his undergraduate days in a somewhat different way: "Shaw and Wells had been my gods at boarding school and I was still very much under their influence. Don't you remember those Shawesque articles that I used to write about campus problems? I considered myself a social reformer. *Fabian Essays,* which I read at college, made a great impression on me. And, whatever I may have said at some point, I very much admired some of Masefield. . . ." [26] It was Wilson who reviewed Compton Mackenzie's *Sinister Street* for the *Nassau Lit.* Wilson's literary interests had developed at an earlier age than Fitzgerald's, but both young men went through the same process of literary development. The success of a writer in finding his own voice depended—in their generation as in the present generation—not so much on his ability to acquire literary tradition as in his capacity to shake it off.

There is no doubt that the novelist Fitzgerald most admired, as an undergraduate, was H. G. Wells. The novelist to whom Fitzgerald should rather have turned, it has been assumed, was Henry James. And the controversy over the nature of the novel that Wells and James engaged in between 1911 and 1915—part of it in *Boon*, one of Wells's books that Fitzgerald certainly did read—has come neatly to symbolize the wrong and the right road, respectively, for the modern novelist to take. But the restricted technical terms of the dispute which have been applied to Fitzgerald's development fail to do justice to his youthful interest in writing fiction. From the perspective of a young writer seeking an independent voice, James before the First World War must have appeared as a dubious model. He had created in the New York Edition his own forbidding monument, and then turned himself into an English country squire; for disciples he had acquired a coterie of lady novelists who proclaimed their exquisite sensibilities. Of James, Wells wrote in *Boon*, "he is eager to accept things—elaborately. You can see from his books that he accepts etiquettes, precedences, associations, claims." [27] However unfair this is to James, it differs little from the impression one might then have got independently—short of actually reading James.

To young persons Wells as a man and as a writer was a much more exciting figure. In 1915 he seemed the most original new voice of the age; from a historical point of view Fitzgerald's preference was intelligent and, in a way, inevitable. "Thinking people who were born about the beginning of this century are in some sense Wells's own creation," George Orwell once wrote. ". . . I doubt whether anyone who was writing books between 1900 and 1920, at any rate in the English language, influenced the young so much." [28] Through Wells, Fitzgerald first came into contact with those modern philosophers whose names he began to invoke in his letters—Schopenhauer, Bergson, William James. In addition Wells was an outsider, a breaker of pretensions, an individualist standing outside the establishment. "He abhors 'personages,' " Van Wyck Brooks wrote in 1915 in his *The World of H. G. Wells*—a book that indicates how important Wells was to the emerging new mood in American literature which Brooks among others was helping to form. "For the personage is one who, in some degree, stands on his achievement, and to Wells man, both in his love and in his work, is experimental: he is an experiment toward an impersonal synthesis, the well-being of the species. It is true that this idea of man as an experiment does not conflict with a very full development of personality. It consists in that; but personality to Wells is attained purely through love and work, and thus it comes to an end the moment it becomes static, the moment one accepts the laurel wreath, the moment one verges on self-consequence." [29] The idea of heroism that Fitzgerald encountered in Wells's fiction represented an absolute and inescapable challenge to the concept of the romantic hero in genteel American literature.

For about half a century the genteel tradition had dominated American literature. It had shaped and directed the movement toward realism in most of its phases, and the naturalists of the turn of the century—with the exception of Theodore Dreiser, whose first novel, *Sister Carrie,* was suppressed—had published under its wary surveillance. The two greatest novelists of the period, Mark Twain and Henry James, in their separate ways fought against the genteel tradition, yet each had suffered in his career because of its demands. But in the circumstances of the First World War, as the genteel romantic hero attained his apotheosis on the battlefield, the influence of the genteel tradition on American literature reached a climax, and died. Writers who experienced the war, writers who experienced the atmosphere at home, were faced more distinctly than ever before with the decision of whether to celebrate or to oppose the values of their society. As what they saw and what they knew came more sharply into conflict with accepted ideas, the choice grew more definitely into a simple yes or no, to write as a propagandist or to stand separate and alone as an artist. Fitzgerald's formative years as a writer of fiction overlapped with America's entry into the war, and it was inevitable that he should bear to some extent the burden of this conscious choice. It is from this point of view, the conflict between taking over genteel standards or challenging them, that Fitzgerald's stories in the *Nassau Lit* between January and October, 1917, become significant. Fitzgerald was as yet unable to abandon completely the conventions of the genteel tradition, though his experience and his adopted attitudes were drawing him away from them. In a way he compromised, and in compromising he created a new type of character in American literature—a character who brought together, in an imperfect and volatile balance, the old ideals and a new mode of behavior. The post-war age called her the flapper; in literature she may better be named the genteel romantic heroine. She is a young woman who dares to use her independent will for what she wants, and is not punished for it, either by depiction as an odious character or by the author's censure. The only model for her in American literature is Gertrude Wentworth in *The Europeans,* who triumphs over genteel repression in Henry James's satire on genteel values; but at that moment Fitzgerald no doubt had never heard of her.

Fitzgerald's genteel romantic heroine appears, still in her teens, in two *Nassau Lit* stories that Fitzgerald later extensively revised and used in *This Side of Paradise.* At sixteen she is Isabelle in "Babes in the Woods," out to win the heart, for the sake of her ego, of the attractive college boy on the last night of his holiday. When Isabelle's hostess says, "I guess he knows you've been kissed," Fitzgerald interpolates for Isabelle: "She wasn't quite old enough to be sorry nor nearly old enough to be glad." Her first kiss with him is frustrated, and she goes to bed muttering into her pillow, "Damn!" [30] A year or two older she is Helen Halycon in "The Debutante," who smokes and carries a silver flask and tells her mother, "You can't run everything now, the way they did in the early nineties"; and when her father joshingly asks her, "about to fit into the wide, wide world?" she replies: "No, daddy, just taking a more licensed view of it." To her dejected suitor, John Cannel, she says, "I like to run things, but it gets monotonous to always know that I am the key to the situation." [31] Far too much in love with her, Cannel—in the Tarkington manner—has lost his will, and his imagination has grown morbid; in him the genteel romantic hero has turned into a pathetic figure.

The genteel romantic heroine wants her man to be a hero, but in the very act of giving him her love she destroys his capacity for heroism. This is the serious dilemma posed as a theme in the two most ambitious stories in the *Nassau Lit* group, "Sentiment—and the Use of Rouge," and "The Pierian Springs and the Last Straw." In "The Pierian Springs . . ." George Rombert, uncle of the young narrator, is a scandalous author, "a Romeo . . . a combination of Byron, Don Juan, and Bernard Shaw, with a touch of Havelock Ellis for good measure. He was about thirty, had been engaged seven times and drank ever so much more than was good for him." With his fierce willfulness and his skill as an entertainer, he is an exemplar of the genteel romantic hero, unredeemed by society though he is entering dangerous middle age. He was drunk when the narrator encountered him, "but he was perfectly conscious of himself and the dulling of faculties was only perceivable in a very cautious walk and a crack in his voice that sank it occasionally to a hoarse whisper. He was talking to a table of men all in various stages of inebriation, and holding them by a most peculiar and magnetic series of gestures. Right here I want to remark that this influence was not dependent so much upon a vivid physical personality but on a series of perfectly artificial mental tricks, his gestures, the peculiar range of his speaking voice, the suddenness and terseness of his remarks." But within himself George Rombert is a bitter man. Years before his stupid behavior had cost him the love of his life, and he had gained his revenge ever since by writing novels about bad women and conducting affairs with debutantes. Then in a sudden gesture he takes the boy to meet his old sweetheart, now a widow. In her company he astonishes the narrator by acting like a "naughty boy to a stern aunt," and then, flaring into sudden anger and violence, he twists off her wedding ring and stamps on it, breaking her finger. The man and boy rush out, and the narrative ends.

Yet Fitzgerald cannot leave his genteel romantic hero, with his clever disruptive pen and his anti-social animus, as an outcast who may threaten social order. He continues: "The story ought to end here. My Uncle George should remain with Mark Anthony and De Musset as a rather tragic semi-genius, ruined by a woman. Unfortunately the play continues into an inartistic sixth act where it topples over and descends like Uncle George himself in one of his more inebriated states, contrary to all the rules of dramatic literature. One month afterward Uncle George and Mrs. Fulman eloped in the most childish and romantic manner the night before her marriage to the Honorable Howard Bixby was to have taken place. Uncle George never drank again, nor did he ever write or in fact do anything except play a middling amount of golf and get comfortably bored with his wife." The genteel romantic hero wins his woman and a firm social place; society has tamed him. But he did not write again, and this renders the story significant beyond its value as a portrayal of genteel romantic stereotypes. By making George Rombert a writer, Fitzgerald gave his genteel hero's passage from revolt to acceptance —so badly tacked on at the end— a deeper meaning, suggestive of the myth of Philoctetes that Edmund Wilson used later as the theme of his book of essays, *The Wound and the Bow*. The wound makes the writer; heal the wound, and the Pierian Springs—the reputed home of the Muses—dry up. Fitzgerald gave this story of the genteel romantic hero its standard ending, but he was capable by this point, both as an intellectual and as an artist, of treating it with irony. "You see"—this is his last line— "I claim that if Dante had ever won— but a hypothetical sixth act is just as untechnical as a real one." [32] As a writer, George Rombert wins the girl only to throw away the creative talent which gives him any claim to heroism in our eyes.

"Sentiment—and the Use of Rouge" is set in wartime England, and what it loses in authenticity it gains in candor. Clay Harrington Syneforth, a young aristocrat, comes back after two years away at the front and is deeply disturbed by the sudden turn to moral laxness he sees everywhere. "He found that he had come to picture England as a land of sorrow and asceticism and while there was little extravagance displayed tonight, he thought that the atmosphere had fallen to that of artificial gaiety rather than risen to a stern calmness . . . there was something in the very faces of the girls, something which was half enthusiasm and half recklessness, that depressed him more than any concrete thing." But when he criticized his sister's use of rouge on her face, his mother answered, "Really, Clay, you don't know exactly what the standards are, so you can't quite criticize." At a dance Clay meets Eleanor Marbrooke, the fiancé of his brother who was killed in the war. Clay is stiff and moral, and they talk.

Eleanor: "I believe you're a sentimentalist. Are you?"

Clay: "Tonight, I am—almost—for the first time in my life. Are you, Eleanor?"

Eleanor: "No, I'm romantic. There's a huge difference; a sentimental person thinks things will last, a romantic person hopes they won't."

Fitzgerald is re-defining for himself the vocabulary of the genteel tradition. Eleanor forces Clay to take her to his bachelor apartments. He talks of "compromising" her. "Compromise!" she exclaims. "What's that to words like Life and Love and Death and England. Compromise! I don't believe anyone uses that word except servants." He is helpless before her, and she seduces him. Why? "It's this—," she tells him, "self-sacrifice with a capital S. Young men going to get killed for us—We would have been their wives—we can't be—therefore we will be as much as we can." In the genteel American vocabulary self-sacrifice meant giving up life to preserve morality. Eleanor has turned it around to say, morality must be sacrificed to life—and perhaps to lust. "How about old ideas, and standards of women and that sort of thing?" Clay asks. "Sky-high, my dear," answers Eleanor, "dead and gone." He tries to salvage morality by saying that their act was Love, similar to Life and Death, but she cuts him off: "not that."

Clay returns to the front, and together with an Irish Sergeant O'Flaherty he is mortally wounded. O'Flaherty represents Fitzgerald's Celtic patriotism, and as he dies he tells Clay, "Blood on an Englishman always calls rouge to me mind. It's a game with him. The Irish take death damn serious. . . . I may get killed for me flag, but I'm goin' to die for meself." [33] He dies, and then Clay dies, sentimental about love and war, confused and helpless before sex and before death; in his last conscious moments Clay thinks of God as an old sports referee. Genteel sentimentality is the rouge that puts on reality a falsely pretty face. Fitzgerald is less ambiguous in his criticism of genteel ideals than in his treatment of morality on the home front; but if one may still accuse him of sentimentality toward his willfully immoral women, it was at least part of his effort to set himself free from false conventions. From his sensitivity to social change and his developing self-consciousness as a writer, he was discovering the weakness of genteel American ideals. One of his stories of this period, "Tarquin of Cheepside," in a way symbolizes the opportunities and the difficulties he faced through this new self-awareness. Tarquin violates a woman, runs and hides from his pursuers, then writes furiously through the night. What he writes is "The Rape of Lucrece." Tarquin is Shakespeare, and he proclaims in answer to the criticism of his protector, "I am responsible only to myself for what I do." [34] To break the confines of the genteel tradition, to be truly an artist in America of 1917, one had to accept the possibility of also becoming an immoral man.

There was still the problem of what form of literary art to concentrate upon, and how to get it published. In 1917 Fitzgerald gave over most of his writing energy to poetry. Three years later, as a successful first novelist and short-story writer, writing about himself for *The Saturday Evening Post,* he regarded that effort with humorous self-irony: "I had decided that poetry was the only thing worthwhile, so with my head ringing with the meters of Swinburne and the matters of Rupert Brooke I spent the spring doing sonnets, ballads, and rondels into the small hours. I had read somewhere that every great poet had written great poetry before he was twenty-one. I had only a year and, besides, war was impending. I must publish a book of startling verse before I was engulfed." [35] Shane Leslie may have encouraged him in this ambition. Leslie had been close to Rupert Brooke at Cambridge, and though he recalled a generation later that he had hoped Fitzgerald would be the American Robert Hugh Benson, back in 1918 he had also referred to Fitzgerald as an American Rupert Brooke.[36] Collegiate poets were bringing out books of verse in 1917, no doubt from the same ambition and uncertainty; Fitzgerald's classmate John Peale Bishop and Stephen Vincent Benét at Yale both published books of poetry in the fall. But they had had a comparatively long foreground as poets; Fitzgerald was just beginning and was by no means so dedicated to verse. In the summer of 1917 he spent a month with Bishop and wrote, as he told Edmund Wilson, "a terrific lot of poetry mostly under the Masefield-Brooke influence. . . . I sent twelve poems to magazines yesterday. If I get them all back I'm going to give up poetry and turn to prose." [37] One of the poems was accepted by the magazine *Poet Lore,* but the war cut off Fitzgerald's poetic career. He took up a commission in the Army in November 1917, and by Christmas he was writing to Leslie from Ft. Leavenworth, Kansas, "the reason I've abandoned my idea of a book of poems is that I've only about twenty poems and can't write any more in this atmosphere." [38] It was not a great loss. Very few of the images and none of the ideas in Fitzgerald's collegiate verse are worth remembering, and the impression is strong that Fitzgerald was more interested in quickly publishing a book than in writing poetry. For no sooner had he given up his hope for a book of poems than he was hard at work on a novel.

This is how, in 1920, he described the shift in his literary intentions:

By autumn I was in an infantry officers' training camp at Fort Leavenworth, with poetry in the discard and a brand-new ambition— I was writing an immortal novel. Every evening, concealing my pad behind Small Problems for Infantry, I wrote paragraph after paragraph on a somewhat edited history of me and my imagination. The outline of twenty-two chapters, four of them in verse, was made, two chapters were completed; and then I was detected and the game was up. I could write no more during study period.

This was a distinct complication. I had only three months to live— in those days all infantry officers thought they had only three months to live—and I had left no mark on the world. But such consuming ambition was not to be thwarted by a mere war. Every Saturday at one o'clock when the week's work was over I hurried to the Officers' Club, and there, in a corner of a roomful of smoke, conversation and rattling newspapers, I wrote a one-hundred-and-twenty-thousand-word novel on the consecutive week-ends of three months. There was no revising; there was no time for it. As I finished each chapter I sent it to a typist in Princeton.

Meanwhile I lived in its smeary pencil pages. The drills, marches and Small Problems for Infantry were a shadowy dream. My whole heart was concentrated upon my book.[39]

It was obviously an act not so much of art as of expediency. Haste marked its conception and its composition. Whatever was available should go in: the poems, "Babes in the Woods," from the *Nassau Lit*, Father Fay's long story about seeing an apparition. With a dash of braggadocio in his letters he made a virtue out of his necessity. "I'm sandwiching the poems between reams of autobiography and fiction," he wrote Leslie, who had offered to show the book to his own American publisher, Charles Scribner's Sons. "It makes a pot-pourri, especially as there are pages in dialogue and in *vers libre*, but it reads as logically for the times as most public utterances of the prim and prominent." [40] And to Wilson: "It rather damns much of Princeton but it's nothing to what it thinks of men and human nature in general. I can most nearly describe it by calling it a prose, modernistic 'Childe Harold' and really if Scribner's takes it I know I'll wake some morning and find that the debutantes have made me famous overnight. I really believe that no one else could have written so searchingly the story of the youth of our generation. . . ." [41] Fitzgerald's allusion to Lord Byron indicates that he may have discovered in the early-nineteenth-century romantics a more relevant and sustaining literary tradition for himself; he had already begun at Princeton his life-long admiration for the poetry of John Keats, whose themes and images were to be of great importance in Fitzgerald's later fiction. But the bravado of his letters reflects more a vague desire than a conscious intention. In the manuscript portion which survives from that unpublished first novel, "The Romantic Egotist," there are few traces of defiant Byronic self-exaltation.[42] Writing in such unreflective haste, Fitzgerald took the events of his own past experience at their face value and created a character who represents —as much as Fitzgerald did in his own boyhood—the conventional romantic hero of genteel American literature.

Still, if Stephen Palms of "The Romantic Egotist" portrays a standard genteel romantic hero, that figure has attained in him an advanced state of decline; for Stephen Palms has raised the unconscious social ambition and social conformity in the genteel romantic hero to an acute level of conscious thought. Stephen's egotism has nothing to do with the self in any Cartesian sense, nor with the self-creative, socially destructive egotism of a Napoleon, which fascinated and appalled the romantic temperament. "I had a definite philosophy," Stephen Palms says, "which was a sort of aristocratic egotism." His form of egotism, that is, represented at heart a desire for high social position. Stephen Palms constantly interprets the nuances of his social situation. As a youth he looks at life much as had Tom Sawyer: ". . . hotel life made me rather inclined to the view that life was a series of tricks 'pulled off' with more or less success by the individual." Gradually his social sense develops. "I am capable now of the utmost snobbishness and class hypocrisy, but was not so until later in life. I think I always believed that social barriers were made by the strong to bolster up their weak retainers and keep out the almost-strongs. Father had a distinct class sense—I suppose because he was a Southerner. He used to tell me things as precepts of the 'School of Gentlemen' and I'd use them as social tricks with no sense of courtesy whatever. For instance, he told me once, that when he had entered a crowded room, he had walked through the dozen or so present without speaking, although he knew them all, and going to the old grandmother wished her a very good evening. He told me that people complimented him on this act of courtesy for months, and the host and hostess were his friends almost through life." At prep school it first became clear to him, "my object was to pass as many people as possible and get to a vague 'top of the world.'" Finally at college he comes into his own: "class was the first thing you noticed at Princeton . . . all the petty snobbishness within the prep-school, all the caste system of Minneapolis, all were here magnified, glorified and transformed into a glittering classification. . . . I liked the idea of a big competition for success of classes and caste within classes and the triumph of ability and personality." Ability and personality, of course, were what finally mattered; wealth and birth merely qualified one for the race. For all the infinite gradations of the social system at any given moment, it was remarkably fluid with the passage of time. The genteel American aristocracy always kept its doors open to talent that was willing to conform. Once Stephen's social antennae were fully developed, once he had his social techniques well in hand, it was time to look inward, to see what he had to offer in the way of content.

Looking within himself, he was not absolutely reassured. "I considered that I was a fortunate youth," he analyzed himself, "capable of expansion to any extent for good or evil. I based this, not on latent strength, but upon facility and superior mentality." He gave himself credit for being handsome, potentially a great athlete, an extremely good dancer; talented, ingenious, quick to learn; personable, charming, magnetic, and poised. "I was convinced that I had . . . the ability to dominate others. Also I was sure that I exercised a subtle fascination over women." But there were debits on the ledger, too. He thought himself unscrupulous, cold, cruel, lacking honor, selfish, desirous of influencing people even to evil, in short, morally rather worse than most; a slave to moods, liable to lose his poise, surly and sensitive, by no means the "Captain of my fate." "Generally," he said, "I knew that at bottom I lacked the essentials. At the last crisis, I knew I had no real courage, perseverance or self-respect." [43] On a certain level this sounds like very harsh self-criticism indeed. But it may also be read as a candidly self-conscious, though otherwise normal, statement of the qualities required for genteel romantic heroism. All of the good attributes of the genteel romantic hero are there. Naturally, being willful, he appears on the surface morally worse than others; naturally, being imaginative, he should be more subject to moody ups and downs. Saying that he lacks "the essentials" is simply another way of expressing his willingness to conform. The last crisis of which he speaks may symbolize the moment of passage to maturity, when the genteel romantic hero gives up his opposition and accepts the proffered social place.

Yet one element in this self-appraisal jars with such a simple reconciliation. The genteel romantic hero may very aptly be defined, by using one of H. G. Wells's terms, as a young man growing up to be a "personage." In his study of Wells, Van Wyck Brooks described a personage as one who "stands on his achievement"—"personality . . . comes to an end the moment it becomes static, the moment one accepts the laurel wreath, the moment one verges on self-consequence." [44] George Rombert, in Fitzgerald's short story "The Pierian Springs and the Last Straw," lost his personality when he stood on his achievement. Stephen Palms looks at the situation from a slightly different point of view. "There seemed to have been a conspiracy to spoil me," he says, "and all my inordinate vanity was absorbed from that. All this was on the surface, however, and liable to be toppled over at one blow by an unpleasant remark or a missed tackle; and underneath it, came my own sense of lack of courage and stability." [45] How thoroughly Fitzgerald absorbed Wells's definition and applied it to himself may be seen in a letter he wrote to a young cousin shortly after finishing "The Romantic Egotist": "A personage and a personality are quite different—I wonder if you can figure the difference. Your mother, Peter the Hermit, Joan of Arc, Cousin Tom, Marc Antony and Bonnie Prince Charlie were personalities. You and Cardinal Newman and Julius Caesar and Elizabeth Barrett Browning and myself and Mme. DeStael were personages. Does the distinction begin to glimmer on you? Personality may vanish at a sickness; a personage is hurt more by a worldly setback." [46] Stephen Palms knows then, with his exacerbated social- and self-awareness, on what a precarious foundation of social etiquettes, precedences, associations, claims—all those arrangements that H. G. Wells accused Henry James of too elaborately accepting—the conventions of the genteel romantic hero rest; and though he possessed "a sense of infinite possibilities that was always with me whether vanity or shame were my mood," he was right sometimes to be pessimistic about his situation.

It must have been Fitzgerald's capacity to make articulate the unstated conventions of the genteel romantic hero—and also to bring them into doubt—that attracted the attention of the Scribner's editors, though they turned down "The Romantic Egotist." Maxwell Perkins liked the manuscript and wanted to ask Fitzgerald to rewrite it in the third person; Edward L. Burlingame described it as "hard sledding"; and William Crary Brownell, chief editor of the firm, a leading conservative critic, author in 1917 of a book, *Standards,* defending the genteel tradition—in the words of Scribner's official historian—"could not stomach it at all." [47] In 1918 Fitzgerald was not yet able to break away from the genteel tradition; rather, it rejected him.

CHAPTER TWO

The impetus of F. Scott Fitzgerald's collegiate literary career was spent by the time he was discharged from the Army early in 1919, and he had failed to make from it any larger success. The novel he had completed on weekends at Ft. Leavenworth, Kansas, had been returned in August 1918 by Charles Scribner's Sons, the publishing firm to which Fitzgerald's friend Shane Leslie had submitted it. Maxwell Perkins at Scribner's had given Fitzgerald detailed suggestions for revision, but Fitzgerald lacked the time and the concentration to do more than a quick patch-up job. Within a few weeks he had sent in a partially revised version, and in October 1918 the novel was again refused. At Fitzgerald's request Perkins passed the manuscript on to another, less conservative publishing house, but there it evoked even less interest. Fitzgerald settled in New York, tried without success to catch on as a reporter on one of the New York papers, and finally went to work as an advertising copy writer.

In the evenings he wrote. He had still not settled his literary aspirations on a particular form, and though he concentrated mainly on short stories he also wrote movie scripts, song lyrics, poems, sketches, and jokes—whatever had a chance of being placed somewhere. He thought up advertising promotions; he even considered trying to break in as a song writer. Over four months he had built up an inventory totaling, in short stories alone, nineteen. The longest time he

31

spent on one was three days. No wonder his rejections came back so promptly. He was disappointed when he made his first sale, in June 1919 to *The Smart Set,* and it turned out the story they took was "Babes in the Woods" from the *Nassau Lit.* But Fitzgerald had carefully gone over "Babes in the Woods" and extensively revised it for the novel, so it was a much more finished story than could have been any of the new ones he was turning out so rapidly. The headlong haste with which he must have written his free-lance pieces in those four months is even more strikingly apparent in the fact that in that period he traveled three times to Montgomery, Alabama, and lost several weeks to a drunken spree. Under other circumstances a sale to so important a literary periodical as *The Smart Set* might have been a happy conclusion to so brief an apprenticeship, and the successful start to a writing career. But Fitzgerald was deeply involved in his courtship of Zelda Sayre, and a check for thirty dollars from *The Smart Set* symbolized neither the wealth nor the success he felt he must attain to win her as his wife. Early in July he went home to St. Paul to give "The Romantic Egotist" the thorough revision he had been unable to accomplish before. Whether he was motivated by long-range literary strategy or by a long-shot hope for sudden fame and money enough to impress Zelda Sayre, his decision was a sound one. Fitzgerald may have possessed the talent to be a writer, but up to that point he had demonstrated neither the patience nor the care to be a good one. Two months later the revision was completed; ten weeks after he left New York Scribner's accepted *This Side of Paradise* for publication in the spring.

By the time *This Side of Paradise* came out in March 1920, Fitzgerald had thrown himself so fully into the literary life of the early post-war period—had become so suddenly aware of Mencken and Dreiser and literary realism and of writers like James Branch Cabell —it was quite forgotten that his novel was not a product, at least in conscious intention, of that literary atmosphere. From the moment he left Princeton in the fall of 1917 to the time of his departure from New York in the summer of 1919 Fitzgerald had given over his nonworking hours so completely to his own writing that he must have had little time to read. On the train back to St. Paul he read Hugh Walpole's *Fortitude,* and the writers on whom he could draw when he sat down to rewrite "The Romantic Egotist" were still H. G. Wells,

Compton Mackenzie, Booth Tarkington, Robert Hugh Benson, and more distantly, Walpole, Shaw, Wilde, Brooke—the same writers who were in his mind when he began it. Amory Blaine, Fitzgerald's new hero, was "rather surprised by his discovery through a critic named Mencken of several excellent American novels: 'Vandover and the Brute,' 'The Damnation of Theron Ware,' and 'Jennie Gerhardt.' " [1] Fitzgerald explained this reference when he inscribed a copy of *This Side of Paradise* for Mencken. "As a matter of fact, Mr. Mencken, I stuck your name in on page 224 in the last proof," Fitzgerald wrote, ". . . partly, I suppose, as a vague bootlick and partly because I have since adopted a great many of your views. But the other literary opinions, especially the disparagement of Cobb, were written when you were little more than a name to me—" [2] Fitzgerald had not been aware of Mencken's pre-eminent position as a critic of American literature when that spring he submitted the short stories to the editors of *The Smart Set*, of whom Mencken was one.

Near the end of his revision Fitzgerald wrote a preface to *This Side of Paradise*. It was a personal rather than a literary document, and Fitzgerald offered it more to Scribner's editors than to any future novel-reading public. "The preface I leave to your discretion," he told Perkins in the cover letter with the completed manuscript, "—perhaps it's a little too clever-clever." [3] And Perkins discreetly dropped it out. But the preface is a unique record of Fitzgerald's literary consciousness while he was writing *This Side of Paradise*, and as it has not heretofore been discussed by students of Fitzgerald, it will be useful to restore it momentarily to its place as an introduction to the novel.

Fitzgerald's preface was not, like a Hawthorne preface, an occasion for questioning the strictures of literary convention or proposing a new way of looking at literary forms. Rather it was a ritual act of rejection: a public sloughing off of his immediate past, displaying what Edmund Wilson noticed in his early essay on Fitzgerald for *The Bookman*, Fitzgerald's early capacity to throw off his unsuccessful work with a swift self-irony and self-depreciation. [4] The first sentence establishes his superior tone of condescension toward his literary past: "Two years ago when I was a very young man indeed, I had an unmistakable urge to write a book." This book, the first version of "The Romantic Egotist," written at Ft. Leavenworth, he puts down as "a tedious casserole of a dozen by Mackenzie, Wells, and Robert Hugh Benson, largely flavored by the great undigested butter-ball of *Dorian Gray*." One is left with the impression that the writing of "The Romantic Egotist" was in the nature of a bodily function, in which his mind was not involved. It was returned by the publisher "with the complaint that the hero failed in the end to find himself, and that this defection would so certainly disappoint the reader as to predestine the book to failure." One may take it that Fitzgerald means "defect," but the word "defection" in reference to "The Romantic Egotist" has its own symbolic appropriateness.

"I pondered the difficulty for several weeks," Fitzgerald continues, "—how could I intrigue the hero into a 'philosophy of life' when my own ideas were in much the state of Alice's after the hatter's tea-party." Into this intellectual vacuum, he intimates, only fools may tread:

> At length I took a tip from Schopenhauer, Hugh Walpole and even the early Wells—begged the question by plunging boldly into obscurity; astounded myself with an impenetrable chapter where I left the hero alone with rhapsodic winds and hyper-sensitive stars . . . and finding that I had merely dragged the hero from a logical muddle into an illogical one, I dispatched him to the war and callously slew him several thousand feet in the air, whence he fell "not like a dead bird, but as a splendid life-bound swallow****down****down****"

Fitzgerald's epitaph on this version is pithy: "The book finished with four dots—there was a fifth dot but I erased it."

Eventually, in a fanfare of capitalized words, the root of the trouble came clear to him.

> All I had written of things I was interested in: THE INFLUENCE OF NIGHT, RATHER BAD WOMEN, PERSONALITY, FANATICISM, THE SUPERNATURAL, and VERY GOOD WOMEN, was quite above the average. All I had written of subjects with which I was thoroughly cognizant: THE "PREP" SCHOOL, COLLEGE, THE MIDDLE WEST, NATURE, QUAINT STUPID PEOPLE, and MYSELF, was, because I was quite bored with all of them, well below the average. My course was obvious, my inspiration was immediate.

34

Virtuously resisting the modern writer's tendency to dramatize himself, I began another novel; whether its hero really "gets anywhere" is for the reader to decide.[5]

Neither the course nor the inspiration is made quite visible to the reader of the preface, but the message of this document is clear enough. It is addressed directly to Maxwell Perkins, and its practical purpose was to warn him to expect, not simply a further revision, but a novel new in conception, quite different in tone from the old. In his letter of acceptance Perkins responded, "Viewing it as the same book that was here before, which in a sense it is, though . . . extended further, I think that you have improved it enormously." [6] From the point of view of Fitzgerald's collegiate fiction and the unpublished versions of the novel, *This Side of Paradise* represented for Fitzgerald's development a remarkable advance.

II

Fitzgerald considered three titles for his novel. The two he rejected —"The Romantic Egotist," left over from the earlier manuscript, and "The Education of a Personage"—suggest the unique character and personal destiny of the novel's young hero. The one he chose directs the reader to widen his attention to a place, on the map and in history. *This Side of Paradise* portrays one young man's education, but it is the story of two developments, the young man's and his society's together. Self and society are held in focus together, even in the moments when the novel plunges most deeply into the minds and hearts of the young. This generation had "grown up to find all Gods dead, all wars fought, all faiths in man shaken. . . ." No line from *This Side of Paradise* is better known and more often quoted; but it is often fragmented, and this is what is left out: "a new generation dedicated more than the last to the fear of poverty and the worship of success; grown up to find all Gods dead . . ." (282). If it is a novel of revolt against society—"a gesture of indefinite revolt," Edmund Wilson called it in his 1922 sketch of the early Fitzgerald [7]—its hero in fact embraces the conventions of the society he grew up in, only to find them without value for the post-World War One society in which he must live. And his withdrawal from society is not so much a rejection as a strategic act, a temporary retreat to find a new and firmer foundation within himself from which to build out into his society again.

"Virtuously resisting the modern writer's tendency to dramatize himself," so Fitzgerald in his unpublished preface described his strength to resist temptation, "I began another novel; whether its hero really 'gets anywhere' is for the reader to decide." [8] These words may be taken merely as a tactical denial that the novel is what it so obviously has seemed to readers then and later, a scarcely veiled autobiography in fiction; and the second clause may be read as an extended and slightly ironic metaphor, meaning, whether F. Scott Fitzgerald really "gets anywhere" is for the editors of Scribner's to decide. But it is more useful to understand this sentence as Fitzgerald most probably intended it, as a claim for credit, as an indication that he had attained in tone and in content the detachment and the coherence the publishers had required of him. If the inspiration for incidents in the novel had come out of Fitzgerald's personal experience, to readers of Fitzgerald's collegiate stories it would have been obvious that they were being altered by a second, in many cases a third, transformation into art. The young men to whom Fitzgerald had boasted "I really believe that no one else could have written so searchingly the story of the youth of our generation" might have seen that he had brought together in the novel the fragmented and contradictory insights into genteel values and had tried to make them cohere in the portrait of Amory Blaine.[9] *This Side of Paradise* may be read as social history, as a humorous, vain, and naïve attempt to portray a humorous, vain, and naïve generation. But it is also something more—if not a novel of ideas, then a novel of feelings, of intuited and empirical responses to cultural traditions and conventions that existed only in intuitions and social practices, but which once had their origin in theology and social thought. *This Side of Paradise* is Fitzgerald's full-scale attempt to test the validity of the genteel conceptions of heroism he and his generation had inherited. It is not a novel of ideas, in part because it was written at a time when other persons, older and more experienced than Amory Blaine, were discovering that their ideas also were "still in riot." *This Side of Paradise* has been looked at as a beginning, as the first flare of 1920 that illuminated the road of the decade ahead. But the events of the novel take place almost exactly within the years 1910 to 1920, and it would be as useful to regard it as an ending, as an attempt to evaluate the experiences of the decade past, when many American values and institutions came under scrutiny. To alter a phrase from Walter Lippmann, who had also been trying to break through false assumptions and conventions in the decade before 1920, *This Side of Paradise* is a preface to a novel of ideas.

This half-intellectual, half-emotional thrust, the slowly rising tension of the desire to break through the shell of old conventions and discover the true self underneath, plays the determining role in shaping the form and content of the novel. Fitzgerald had barely begun to direct his attention to the problems of the craft of the novel. Students of his technique assume he was aware at least of the "saturation" side of the H. G. Wells–Henry James debates between "saturation" and "selection" in the form of the novel, but he was hardly mature enough either as an artist or as an intellectual self-consciously to take sides, as he was later to do. The "saturation" form of the novel suited his needs because he had not yet acquired a point of view firm enough to take advantage of the "selection" form; he did not possess the intellectual foundation, that is, to know what to include and what to exclude. In *This Side of Paradise* Fitzgerald seeks to discover that foundation. Had he come upon it before writing the novel, he might have achieved a more perfect work of art, and a more precisely articulated gesture of revolt. But the value of the novel lies in its capacity to demonstrate, not a completion, but a process. "It was always the becoming he dreamed of, never the being," Fitzgerald says of his hero, Amory Blaine (17-18). Amory's quickening realization that he must struggle against constricting forms of social and intellectual commitment to keep alive this process gives this otherwise diffuse novel its particular movement and urgency.

Fitzgerald began *This Side of Paradise* with the same collection of short stories, poems, and plays that provided the interludes of action between the hero's monologues of self-analysis in "The Romantic Egotist." His chief concern with form was to attain the detachment demanded of him by the Scribner's editors. To accomplish this he turned from a first to a third person form of narrative, but the point of view, except for a few lapses, remains that of the young hero. The first and most pervasive difficulty in getting at the meaning of the novel is presented by the inconsistencies in this point of view. It assumes the perspective at times of personal, internally developed values, and at other times of generalized social values. The narrative voice alternates without apparent reason between the form of a soliloquy and the form of a dramatic monologue. The difference between the two forms has been precisely defined by Robert Langbaum in *The Poetry of Experience*.[10] The soliloquist seeks a point of view while the speaker of the dramatic monologue starts with one. The meaning of the soliloquy depends upon how much the soliloquist has been able to see in terms of a general perspective. But the meaning of the dramatic monologue is understood indirectly, by judging the limitations and distortions of what the speaker sees. We understand something other than what the speaker understands, and our understanding comes through what he conceals and distorts, as well as by what he reveals.

Amory Blaine speaks in both types of voices. The confusion in *This Side of Paradise* between the soliloquy and the dramatic monologue as forms of narrative recalls a similar confusion in Hawthorne's *Blithedale Romance*, one of the first American novels to display an awareness of the possibilities in point of view, and an important influence on the first novelist to expound the "doctrine of point of view," Henry James. Coverdale, the narrator of *The Blithedale Romance*, also engages in soliloquies of self-analysis, yet the reader must judge the meaning of the novel from a perspective, as with the dramatic monologue, that judges Coverdale's point of view as well. The difficulty in the case of both Hawthorne and Fitzgerald extends beyond a failure of literary form into the very definition of character which the society provides. The confusion between forms in *The Blithedale Romance* and *This Side of Paradise* reflects the tension in the genteel American tradition between an ideological commitment to the independent individual will and a practical desire for individuals to submit to social conventions and control. The solution of genteel American society was to make generalized social values appear as if they were formed internally by personal choice. This is the solution that Hawthorne succumbed to; that Henry James satirized in *The Europeans* and used as the material for tragic drama in *The Portrait of a Lady;* that F. Scott Fitzgerald had to overcome intellectually and artistically in *This Side of Paradise*.

III

Fitzgerald achieved his tone of detachment through the invention of Amory's mother, Beatrice O'Hara Blaine. Beatrice as a character may be quite unbelievable; in a way Fitzgerald accounts for this, with his peculiar blend of nostalgia, irony, and sense of social history, by placing her culturally in an already by-gone era, the gilded age. "All in all Beatrice O'Hara absorbed the sort of education that will be quite impossible ever again; a tutelage measured by the number of things and people one could be contemptuous of and charming about; a culture rich in all arts and traditions, barren of all ideas, in the last of those days when the great gardener clipped the inferior roses to produce one perfect bud" (4). But for his purposes she is indispensable. With her aristocratic elegance and her egotistic disdain for convention she provides him with a vantage point otherwise, in an American context, almost unobtainable, a social stature apparently superior to and beyond the conventional judgment by upper-middle-class genteel values. We are nevertheless not supposed to take Beatrice Blaine too seriously. In the first five pages of the novel Fitzgerald speaks in a voice of light social satire, mingling high irony with low comedy; lines such as "the history of her constitution and its many amendments" (6), "next to doctors, priests were her favorite sport" (7), "You will admit that if it was not life it was magnificent" (8), set the tone. Fitzgerald makes clear that Amory regards his mother from the same point of view; "he had no illusions about her" (5). But Fitzgerald's young hero is his mother's son. "Amory Blaine inherited from his mother"—this is the first sentence of the novel—"every trait, except the stray inexpressible few, that made him worthwhile" (3). Later when he begins to try on the various masks of social convention, the term "the fundamental Amory" is introduced to refer us back to the core of his character formed by his mother. If we are not to take Beatrice Blaine quite seriously, we are not permitted entirely to dismiss her values either. And if Beatrice can be both "contemptuous of and charming about" Midwestern American society, her son, who must make a place for himself in it, can treat his position with amusement and candor, too.

The first episode of the novel, "A Kiss for Amory," immediately following on the introduction of the Blaines, brings out clearly the elements of Fitzgerald's new style and themes. Fitzgerald discovered his first conscious voice in writing *This Side of Paradise*. In his collegiate stories there had been glimpses of it, but even the phrases and sentences he carried over unaltered from his early work took on a different color in the context of a controlling voice. The lyrics Fitzgerald wrote for Princeton's Triangle Club shows may give clearer signs of his developed style. The superior, ironic voice of "A Kiss for Amory," the comic metaphors, the active verbs and adverbs that directly appeal to visual and aural senses, all suggest the tone of musical comedy. For the first time in Fitzgerald's fiction the language comes alive, broadening themes, implying meanings on its own.

The themes of this short episode derive in part from the conventions of genteel boys' stories and in part from distinctive aspects of Amory Blaine's character. Amory "had been two months in Minneapolis, and his chief struggle had been the concealing from 'the other guys at school' how particularly superior he felt himself to be, yet this conviction was built upon shifting sands" (8). He had discovered, that is, that the road to power and popularity lay through athletics, his weakest point, and he was gamely trying to conform to the norm. Meanwhile, he had received from Myra St. Claire an invitation to a bobbing party. "His lips curled when he read it" (8). He put the invitation in his pocket, "where it had an intense physical affair with a dusty piece of peanut brittle"(9). The day comes for the party, and Amory's first encounter with Minneapolis society is a series of comic reversals. Amory arrives fashionably late, with his mother's cadenced excuses on his tongue. "A butler (one of the three in Minneapolis) swung open the door" (10). But the party had already moved off to the local country club, and Myra waits for him alone. The butler says "ain't," "yeah," and "what" as a personal pronoun (10). After an initial shock of social horror and despair, Amory swiftly assumes the role of the imaginative genteel hero. " 'Well—I'll tell you. I guess you don't know about the auto accident,' he romanced" (10). This is a desperate play. The butler sees through it. Myra's social ruffle is not smoothed. Nevertheless, Amory's will is strong, his imagination fertile. "As they stepped into the machine he hurriedly slapped the paint of diplomacy over a rather box-like plan he had conceived" (11). He assumes a debonair Continental air. And suddenly to Myra he represents "the quintessence of romance" (11). His thirteen-year-old imagination conjures up for her thirteen-year-old imagination a world of sin unknown to the Penrods and Willie Baxters of Booth Tarkington's fictional genteel world; he smokes, he goes to burlesque shows. Myra is enthralled. Amory is stirred. His imagination leaps to puppy love, his will strains against the conventions. Myra directs her chauffeur to by-pass the bobbing party and take them, alone together, to the country club.

Here Fitzgerald's control falters. He slips for the first time into unabashedly sentimental romanticism. "Overhead the sky was half crystalline, half misty, and the night was chill and vibrant with rich tension. From the country club steps the roads stretched away, dark creases on the white blanket; huge heaps of snow lining the sides like the tracks of giant moles" (13). Trying to recover distance, the author's voice first obtrudes into Amory's point of view, then swings momentarily to Myra's. "Then their lips brushed like young wild flowers in the wind" (14). Suddenly Amory becomes disgusted with himself. "He wanted to creep out of his body and hide somewhere safe out of sight, up in the corner of his mind" (14). Myra's will asserts itself: " 'Kiss me again.' Her voice came out of a great void" (14). Their playful touch suggests a somehow ominous mystery. The scene dissolves in a comedy of childish pique and a surprise reversal, as Myra swiftly assumes a previously unrecognized social poise. Amory joins the party and recovers his mood of generalized romanticism. In the genteel world that Amory still inhabits imagination gives more pleasure than the act.

Gradually Amory evolves his adolescent code of egotism. In form and in substance it is exactly the aristocratic code proclaimed by Stephen Palms in "The Romantic Egotist." But Fitzgerald marches Amory up to his philosophy of life in a costume—"his first long trousers, set off by a purple accordion tie and a 'Belmont' collar with the edges unassailably meeting, purple socks, and handkerchief with a purple border peeping from his breast pocket" (18)—that enables us to take Amory, from his age and social standing, with the proper grain of salt. The change in tone from the earlier manuscript to the published novel is most strikingly illustrated here:

"The Romantic Egotist": "I considered that I was a fortunate youth capable of expansion to any extent for good or evil. I based this, not on latent strength, but upon facility and superior mentality." [11]

This Side of Paradise: "Amory marked himself a fortunate youth, capable of infinite expansion for good or evil. He did not consider himself a 'strong char'c'ter,' but relied on his facility (learn things sorta quick) and his superior mentality (read a lotta deep books)" (18).

Amory Blaine's egotism is in no way diminished from his predecessor's; rather by the specifying details and the limiting irony of the adolescent speech it is made more plausible and more likable. Otherwise it follows point-by-point the earlier code. Amory is handsome, an athlete of possibilities, a supple dancer; socially he is personable, magnetic, poised, blessed with "the power of dominating all contemporary males, the gift of fascinating all women" (18); mentally, he is completely, without question, superior. Amory has faults, too, the same ones that made Stephen Palms so sensitive. But where Stephen's pros and cons were displayed with the cold numerical balance of an accounting ledger, Fitzgerald lists Amory's faults one after another connected by three dots: "unscrupulousness . . . the desire to influence people in almost every way, even for evil . . . a certain coldness and lack of affection, amounting sometimes to cruelty . . . a shifting sense of honor . . . an unholy selfishness . . . a puzzled, furtive interest in everything concerning sex" (18-19). The haste and abruptness of the words convey Amory's own emotional self-doubt.

But once again breaking off from Amory's point of view, Fitzgerald makes clear that the faults are at least in part figments of Amory's "Puritan conscience," which later in life he was to slay (18). The ambition, vanity, and "sense of people as automatons to his will" with which Amory concludes his egotistic code are thus as provisional as the faults which create them or spring from them (19). Fitzgerald makes one more significant change from the earlier manuscript in the code of the young egotist. Stephen Palms chose the term "egotist" to describe himself rather than an "out-and-out stiff lump of conceit" because he believed himself to be a combination of vanity and self-knowledge.[12] Amory Blaine's vanity is unmixed, "tempered with self-suspicion if not with self-knowledge" (19). Here the difference between the themes of the two manuscripts is made precise. Stephen Palms knew himself and made his progress through a tale of social rise and placement. Amory Blaine is capable from the start of placing himself in society and is saved by the grace of his own self-doubt. The hero of *This Side of Paradise* proceeds, not from self into society, but away from society into his own first form of self-possession.

Yet in his adolescence the aristocratic egotist has only begun to pass through the shaping hands of society. Already he possessed a disconcerting self-awareness of the process by which he might be molded to the norm. Beatrice asks Amory if his years in Minneapolis were *horrible*—her italics—and he answers, " 'No, Beatrice. I enjoyed them. I adapted myself to the bourgeoisie. I became conventional.' He surprised himself by saying that, and he pictured how Froggy would have gaped" (21). Amory's heightened sense of his own early desire and necessity to adopt established values lays the foundation for the significance of the novel's social observation. Amory is a soliloquist; he is gradually discovering the facts and values of his social environment, and the reader comes to expect from him direct perception rather than judgment. Fitzgerald's failure to sustain this voice—rather his effort to find a voice which could project values instead of simply reporting them—leads to the confusion about Amory's point of view. The difficulty is symbolized by the fact that the first book of the novel completes Amory's formal schooling, but the second book comprises his "education."

"But for the next four years," Fitzgerald writes, "the best of Amory's intellect was concentrated on matters of popularity, the intricacies of a university social system and American Society as represented by Biltmore teas and Hot Springs golf links" (26). The best of Amory's intellect was also, by his own definition, distinctly philosophical. He demonstrated, to his own satisfaction, an abstract, theoretical, and generalizing mind. Few others have derived the same satisfaction from Amory Blaine's speculations. "Your hero as an intellectual," Edmund Wilson told Fitzgerald, "is a fake of the first water and I read his views on art, politics, religion and society with more riotous mirth than I should care to have you know." [13] It would be difficult to sustain an interest in Amory's philosophical progress through the first book of *This Side of Paradise*, it is true, had Fitzgerald not repeatedly shifted the focus away from his hero and into the general social setting. The distinctively social scenes in the first book also contain most of the dramatic action, and in these—the Triangle Club and "Petting" episodes, the stages of the romance with Isabelle, the Asbury Park excursion and the climactic events of Princeton social life—Amory figures, as one might expect from a soliloquist, more as a representative type than as a character autonomously conceived. But in the abstract posturing of Amory's intellectual self-analysis there is a tension that provides the underlying movement and the vitality of the book. For, however much Amory rests contented in the certainties of social place and social convention, still he resists conceding himself wholly to society's mold.

Amory's intellectual resistance took form first as the philosophy of the slicker. The "slicker" was created by Amory and a friend at their preparatory school, St. Regis', to set apart their form of self-proclaimed superiority from the conventions of prep school popularity. "This was a first real break from the hypocrisy of school tradition. The slicker was a definite element of success, differing intrinsically from the prep school 'big man'" (35). But the slicker was also the genteel romantic hero in one of his many masquerades. His principal talent was a "clever sense of social values" and his primary goal in life was worldly success (36). Amory, it is true, committed himself at the same time to a more exalted ideal than that of the slicker. "Amory's secret ideal had all the slicker qualifications, but, in addition, courage and tremendous brains and talent—also Amory conceded him a bizarre streak that was quite irreconcilable to the slicker proper" (35). It would be a mistake to read too much into this vague idealism; Amory seems merely to have added to his slicker philosophy a dash of romantic Catholic mysticism.

IV

The philosophy of the slicker was to stay with Amory until his junior year at Princeton. "Spires and Gargoyles," the second chapter, carries Amory through his first two Princeton years much more in his social than in his intellectual guise. As a social recorder Fitzgerald brought to Amory's social life, particularly to his romance with Isabelle Borgé, all his developed irony and detachment. Their courtship is shaped by images of sports and warfare. The quality of their emotional responses is conveyed by incidents such as this one: "He fancied, but he was not sure, that her foot had just touched his under the table. But it might possibly have been only the table leg. It was so hard to tell. Still it thrilled him" (65-66). Amory himself is at this point so committed to the conventions of the social order that he is able to look at himself as distantly as if he were another person. "As he put in his studs he realized that he was enjoying life as he would probably never enjoy it again" (88). Yet the fundamental Amory remains intact behind the beautiful tapestries of Princeton and Cottage Club and his romance. The fundamental Amory appears in the "Petting" section; it is the social Amory who can find it "rather fascinating to feel that any popular girl he met before eight he might possibly kiss before twelve," the fundamental Amory who considered that this possibility "stood for a real moral letdown" (59). Fitzgerald's hesitation between two forms of narrative voice is mirrored, and in a way explained, by his capacity to keep in focus two perspectives on the same event. This is an early and in part undeliberated instance of the "ability to hold two opposed ideas in the mind" which Fitzgerald later considered a principal source of his intelligence and artistry.[14]

One of the most perplexing episodes of the novel arises from Fitzgerald's double perspective, and more particularly from the incapacity of his devices, or his perception, to deal with issues more profound than egotism and social convention. The episode which has repelled or confused readers of the novel, "The Devil," from a later chapter, is in part derived from the romantic supernaturalism of Roman Catholic writers like Msgr. Benson. But it also has its roots in two earlier scenes from "Spires and Gargoyles": "Carnival," the account of a trip to Asbury Park, and "Under the Arc-Lights," the fatal auto crash. In the "Carnival" section Amory drives down to Asbury Park with five classmates to return a stolen car. Once there, the boys turn their errand into two days of pranks and irresponsible fun, tricking waiters, sneaking into movies, sleeping out of doors. Amory's omnipresent observer's eye watches over them: "He wondered how much each one contributed to the party, for there was somewhat of a spiritual tax levied. Alec and Kerry were the life of it, but not quite the centre. Somehow the quiet Humbird, and Sloane, with his impatient superciliousness, were the centre" (77). It was Humbird who personified Amory's philosophical ideals.

Dick Humbird had, ever since freshman year, seemed to Amory a perfect type of aristocrat. He was slender but well-built—black curly hair, straight features, and rather a dark skin. Everything he said sounded intangibly appropriate. He possessed infinite courage, an averagely good mind, and a sense of honor with a clear charm and *noblesse oblige* that varied it from righteousness. He could dissipate without going to pieces, and even his most bohemian adventures never seemed "running it out." People dressed like him, tried to talk as he did. . . . Amory decided that he probably held the world back, but he wouldn't have changed him. . . .

He differed from the healthy type that was essentially middle class— he never seemed to perspire. Some people couldn't be familiar with a chauffeur without having it returned; Humbird could have lunched at Sherry's with a colored man, yet people would have somehow known that it was all right. He was not a snob, though he knew only half his class. His friends ranged from the highest to the lowest, but it was impossible to "cultivate" him. Servants worshipped him, and treated him like a God. He seemed the eternal example of what the upper class tries to be. (77-8)

Once when he looked at Humbird, Amory was reminded of the photographs of English officers killed in the war. But a friend told him "the shocking truth" (78). Humbird's father was a classic American *nouveau riche,* a grocery clerk who grew rich in real estate speculation out in the West and moved his new fortune to New York. "Amory had felt a curious sinking sensation" (78).

Two months later Humbird lies dead in a shabby New Jersey parlor. They had been on a drinking party in New York. Amory returned in one car, Humbird at the wheel of the other. "Dick was driving," one boy sobbed, "and he wouldn't give up the wheel; we told him he'd been drinking too much—then there was this damn curve—oh, my *God! . . .*" (86). Hardening himself, Amory touches Humbird's lifeless hand. "All that remained of the charm and personality of the Dick Humbird he had known—oh, it was all so horrible and unaristocratic and close to the earth. All tragedy has that strain of the grotesque and squalid—so useless, futile . . . the way animals die. . . . Amory was reminded of a cat that had lain horribly mangled in some alley of his childhood." (86-7)

A year later Amory encounters the devil, whose shadowy presence forewarns him from sleeping with a chorus girl. He runs out, and

46

the devilish footsteps pursue him—and lead him on. He stops, and calls out: "I want someone stupid. Oh, send someone stupid!" (115). "When he called thus it was not an act of will at all—will had turned him away from the moving figure in the street; it was almost instinct that called, just the pile on pile of inherent tradition or some wild prayer from way over the night. Then something clanged like a low gong struck at a distance, and before his eyes a face flashed over the two feet, a face pale and distorted with a sort of infinite evil that twisted it like flame in the wind; *but he knew, for the half instant that the gong tanged and hummed, that it was the face of Dick Humbird"* (116). And then he was safe.

"The Devil" episode has sometimes been regarded as a wildly extreme moral response—what response could be more extreme?—to a fictional situation which projects unreal fantasies of sexual possibilities along with immature sexual squeamishness. For all the truth in this, the vision of Dick Humbird as the climax of the encounter with the Devil suggests that the episode belongs in a wider perspective. Dick Humbird is seen, through Amory's double vision, in two ways. First he is the perfect upper-class young gentleman, whose catalogue of impeccable virtues concludes with the final stamp of true aristocracy—servants worshipped him and treated him like a god. Of course he is not truly aristocratic in any precise sense, as Amory learned to his chagrin. But there are several curious aspects of Amory's admiration for Humbird, as well as of his chagrin. Amory himself was the child of what passes for American aristocracy, despite his more recent overlay of middle-class convention; presumably his experience and judgment would keep him from being fooled by such a parvenu upstart. Yet even when he learns the truth about Humbird's social background, the exceptionally fine quality of Humbird's character remains unquestioned. Perhaps Humbird's unusual and attractive personality should lead to different judgments about the qualities of social classes in America.

The next time Humbird is mentioned, he is dead. The explanation of the accident suggests that, through stubbornness and pride and reckless irresponsibility, Humbird has killed himself. One might place Humbird beside the slain English officers with whom Amory has compared him, as an aristocratic member of a dying order, an anachronism too fine to survive in the swift violence of a changing world. But Fitzgerald explicitly describes Humbird's death as un-aristocratic and squalid; Amory is reminded of a dead alley cat. The nature of Humbird's death helps Fitzgerald avoid the problems raised by Humbird's character in life.

The second part of Fitzgerald's double judgment on Dick Humbird is made uncomfortably explicit in "The Devil" episode. The images of decay and fire, death and Hell—the calcium pallor of the street where the showgirls live, temptation like a warm wind, the divan "alive like heat waves over asphalt, like wriggling worms" (114)—build up to the climactic moment when Amory sees the face of Dick Humbird, "pale and distorted with a sort of infinite evil" (116). Humbird had been condemned to Hell; and seeing Humbird's face contorted with evil saves Amory from a similar end. It is a harsh fate for a young man who had been presented in such glowing terms, terms central to Amory's philosophy of the aristocratic egotist. This obvious but artistically crude judgment on Dick Humbird suggests how tenuous was Fitzgerald's hold on his own abstract ideas of superiority, how closely tied he was still to the moral and economic stereotypes of the genteel culture. For all its warnings against the sexual enticements of showgirls like Axia Marlowe, "The Devil" episode is primarily important for its effort to exorcise the appeal, and the threat, of Dick Humbird's wealth, personality, and charm.

The rise and fall of Dick Humbird give greater meaning to the next phase of Amory's intellectual development than the specific events which call it forth. At the start of chapter three, "The Egotist Considers," Amory suffers two sudden failures. His romance with Isabelle Borgé collapses. An academic failure deprives him of his extra-curricular honors at Princeton. The break with Isabelle begins with her fit of pique, and Amory comes out of it partly amused and partly unscathed, "aware that he had not an ounce of real affection" for her (91). The academic failure is judged by conventional group values—"They're rather off you at the club, you know; every man that doesn't come through makes our crowd just so much weaker"—to which Amory can rise superior: "I hate that point of view" (98). Thus the double failure is presented as an act of discarding useless objects, as a snake wriggles out of an old skin. "That had been his nearest approach to success through conformity. The fundamental Amory, idle, imaginative, rebellious, had been nearly snowed under.

48

He had conformed, he had succeeded, but as his imagination was neither satisfied nor grasped by his own success, he had listlessly, half-accidently chucked the whole thing and become again: . . . the fundamental Amory" (99).

But "the fundamental Amory" quickly moves into new intellectual paths that directly respond to Dick Humbird's challenge. From Monsignor Darcy, Amory discovers an antidote to the charm of Humbird's personality, the "personage"—in language that echoes and expands upon a concept already explored in Fitzgerald's early stories and letters. "A personality," Msgr. Darcy said, "is what you thought you were, what this Kerry and Sloane you tell me of evidently are. Personality is a physical matter almost entirely; it lowers the people it acts on—I've seen it vanish in a long sickness. But while a personality is active, it overrides 'the next thing.' Now a personage, on the other hand, gathers. He is never thought of apart from what he's done. He's a bar on which a thousand things have been hung—glittering things sometimes, as ours are, but he uses those things with a cold mentality back of them" (104). The young college leader to whom Amory next gives allegiance is the class revolutionary, Burne Holiday, who had begun a campaign to abolish the Princeton eating clubs.

> Broad-browed and strong-chinned, with a fineness in the honest gray eyes that were like Kerry's, Burne was a man who gave an immediate impression of bigness and security—stubborn, that was evident, but his stubbornness wore no stolidity, and when he talked for five minutes Amory knew that this keen enthusiasm had in it no quality of dilettantism.
>
> The intense power Amory felt later in Burne Holiday differed from the admiration he had had for Humbird. This time it began as purely a mental interest. With other men whom he had thought as primarily first-class, he had been attracted first by their personalities, and in Burne he missed that immediate magnetism to which he usually swore allegiance. (122-3)

Burne's reform movement gives a concrete focus to Amory's sense that Princeton is going through a period of social change. At the same time he provides Amory with a new perspective on the sudden wealth that had thrust the Humbirds so swiftly into the upper class. Burne was interested in economics, and he was on the way to becoming a socialist and a pacifist. When Amory split with Burne it was over the question of will. Burne equates a strong will with good, a weak will with evil. Amory believes that a strong will can lead a man to evil—his example is the superman. "It seemed to him that life and history were rife with the strong criminal, keen, but often self-deluding; in politics and business one found him and among the old statesmen and kings and generals; but Burne never agreed and their courses began to split on that point" (131). In a sense it is Amory's belief in the superman that leads him to differ further with Burne on the issue of the war. Amory sees a Nietzschean dynamism in the German war effort, materialism and "tremendous licentious force" (150)—terms familiar from Shane Leslie's discussion of the war in *The Celt and the World.* "This," Amory said of the Allied effort in the war, "is the great protest against the superman" (152).

But Fitzgerald knew also, from Shane Leslie's Celtic point of view, that the war had brought all the Anglo-Saxon certainties, all the Victorian values and social arrangements, into question. Amory Blaine goes off to war, not to help preserve the old, but to clear away all obstacles to the new. Amory's parting shot to the Victorian era is a poem suggested by a lecturer's remarks on Swinburne's *A Song in Time of Order.* Amory's generation went off to war and learned there the songs for a time of disorder.

V

Fitzgerald sent Amory Blaine off to the battlefields of France though he himself had never gotten to them. But the war in *This Side of Paradise* is no more than a hyphen between prewar and postwar, an episode in Amory's development that serves to make authentic Amory's experience rather than to shape it. Fitzgerald's interest is not in how the war affects his hero, but in how the home front changed while the war was going on "over there." American society had been transformed in the months between May 1917 and February 1919, Amory's "interlude" abroad. War had not altered him at all.

Not the war itself, but events connected with it, had deprived Amory of his precarious ties to the American aristocracy. During the war his mother died, and from "speculation, extravagance, the democratic administration, and the income tax" the family fortune had melted away (162). Amory is now a poor relation of the genteel world, who must work for his living, with no prospects of sudden wealth ahead. The mother of Amory's first postwar romance, Rosalind Connage, describes Amory as "a dreamer, a nice, well-born boy, but a dreamer—merely *clever*" (190-91). Fitzgerald's "stage-notes" add, "(*She implies that this quality in itself is rather vicious*)" (191). This intrusion warns us not to expect the genteel hero to devise some imaginative reversal of his fortunes. For even should he win the girl there would be no prize of prestige or position to go along with her. The Connage family is in hardly less precarious a financial position than Amory himself. In rewriting "The Debutante," from the *Nassau Lit* story to the first chapter of Book Two of the novel, Fitzgerald added a new dimension of social observation to his portrait of the genteel romantic heroine. As Mrs. Connage says, "Rosalind, you've been a very expensive proposition" (177). The young girl of will and imagination needs wealth to create a sphere in which she can use them. Wealth can no longer be taken for granted. The Connages may have to move to a smaller house. Their younger daughter is in danger of losing her "advantages" (178). No wonder the generation grown up to find all Gods dead and all faiths shaken also feared poverty and worshipped success all the more. If the debutante is to have the wealth she requires, she must marry it. No longer will the genteel hero's cleverness win the girl.

And there is now no question, as there was in Fitzgerald's last collegiate stories, whether the young man is enough of a genteel hero truly to deserve the girl. Amory Blaine rises obviously superior to the heroines whose love he conquers, only to lose. The role of the strong-willed girl in the first version of "The Debutante," Helen Halycon, is shifted to Rosalind in the novel, but the role of the whining self-pitying suitor goes to a dull, weak-willed suitor, Howard Gillespie. It is to Gillespie that Rosalind brags of her power—"Given a decent start any girl can beat a man nowadays" (181)—and Gillespie whom she rebukes for being a coward. Amory, curiously, is made superior to Rosalind by an exchange of roles from another early story, "Sentiment—and the Use of Rouge." In that story Clay Syneforth is the sentimental one, Eleanor Marbrooke is willfully strong. In the novel Amory speaks Eleanor's most important line.

Rosalind becomes the sentimental partner, Amory the one who loathes sentiment. "I'm romantic," he tells her, as Eleanor told Clay in only slightly different words, "—a sentimental person thinks things will last—a romantic person hopes against hope that they won't" (177). Amory says the same thing to his next romance, Eleanor Savage. After the second time Fitzgerald parenthetically remarks, "(This was an ancient distinction of Amory's)" (229). "Ancient" must ironically refer to the Rosalind affair. The distinction had earlier not been necessary. Before the First World War, the sentimentalists and the romantics alike thought things would last.

Amory of course had always been a romantic. But his "ancient distinction" explicitly redefines and rejects the role he had played before the war; the genteel romantic hero is now defined as a sentimentalist, one who founded his judgments upon social values and social arrangements he falsely assumed to be permanent. Amory's newly devised version of the romantic hero provides no ready-made judgments. Rather, as in the original meaning of the romantic impulse, it requires Amory to redefine himself on the basis of his own experience.

Book Two of *This Side of Paradise,* "The Education of a Personage," marks the shift in Fitzgerald's narrative voice from soliloquy to dramatic monologue, from the general social perspective to the individual perspective. If the narrative voice alternates between the two modes in a confusing way during the first half of the novel, by the second book confusion has given way to chaos: "life had changed from an even progress along a road stretching ever in sight, with the scenery merging and blending, into a succession of quick, unrelated scenes" (233). The general social perspective had been rejected. As yet there was no coherent individual perspective to take its place. Amory Blaine's experiences in the second book, moreover, are negative experiences. Amory learns the points of view he must avoid. "The Education of a Personage" is an education in how to put on and throw off useless masks. What was once progress seems not so much "a succession of quick, unrelated scenes" as a definite process of decline. Fitzgerald's wit and irony cannot provide a detached perspective toward material over which he lacks a controlling form. The clever dialogues on contemporary books and writers, part of which were written into the galley proofs of the novel apparently in an effort to enliven the final chapters, only diffuse their tone all the more.

Yet the dead husks one by one are stripped away, and the new seed laid bare at last. Society has changed around Amory. A new emphasis on wealth has made the imaginative romantic qualities of the genteel hero appear as if they were something "vicious." Amory's old role in the social system is no longer valid, and so, during his "experiments in convalescence," he breaks away from conventional ideas and literary values as well. "Well," Amory considered, "I'm not sure that the war itself had any great effect on either you or me —but it certainly ruined the old backgrounds, sort of killed individualism out of our generation" (213).

In his brief romance with Eleanor Savage, Amory explores the opposite pole from social conformity—the absolute, unfettered romantic will—and rejects it too. The Eleanor chapter, "Young Irony," is the only chapter of the novel set in "nature," in the country, away from schools and cities. "Eleanor was, say, the last time that evil crept close to Amory under the mask of beauty" (222). This introduction to the last romance prefigures Amory's later rejection of the romantic vision of beauty, exemplified for Fitzgerald by Keats's lines in the "Ode on a Grecian Urn." With Eleanor "his imagination ran riot and that is why they rode to the highest hill and watched an evil moon ride high, for they knew then that they could see the devil in each other" (222). Wherever Amory was eventually to find his truth, thereafter it would forever be severed from beauty.

Eleanor knows Amory as the boy who walks the hedgerows reciting Poe. He meets her in a sublimely romantic thunderstorm, while she recites Verlaine. He is Byron's Don Juan, she is "a graceful, facile Manfred" (235)—a feminine counterpart of Byron's hero who became the symbol for nineteenth-century readers of absolute romantic will. But the romantic will turns its back on too much that Amory values. To him, its lonely despair rejected sentiment and faith too completely. "I'm hipped on Freud and all that," Eleanor says one night on a ride, "but it's rotten that every bit of *real* love in the world is ninety-nine percent passion and one little soupçon of jealousy" (238). Fitzgerald's 1920 readers may have thrilled to that line; but Fitzgerald did not intend to let it stand unchallenged for more than a moment. For it is only the first step in Eleanor's more and more vehement defiance. " 'I'll tell you there *is* no God. . . .' She let go her reins and shook her little fists at the stars" (239). Amory finds he must object. At once Eleanor's will erupts into self-destructive violence. She tries to hurl herself over a cliff. At the last moment she saves herself, but her horse goes over and is killed. Suddenly Eleanor confesses: "I've got a crazy streak . . . twice before I've done things like that. When I was eleven Mother went—went mad—stark, raving crazy. We were in Vienna——" (240). The absolute romantic will turns on itself like a self-devouring reptile. It leads to its negation, belief in nothing, prostration before crude material power; and one more step beyond lies madness.

When Eleanor told Amory her Freudian perspective on sex, he responded, "You see every one's got to have some cloak to throw around it. The mediocre intellects, Plato's second class, use the remnants of romantic chivalry diluted with Victorian sentiment . . ." (238). On his return to the urban world Amory finds himself confronted with a sexual situation to which only this conventional genteel response seems appropriate. In Atlantic City he meets his old Princeton friend, Alec Connage, Rosalind's brother. Alec offers Amory half of a suite in a hotel. Amory wakes up in the middle of the night to find Alec sleeping with a girl in the other room. Hotel detectives are about to arrest Alec for violation of the Mann Act. Once again Amory feels the shadowy presence of evil around him. For a span of seconds he reflects.

> The first fact that flashed radiantly on his comprehension was the great impersonality of sacrifice—he perceived that what we call love and hate, reward and punishment, had no more to do with it than the date of the month. . . . Now he realized the truth: that sacrifice was no purchase of freedom. It was like a great elective office, it was like an inheritance of power—to certain people at certain times an essential luxury, carrying with it not a guarantee but a responsibility, not a security but an infinite risk. Its very momentum might drag him down to ruin—the passing of the emotional wave that made it possible might leave the one who made it high and dry forever on an island of despair. (247-8)

Amory seizes on the act of self-sacrifice, the cornerstone of genteel morality. But he turns it on its head. "Sacrifice by its very nature was arrogant and impersonal; sacrifice should be eternally supercilious"

(248). Amory sacrifices himself for Alec Connage not in a gesture of genteel acceptance, but in disdainful defiance of the genteel code. For whatever significance it has, in the act he gains release at last from the mystic evil that has dogged him.

Now the egotist must complete his metamorphosis into a personage. What little that remains of Amory's genteel heroism has evaporated into air. He is floating free of all encumbrances at last. Perhaps he shall fall; this is the warning message of the impressionistic realism of the New York street scenes. Perhaps he shall rise. But if he rises it will be from some new principle of motion, as yet unknown. He "had grown up to a thousand books, a thousand lies; he had listened eagerly to people who pretended to know, who knew nothing" (262). Hereafter all inquiries will start with himself. The death of Monsignor Darcy suddenly makes clear to him how he may act. "He found something that he wanted, had always wanted and always would want—not to be admired, as he had feared; not to be loved, as he had made himself believe; but to be necessary to people, to be indispensable; he remembered the sense of security he had found in Burne. . . . Amory felt an immense desire to give people a sense of security" (266). The monsignor had first planted in Amory's mind the concept of the "personage." Now Amory revises the definition. To Monsignor Darcy the personage was one who gathered his accomplishments around him as if they were possessions. He represented order and stability. Thus he was even more of a genteel figure than the "personality." The term "personage" meant almost precisely the same thing to Monsignor Darcy as it did to H. G. Wells; and for Wells "personage" was a term of opprobrium.

Amory retains the title but gives it an opposite meaning. For Amory the personage is one who gives away, one who creates, one who constructs. He is the figure who dreamed, as Fitzgerald said of Amory when the novel began, always of the becoming, never the being. Thus Fitzgerald reversed Wells's definition. He took the title "personage" away from the genteel hero and applied it to a new form of heroism, fitting Wells's description of the extraordinary man. "He is an experiment toward an impersonal synthesis, the well-being of the species"; so Van Wyck Brooks phrased Wells's view.[15] Fitzgerald's personage fulfills himself not in a static sense of achievement, but through a continual process of action.

In the auto ride toward Princeton near the end of the novel, Amory describes his new version of the personage: ". . . the man who, being spiritually unmarried, continually seeks for new systems that will control or counteract human nature. His problem is harder. It is not life that's complicated, it's the struggle to guide and control life. That is his struggle. He is a part of progress—the spiritually married man is not" (272). Amory's gesture of revolt thus shifts without hesitation into a gesture of commitment. He has broken, not with society, but with an accommodation to a social perspective which denies his own distinctive human values. He has given up a passive but secure place in the social order for an active and problematic role in creating constructive social change. He has turned his back on a system of values which exalts the individual will in theory but in practice constricts it. Now he must make a direct confrontation with the capacity of his will to create values for himself. If he has not yet become a "personage," he has at least attained the ground from which he may begin to work. In the auto-ride episode Amory's point of view, for the first time in the novel, is distinctly his own; for the first time also, he speaks in the voice of the dramatic monologue.

Amory talks to the two men as if he were a socialist. It has disconcerted some readers that Amory should discover a new panacea so quickly in place of the old. But it is necessary to understand Amory's point of view now, as Langbaum wrote of the dramatic monologue in *The Poetry of Experience,* "not through his description of it but indirectly, through seeing what he sees while judging the limitations and distortions of what he sees." [16] From this perspective it is possible to see that Amory is arguing in favor of socialism primarily because it is unconventional. He is shocking himself, as well as the little man in the car, by his bravado. Socialism happens to be the arguing point most readily at hand with which Amory can test his new freedom. He has no need just yet to find a harness. The old and outworn systems are behind him. His will is freed both from genteel social conventions and the extremes of romantic despair. Nothing matters but the pleasure of the chase. "Even if, deep in my heart, I thought we were all blind atoms in a world as limited as a stroke of a pendulum, I and my sort would struggle against tradition; try, at least, to displace old cants with new ones. I've thought I was right about life at various times, but faith is difficult. One thing I know. If living isn't a seeking for the grail it may be a damned amusing game" (278). He remains as willful and imaginative as the genteel hero, but his will is not clouded by sentiment, nor his imagination by a dangerous reliance on a sense of beauty. No false visions remain to constrain him. The world is open to his will. "He stretched out his arms to the crystalline, radiant sky. 'I know myself,' he cried, 'but that is all' " (282).

This Side of Paradise ends thus with a thrust into the future. The process of the novel does not itself end; rather it is to be renewed on a different plane. Fitzgerald succeeded in creating a new definition of individualism in contrast to the individualism of the genteel tradition; and it led, neither to despair nor to rebellion, but to an even more responsible commitment to a social order. Perhaps this success explains part of the novel's surprising popularity; *This Side of Paradise* appealed in 1920 to radicals and conservatives together. But Fitzgerald's new idea of the fundamental self is more an act of faith than of demonstrated proof. Amory Blaine does not "know himself" in any classic sense. He has arrived at his new form of individualism through a reversal of the Cartesian reasoning, "I think, therefore I am." He had knocked away all his props of social place and social convention and found himself still standing. Therefore he could say, "I am." But what he was to think had not yet come to him.

CHAPTER THREE

Within a week after *This Side of Paradise* was accepted for publication, F. Scott Fitzgerald read a novel that gave his literary opinions a sudden new turn. The novel was *Salt*, by Charles G. Norris. Fitzgerald wrote about his response to it in an effusive and chaotic letter to a college girl acquaintance—a letter otherwise remarkable for the way it brought together nearly all the literary forms and intellectual poses from Fitzgerald's collegiate years. For the girl's benefit, Fitzgerald cast himself as a genteel romantic hero. He wanted, by entertaining her, to please her, and also, by his willful defiance, to shock her. The letter begins with poetic doggerel and musical comedy chorus lyrics. Later it pessimistically rejects religious and moral sanctions, then abruptly shifts into the language of youthful romance. It ends with a low-brow joke. Fitzgerald ostensibly was writing to proclaim his great success. "Most beautiful, rather-too-virtuous-but-entirely-enchanting Alida: Scribners has accepted my book. Ain't I smart!" Yet he confesses at once, "But *hic jubilatio erat totam* spoiled for *meum par lisant une livre, une novellum,* (*novem*) *nomine* Salt *par* Herr C. G. Norris—a most astounding piece of realism, it makes *Fortitude* look like an antique mental ashcan and is quite as good as *The Old Wives' Tale.* Of course, I think Walpole is a weak-wad anyhow. Read *Salt*, young girl, so that you may know what life B." [1] Fitzgerald does not make clear whether Norris's realism spoiled his happiness by depressing his emotions or by surpassing him in literary skill. Perhaps when he came upon the new realism just at the moment of his first success, Fitzgerald was convinced that *Salt* did both.

Salt may have been the first novel—at least the first new novel—Fitzgerald had read since he went through *Fortitude* ten weeks earlier coming home on the train from New York. No matter what precise value Fitzgerald gave to *Salt*, he vastly overvalued it. But the novel does bear an uncanny resemblance to *This Side of Paradise*, in a way that might have forced Fitzgerald to make a comparison unfavorable to himself. For *Salt* reveals how much *This Side of Paradise* dissembles; how much Fitzgerald avoided confronting the implications of his subject, how successful he was in putting on everything a sweet face. *Salt* implies that, for all its rhetorical overthrowing of the genteel tradition, *This Side of Paradise* is essentially a novel written in the sentimental mode. *Salt* tells much the same story, and tells it straight.

There is no confusion in *Salt*, as there is in *This Side of Paradise*, about the provenance of an American aristocracy. Griffith Adams, the novel's protagonist, carries the blood of the Massachusetts Adams dynasty in his veins. His mother is as attractive and as roaming as Beatrice was, but she takes as her third husband an Italian adventurer, and dies penniless, deserted, and duped. Rather than enrolling at Harvard, as one might expect, Griffith goes to a big Midwestern state university, where imagination and individuality are beaten out of him by fraternity life. Griffith wastes his time, is caught trying to steal examination papers, and leaves the university without graduating. He goes to New York, works for a railroad, and is fired for participating in a graft scheme. He marries a girl from a class far below his own, and she dies soon after giving birth to a child. Griffith Adams was a "blotter," who could act only in response to the flow of experience.[2] His hard knocks prepared him for the discovery that his will was chained down by false conventions. "I had to unlearn what I'd been taught," he says, "and through hard experience find out for myself the real values and truths of life."[3] Much more than Amory Blaine, Griffith Adams deserved the epigram from Oscar Wilde—"Experience is the name so many people give to their mistakes"— that graced the title page of *This Side of Paradise*.

Finally, at the end of the novel, Griffith performs his first autonomously willed act. Confronted with the love of two women, one rich and one poor, he chooses the poor one.

Salt had only one literary lesson it could teach Fitzgerald, and that was candor. Two years later when he reviewed another novel by Charles G. Norris, Fitzgerald had long outgrown whatever momentary interest he had felt for the writer. He could praise Norris only as the man who, by chance, had torn the draperies from Fitzgerald's window on the literary world.

> Although not one of the first I was certainly one of the most enthusiastic readers of Charles Norris's "Salt"—I sat up until five in the morning to finish it, stung into alertness by the booming repetition of his title phrase at the beginning of each section. In the dawn I wrote him an excited letter of praise. To me it was utterly new. I had never read Zola or Frank Norris or Dreiser—in fact the realism which now walks Fifth Avenue was then hiding dismally in Tenth Street basements. No one of my English professors in college ever suggested to his class that books were being written in America. Poor souls, they were as ignorant as I—possibly more so. But since then Brigadier General Mencken has marshaled the critics in acquiescent column of squads for the campaign against Philistia.[4]

Mencken's personal share in Fitzgerald's literary destiny must have become clear to Fitzgerald not long after he read Salt. Mencken —or George Jean Nathan, his co-editor—had taken "Babes in the Woods" for The Smart Set before Fitzgerald had left New York; it had appeared in the September 1919 number, before Charles Scribner's Sons had received the manuscript of This Side of Paradise. "The Debutante," like "Babes in the Woods" an excerpt from the novel, came out in the November issue; "Porcelain and Pink," a minor playlet, appeared in the January 1920 Smart Set, and the February number printed two Fitzgerald short stories, "Benediction" and "Dalrymple Goes Wrong." Fitzgerald thus had appeared five times in The Smart Set before any other magazine had printed his fiction—and a sixth time before This Side of Paradise was published. Mencken, Nathan, and The Smart Set had launched Fitzgerald into the world of literature. Sometime during the same period Mencken's books began to launch Fitzgerald into a new world of ideas.

Fitzgerald first became aware of Mencken around January 1920. It was then that he inserted Mencken's name into the galley proofs of *This Side of Paradise*. Writing Maxwell Perkins about his interest in the novelist Frank Norris, Fitzgerald added: "Another of my discoveries is H. L. Mencken, who is certainly a factor in present day literature. In fact I'm not so cocksure about things as I was last summer—this fellow Conrad seems to be pretty good after all." [5] Other remarks about Conrad and Theodore Dreiser in Fitzgerald's letters through the early part of 1920 seem to derive from the essays in Mencken's *A Book of Prefaces*. After his marriage in April 1920 Fitzgerald and his wife became friends with George Jean Nathan. Late in the summer Nathan introduced them to Mencken, and the co-editors of *The Smart Set* were occasional visitors at the Fitzgeralds' suburban Connecticut home. The following winter *The Bookman* gave Fitzgerald Mencken's *Prejudices: Second Series* to review. This interesting review—interesting not only for Fitzgerald's praise of Mencken, but also for his perceptive insight into Mencken's intellectual dilemmas—was published in March 1921.[6] It indicates that Fitzgerald had also read, from Mencken's already considerable corput, the first series of *Prejudices* and *A Book of Burlesques*. With Teutonic efficiency Mencken had completed his intellectual conquest of Fitzgerald in hardly more than a year.

But the question of influence on a creative writer is never quite so cut and dried. Over the next few years Fitzgerald made up two reading lists in which Mencken and Mencken's interests figure significantly, but not in ways one might expect. The first list, "The Ten Books I Have Enjoyed Most," has been dated around the autumn of 1922. It places one of Mencken's books second, behind Fitzgerald's perennial favorite, *The Notebooks of Samuel Butler*. Fitzgerald's choice from among Mencken's works was *The Philosophy of Friedrich Nietzsche,* and his comment was: "A keen hard intelligence interpreting the Great Modern Philosopher." One may wonder whether Fitzgerald was more interested in Mencken or Nietzsche—especially in light of a second list made up five years later. Entitled "Scott Fitzgerald Lays Success to Reading," it gives the books that influenced him most during his even-numbered years from fourteen to thirty. The titles for ages fourteen to twenty-two tell the familiar story: at fourteen, *The Varmint*, by Owen Johnson;

at sixteen, Robert Hugh Benson's *The Lord of the World;* at eighteen, *Dorian Gray;* at twenty, *Sinister Street;* at twenty-two, *Tono-Bungay.* For the most influential book at age twenty-four—Fitzgerald celebrated his twenty-fourth birthday soon after he met Mencken in the fall of 1920—he put down, not a Mencken title, but a Nietzsche title: *The Genealogy of Morals.*[7]

Meanwhile, in the third of a year between completing *This Side of Paradise* and inserting Mencken's name into the proofs of the novel, Fitzgerald wrote and sold thirteen short stories. It is to these one first must look to see in what directions Fitzgerald's art and intellect turned after *This Side of Paradise.* From a financial point of view, at least, these stories were spectacularly successful. Fitzgerald still wanted an income; the stories supplied it. But problems of adjustment to a professional career still remained to be solved, choices of forms and of roles still to be made. For all the prestige it gave, *The Smart Set* could not pay more than $40 a story; *Scribner's* magazine paid $150; *The Saturday Evening Post* paid $400 to start, quickly jumped to $600; and agents were eager to buy *Post* stories at even higher rates for the movies. What income the novel would bring was problematic. To live well as a writer one might want to sell to the *Post* and to the movies; to live with one's conscience was another matter. Trite as this issue may seem, it was a vital one for Fitzgerald in these early months of self-definition. He was only too ready at times to take the cue from others and depreciate himself. This was a case when his self-disparagement came without prompting.

It may be that Fitzgerald was troubled by his failure to start a new novel. In fact he began three different novel-length projects within a month after completing *This Side of Paradise.* When these came to nothing, he started a fourth around January 1920. But that too quickly petered out. One of the early efforts was to be a literary notebook modeled after Samuel Butler. The others, to judge from their titles and Fitzgerald's sketchy remarks in his letters, were to be works of realism in the fashion of Norris's *Salt.* The first was called "The Demon Lover," the second "Drunkard's Holiday," and the third "Darling Heart." While this last one was lying moribund early in February 1920, Fitzgerald began a letter to Perkins,

I certainly touched the depths of depression tonight. The action on that book, *Madeline*, has knocked hell out of my new novel, *Darling Heart*, which turned completely on the seduction of the girl in the second chapter. I was afraid all along because of *Susan Lenox*, and the agitation against Dreiser but this is the final blow. I don't know what I'll do now—what in hell is the use of trying to write decent fiction if a bunch of old women refuse to let anyone hear the truth!

Then he abruptly shifted his tone to talk about his discovery of Frank Norris.

I've fallen lately under the influence of an author who's quite changed my point of view. He's a chestnut to you, no doubt, but I've just discovered him—Frank Norris. I think *McTeague* and *Vandover* are both excellent. I told you last November that I'd read *Salt* by his brother Charles and was quite enthusiastic about it. Odd! There are things in *Paradise* that might have been written by Norris—those drunken scenes, for instance—in fact, all the realism. I wish I'd stuck to it throughout! [8]

Fitzgerald identified himself so completely with the school of literary realism that the success of his sentimental short stories embarrassed him as often as it delighted him. In September he had informed Perkins, "Also I'm writing short stories. I find that what I enjoy writing is always my best...." [9] By January he assured Perkins he was starting a new novel, "but I don't want to get broke in the middle and start in and have to write short stories again—because I don't enjoy it and just do it for money." [10] He desired money and he wanted to be a realist. It was like walking on two stilts of different length; he found it very difficult to co-ordinate them. "Now my novels," he wrote his agent, Harold Ober, "at least my first one, are not like my short stories at all, they are rather cynical and pessimistic—and therefore I doubt if as a whole they'd stand much chance of being published serially in any of the uplift magazines ... How about it— ... do you think a story like C. G. Norris's *Salt* or Cabell's *Jurgen* or Dreiser's *Jenny Gerhardt* would have one chance in a million to be sold serially? I'm asking you for an opinion about this beforehand because it will have an influence on my plans." [11] Norris and Cabell and Dreiser represented the company he wanted to travel with, though it is certain he had then read, of the three novels he named, only *Salt*. But meanwhile he was quickly revising two of the stories he had even more hastily written back in the summer of 1919, and the *Post* bought them together for $1,000. Soon he was to call both stories "trash." Of the thirteen stories he wrote between September and January he was to reject, as "trash," or with adjectives meaning the same thing, six in all. Two others were slight little playlets for *The Smart Set*, and another much-revised story, "The Smilers," eventually got into *The Smart Set*, where Fitzgerald let it forever remain. Thus only four of the thirteen stories did he consider worthy of respect. The day after Christmas 1919, he confessed to the editor of *Scribner's* magazine, "I'm in the most frightful literary slump—and I'm writing a movie to see if I can rest up my brain enough to start a new novel and also get the wherewithal to live until I finish it." [12] If one could not walk on stilts of different length, the best thing was to throw them down and hitch a ride, like Amory Blaine, in a rich man's limousine.

Still, one should be even more critical of Fitzgerald had these early stories been uniform in quality and consistent in their point of view. The wide gap between the strongest and the weakest of these stories was created in part by the turmoil in Fitzgerald's mind over conflicting intellectual and professional commitments. But it also represents the fertility of his imagination, his willingness to take risks, and most important, his capacity to question and criticize within his art his own newly developed points of view. Fitzgerald was stretching the truth when he told Harold Ober that *This Side of Paradise*, unlike his stories, was "cynical and pessimistic"; rather it ended with a positive commitment on a note of guarded optimism. Yet the two new stories Fitzgerald wrote immediately after finishing the novel, "Dalrymple Goes Wrong" and "Benediction"—two of the four early stories that escaped his condemnation—did in fact treat with cynical pessimism the individualistic credo he had developed at the end of the novel. Therein lies whatever permanent value they possess.

"Dalrymple Goes Wrong" represents the unimagined dark side of the willful independence Amory Blaine developed in *This Side of Paradise*. Bryan Dalrymple returns from the First World War, like Amory, and takes up the task of losing his illusions about the values of conventional society. But as he learns to free his will from restricting modes of conduct, Dalrymple lacks the imagination that made it possible for Amory to create a willful moral code of conduct on his own. Dalrymple instead turns to a conventional form of anti-social behavior. Though his daytime life remains as plain and color-less as before, at night he begins a life of crime. At times he found it difficult to square his behavior with his conscience. "The tremen-dous pressure of sentiment and inherited tradition kept raising riot with his attitude. He felt morally lonely." [13] But he succeeds at last in conquering his moral loneliness, by turning it into a positive credo. "Other men who broke the laws of justice and charity lied to all the world. He at any rate would not lie to himself. He was more than Byronic now: not the spiritual rebel, Don Juan; not the philosophical rebel, Faust; but a new psychological rebel of his own century—defying the sentimental a priori forms of his own mind——" (166). There is no difference between this self-definition and that of Amory Blaine—except that Dalrymple is committed, not to construc-tion, but to destruction. Eventually, "He found that it was on the whole better to give up considering himself as a rebel. It was more consoling to think of every one else as a fool" (170). The conven-tional society recognizes Dalrymple's new attitude of willful supe-riority without a glimmer of its origin. At the ironic ending the community he defied accepts him as its future leader.

The other story, "Benediction," took its setting and its frame from the old *Nassau Lit* story, "The Ordeal." But in the new story the spiritual crisis of a seminary novice is transferred to a nineteen-year-old girl. "Benediction" begins as Lois Moran, en route to visit her older brother at a Maryland seminary, has agreed by implication to go to bed with her boy friend when she returns. At the seminary Lois is surprised to find her brother Kieth much stronger and hap-pier and more confident than she had expected. Kieth was sweet; and Lois suddenly discovers that "real sweetness is a sort of hard-ness—and strength" (148). "Hard" is a major new word in Fitzger-ald's vocabulary of personal virtues. Dalrymple learned to be "hard." Lois Moran considered herself "hard"; but if Kieth too was hard, then her boy friend was made of "soppy softness" (148). Kieth explains to Lois how he has learned to be strong. "No, I don't think that to help others you've got to show yourself at all. Real help comes from a stronger person whom you respect. And their sympathy is all the bigger because it's impersonal. . . . It's like that idea of saving your life by losing it. You see we sort of feel that the less human a man is, in your sense of human, the better servant he can be to humanity" (149). Like Dalrymple's self-definition, this too closely resembles Amory's secular code. But Kieth is a seminarian, and his creed is not merely temporal. At the Benediction service, Lois, with future immorality in her heart, sees evil in a candle flame snuffed out by faith. As they part Kieth begs for her support. She sobs, "You've got me, Kieth" (155). Faith and morality have won out over doubt and immorality—or so it seems. The strong shall help the strong, Kieth had implied; but his request to her is too sentimental and romantic, his strength giving in to her weakness in an effort to turn her weakness into strength. Lois returns to Baltimore and writes a telegram cancelling her rendezvous with her lover. But the last line of the story gives it an ironic twist. " 'Tore it up, eh?' said the second clerk" (156). Constructive morality can offer nothing to compare with a love affair.

In "The Ice Palace," a third story that survived Fitzgerald's harsh self-criticism, the plot turns partly on a rejection of Amory Blaine's form of self-expression—making oneself indispensable to others, giving them a sense of security. Sally Carrol Happer, the Southern belle who becomes engaged to a Northerner, admits, "I'm the sort of person who wants to be taken care of after a certain point, and I feel sure I will be" (60). But she soon discovers that the desire of her Northern fiancé to take care of her masks the selfishness and lack of human kindness of which Amory himself had boasted. Her hours of wandering lost in the ice palace symbolize the death of her spirit that awaits her in the North; she breaks off the engagement and goes home. So far, then, as Amory Blaine's form of individualism represented a workable alternative to sentimental or conformist values, Fitzgerald seems quickly to have rejected it. Intellectually he was back at ground zero. As a stylist he had grown more and more clever and subtle. But the artist cannot escape taking some point of view; the question now became, would the point of view be created in Fitzgerald's mind, or would his stories reflect, like mirrors, the prejudices of his readers. Booth Tarkington, who had once been for Fitzgerald the model of a Princeton writer, remained for him the living example of a professional. Tarkington was a brilliant success in fiction and as a playwright; he was a man made wealthy by his writings; he was ranked as one of the most "naturally" gifted of all American writers; and he was put down already in 1920 by the serious critics as a sentimentalist, a man who had wasted his talent writing trivia.

The last of the four stories Fitzgerald considered "worth reading" —this is how he designated them in inscribing *Flappers and Philosophers* for H. L. Mencken [14]—"The Cut-Glass Bowl," was Fitzgerald's first exercise in the school of realism. A cut-glass bowl has been given to a woman by a rejected suitor, who chose it as an appropriate gift because it was "as hard as you are and as beautiful and as empty and as easy to see through" (97). She is an immoral woman, and the bowl figures in a series of family disasters. Finally the woman tries to throw the bowl out of her life. She trips, and falls on the bowl as it smashes to pieces. In the end we are to assume she bleeds to death. Fitzgerald may have included it in his list of stories "worth reading" because he felt Mencken would appreciate its realism, or because he was proud of its realism. But "The Cut-Glass Bowl," with its inexorable march to a ruthless punishment, belongs to that branch of fiction Mencken himself called pseudo-realism, that uses the fashion of realism as a cloak for sentimental moral judgments.

Then what can be said for the remainder of the stories, which Fitzgerald considered not worth reading? "Head and Shoulders" is a clever little story about an intellectual genius and a chorus girl who marry and reverse their roles. It is lightly anti-intellectual and takes for its theme the moral that life plays strange tricks. But there is a suppressed cruelty and despair in the situation; and the weakness of Fitzgerald's treatment may be suggested by comparing it to the 1930 German film *The Blue Angel*. "The Four Fists" is about a man who gets socked in the nose four times when he commits immoral acts. The fourth time he changes his business plans and does something moral; "some instinct in him, stronger than will, deeper than training, had forced him to do what would probably end his ambitions and his happiness" (188). But no, of course, morality makes him wealthier and more important and happier than ever. "The Camel's Back," of which Fitzgerald boasted that he wrote it in one day, and later wrote "I like it least of all the stories" in his second collection, turns on an acute feeling of class-consciousness and is marked by scarcely contained threats of violence against social inferiors.[15] "Bernice Bobs Her Hair" is a comic story built around feelings of social superiority and indifference, and ends with a physical act of revenge. There are many definitions of the true purpose of fiction in the modern age, but none includes the purpose that Fitzgerald's humorous early stories largely served: the vicarious satisfaction of sentimental inclinations and latent animosities.

There remains yet one story from this first group of thirteen. "The Offshore Pirate" was the last Fitzgerald wrote, the most amusing, and in many ways the most interesting. In his list for Mencken, Fitzgerald put it neither with the four stories "worth reading" nor with the four "trash" stories, but stuck it like a balance between them. He called it "amusing"; later he was to reject it as cheap. It is cheap, but only the last page reveals this to a first reader. Yet for an understanding of Fitzgerald's mind and art the story is more important than any other from this early group; one could do without *This Side of Paradise* and the full dozen other stories more readily than "The Offshore Pirate." As much as it is clever and entertaining it is also ideological, indeed it is dialectical; it incorporates a debate over values more substantive than any in the novel. "The Offshore Pirate" not only retreats from the skepticism with which earlier stories had treated Amory Blaine's solution to life's problems; it retreats also from Amory's solutions. All the issues that *This Side of Paradise* apparently resolved are here open to question once more. And this time Fitzgerald brought to them not only his innocence and earnestness, but also his new preference for realism, strangely mingled with the tricks and evasions he had quickly absorbed as a budding writer for the slicks.

"The Offshore Pirate" is the story of a genteel romantic hero, restored to his full glory, as if the war had never taken place. The story is set in a classic genteel conventional pattern. For the first time since finishing the novel, Fitzgerald reverted in style to his vague and sentimental romantic-poetic prose. A beautiful, willful, temperamental young girl, Ardita Farnam, is cruising with her uncle on a yacht off the Florida coast. She is fed up with stuffy, boring, moralizing, conventional suitors. She has taken up with a bad man, because he seems the only one who can give her life the romance and power

68

she desires. "He's the only man I know, good or bad," she says, "who has an imagination and the courage of his convictions" (20). The task of her suitor from the conventional upper class—though neither Ardita nor the reader is aware of this until the end—is to prove that he is equally as imaginative and courageous, though also good. Ardita is left alone on the yacht, and in a moment it is boarded and taken over by a handsome young man with a crew of faithful Negroes— otherwise known, in jazz circles, as Curtis Carlyle and his Six Black Buddies. Curtis and his crew have apparently staged a large robbery and are using the Farnam yacht for their get-away. "Ardita scrutinized him carefully—and classed him immediately as a romantic figure. He gave the effect of towering self-confidence erected on a slight foundation—just under the surface of each of his decisions she discerned a hesitancy that was in decided contrast to the arrogant curl of his lips" (25). Curtis tells his life story. He was a poor boy who grew up in the Negro slums of a Tennessee town. "There were inevitably a dozen pickaninnies streaming in his trail, passionate admirers whom he kept in tow by the vividness of his imagination and the amount of trouble he was always getting them in and out of" (27). Indeed he was a Huck Finn who grew old. He had become an extremely successful Broadway musician and entertainer. But he wanted more, much more.

> He wanted to have a lot of money and time, and opportunity to read and play, and the sort of men and women round him that he could never have—the kind who, if they thought of him at all, would have considered him rather contemptible; in short he wanted all those things which he was beginning to lump under the general head of aristocracy, an aristocracy which it seemed almost any money could buy except money made as he was making it. He was twenty-five then, without family or education or any promise that he would succeed in a business career. He began speculating wildly, and within three weeks he had lost every cent he had saved.
> Then the war came. He went to Plattsburg, and even there his profession followed him. A brigadier-general called him up to headquarters and told him he could serve the country better as a band leader— so he spent the war entertaining celebrities behind the line with a headquarters band. It was not so bad—except that when the infantry came limping back from the trenches he wanted to be one of them.

The sweat and mud they wore seemed only one of those ineffable
symbols of aristocracy that were forever eluding him. (28-9)

Curtis is extraordinarily class-conscious; and Ardita finds it extraordinarily stuffy and boring. She believes in the credo of Amory Blaine:
"Courage to me means ploughing through that dull grey mist that
comes down on life—not only overriding people and circumstances
but overriding the bleakness of living. A sort of insistence on the
value of life and the worth of transient things" (37). Curtis argues
that this attitude is determined by her class and social position, and
thus is one he cannot share. The sheer brazenness of his adventure
draws her to him, despite the "caste nonsense in his head" (40). But
he knows that two so disparate in their views of money could never
make a go of love. "Oh, blessed are the simple rich, for they inherit
the earth!" (40). Soon a coastal patrol finds them at their island
hideout. They await capture.

> Suddenly against the golden furnace low in the east their two grace-
> ful figures melted into one, and he was kissing her spoiled young
> mouth.
> "It's a sort of glory," he murmured after a second.
> She smiled up at him.
> "Happy, are you?"
> Her sigh was a benediction—an ecstatic surety that she was youth
> and beauty now as much as she would ever know. For another instant
> life was radiant and time a phantom and their strength eternal—then
> there was a bumping, scraping sound as the rowboat scraped along-
> side. (44)

Then it is revealed to Ardita that Curtis Carlyle is none other than
Toby Moreland, the conventional suitor she has refused to see. She
is radiant, pleased beyond belief. " 'What an imagination!' she said
softly and almost enviously. 'I want you to lie to me just as sweetly
as you know how for the rest of my life' " (46). Imagination and
convention march to the altar side by side; it is almost an archetypal
genteel romance. "Curtis Carlyle's" life and aspirations are left to
dangle; the end implies that only an aristocrat could have devised
the adventure and conceived the tale, yet the pathos and the realism
of the tale remain. On the other side, much of the humor and color
in the story comes from Negro songs, Negro dialect, and the incon-
gruities of the Six Black Buddies. But Fitzgerald uses them as stereo-

types marked by insensitivity and prejudice, capped by a remark of Toby's father: "We've been keeping pretty close to you in case you should have trouble with those six strange niggers" (45). The crassness and the blind sentimentality that lie just below the surface leave this story amusing to skim through—as its *Saturday Evening Post* readers were no doubt accustomed to do—but distasteful to consider. Yet for Fitzgerald's development it is of greatest significance, for it weds the refurbished concept of the genteel romantic hero to the idea, developed by Amory Blaine and re-expressed by Ardita Farnam, of unconventional, individualistic self-creation. And in that state the fused idea was to remain until Fitzgerald took it up again; for immediately after finishing "The Offshore Pirate" he turned to other things.

The next thing was "May Day." How and why Fitzgerald came to write "May Day" after a baker's dozen of popular, largely undistinguished short stories is a matter only for conjecture. When he wrote his agent Ober early in January 1920—"The excellent story I told you of probably won't be along for two or three weeks. I'm stuck in the middle of it" [16]—most probably he was referring to "The Offshore Pirate." In the letter to Perkins from New Orleans early in February, where he complained about the effect of censorship on his projected novel, and first mentioned his interest in Frank Norris and Mencken, Fitzgerald also speculated on his writing plans for the rest of the year. He would discard the threatened novel, and not begin "my fall novel" until June—with the idea of finishing it in August. Meanwhile, he would write three stories a month, one each for *The Smart Set, Scribner's,* and the *Post.*[17] One may take this simply for ambitious day-dreaming that he was careless in committing to paper. In fact during the following twenty months Fitzgerald wrote, besides "May Day," only three stories; all were written and published in the fall and winter of 1920-21, none appeared in Fitzgerald's "only three magazines."[18] "May Day" was the single product of the first half of 1920. Begun apparently in New Orleans, it was completed late in March in Princeton, where Fitzgerald had gone to prepare for his marriage to Zelda Sayre. *The Smart Set* printed "May Day" in July.

Fitzgerald has given us the clues to understand how nine months of full-time writing should have given birth suddenly to a novella unlike anything that had come before; our only obligation is to use them with care. "May Day" marks the first of several important advances, or turns, in Fitzgerald's career, where latent developments in style and thought suddenly came to fruition in his art. The question of influence, once more, is a delicate one. Did he borrow the fuel, or borrow merely a spark to ignite his own? Later, more significant, shifts in the direction of his art need to be traced in some detail. In the case of "May Day," new aspects of style and theme surely were inspired by his reading of Frank Norris and Mencken. Fitzgerald's adoption of Mencken's views—the adoption he spoke of when he inscribed *This Side of Paradise* to Mencken—comes out quite obviously in a letter he wrote in June 1920 to President Hibben of Princeton. "My view of life, President Hibben," said Fitzgerald, "is the view of the Theodore Dreisers and Joseph Conrads—that life is too strong and remorseless for the sons of men." [19] There is no definite indication that Fitzgerald had read either Dreiser or Conrad by June 1920; rather he is quoting directly from Mencken's *Book of Prefaces*.[20] From Norris's *Vandover and the Brute* Fitzgerald no doubt took the theme of the degenerating pseudo-artist for the character of Gordon Sterrett in "May Day." From *McTeague: A Story of San Francisco* he may well have been inspired to try a more expansive social setting, to widen his range of characters—in short, to tell rather than just imply the story of a place and time. Yet these are simple technical borrowings compared to the influence Norris and Mencken must have had on Fitzgerald's self-awareness as an artist. They were the first American literary men against whom he judged his own ambitions as a writer. For the first time Fitzgerald recognized that the editor of *The Smart Set*, who had so amiably welcomed his work, was one of America's most important critics, with high and demanding standards of art. And the young *Saturday Evening Post* author, whose cleverness and sentimentality were beginning to mark him as his generation's Tarkington, must have read Frank Norris's views on "The True Reward of the Novelist," quoted by Charles G. Norris in his introduction to *Vandover*.

> Once more we halt upon the great word—sincerity, sincerity, and again sincerity. Let the writer attack his . . . novel with sincerity and he cannot then go wrong . . . His public may be small, perhaps, but he will have the better reward of the knowledge of a thing well done.

Royalties on editions of hundreds of thousands will not pay him more to his satisfaction than that. To make money is not the province of the novelist. If he is the right sort, he has other responsibilities, heavy ones. He of all men cannot think only of himself or for himself. And when the last page is written and the ink crusts on the pen point and the hungry presses go clashing after another writer, the "new man" and the new fashion of the hour, he will think of the grim, long grind, of the years of his life that he has put behind him, and of his work that he has built up volume by volume, sincere work, telling the truth as he saw it, independent of fashion and the gallery gods, holding to these with gripped hands and shut teeth—he will think of all this, then, and he will be able to say: "I never truckled; I never took off the hat to Fashion and held it out for pennies. By God! ... I told them the truth; I knew it for the truth then, and I know it for the truth now." And that is his reward—the best that a man may know; the only one worth striving for.[21]

One should read "May Day" not so much for what Fitzgerald may have borrowed from Norris and Mencken, but for what their standards helped him to bring out from himself. What truths was he capable of telling, if he tried? And what kind of art does the truth make?

"There had been a war fought and won and the great city of the conquering people was crossed with triumphal arches and vivid with thrown flowers of white, red and rose."[22] Thus "May Day" begins. The indefinite time and setting of the prologue serve several purposes for Fitzgerald. Not only does the prologue provide the story with overtones of universal meaning. It attains also for Fitzgerald a necessary and highly useful detachment from the actual time and place of his story, New York City on May 1, 1919. Moreover, the archaic, formal, slightly ornate language of the prologue broke Fitzgerald free from his conventional style and tone; and in the language of the novella he took full advantage of his opportunity. "May Day" is simpler in style than any work of fiction Fitzgerald had written before. The language is descriptive and direct, where in Fitzgerald's earlier stories it had been weighted with value judgments, and rather vague. It is primarily a language of action. Persons are described more by movement and act than by interior states of mind. The language is sensual; it is full of textures, odors, colors. There is an extraordinary awareness of physical presence. The characters are not merely ideas, but three-dimensional figures, moving on a stage. Edith Bradin does not simply dance, she performs an intricate dialogue with a series of partners that conveys information about her social and intellectual position more effectively than an explanatory narrative.

> A fat man with red hair cut in.
> "Hello, Edith," he began.
> "Why—hello there——"
> She slipped, stumbled lightly.
> "I'm sorry, dear," she murmured mechanically. (46)

But the most pervasive aspect of physical description in "May Day" is its concentration on the human body; and it is this emphasis of style that gives the novella its primary moral and intellectual meanings.

As "May Day" weaves together the destinies of nearly a dozen major and minor characters, two principal focal centers for the story emerge, one a linear progression, one a personal point of view. The linear progression is in fact a linear retrogression, the degeneration of Gordon Sterrett, the pseudo-artist; or rather it is a display of the consequences of a degeneration that has already been accomplished, and has only in the story to reap its inexorable ends. Immediately after the prologue Gordon Sterrett is introduced in the language of physical decay: "his eyes were framed above with unusually long eyelashes and below with the blue semicircle of ill health, this latter effect heightened by an unnatural glow which colored his face like a low, incessant fever" (26). Sterrett had been drinking, let his talent go, got involved with a cheap girl, lost his job, and was in desperate need of money. "You seem to be sort of bankrupt," a friend tells him, "—morally as well as financially. . . . there's a regular aura about you that I don't understand. It's a sort of evil" (28). This description of Gordon Sterrett combines the mystic element in Fitzgerald's old idea of evil with the social dimension of his later concept of moral bankruptcy—but neither gives depth or meaning to Gordon Sterrett's character. The idea for Sterrett is the most obviously derived element in "May Day," and also the least interesting. It comes from the character of Vandover in Frank Norris's *Vandover and the Brute,* who was also an upper-class pseudo-artist who drank, let his talent go, lost his money, and got in trouble with a girl. But while Vandover's decline takes place in Norris's novel through a lengthy Calvinistic struggle between the good and the beast in man, Sterrett's decline has already been accomplished when Fitzgerald's story begins. His suicide at the end is simply the last step of an already determined solution to a naturalistic equation; and the story of Gordon Sterrett contributes to "May Day" only a thread by which to tie together start and finish, and a non-moral language which yet provides a moral context as it spreads beyond into the lives of others.

The second focal center, the personal point of view, belongs to Edith Bradin. She is the only major character in "May Day" whose perception is capable of extending beyond her own person, and much of the moral meaning of "May Day" derives from the occasions when her vanity overcomes her wider perception. Edith was in love with her own body.

> She thought of her own appearance. Her bare arms and shoulders were powdered to a creamy white. She knew they looked very soft and would gleam like milk against the black backs that were to silhouette them tonight. The hairdressing had been a success; her reddish mass of hair was piled and crushed and creased to an arrogant marvel of mobile curves. Her lips were finely made of deep carmine; the irises of her eyes were delicate, breakable blue, like china eyes. She was a complete, infinitely delicate, quite perfect thing of beauty, flowing in an even line from a complex coiffure to two small slim feet. . . . closing her eyes she drew in a deep breath of pleasure. She dropped her arms to her side until they were faintly touching the sleek sheath that covered and suggested her figure. She had never felt her own softness so much nor so enjoyed the whiteness of her own arms.
>
> "I smell sweet," she said to herself simply, and then came another thought—"I'm made for love." (43-4)

Edith was also "falling in love with her recollection of Gordon Sterrett" (43). He had taken her up to New Haven in his senior year. "There was a quality of weakness in Gordon that she wanted to take care of; there was a helplessness in him that she wanted to protect" (44). But when she meets Gordon Sterrett at the dance she sees at once that he has sunk far too deeply into degeneration. She turns cool. "—Love is fragile—she was thinking—but perhaps the pieces are saved, the things that hovered on lips, that might have been said. The new love words, the tendernesses learned, are treasured up for the next lover" (49). Edith Bradin's love for Gordon Sterrett dies, with the suggestion that the emotion of love for another may be no more than a desire to express one's vanity, one's competence, romantic skills. Edith leaves the dance and goes to see her brother Henry who is working late as an editor of a radical paper. She tries to dissuade him from his idealistic self-sacrifice.

> "I wish you'd—you'd come back to Harrisburg and have a good time. Do you feel sure that you're on the right track—"
> "You're wearing beautiful stockings," he interrupted. "What in earth are they?"
> "They're embroidered," she replied, glancing down. "Aren't they cunning?" She raised her skirts and uncovered slim, silk-sheathed calves. "Or do you disapprove of silk stockings?" (60)

Pleasure in her physical self quickly blunts her concern for her brother. But at that moment the novella's concentration on the human body takes a violent turn. A gang of soldiers, out roaming the streets beating up socialist May Day orators, breaks into the radical paper's office. In the melee one soldier is pushed out a window and crushes his skull on the pavement below; and when the police come Henry Bradin, Edith's brother, is discovered sitting on the floor with a leg broken.

The soldiers, two soldiers in particular, make up a third focal point of "May Day," as well as a second major aspect of Fitzgerald's borrowed naturalism. Whatever contact Fitzgerald may have had in the Army with lower-class enlisted men, Carrol Key and Gus Rose are drawn not so much from life as in naturalistic physical terms taken from Frank Norris's *McTeague*. Gordon Sterrett represents the degeneration of one pseudo-artist; Key and Rose represent "generations of degeneration" (35). The paths of Key and Rose run together with the paths of the other characters, adding a comic note and also a social perspective to the aristocratic pretenses of the Yale fraternity men, and a pathos to the social and personal violence. The soldier who fell from the melee at the radical paper and crushed his skull was Carrol Key; and later it was Rose whose animal nostrils breathed in the odor of decay from Gordon Sterrett. At the true end of the story—Gordon Sterrett's suicide comes really as an anti-climax—Rose is made to stand alone as the person responsible for violence. In the

Biltmore lobby he watches stupidly as Philip Dean and Peter Himmel, who had been Edith Bradin's escort, drunkenly cavort as "Mr. In and Mr. Out." Edith enters with her brother's co-editor of the radical paper. Pointing at Rose, she cries, " 'There's the soldier who broke my brother's leg,' " and the editor makes a "lightning-like spring" (73). In the end Edith's desire for love and the editor's radical principles—the only positive values in a story marked by physical degeneration, physical vanity, and physical violence—are themselves reduced to revenge and violence.

In "May Day" Fitzgerald proved that his imagination and his breadth of vision were greater than he had theretofore demonstrated. But he did not show that his imagination and his breadth of vision were under control. One reason why the novella has proven such rich material for critics is that its themes and motivations seem often so contradictory. It has sometimes been argued, for example, that Gordon Sterrett is the victim of society and of poverty. But there is no evidence in the story that Gordon Sterrett is the victim of anything more than natural weakness; and his poverty is not a cause of his degeneration, but its result. Equally, Edith Bradin represents the one internal center of consciousness in the story, but her point of view is undercut as much as all the others. The reader is permitted to share only one perspective on events, the author's detached and ironic point of view.

There is one passage in "May Day" that has attracted particular attention, a passage which stems from this naturalistic irony and perhaps from something more. It comes in the all-night restaurant, where Gordon and his cheap girl, the soldier Rose, and the college drunks Dean and Himmel have gathered. Himmel has been ejected for flinging hash around.

> But the commotion upon his exit proper was dwarfed by another phenomenon which drew admiring glances and a prolonged involuntary "Oh-h-!" from every person in the restaurant. The great plate-glass front had turned to a deep creamy blue, the color of a Maxfield Parrish moonlight—a blue that seemed to press close upon the pane as if to crowd its way into the restaurant. Dawn had come up on Columbus Circle, magical, breathless dawn, silhouetting the great statue of the immortal Christopher, and mingling in a curious and uncanny manner with the fading yellow electric light inside. (67)

This has been treated, in many ways justly, as a passage of profound moral meaning and historical significance. "Magical, breathless dawn" silhouettes "the great statue of the immortal Christopher." It mingles in a curious and uncanny manner with the electric light. Here are the heartfelt yearnings for the greater than real, the new dawn, the virgin offering of nature, linked inextricably with Columbus and his discovery of the New World. But, however significant this vision and this theme were later to become in Fitzgerald's fiction, in "May Day" they cannot yet be separated from the language and meanings that surround them.

One way to place them properly in their context is to recall an advertisement for "Edison Mazda" light bulbs, painted by the artist Maxfield Parrish, which appeared in the *Ladies' Home Journal* for January 1918.[23] In the painting dawn is rising over a mountain lake. A lightly-clad, golden-haired beauty of nature sits on a rock in the center foreground, watching with sublime awe as golden dawn strikes the mountainside, driving back the "deep, creamy blue" of a Maxfield Parrish moonlight, quite as Fitzgerald has described it. Beneath the scene an epigraph from Shakespeare appears:

> And Night is fled
> Whose Pitchy Mantle over-veil'd the earth.

The purpose of the painting, and the epigraph, was to sell electric light bulbs. It would be farfetched to suggest that Fitzgerald had this advertisement in mind when he wrote his passage of dawn, though of course he knew well enough the blue of a Maxfield Parrish moonlight. But with this painting in mind—and Fitzgerald's drawing on Parrish's name—it is possible to see that such "magical, breathless" dawns are false and sentimental dawns, and that if nature produces dawns equally as beautiful as the commercial artist can, they are equally to be distrusted. Nature plays many cruel jokes on men, and an appeal to romantic sentiment is chief among them. This passage is not an evocation of romantic wonder, but a heavily ironic deflation of it. Fitzgerald would have to alter his point of view and develop his control before he could, or would wish to, draw from this romantic vision a radically different moral value. Meanwhile, it was to lie waiting, like other seeds sown earlier, until Fitzgerald turned over new ground.

CHAPTER FOUR

F. Scott Fitzgerald began his second novel, *The Beautiful and Damned,* in July 1920. Late in March he had completed "May Day," just before *This Side of Paradise* was published; and on April 3 he and Zelda Sayre were married in New York. April was given over to a honeymoon and parties in New York and Princeton. By May the Fitzgeralds rented a cottage in Westport, Connecticut, where the parties continued through June. Finally by July he settled down to work again. It had been his belief, expressed in an earlier letter to Maxwell Perkins, that his "fall novel" could be finished up in three months; and he assumed the same length of time when work was actually begun.[1] But the first draft took him ten months. By May 1921 it was finished, and the Fitzgeralds sailed to Europe for the summer. It ran as a serial in *The Metropolitan Magazine* starting in September. Soon after that the Fitzgeralds were back in St. Paul awaiting the birth of their child. Fitzgerald devoted October and November to going over *The Beautiful and Damned* for book publication. It came out the following March.

The success and the notoriety of *This Side of Paradise* had thrust Fitzgerald, by the summer when he began to write *The Beautiful and Damned,* into New York literary life. George Jean Nathan and H. L. Mencken now became his good friends. Editors and critics like Burton Rascoe of the New York *Tribune* sought him out for reviews and opinions. James Branch Cabell, author of *Jurgen* and in 1920 among the most famous of living American novelists, entered into a genial exchange of letters with him. Fitzgerald began to speak out about the novels of his contemporaries; he even began to read them. Almost as soon as his professional career was launched he had earned a place among a group of leading writers and critics who seemed to share his values and aims; but whatever pleasure he derived from this swift acceptance, it may not have been wholly the best thing for him. It was obviously a great advantage for Fitzgerald to learn, as he put it in his review of Charles G. Norris's *Brass,* "that books were being written in America." [2] But he was not yet certain what kind of American book he wished to write, nor even what kind he liked to read. He may have been strengthened by the companionship and sense of solidarity drawn from his literary loyalties; but any commitment to group values could only retard, rather than push forward, his development of a self-sustaining literary and intellectual point of view. There are suggestive insights into this problem to be gained from the triangular correspondence that took place late in 1920 among Fitzgerald, Rascoe, and Cabell.

Fitzgerald entered the exchange—Rascoe and Cabell were old friends—when Rascoe sent him a copy of "Fanfare," the Knopf advertising pamphlet on Mencken. Mencken and Nathan had been "up at the apartment drinking with us the other night," Fitzgerald said in reply, "and he [Mencken] was quite enthusiastic about *Main Street.*" Then Fitzgerald went on to add his opinion of another widely publicized first novel of the "post-war generation," Floyd Dell's *The Moon-Calf.* "This *Moon-Calf* is a wretched thing without a hint of glamor," he wrote, "utterly undistinguished, childhood impressions dumped into the reader's lap with a profound air of importance, and the sort of thing that Walpole and Beresford (whom I abominate) turn out twice a year with great bawlings about their art. I'd rather be Tarkington or David Graham Phillips and cast at least some color and radiance into my work! Wouldn't you?" [3] Fitzgerald appears to be taking his stand here for sentiment and against realism; and he must have reinforced this impression when he wrote to Rascoe a short time later, "I still think *Moon-Calf* is punk, *Poor White* is fair, and *Main Street* is rotten." [4] But Rascoe was not reading these pronouncements for their philosophical import. After Fitzgerald's first letter he wrote to Cabell, "They tell me, too, that Floyd Dell's *Moon-Calf* is a good piece of work, despite the letter I have today from F. Scott Fitzgerald denouncing it a shade too fervently to be disinterested. . . . (From what I have been able to gather the themes of *Moon-Calf* and of *This Side of Paradise* are parallel, Dell's being only, as Fitzgerald puts it, without glamour.)"[5] To Rascoe, no doubt, there was no such thing as a disinterested opinion about a book; he had been a literary editor too long to harbor that illusion.

Fitzgerald was never to waver in his dislike for *Moon-Calf;* rather it must have grown when Knopf advertised it as "The most brilliantly successful first novel of many years."[6] But his views on Sinclair Lewis and Booth Tarkington did waver, and he appears too often like a good ideologue gamely trying to follow the literary party line. He came to write Cabell after Zelda Fitzgerald had procured from the novelist an autographed first edition of *Jurgen.* The thank-you note provided Fitzgerald another opportunity to take a poke at Floyd Dell. "I'm all for *Salt, The Titan,* and *Main Street.* At *Poor White* I grow weary—but at *Moon-Calf*—My God! . . . I appreciated your qualified tribute to Tarkington in *Beyond Life.* I agreed with it perfectly."[7] Fitzgerald may truly have believed that *Main Street* was "rotten" and "I'd rather be Tarkington," as he had written Rascoe. But Lewis had dedicated *Main Street* partly to Cabell; and in *Beyond Life* Cabell had gently played at Tarkington with razors:

> Mr. Tarkington has not mere talent but an uncontrollable wizardry that defies concealment, even by the livery of a popular novelist. . . . Mr. Tarkington is a gentleman whose ability none of us have any choice save cordially to love, and to revere. It is for that reason I resent its waste, and voice my resentment unwillingly. In short, I throw my brick with one hand, and with the other remove my hat. . . . the fact remains that out of forty-nine years of living Mr. Tarkington has thus far given us only *Seventeen.* Nor would this matter were Mr. Tarkington a Barclay or a Harrison, or even the mental and artistic equal of the trio's far more popular rival, Mr. Harold Bell Wright. But Mr. Tarkington has genius. That is even more tragic than the "pleasant" ending of *The Magnificent Ambersons.* . . .[8]

The end of Fitzgerald's variegation on *Main Street* came a month later when he wrote a letter of congratulation to Sinclair Lewis. The language is worth regarding. "Dear Mr. Lewis," he said, "I want to tell you that *Main Street* has displaced *Theron Ware* in my favor as the best American novel. The amount of sheer data in it is amazing! As a writer and a Minnesotan let me swell the chorus—after a third reading." [9] This is rather equivocal praise. Fitzgerald had just then read *The Damnation of Theron Ware* for the first time; and "sheer data" was not the kind of stylistic quality Fitzgerald was likely to admire. But no doubt it reflects the equivocations in his own mind between the Tarkington path and the path—to leave his contemporaries aside—of Frank Norris. His uneasy absorption of two professional manners into one comes out in this curious manifesto to relatives in St. Paul: "Still, as you know, I really am in this game seriously and for something besides money, and if it's necessary to bootlick the pet delusions of the inhabitants of *Main Street* (Have you read it? It's fine!) to make money, I'd rather live on less and preserve the one duty of a sincere writer—to set down life as he sees it as gracefully as he knows how." [10] For Norris that one duty was to set down life as *truthfully* as he knew how. What, since "May Day," had happened to truth?

Truth, principally, was no longer an issue. It had been discovered, catalogued, and stored away; the novelist's new duty was not to find it, but to tell it well. At the time Fitzgerald began *The Beautiful and Damned*, these were his views; and thus his early plans for the novel represent no new intellectual or artistic development, but simply reiterate the least interesting and most obviously borrowed themes of "May Day." His first statement on the subject of the novel came August 12, 1920, in a letter to Charles Scribner II. "My new novel," he explained, "called *The Flight of the Rocket*, concerns the life of one Anthony Patch between his 25th and 33d years (1913-1921). He is one of those many with the tastes and weaknesses of an artist but with no actual creative inspiration. How he and his beautiful young wife are wrecked on the shoals of dissipation is told in the story. This sounds sordid but it's really a most sensational book and I hope won't disappoint the critics who liked my first one. I hope it'll be in your hands by November 1st." [11] Here, all over again, is the character of Vandover from Frank Norris's *Vandover and the Brute;* here, all over again, is the idea derived from Conrad through Hugh Walpole through Mencken's *Book of Prefaces*, "that life is too strong and remorseless for the sons of men." In a later letter to Shane

Leslie, Fitzgerald promised that the new novel would be "much more objective" than *This Side of Paradise*.[12] But Fitzgerald felt objective because others were doing the subjective thinking for him.

Those others, of course, were Frank Norris and H. L. Mencken. Had Leslie been a reader of Mencken, the very next sentence would have given Fitzgerald's objectivity away: "I am now working on my second novel—much more objective this time and hence much harder sledding. But the bourgeoisie are going to stare!" This latter sentence is pure "Menckenese," the first direct copying of Mencken's style in any of Fitzgerald's writing, if the sentence Mencken quoted from Hugh Walpole is excepted. But as Fitzgerald absorbed Mencken's ideas he absorbed Mencken's way of expressing ideas as well. And later, of course, Fitzgerald's correspondents would not need to know Mencken's language to read into Fitzgerald the shaping hand of a mentor. To his relatives the McQuillans he described Mencken as "my current idol"; and to James Branch Cabell he wrote, "I have just finished an extraordinary novel called *The Beautiful Lady Without Mercy*"—the second working title of *The Beautiful and Damned*— "which shows touches of your influence, much of Mencken, and not a little of Frank Norris." [13] This reference to Cabell's influence is obviously flattery, most probably false; Fitzgerald had read little or nothing by Cabell at that point. But "much of Mencken, and not a little of Frank Norris" nicely reveals his literary and intellectual debts.

Fitzgerald was not the only writer in 1920 who thought with perfect fluency because he had fallen wholly under the spell of Mencken's ideas. As a critic Mencken exerted far more immediate influence on writers and readers in 1920 than any American critic has since; the explanation has primarily to do with particular historical circumstances that cannot be repeated. He had published and encouraged, as an editor and reviewer, the writers who emerged as major figures after the war, among them Dreiser, Lewis, and Sherwood Anderson. His study of the American language, undertaken during the war and published in 1919, encouraged writers to break from genteel convention and listen to the spoken language of the day. Above all, his attacks on American patriotism, puritanism, and middle-class values expressed the mood of rejection that young intellectuals after the war felt toward American society. None of

Mencken's literary followers could have guessed in 1920 that the master was tiring of literature, considered that his useful work had been done, and wanted to turn to political and social topics; not even Mencken himself could have foreseen the extraordinary popularity he attained among people who misinterpreted him, indeed who were meant to be his victims; it would have been difficult to believe in 1920 that from the perspective of the next generation Mencken's contribution to the truly creative and original aspects of postwar American literature would be rather small. In 1920 most American writers would have valued Mencken's praise above that of any other critic; and in the August 1920 *Smart Set* Mencken began his review of *This Side of Paradise* by calling it, "the best American novel that I have seen of late."

Mencken's review of *This Side of Paradise* appeared just as Fitzgerald was getting his second novel under way; and though when their friendship blossomed the writer and the critic must have talked occasionally about Fitzgerald's work, the review came at a decisive point in Fitzgerald's planning. As a document of Mencken's public opinion on Fitzgerald, therefore, it may stand in lieu of their unrecorded private conversations. "In 'This Side of Paradise,'" Mencken wrote, Fitzgerald "offers a truly amazing first novel—original in structure, extremely sophisticated in manner, and adorned with a brilliancy that is as rare in American writing as honesty is in American statecraft." This is a fair sample of Mencken's 1920 reviewing style, in its vagueness and its political and social similies. It must have flattered Fitzgerald to be so singled out as one of the elect; yet in praising Fitzgerald's sophistication and "artistry" Mencken had picked elements of style and point of view that Fitzgerald had rejected, in all but his *Saturday Evening Post* stories, in favor of greater realism in language and theme.

Mencken's discussion of content took the same form. "The first half of the story is far better than the second half. It is not that Fitzgerald's manner runs thin, but that his hero begins to elude him. What, after such a youth, is to be done with the fellow? The author's solution is anything but felicitous. He simply drops his Amory Blaine as Mark Twain dropped Huckleberry Finn, but for a less cogent reason. But down to and including the episode of the love affair with Rosalind the thing is capital, especially the first chapters. Not since

Frank Norris's day has there been a more adept slapping in of preliminaries."[14] Again, Mencken makes a highly favorable comparison with a writer Fitzgerald greatly admired, Frank Norris; and the reference to *Huckleberry Finn*, though more equivocal, also must have been flattering. But whatever generic relationship Fitzgerald's characters bear to Mark Twain's boy heroes, Fitzgerald had not given up on Amory Blaine's development the way Mark Twain seemed to give up on Huckleberry Finn. In fact Amory is more centrally isolated a character in the second half of *This Side of Paradise* than he was in the first. What Mencken found unsatisfactory, then, was Fitzgerald's positive answer to Amory's dilemmas, the credo of constructive individualism. In content, also, Mencken chose to praise aspects of the novel that most closely adhered to genteel character stereotypes and conventional norms. Mencken's favorable review of *This Side of Paradise* is thus not without its ironies. Had Fitzgerald followed the criticism of the great "sham-smasher," he would have paradoxically been pushed even deeper into the genteel Tarkington groove.

Fitzgerald may not have been aware of the inconsistencies between his aims and Mencken's, though they were re-emphasized when Mencken reviewed *Flappers and Philosophers* in the December 1920 *Smart Set*. After Fitzgerald had sent Mencken the book of stories with its self-disparaging inscription, Mencken had encouragingly written, "I suspect that it is a great deal better than you think it is."[15] But in the review Mencken took even wider license from Fitzgerald's denigrating hints; with his three-way division into "worth reading," "amusing," and "trash," Fitzgerald may also have suggested Mencken's opening metaphor: "F. Scott Fitzgerald in 'Flappers and Philosophers' . . . offers a sandwich made up of two thick and tasteless chunks of *Kriegsbrot* with a couple of excellent sardines between. In brief, a collection that shows both the very good and the very bad. . . . From 'Benediction' the leap to 'The Offshore Pirate' and other such confections is like the leap from the peaks of Darien to the slums of Colon. Here is thin and obvious stuff, cheap stuff—in brief, atrociously bad stuff." Mencken posed two alternatives for Fitzgerald's future. "Will he proceed via the first part of 'This Side of Paradise' to the cold groves of beautiful letters, or will he proceed via 'Head and Shoulders' into the sunshine that warms Robert W.

Chambers and Harold McGrath?"[16] By December 1920 Fitzgerald was deep into *The Beautiful and Damned,* and Mencken's choice of "cold groves" or "sunshine" must have seemed to him equally unacceptable places to be.

Whether it was through some unarticulated sense of these discrepancies, or through a more general desire not to be completely swept off his feet, Fitzgerald was seeking by the end of 1920—even as he was paying greater homage to Mencken—ways to maintain his distance and his critical perspective. When Burton Rascoe sent to Fitzgerald his "Fanfare" pamphlet on Mencken, Fitzgerald replied, "why has no one mentioned to him or of him that he is an intolerably muddled syllogism with several excluded middles on the question of aristocracy? What on earth does he mean by it? Every aristocrat of every race has come in for scathing comment yet he holds out the word as a universal panacea for art."[17] Fitzgerald had had his own ideas on aristocracy; though the kind of aristocrat Fitzgerald had criticized through Dick Humbird in *This Side of Paradise* was properly called by Mencken a "plutocrat." At that time Rascoe was asking his correspondents to help him distinguish Mencken's "oft-repeated code of honor" from the fundamentals of Christian ethics.[18] To this inquiry Fitzgerald answered, "Mencken's code of honor springs from Nietzsche, doesn't it?—the agreement among the powerful to exploit the less powerful and respect each other. To me it has no connection with Christian ethics because there is no provision for any justice to 'the boobery.'"[19] There were thus three subjects on which Fitzgerald potentially might come to disagree with Mencken: art, aristocracy, and ethics. He had sensed their differences even as he fell more deeply under Mencken's influence. But in the winter of 1920-21, with no competing intellectual interest on his horizon, Fitzgerald linked himself more closely with Mencken than ever.

Until that winter Fitzgerald had tried to keep separate in his mind the standards of fiction set for him by Mencken, and the standards set by the editors of high-paying popular magazines. By New Year's Eve, 1920, the wall had been broken through, and Mencken's values poured over in a flood to wash out the other. "Here . . . am I with six hundred dollars' worth of bills and owing Reynolds $650.00 for an advance on a story that I'm utterly unable to write," he confessed that day to Perkins. "I've made half a dozen starts yesterday and today and I'll go mad if I have to do another debutante, which is what they want." [20] In fact he wrote no short fiction for the next nine months; and the stories he wrote and published while *The Beautiful and Damned* was under way are of almost no value except as they reflect his difficulties with the short form. There were five. Two, "Jemina" and "Tarquin of Cheapside," do not strictly count, for they were slightly revised versions of stories dug out of the *Nassau Lit.* "The Jelly-Bean" and "The Lees of Happiness" were written before the novel was begun; "His Russet Witch" (retitled "O Russet Witch!" for book publication) was done in time taken from the novel. These three represent Fitzgerald's fiction at its weakest. They are of interest chiefly because they seem to be serving the function of dreams, to express and so clear the mind of its tag ends, anomalies, and contradictions.

"The Jelly-Bean" was the last of what Fitzgerald called his first manner, the "flapper" stories. The "flapper" in Fitzgerald's commercial stories had never been so interesting as the cruder but more imaginative conception, in several of the Princeton stories, of the genteel romantic heroine. Fitzgerald gave the intellectual and moral qualities of those early heroines to his later heroes, and the "flapper," whatever her value as a well-observed social phenomenon, represents either conventional morality, or is immoral. Nancy Lamar, the "flapper" in "The Jelly-Bean," was the first "flapper" Fitzgerald observed through the eyes of his post–"May Day" realism.

> "You hard?"
> "Like nails." She yawned again and added, "Give me a little more from that bottle." [21]

Nancy Lamar drinks corn liquor from a bottle, swears, gambles, and writes bad checks. Her head is filled with wild romantic notions derived from Lady Diana Manners (in John Davidson's *Ballad of a Nun*) and sentimental English novels. "Nancy had a mouth like a remembered kiss and shadowy eyes and blue-black hair inherited from her mother who had been born in Budapest" (20). There is a suggestion here that she belongs to the convention of dark ladies in romantic fiction; and also that "Jewish blood" flows in her veins. Thus the reader is prepared for her punishment; but though her sudden marriage at the end of the story to a man she does not love is presented as a punishment, Nancy Lamar's new husband also happened to be an extremely wealthy man. One need not worry so over her future.

The more interesting aspect of Nancy's marriage is its effect on Jim Powell, the "Jelly-Bean." Jim was an idler, a corner loafer; his "unconscious ennui," his "half-frightened sense of adventure" are suggestive of the character of Huck Finn in its first form, in *Tom Sawyer* (19). Like Curtis Carlyle in "The Offshore Pirate," Jim is an effort to portray the lower class outsider, the economic outcast, the "running-mate of poor whites" (19). But as Curtis Carlyle is a bogus concoction of the aristocrat Toby Moreland, Jim Powell too comes from the best Southern landed blood, fallen on hard times. It was Nancy Lamar's presence that pulled Jim out of his ennui, sparked in him "a vague and romantic yearning" (23). For twice helping her out of bad scrapes he earned her kiss, and it seemed "an enchanted dream" (30). Then he learned of Nancy's marriage, and felt broken. "All life was weather," the story ends, "a waiting through the hot where events had no significance for the cool that was soft and caressing like a woman's hand on a tired forehead. Down in Georgia there is a feeling—perhaps inarticulate—that this is the greatest wisdom of the South—so after a while the Jelly-bean turned into a pool-hall on Jackson Street where he was sure to find a congenial crowd who would make all the old jokes—the ones he knew" (34). Through this last touch of "Dreiser-Conrad realism" the reader is left to ponder the meaninglessness of life. The sentimental reader gains his pleasure from flapper deviltries and romantic yearnings; and the realistic reader rises superior at the end. One can eat his cake and have it too; but only at the cost of cold and lifeless characters, for whose ignorance one is led to feel, not pity, but something closer to contempt.

"The Jelly-Bean" represented in fact a watershed. In form and subject matter it belongs to the earlier group of stories. The next two stories belong to the period and the mood of *The Beautiful and Damned*. Much of their interest derives from the fact that Fitzgerald used them to experiment with the themes of the novel, particularly the theme of marriage; they also provide the first evidence of Fitzgerald's new concern with time.

"The Lees of Happiness" tells the story of a marriage between beauty and intellect. Fitzgerald had already taken up this subject in the story "Head and Shoulders," and was working it out again in his new novel. Where "Head and Shoulders" treated the idea frivolously, "The Lees of Happiness" turns it into heavy-handed naturalism. Jeffrey Curtain, a famous author, marries Roxanne Milbank, a famous actress, and they prepare to live happily ever after. But fate will not let them be. "A blood clot the size of a marble had broken" in Jeffrey's brain.[22] He was to live for years as a speechless, sightless, motionless vegetable; and Roxanne was to care for him faithfully every day for all those years. This loyal but tragic love is made even more remarkable by contrast with the marriage of Jeffrey Curtain's friend Harry Cromwell. Harry's wife, Kitty, is a thoughtless self-serving egotist who eventually divorces Harry to marry a wealthy man who can provide her with the luxury she craves. Kitty Cromwell is a negative projection of Gloria Gilbert of *The Beautiful and Damned.* She expresses Gloria's values—" 'Harry doesn't care about going out.' Spite crept into her voice. 'He's perfectly content to let me play nursemaid and housekeeper all day and loving wife in the evening.'" (129)—without Gloria's beauty or glamor. Roxanne Curtain possesses the beauty and glamor, but it is to her, and not to Kitty, that life has dealt its harshest blows. Roxanne portrays other aspects of Gloria Gilbert. The curious suggestion is made about her, as was to be made about Gloria in the novel, that she possessed the temperament of an adolescent, even of "a little girl" (124). And Roxanne, like Gloria, can love what is past and never to return. " 'You can't love that,'" Harry says, referring to the "expressionless mummy" that was Jeffrey Curtain. " 'I can love what it once was,'" Roxanne answers. " 'What else is there for me to do?'" (135, 136). In "The Lees of Happiness" the bad succeed and the good fail. To Roxanne Curtain and Harry Cromwell "life had come quickly and gone, leaving not bitterness, but pity; not disillusion, but only pain. There was already enough moonlight when they shook hands for each to see the gathered kindness in the other's eyes" (139). They are not "hard" in the way Fitzgerald's flappers are "hard"; but they are strong enough to preserve their values despite their plight. Though the story is limited by its inexorable naturalism, Fitzgerald has dropped his tone of superior irony; for the first time in his "realistic" stories there are characters one may pity and admire.

"O Russet Witch!" is also, in a way more surreal than real, a story of beauty and intellect. Merlin Grainger is a bookstore clerk who throughout forty years of life continually encounters a "Caroline" who represents, so he believes, "my romantic yearning for a beautiful and perverse woman." [23] But Merlin's "Caroline" is really a beautiful society woman, Alicia Dare; and all the magic fantasy moments in Merlin's four decades of romantic imagining were actual true life antics of Alicia Dare. When he learns this, Merlin is crushed. "He knew now that he had always been a fool. 'O Russet Witch!' But it was too late. He had angered Providence by resisting too many temptations. There was nothing left but heaven, where he would meet only those who, like him, had wasted earth" (119). This didactic ending unfortunately is not true to the story. "O Russet Witch!" is a story about the need for fantasy to give color to drab lives, and also about fantasy's inevitable disruptive effects on stolid middle-class respectability. Merlin Grainger's life is portrayed in its mundane aspects by a realistic treatment and in its fantasy visions by an interesting kind of surrealism. The sentimental moralizing at the end has no foundation either in the story's realism or in its fantasy; to suggest that Merlin, by not resisting the temptations of "Caroline"— Alicia Dare, could have attained her or what she symbolized, is to render both the realism and the fantasy meaningless.

These last two stories were relative failures; Fitzgerald was to admit it in the annotated table of contents to *Tales of the Jazz Age*, where they were reprinted.[24] He refused to give the editors yet another debutante story. And by the end of 1920 he had fallen several hundred dollars into debt. A stable income from professional writing did not then seem assured; and even if it were, there was no proof that Fitzgerald could live within it. Under these circumstances it is not surprising that he was attracted to the new medium, motion pictures, which seemed to have at its disposal sums of money the literary world could not come close to matching. In the previous winter he had sold "Head and Shoulders" to the Metro studios for $2,500; later Metro also bought "The Offshore Pirate" and Fox purchased "Myra Meets His Family." [25] Apparently he had also tried his hand at writing directly for the films. Here then was a source of income paying four or five times as much as the highest-paying magazine. "I have written numerous short stories to be published by Scribner's this fall, under the title of *Flappers and Philosophers*," he wrote Shane Leslie in August 1920. "I am living royally off the moving picture rights of these same stories." [26] When Mencken reviewed the book of stories it turned out that the two stories he singled out to condemn as "confections" were "Head and Shoulders" and "The Offshore Pirate"; the third story sold to the movies, "Myra Meets His Family," Fitzgerald had not even considered good enough to include in the book. [27]

This slap from Mencken did not deter Fitzgerald from pursuing the financial possibilities in the movies. In his hard-hearted, let-the-philistines-be-damned letter to his aunt and uncle McQuillan, Fitzgerald wrote, "I am waiting to hear from a scenario I outlined on Griffith's order for ___ ___ —who is a colorless wench in the life as is her pal, ___ ___. But I am not averse to taking all the shekels I can garner from the movies. I'll roll them joy pills (the literary habit) till doomsday because you can always say, 'Oh, but they put on the movie in a different spirit from the way it was written!'" [28] Whatever pose this represents, it is not the embattled but high-principled artist; whatever contradictions it entailed, Fitzgerald was capable of supporting them. If he planned *The Beautiful and Damned* as a slap at bourgeois conventions, immediately when the novel was completed he planned, as he wrote James Branch Cabell in February 1921, "to sell my soul . . . and go to the coast to write one moving picture." [29] Apparently nothing came of any of these plans. But Fitzgerald's interest in motion picture work revived in spurts over the next five years; finally in 1927 he went to Hollywood for a brief trial as a screenwriter. If Fitzgerald's interest in movies was founded on anything more than money, probably it was his own self-definition as an entertainer. However much Norris and Mencken had taught him to think first of truth and art, Fitzgerald had not lost his old idea of serving, through his talents as an entertainer, as a spokesman or a popular leader. And however much he had learned from Mencken to despise the bourgeoisie, he was always concerned with who was in his audience—and how many. Inevitably the growth of the movies into the most popular of art forms should have held his attention.

There remains one final issue to be raised from this period before *The Beautiful and Damned* was completed. Between the first draft of the novel, and its revision, the Fitzgeralds went to Europe. They were abroad for less than two months in England, France, and Italy, and from the evidence that exists, at this moment when other young American writers were gathering on the docks to expatriate themselves, Fitzgerald hated Europe. From London, as the trip was ending, Fitzgerald wrote Edmund Wilson:

> God damn the continent of Europe. It is of merely antiquarian interest. Rome is only a few years behind Tyre and Babylon. The negroid streak creeps northward to defile the Nordic race. Already the Italians have the souls of blackamoors. Raise the bars of immigration and permit only Scandinavian, Teutons, Anglo-Saxons and Celts to enter. France made me sick. Its silly pose as the thing the world has to save. I think it's a shame that England and America didn't let Germany conquer Europe. It's the only thing that would have saved the fleet of tottering old wrecks. My reactions were all philistine, anti-socialistic, provincial and racially snobbish. I believe at last in the white man's burden. We are as far above the modern Frenchman as he is above the Negro. Even in art! Italy has no one. When Anatole France dies French literature will be a silly jealous rehashing of technical quarrels. They're thru and done. You may have spoken in jest about New York as the capital of culture but in 25 years it will be just as London is now. Culture follows money and all the refinements of aestheticism can't stave off its change of seat (Christ! what a metaphor). We will be the Romans in the next generations as the English are now.[30]

So for the time being Fitzgerald would go home in order, as Mencken said of himself, not to miss any of the show.[31]

II

F. Scott Fitzgerald's second novel is about the American show, and how to live it through. *The Beautiful and Damned* is the novel of ideas to which *This Side of Paradise* had been the preface. There is little enough in common between Fitzgerald's first and his second novel, but they share most significantly almost exactly the same span of time: the decade from 1910 to 1920. *This Side of Paradise* takes its mood and its themes, not from the early atmosphere of the twenties in America, but from the problems and aspirations of the decade before; but if the mood and themes of *The Beautiful and Damned* can be placed chronologically, they belong to a decade even earlier. As a young man's novel—Fitzgerald was still only twenty-five when it was published—*The Beautiful and Damned* is a companion volume, not to *Three Soldiers* and *The Enormous Room* and other young men's novels of 1922, but to the young Frank Norris and the young Dreiser and the early Conrad. *This Side of Paradise* represented an advance over Fitzgerald's collegiate writing; *The Beautiful and Damned* marks neither a development nor a retrogression in Fitzgerald's work, so much as a recapitulation, out of order, of a by-passed state of growth.

The charm of *This Side of Paradise* lay in its sense of mastery and self-assurance; the languor in *The Beautiful and Damned* comes from its sense of drift and self-despair. In *This Side of Paradise* Fitzgerald devised a set of values by which to meet the postwar world; in his second novel these values are given notice only once, in Tudor Baird, "a relic of a vanishing generation which lived a priggish and graceful illusion and was being replaced by less gallant fools." [32] Tudor Baird is killed in the next sentence. These values were developed in *This Side of Paradise* through—and partly despite—shifts in the narrative voice between the soliloquy and the dramatic monologue. The speaker of the dramatic monologue in *This Side of Paradise*, when it was finally attained, was the novel's central character, Amory Blaine; in that novel Fitzgerald had achieved detachment by putting Amory's first-person point of view into the third person. The voice of the dramatic monologue is established early and maintained throughout *The Beautiful and Damned;* yet the speaker in the novel, the spokesman of a fixed point of view, is not one of the characters, but the author himself. In its chronology and social background *The Beautiful and Damned* may be called the least autobiographical of Fitzgerald's five novels; yet in no other novel is the reader invited so persistently to pay attention to the author's voice and character.

Unfortunately, where Fitzgerald is most exposed he is also most vulnerable; where he shows himself the most, he is least himself. Readers of *The Beautiful and Damned* who thought they were getting F. Scott Fitzgerald's latest views on the Jazz Age were wrong. They were getting H. L. Mencken's views and a prediction, perhaps, of what Frank Norris's opinions might have been. Whatever value Fitzgerald may have derived from his discovery of Norris and

Mencken had been spent before the novel, for in *The Beautiful and Damned* his own voice is almost wholly lost among their echoes. Fitzgerald had merely borrowed from Norris's *Vandover* the general conception of Gordon Sterrett in "May Day"; for his hero in the novel, Anthony Patch, he took over many details as well, from Vandover's passion for the bath to his animal behavior. For his stories Fitzgerald had adopted some of Mencken's views; in the novel he uses Mencken's characteristic language. *The Beautiful and Damned* is filled with musical metaphors; they were a fixture of Mencken's style, though Fitzgerald had never used them before.

Mencken's domination of the novel's social point of view is so complete that even Fitzgerald's sense for history and social nuance was crudely blunted. A perceptive awareness of social change had been one of the exceptional qualities of *This Side of Paradise*. Though *The Beautiful and Damned* covers almost precisely the same period as the earlier novel, it is almost completely insulated from an awareness of social change. The novel moves from prewar days through the First World War into the twenties, but little in it bears any intrinsic relationship to the historical circumstances under which it occurs. In the end Anthony and Gloria Patch win Adam Patch's fortune because Prohibition had brought about a reaction against reformers, and the judge may have thought "Adam Patch made it harder for him to get liquor" (419); but Mencken in his review of the novel quite correctly dismissed this as a *deus ex machina*.[33]

The Beautiful and Damned indeed is crowded with observations on American social life. But none forms a creative insight within the work of art; rather each is, as Fitzgerald said of one such observation, "a study in national sociology" (70). At times the style incorporates the opaque and banal clichés of popular social history: "Babe Ruth had smashed the home-run record for the first time and Jack Dempsey had broken Jess Willard's cheek-bone out in Ohio. Over in Europe the usual number of children had swollen stomachs from starvation, and the diplomats were at their customary business of making the world safe for new wars. In New York City the proletariat were being 'disciplined,' and the odds on Harvard were generally quoted at five to three. Peace had come down in earnest, the beginning of new days" (391). At other times it adopts Mencken's particular form of commentary on American social types and social values: "In April war was declared with Germany. Wilson and his cabinet—a cabinet that in its lack of distinction was strangely reminiscent of the twelve apostles—let loose the carefully starved dogs of war, and the press began to whoop hysterically against the sinister morals, sinister philosophy, and sinister music produced by the Teutonic temperament" (306). Mencken's style and his views were developed to serve distinctive journalistic and moral purposes; the reader who wants to judge their strength and cogency had better try them in Mencken's books, rather than Fitzgerald's. It is difficult to escape the conclusion that *The Beautiful and Damned* is a product of careless haste and intellectual confusion. Originality might have been its redeeming quality; but the excessive and literal nature of its borrowing dominates the novel. What remains is to discover how Fitzgerald's distinctive style and themes entered into the novel, and what significance they hold for his mind and art as a whole.

In his review of *This Side of Paradise* Mencken had singled out the first chapter for particular praise. "Not since Frank Norris's day," he wrote, "has there been a more adept slapping in of preliminaries." [34] Fitzgerald attempted to match Mencken's standard in *The Beautiful and Damned* with a first chapter equally adept; this chapter brings together in a remarkable way Fitzgerald's confusing and contradictory styles and themes. Up to the last two pages of the chapter its purpose is to "slap in the preliminaries" of the novel's hero, Anthony Patch. The opening page prepares the reader for a continuation of *This Side of Paradise;* in a style marked half by banter, half by romantic yearning, Anthony is presented almost exactly as Amory Blaine in the first novel had been left, as "a distinct and dynamic personality, opinionated, contemptuous, functioning from within outward—a man who was aware that there could be no honor and yet had honor, who knew the sophistry of courage and yet was brave" (3). Yet immediately on turning the page one encounters the style and perspective of H. L. Mencken—the series of unusual and oddly juxtaposed adjectives and descriptive nouns, the affectation of medical bluntness about life, a snidely historical tone implying the ignorance and fatuousness of most endeavor—utilized to bring forth Anthony's family background, and especially his grandfather, the notorious reformer Adam Patch, for whose "will to power was substituted a fatuous puerile desire for a land of harps and canticles on earth" (15). There is only one indication that Fitz-gerald is trying to speak in his own voice, and there he revives an old confusion: "Virginians and Bostonians to the contrary notwith-standing, an aristocracy founded sheerly on money postulates wealth in the particular" (4). An aristocracy founded sheerly on money is not an aristocracy at all, but a plutocracy; this had been one of Mencken's points in his essay on "The National Letters," as else-where.[35] By introducing this misunderstanding into the novel Fitz-gerald rendered suspect his themes that were founded on the aristo-cratic virtues of his characters.

When Anthony returns to the scene a page or two later he has already lost all trace of his first description and has been transformed into a lesser Vandover—a wealthy, lazy Harvard man, a dilettante and dabbling aesthete, whose pleasure in beauty was most fully expressed in a weak and sentimental eroticism. Fitzgerald then went back to *This Side of Paradise* for the dramatic form of dialogue he used to introduce Anthony's friends Richard Caramel and Maury Noble and their intellectual points of view. Caramel is the function-ing creator, a writer; Maury, the complete cynic; Anthony, the man pathetically torn between creativity and passive cynicism, ready to slip into the purposeless abyss that lies between them. They begin the principal intellectual debate of the novel, on the nature of art and artists; and it becomes obvious at once that Fitzgerald is talking consciously about himself. There is a hint that Anthony's asceticism and detachment are in fact masks to cover a deep fear of uncon-trollable natural force, "the threat of life" (27). But this fearful aspect of man's helplessness before natural force is quickly dissolved into something of a cosmic joke. The "Flash-Back in Paradise" intro-duces universal themes, jazz age and flapper themes, and inadver-tently deals another blow to the concept of artistocracy on which Fitzgerald later will insist.

> THE VOICE: . . . You will be disguised during your fifteen years as what is called a "susciety gurl."
> BEAUTY: What's that? . . .
> THE VOICE: (*At length*) It's a sort of bogus aristocrat. (29)

With the "meaninglessness of life" and the borrowed disdain for middle-class values so dominant in the novel, it is curious that the opening page should introduce Anthony Patch so strikingly in language reminiscent of *This Side of Paradise*. The values of the genteel romantic hero come up only once in *The Beautiful and Damned*, merely, with the death of Tudor Baird, to record their demise. Yet in an implicit way the qualities of genteel romantic heroism—either in their sentimental form or in the constructive reinterpretation made by Amory Blaine in *This Side of Paradise*—echo everywhere in the novel. In one sense the genteel hero has been broken up among the major male characters in the novel. Dick Caramel represents the entertainer; Maury Noble, the man who can give others—at least Anthony—a sense of security; Joseph Bloeckman, the Jewish movie producer, the entrepreneurial aspect of giving pleasure to others; certainly all three represent the drive for wealth and conventional success. Anthony Patch, oddly, least of all the male characters possesses qualities of the genteel hero; his presumably is the superior intelligence, a capacity more claimed for him than demonstrated. Yet in the more important sense it is around Anthony that the values of genteel romantic heroism echo most significantly.

In the late nineteenth century the genteel romantic hero had been one way, in literature, of getting around the social and scientific issues raised by Darwinian naturalism; Mark Twain's progression from *Innocents Abroad* to *Tom Sawyer* demonstrates how the genteel romantic hero had served as the answer, for a time, to his intellectual dilemmas. Thus in so thoroughly adopting naturalism Fitzgerald had thrust himself back in time into an intellectual position where genteel heroism was not an adequate answer. Anthony Patch represents that intellectual position; the literary genre of "the meaninglessness of life" may have been fashionable in the early twenties, as Edmund Wilson in his portrait of Fitzgerald said, but the moral issues of "the meaninglessness of life," for some American intellectuals of the late nineteenth century, had been literally a matter of life and death.[36]

Anthony was burdened by the fear that absolute knowledge was meaningless. "One must understand all"—that was Anthony's desire "—else one must take all for granted" (45)—that was Maury Noble's solution, but Anthony could not grasp it. He was unable to choose between wisdom and weakness. "I can imagine," Anthony said to Dick Caramel, "a man knowing too much for his talent to express.

Like me. Suppose, for instance, I have more wisdom than you, and less talent. It would tend to make me inarticulate. You, on the contrary, have enough water to fill the pail and a big enough pail to hold the water. . . . Say I am proud and sane and wise—an Athenian among Greeks. Well, I might fail where a lesser man would succeed. He could imitate, he could adorn, he could be enthusiastic, he could be hopefully constructive. But this hypothetical me would be too proud to imitate, too sane to be enthusiastic, too sophisticated to be Utopian, too Grecian to adorn" (36). So the meaninglessness of life, once he had succumbed to it, became the justification for his indolence. "I do nothing, for there's nothing I can do that's worth doing" (65). He would wait for "some path of hope . . . some purpose yet to be born" (55-6). Meanwhile he could be aimless and depressed, obsessed with "A self-absorption with no comfort, a demand for expression with no outlet, a sense of time rushing by, ceaselessly and wastefully—assuaged only by that conviction that there was nothing to waste, because all efforts and attainments were equally valueless" (93). He recognized that strength lay in ignorance. When he first went to work in a brokers' office, "He felt that to succeed here the idea of success must grasp and limit his mind. It seemed to him that the essential element in these men at the top was their faith that their affairs were the very core of life" (231). Considering the members of his college class who had become successful, he remembered "the days of his integrity," when "he would have cried that to struggle was to believe, to believe was to limit" (285). But he preferred instead to build his life on "the old illusion that truth and beauty were in some way entwined" (417). Anthony Patch fell in love with Gloria Gilbert.

For Anthony, Gloria was an escape from his intellectual dilemma. "He had realized at last what he wanted—to kiss her again, to find rest in her great immobility. She was the end of all restlessness, all malcontent" (107). Anthony was blinded by love; but it was an illusion even greater to think that an energetic debutante like Gloria would provide him immobility. In Gloria Gilbert, Fitzgerald tried to portray the apotheosis of the postwar debutante. Yet he was not satisfied with a single method of exalting her above mankind's common herd. He tried all he knew. The most obvious one was simply to deify her. This the "Flash-Back in Paradise" accomplished, informing the reader that Beauty would inhabit the soul of a "susciety gurl" (29). Another was to borrow from the romantic way of exaltation; Gloria became the Beautiful Lady Without Mercy from Keats's poem. A third was to borrow the language of H. L. Mencken and make Gloria into a Nietzschean superman, a woman of indomitable will. All three means of exalting Gloria play together in the novel in not too clear a way; and still she remains the simple little Kansas City debutante, anxious for marriage to a man of wealth, happy to be taken care of, wishing only to be "forever and securely safe" (155).

One cannot criticize an author for endowing a character with multiple and conflicting personalities, for he is only being true to human life. But in creating Gloria Gilbert, Fitzgerald seems to have taken as his norm something beyond human life. He meant to give his novel a universal theme, as he had also tried to do in the novella "May Day." But universal language pervades the novel as if it were a medieval fantasy, and ultimately social observation becomes irrelevant; for Anthony and Gloria are playballs of the gods, not responsible for their own conduct, and surely not to be considered as judgments on their place and time. "It never occurred to him that he was a passive thing, acted upon by an influence above and beyond Gloria, that he was merely the sensitive plate on which the photograph was made. Some gargantuan photographer had focussed the camera on Gloria and *snap!*—the poor plate could but develop, confined like all things to its nature" (105-6). *The Beautiful and Damned* might as well be about the Stone Age as the Jazz Age.

The universal theme is pressed so forcefully that whatever validity other themes possess seems quickly to fade. "Her eyes appeared to regard him out of many thousand years . . ." (102). ". . . not knowing that they were but following in the footsteps of dusty generations but comprehending dimly that if truth is the end of life happiness is a mode of it, to be cherished in its brief and tremulous moment" (137). "She did not know that this gesture of hers was years older than history, that, for a hundred generations of men, intolerable and persistent grief had offered that gesture, of denial, of protest, of bewilderment, to something more profound, more powerful than the God made in the image of man, and before which that God, did he exist, would be equally impotent. It is a truth set at the heart of tragedy that this force never explains, never answers—this force intangible as air, more definite than death" (414). It is carried through the imagery of the novel to link nature—the sun, life-giving nature—with the gods who play with destinies. To Anthony, courting Gloria, "She was a sun, radiant, growing, gathering light and storing it—then after an eternity pouring it forth in a glance, the fragment of a sentence, to that part of him that cherished all beauty and all illusion" (73). But that was one of his illusions; the sun was still in his sky, and the morning of their wedding broke "in yellow light through his east window, dancing along the carpet as though the sun were smiling at some ancient and reiterated gag of his own" (151). Soon, for Anthony, Gloria "hung like a brilliant curtain across his doorways, shutting out the light of the sun" (191). The end of the novel, the climax of Anthony's alcoholism and his moral and physical self-destruction, the day when their appeal on Adam Patch's will is to be decided, opens in sunshine. Gloria calls Anthony to see it. "Anthony glanced mechanically out the window ..." (442). She goes with Dick Caramel to the courtroom. Anthony remains behind, "looking down blindly into the sunny street" (443). Dorothy Raycroft, Anthony's Southern lover, suddenly appears. Anthony turns on her in animal rage and drives her out. His mind cracks. Gloria and Dick return with the exciting news that they have won the case, thirty million dollars are theirs. "They found Anthony sitting in a patch of sunshine on the floor of his bedroom" (446). The sun puts the spotlight on Anthony for Fitzgerald's last naturalistic irony. Anthony has reverted in his madness to his childhood stamp collection. "He held up a handful of stamps and let them come drifting down about him like leaves, varicolored and bright, turning and fluttering gaudily upon the sunny air ..." (447).

In the second way Fitzgerald exalted Gloria, the goddess Beauty became, in her romantic guise, the Beautiful Lady Without Mercy. Fitzgerald turned back to his collegiate emulation of the nineteenth-century Romantics. Returning to a romanticism he had once rejected in *This Side of Paradise* gave Fitzgerald another chance to write prose poems—"Her eyes were gleaming ripples in the white lake of her face; the shadows of her hair bordered the brow with a persuasive unintimate dusk. No love was there, surely; nor the imprint of any love. Her beauty was cool as this damp breeze, as the moist softness of her own lips" (102)—which conflicted with the dominant tone of popular sociology and naturalistic irony. It also gave him a dramatic issue that "the meaninglessness of life" could not match. Anthony's love for Gloria may have been an escape, but it would not have been so interesting unless it was also a seeking; the Keatsian motif supplied his answer. "She was beautiful—but especially she was without mercy. He must own that strength that could send him away. At present no such analysis was possible to Anthony" (116).

Gloria is the Beautiful Lady Without Mercy, a theme reiterated almost as often as the universal theme. Yet the romanticism it signifies is much more interesting in relation to Anthony than to Gloria. To Maury and to Anthony alike, Gloria is both the Universal Beauty and the Beautiful Lady Without Mercy. But there is also a *belle dame sans merci* who lived in Anthony's heart; it is she who lies behind the affair with Dorothy Raycroft at his Southern army post. Anthony, the romantic, always let his "superior intellect" slide into a vague aestheticism, and his aetheticism descend into erotic yearning. He could play with a simple girl like the movie usher Geraldine simply to indulge his erotic fancy. But Geraldine was drawn from Mencken's world, Dorothy Raycroft from Fitzgerald's. "For years now he had dreamed the world away, basing his decisions upon emotions unstable as water. The little girl in the white dress dominated him, as she approached beauty in the hard symmetry of her desire" (342). Anthony succumbed to Dot not only because her will was more powerful than his own, but because the intensity of her will had given her a certain beauty in Anthony's romantic eyes. The romantic themes in *The Beautiful and Damned* are less clear than the universal themes, perhaps because they came more from within Fitzgerald than from without. Yet in the contradictions and inconsistencies of the romanticism in *The Beautiful and Damned*, Fitzgerald was working out his more lasting, and more original, themes.

In *This Side of Paradise* Amory Blaine's "ancient distinction" was between the romantic and the sentimental. Only when he shifted from sentimental complacency to a romantic sense of impermanence was Amory capable of action. But for the plot of *The Beautiful and Damned* Fitzgerald turned around this "ancient distinction." The romantic is there caught in the middle between the naturalistic and the sentimental. It is Maury Noble, who truly believes life is mean-

ingless, who can strive for wealth and success; it is Gloria, the sentimental reader of *Penrod*, or Dorothy, the ignorant Southern girl,
who can crave love and by that craving find it; it is Richard Caramel
whose aspiration to do good makes him a successful writer. The
romantic does not know what he wants or how to get it. He is so
frightened by the thought that things will not last that it destroys
him.

The central confusion in the romanticism of *The Beautiful and
Damned* is of time: the present, the future, the past. Anthony becomes aware of his romanticism when he realizes that the moment
is unique and irreplaceable—that things will not last. In a night club
with Gloria, "—Anthony for the moment wanted fiercely to paint her,
to set her down *now*, as she was, as, as with each relentless second
she could never be again." She asks him what he was thinking. " 'Just
that I'm not a realist,' he said, and then: 'No, only the romanticist
preserves the things worth preserving' " (73). From Anthony's earlier impulse to paint her, it would be logical to assume he means
that only a memory or images of moments may be preserved; but he
may mean that his emotion can be preserved through time, or he
may mean nothing at all. For a short time later "a spark of wisdom,
a true perception of his own from out the effortless past," is struck
in Anthony's mind: memory is short. And when Anthony and Gloria
visit the Custis-Lee mansion in Arlington, it is Anthony who cries
out like a sentimentalist, "Don't you want to preserve old things?"
and Gloria who insists on the romantic belief that things will not,
and should not, last.

Fitzgerald added his own comment on how the past is transmitted
to the present with a Mencken-style historical quip. "The grey house
had been there when women who kept cats were probably witches,
when Paul Revere made false teeth in Boston preparatory to arousing
the great commercial people, when our ancestors were gloriously
deserting Washington in droves" (177). History, too, is bunk. Romanticism is again defined as "imminency of action" (214); love,
a chance embrace that exists only in the present, "coolly sought and
quickly forgotten" (207). Yet in the end it is memory that produces
the complicated final ironies. Anthony in fact returns to his past,
but only in madness. As he sails for Europe, successful and wealthy
at last, reminiscences occupy him; and they are false memories, false

memories that as they console him only deepen the reader's ironic sense that life plays many hoaxes and truth is wholly lost. For amid the dialectic between romantic present and sentimental past, it is the future—in the form of the fortune he expects when Adam Patch dies —which is the source of Anthony's undoing. Anthony is made incongruously to believe in the reality of his grandfather's future bequest, though his conviction that life is meaningless gives him no faith in any other aspect of the future. One can accept this from Anthony Patch, but only at the cost of his reiterated intelligence and sophistication. Fitzgerald was toying here with an idea of great interest and importance, the mingling in one mind of romantic ideology with sentimental emotion. This combination, in one of its forms, lay behind the nineteenth-century concept of the genteel hero; in another form it led to Amory Blaine's successful revision of genteel heroism, and in a third form to Anthony Patch's failure; later in other forms it would become an important part of Fitzgerald's three major novels. But in *The Beautiful and Damned* its value was lost in the confusions of Fitzgerald's many themes.

Gloria's "Nietzscheanism" is another source of the confusion caused by the mingling of overlapping and sometimes contradictory themes. It was Fitzgerald's purpose to make the reader see how much Anthony was controlled by Gloria; how he, weak and without will, succumbed to her power even when she did not wish it so. This end was accomplished by the theme of meaninglessness, to escape which Anthony desired to rest in Gloria's immobility; and by the theme of beauty, to which Anthony was susceptible. Anthony's efforts to assert his will against her will are entirely compatible with other aspects of his occasional desire to do something meaningful; it is not necessary to know that Gloria is a "consistent, practising Nietzschean" (161) to account for Anthony's failure. Moreover, this emphasis on her Nietzschean power strains her credibility even more, since she had already been elevated beyond the human to the stature of a goddess or a *belle dame sans merci:* particularly when the traits of character that most distinguish her individuality are sentimental ones—reading a movie magazine, crying over a long-dead kitten, wishing for her mother. In the details of her life Gloria would represent an interesting satire on the postwar debutante, were it not that Fitzgerald went to great pains, not to satirize her, but to elevate her significance. Of the several ways he went about it, the "Nietzschean" theme is the least relevant to any other theme of the novel; the greatest value of Gloria's "Nietzscheanism" lies in what it reveals of Fitzgerald's understanding of Nietzsche. Here is how he defined her code: "The magnificent attitude of not giving a damn altered overnight; from being a mere tenet of Gloria's it became the entire solace and justification for what they chose to do and what consequence it brought. Not to be sorry, not to loose one cry of regret, to live according to a clear code of honor toward each other, and to seek the moment's happiness as fervently and persistently as possible" (26). This is a precise enough statement of certain attitudes toward middle-class values and certain types of behavior that Nietzsche favored; but Anthony and Gloria, as characters and in their actions, misrepresent and abuse their Nietzschean creed.

The novel's racism is also revealing of the confusion of purposes which lies at the heart of *The Beautiful and Damned*. When the reader is asked to admire Fitzgerald's aristocrats he is meant also to admire their racist views; when he is asked to feel contempt for their weakness and blindness he is meant also to condemn their racist views. There is no need to go through every derogatory remark made in the novel about Italians, garlic-eaters, train riders, Negroes, Jewish shopkeepers, the millions "swarming like rats, chattering like apes, smelling like all hell . . . monkeys!" (394). The career of Joseph Bloeckman can stand for the whole. Bloeckman is introduced as an uncouth Jew, typical as much of all stupid, aspiring Americans as of his "race," an object of derision and contempt both in Gloria's and in Anthony's eyes. Bloeckman was a showman, an immigrant boy who had raised himself from circuses through vaudeville into the movie industry. "The moving-picture industry had borne him up with it where it threw off dozens of men with more financial ability, more imagination, and more practical ideas . . ." (97); but as time goes on, as Anthony and Gloria reach their peak of happiness and begin their inexorable slide down, they catch glimpses of Bloeckman on his escalator going up. Year by year he grows in dignity, in manners, in style. Anthony and Gloria, Dick and Maury, all end contemptibly or fatuously; Bloeckman, who began contemptibly, is the only major character who is made to rise in esteem. At the end Anthony, drunk and morally and physically broken, confronts him, now Joseph Black, fit, wealthy, proud. "Not so fas', you Goddam Jew," Anthony shouts (437). Enraged, Bloeckman beats him up. The reader is on Bloeckman's side, contemptuous of Anthony and his prejudices. Yet the curse has been made; Black is still Bloeckman, the immigrant Jew with intent eyes, upward creeping, growing rich as his movies ground out their "ancient moral tale for the edification of the national mind" (398). Bloeckman's part in the novel shows that the racism of Anthony and Gloria does not receive Fitzgerald's unqualified endorsement; rather it shows how adept Fitzgerald could be in the sentimental writer's trick of giving the reader both the discharge of the feeling and the condemnation of it; how skilled he was at having it both ways.

The Beautiful and Damned is not a novel that shows off Fitzgerald's literary skills; but it does talk a great deal about them. The novel is filled with conversation about literature. Some of it is spoken by Anthony, some by Dick Caramel, the novelist; but no reader familiar with Fitzgerald's earlier work or with his career could fail to see that it was about Fitzgerald. His public statements are put into the mouths of characters; *This Side of Paradise* is mentioned by name. There is a certain fascination in reading his remarks about himself; there is also a certain disquiet, for however much he was exorcising in a useful though not particularly artistic way his own fears and self-doubts, he was admitting that his fears and self-doubts went deeper than any of his readers could have suspected.

Dick Caramel is an unpublished writer when the novel opens; but he has already made the leap forward from college tastes that Fitzgerald had not made until after *This Side of Paradise:*

> "He's inclined to fall for a million silly enthusiasms. If it wasn't that he's absorbed in realism and therefore has to adopt the garments of the cynic he'd be—he'd be credulous as a college religious leader. He's an idealist. Oh, yes. He thinks he's not, because he's rejected Christianity. Remember him in college? Just swallow every writer whole, one after another, ideas, technic, and characters, Chesterton, Shaw, Wells, each one as easily as the last." (21)

The next time Anthony talks about Dick he sounds like Fitzgerald's warning conscience:

"So long as he sticks to people and not to ideas, and as long as his inspirations come from life and not from art, and always granting a normal growth, I believe he'll be a big man. . . . He tries to go to life. So does every author except the very worst, but after all most of them live on predigested food. The incident or character may be from life, but the writer usually interprets it in terms of the last book he read. . . . Dick, of course, can set down any consciously picturesque, character-like character, but could he accurately transcribe his own sister?" (46-7).

Dick's first novel, "The Demon Lover," is a great success, though it is damned by all the upright clergymen and public librarians of Mencken's America. Thereafter Dick describes the joys and sorrows of the suddenly successful young writer:

"It's been mighty funny, this success and all," said Dick. "Just before the novel appeared I'd been trying, without success, to sell some short stories. Then, after my book came out, I polished up three and had them accepted by one of the magazines that had rejected them before. I've done a lot of them since; publishers don't pay me for my book till this winter. . . . I'm certainly writing faster and I don't seem to be thinking as much as I used to. . . . I get a thing I call sentence-fever that must be like buck-fever—it's a sort of intense literary self-consciousness that comes when I try to force myself. But the really awful days aren't when I think I can't write. They're when I wonder whether any writing is worth while at all—I mean whether I'm not a sort of glorified buffoon." (188-9)

If one doubted that Fitzgerald was reminiscing about his own problems, he supplies the necessary evidence when Anthony quotes, as Dick's, part of Fitzgerald's "The Author's Apology" to the American Booksellers Convention in 1920.[37] Then Dick was confronted with the same type of financial bait that Fitzgerald had met. "In the two years since the publication of *The Demon Lover,* Dick had made over twenty-five thousand dollars, most of it lately, when the reward of the author of fiction had begun to swell unprecedently as a result of the voracious hunger of the motion pictures for plots. He received seven hundred dollars for every story, at that time a large emolument for such a young man—he was not quite thirty—and for every one that contained enough 'action' (kissing, shooting, and sacrificing) for the movies, he obtained an additional thousand" (222). None of Dick's later stories was up to the quality of the novel, and some, to Anthony, were "downright cheap." "These, Dick explained severely, were to widen his audience. Wasn't it true that men who had attained real permanence from Shakespeare to Mark Twain had appealed to the many as well as to the elect?" (222).

This too was a motive Fitzgerald in the past had shared. Later, when Anthony tries to take up writing, Dick gives him advice based on practical experience: " 'Well, it'd be a year and a half before you'd make any money out of a novel. Try some popular short stories. And, by the way, unless they're exceptionally brilliant they have to be cheerful and on the side of the heaviest artillery to make you any money" (301). By the end Dick Caramel had become a fourth-rate writer. In the novel it is the fall of 1920, and a new best-seller is crowding Dick Caramel's type of fiction out of the market. " 'You know these new novels make me tired. My God! Everywhere I go some silly girl asks me if I've read *This Side of Paradise*. Are our girls really like that? If it's true to life, which I don't believe, the next generation is going to the dogs. I'm sick of all this shoddy realism. I think there's a place for the romanticist in literature' " (421). This is a clever touch, a confession and an exculpation—a play for the sympathy of literary insiders and a titillation for would-be insiders. Failing adequately to display his talents in his second novel, Fitzgerald managed at least to advertise his first one.

CHAPTER FIVE

Of all the new writers who came into prominence in America after the First World War, none emerged so swiftly nor so easily as Fitzgerald. He was good and he was lucky; that combination explains sudden good fortune in any literary generation. But Fitzgerald was as much a representative as an isolated figure of success in the early 1920's. His early success was followed, and surpassed, by similar good fortune among a dozen other writers, some of whom had been publishing novels obscurely for four or eight or ten years. As changes occurred in the dominant modes of literary expression after the First World War, they also took place—if not the same changes precisely —in the tastes of the American reading public. On the most simple level this change in tastes may be charted through the months of 1920 on the list of "Fiction in Demand at Public Libraries" published by *The Bookman*. In June 1920 a novel by Zane Grey led the list, and works by Joseph C. Lincoln, E. Phillips Oppenheim, Eleanor H. Porter, Grace S. Richmond, and Alexander Black followed. By October *This Side of Paradise* was most in demand at public libraries throughout the United States; and in succeeding months novels by Sinclair Lewis, Edith Wharton, Floyd Dell, Willa Cather, and John Dos Passos were at or near the top. These names represent so many diverse literary and intellectual attitudes that no one new taste in literature obviously unites them, except that each in its own way was critical of contemporary American life. In any case by the early twenties the battle for new styles and new subjects in American literature, waged on so many fronts over the previous decade, had been decisively won.

"It would be difficult to imagine a more radical change in a few years," H. L. Mencken wrote in *The Smart Set* in 1922. "There thus remains no impediment whatever to the free functioning of the adolescent American literatus. . . . Let a new Fitzgerald escape from Princeton, and he is received with a cordiality (both spiritual and spirituous) that the president of his university might envy." [1] Fitzgerald may have been the first new success among the reading public simply because it was his fortune to publish a season ahead of the others. And yet Fitzgerald, in his fiction and in his literary personality, possessed qualities he shared with none of the others. Mencken's tribute, with its tone of mingled hospitality and condescension, both expresses and represents the way Fitzgerald became a literary figure of importance: partly through what he stood for and partly by the way he acted; though neither would have made a difference had he not also been a writer of exceptional skill. Yet under the circumstances only a writer of extraordinary self-control and inflexible purpose could have prevented his talent from becoming an object to be manipulated by others who wished to use his values or his personality for their own ends. On the contrary, Fitzgerald, with his instinct for advertising and entertainment, let himself become a prisoner, delighting in it. To a disheartening extent the history of F. Scott Fitzgerald's mind and art, in the first moments of his career as in the last, is the history of his reputation.

Fitzgerald emerged on the literary scene in late 1919 and early 1920 with one foot planted in the past and one foot stepping toward the future. That might explain why his early stories were welcomed both by *The Smart Set* and *The Saturday Evening Post;* but it explains even better why in the course of fifteen spring weeks the *Post* should have run six of his stories about beautiful, young, and willful girls. Fitzgerald's stories were about the antics and the slang and the styles of postwar youth; but whereas in his two *Smart Set* stories youthful values judged prewar standards and condemned them, in the *Post* stories the young, for all their daring new ways, played their games by prewar sentiments and standard rules. This must have been deeply reassuring to conservative readers of any age, for it implied that inevitable change would come without any great disruption in the eternal continuities. It must have been of enormous significance to advertisers in *The Saturday Evening Post* to see that the *Post* could maintain trusted standards, while presenting a picture of the young that would attract younger readers with money to spend; the difficulties of *The Saturday Evening Post* since World War II have demonstrated how important to its earlier success was its appeal to affluent young adult readers, an appeal which Fitzgerald's *Post* stories over a dozen years helped form. And it fitted, in an extraordinary way, with a sentimental desire of the older generation, fostered in part by the world war, to see the younger generation find particularly intense pleasure and happiness.

An undated, unattributed newspaper clipping in Fitzgerald's personal scrapbook suggests how deeply the older generation wanted the young to be compensated for having to fight their idealistic war. It is a society page article about the marriage of Fitzgerald's first love, Ginevra King, to an aviator during the war; society page articles hardly reflect reality, then or now, but they do reflect the attitudes of persons who must also have been attracted to sentimental fiction. This is how the article began:

> What a realization of the supreme power of youth is forced on us by these so-called "war weddings." The old and wise look on with awe at the valorous determination of the young to snatch happiness from the tremendous conflagration which is burning up our outworn failure of a civilization. The flames light up the radiant faces of our boys and girls as, two by two, they join hands and smilingly undertake to cope with the great catastrophe.
>
> In the shadows of the outer circle their elders look on, stretching out detaining but ineffectual hands, in helpless anguish. They are part of a closing chapter. To their sons and daughters belong both the present and the future. Each of these war marriages is a further manifestation of the triumph of youth.[2]

It was this triumph of youth, that young and old alike could glory in, of which Fitzgerald was to become known as the chronicler.

The reviewers of *This Side of Paradise*, which was published in the midst of Fitzgerald's first long run in the *Post*, made this clear. *This Side of Paradise* hardly fit the category of a sentimental story for *The Saturday Evening Post.* It was treated by some as an innovating and original work of art, and liberal weeklies like *The Nation* and *The New Republic* gave it more prominent attention than the usual reviewing media. But in periodicals closer to the book trade and to buyers of best-sellers, which *This Side of Paradise* was to become, the novel was important because it was exemplary, because it carried the news on youth, and the news was good. "The glorious spirit of abounding youth glows throughout this fascinating tale," *The New York Times* said. "We know that [Amory Blaine] is doing just what hundreds of thousands of other young men are doing in colleges all over the country." And to reassure its readers that hundreds of thousands of young college men were not out savoring the pleasures of immorality, the reviewer made clear that there was a "spirit of innocence in so far as actual wrongdoing is implied." [3] *The Booklist* of the American Library Association accepted Amory Blaine's representative nature but would not permit him to stand for all young men: "Amory Blaine, the hero, is a composite photograph of many young Americans who love the unhampered life allowed by plenty of money, fertile imagination, and freedom from parental discipline." [4] The upper-class atmosphere of the novel of course did not hinder its acceptance by sentimental readers. "It is probably one of the few really American novels extant," Harry Hansen, literary editor of the *Chicago Daily News,* was quoted in a double-page advertisement for the book in *Publishers' Weekly.* "Most writers feel that if they want to portray American life they have got to go down to the steel mills or into a mining town. Can you imagine any college man passing up this book?" [5] The *Publishers' Weekly* book reviewer linked *This Side of Paradise* with two safe old favorites—who were also two old Princeton men: "If you enjoy the thrill of discovering a new literary star and like the sort of thing Ernest Poole and Booth Tarkington at their best stand for in our American fiction, don't miss it." [6] It was "a convincing chronicle of youth by youth," said *The Bookman.*[7] "Those who read these pages," *Publishers' Weekly* concluded, ". . . will be apt to thank God that we have young men to write books as they finally lay the volume down." [8]

Fitzgerald spoke for the young, but he spoke as well to the old. As the reviewers read it, *This Side of Paradise* possessed an uncanny capacity to satisfy curiosity and fulfill expectations without unpleasant shocks or surprises. Fitzgerald was at his most clever when he coined the advertising slogan, "a novel about flappers for philosophers." [9] As the *New York Evening Sun* said, *This Side of Paradise* was a novel "in the very contemporary accent of youth, seen in the light of a wisdom he has somehow managed to steal from an overtaken middle age." [10] The style, the poems, the dialogues, the original aspects of the novel's form, could safely be accommodated—according to the *New York Evening Post*—because of the author's youth, the "Byronism that is normal in a man of the author's type." [11] But the tone was far more mature, exceptionally sensitive to the values and desires of older readers. It was realistic, but neither too much nor too little. It was partly representative of youth and partly not. It was not too immoral, nor was it too moral. It was serious, it was also funny. It was honest and true; it was safe. *This Side of Paradise* was almost unanimously praised. It was the old genteel story told, as befitted the desire of the postwar "Reconstruction" period for rebirth, in a new way. "It is the old 'literary material' of self-absorption in the early 'twenties; the old growing pains, old intellectual and emotional adventures mistaken for discoveries, the romantics and heroics, moods, fancies, the favorite stories even, albeit done in new terms and from a more or less new attitude . . . ," the New York *Sun* wrote. "It is the first self-conscious and self-critical offering of the exceptionally 'brilliant' contingent among the American youth whom 1917 overtook in college. You could think of it as the New Youth, more differentiated by the war than even the new Middle Age has realized, talking about itself in public exuberantly and yet with a certain sobriety and conviction youth never had before." [12]

But *This Side of Paradise* had not ended in genteel platitudes; Amory Blaine's final convictions had broken with sentimental values in favor of a new type of constructive individualism. Thus even the reviewers who praised the maturity of Fitzgerald's wisdom had also to call into question his intelligence. "In the last third," said *The Independent*, "he dives so deep that he gets well over his head. . . . [Amory Blaine] exclaims, 'I know myself,' but the reader doubts him." [13] *The Bookman* called it an "unconvincing protestation." [14] "Poor Amory is all dressed up, intellectually and aesthetically, with no place to go," H. W. Boynton wrote in *The Review*. "Perhaps we do not quite share his author's vision of him as a new-made 'personage'

—as one who without at all knowing where he is going is at last discernibly on his way." [15] Of course, none of the genteel reviewers was quite so critical of Amory's views as was H. L. Mencken, whose statement that Fitzgerald "simply drops Amory Blaine" suggests that Mencken did not disbelieve in Amory's ideas, but rather found them nonexistent.[16]

From a modern perspective the highly favorable review in *The Nation* was most perceptive. "Mr. Fitzgerald's mind is still hovering uncertainly on the shores of new seas of thought," *The Nation* wrote. "It is—to risk a bull—rather afraid of wetting its feet. . . . He has not yet reached any thought or perception that is absolutely his own." But *The Nation* recognized that the end of the novel represented not so much a conclusion as a beginning for Amory Blaine's new individualism. "He has not yet come into any self to know. Neither has Mr. Fitzgerald. But he is on the path of those who strive. His gifts have an unmistakable amplitude and much in his book is brave and beautiful." [17] *The New Republic,* in another mostly favorable review, praised the novel's "intellectual honesty" and "sometimes disconcertingly realistic investigation of a sensitive mind growing up in our own present-day civilization." [18] What *The New Republic* meant by honesty and realism was not necessarily what the newspaper reviewers meant by the same words. It was the genteel reassurances expressed by some New York papers that led Heywood Broun to his dissent in the *New York Tribune.* "It seems to us inconceivable," Broun wrote, "that the attitude toward life of a Princeton undergraduate, even a freshman, should be so curiously similar to that of a sophomore at Miss Spence's." [19] But that was just the kind of news, where and when it could be found in *This Side of Paradise,* that would have been most pleasing to sentimental minds.

There is no record of Fitzgerald's precise response to the reviews of *This Side of Paradise* as they came in during April and May and June of 1920; perhaps he could have made no precise response, for those also were the months of his marriage and honeymoon and first half-hearted efforts to end the round of celebration parties and get back down to work. In any case his intellectual stance and his views on literature had shifted so radically in the preceding half year that any discussion of the novel's attitudes must have seemed like ancient history.

What mattered to Fitzgerald was not what the reviews said about his point of view, but that they were so overwhelmingly favorable. In fact he was delighted to be regarded as the spokesman for youth to middle age; his advertising slogan, "a novel about flappers for philosophers," perfectly expressed the role he wanted his novel to play. His instinct for advertising—and self-advertising—took over from and dominated whatever literary or intellectual ends he had once wanted the novel to serve. To publicize *This Side of Paradise* a flyer was tipped into copies of the novel distributed at the May convention of the American Booksellers Association, bearing Fitzgerald's picture and the following statement, entitled "The Author's Apology": "I don't want to talk about myself because I'll admit I did that somewhat in this book. In fact to write it, it took three months; to conceive it—three minutes, to collect the data in it—all my life. The idea of writing it came on the first of last July; it was a substitute form of dissipation. My whole theory of writing I can sum up in one sentence. An author ought to write for the youth of his own generation, the critics of the next, and the schoolmasters of ever afterward. So, gentlemen, consider all the cocktails mentioned in this book drunk by me as a toast to the Book-Sellers Convention." [20] As another way of gaining publicity Fitzgerald wrote an imaginary interview with himself, but Scribner's advertising department declined to use it. Partly it repeated "The Author's Apology"; most of it eventually found its way into the literary dialogues of *The Beautiful and Damned*.[21] He expounded the same views in newspaper interviews where he could. Meanwhile his own drunken antics in New York were becoming as notorious as the antics of his fictional flappers. "They rode down Fifth Avenue on the tops of taxis because it was hot," according to one of Fitzgerald's biographers, "or dove into the fountain at Union Square or tried to undress at the *Scandals,* or, in sheer delight at the splendor of New York, jumped, dead sober, into the Pulitzer fountain in front of the Plaza. Fitzgerald got in fights with waiters and Zelda danced on people's dinner tables." [22] Yet not everyone could be expected to look upon the pleasures of the young generation with benign middle-aged envy and indulgence, and as Fitzgerald took it upon himself to be the spokesman for youth, to be in his own person the symbol of youth, it was natural that the opponents of youthful manners should have singled out him and his book as their target. He was called cocky and impudent, complacent and pretentious; and these were no doubt as true of his attitude as it was of the wealthy and genteel youth he had chosen to represent. But whatever blows Fitzgerald's ego had to take, this kind of publicity, as Maxwell Perkins told him, was "advantageous" for the sales of *This Side of Paradise*.[23]

By August 1920 sales of *This Side of Paradise*, as Fitzgerald wrote to Shane Leslie, had passed thirty thousand copies.[24] In the September *Smart Set* Mencken called Fitzgerald's book "the best American novel that I have seen of late." [25] For the month of October *This Side of Paradise* was number one on *The Bookman's* list of "Fiction in Demand at Public Libraries." A year after he finished the novel, half a year after its publication, Fitzgerald had attained a kind of prominence, both as an artist and as a literary public figure, which no young American has equaled since. He had managed both to express a mood and to embody it; the most striking parallel in recent years may be the youthful success of the Soviet poet Yevgeny Yevtuschenko. For both young men maintained a continuity with the past while providing in their person and their art an exhilarating sense of change, of liberation, of thaw.

But to meet both the standards of literary art and the standards of commercial success—and in novel and short-story forms at the same time—was a trick which required more care, patience, and guile than Fitzgerald in 1920 could command. No doubt Fitzgerald's extraordinary success with *The Saturday Evening Post* contributed to the aura of publicity and precocious power which surrounded *This Side of Paradise* when it was published; but journals like *The Nation* and *The New Republic* acclaimed the novel, quite possibly unaware that it followed rather than preceded Fitzgerald's commercial success in the short story form. It was Scribner's policy, however, to capitalize on the success of a novel by issuing in the following season a volume of the author's short stories. Fitzgerald took his title from the advertising slogan he had coined for the novel, and the collection was called *Flappers and Philosophers*. There were eight stories in it from the thirteen he had up to then published; and the first three in the collection, "The Offshore Pirate," "The Ice Palace," and "Head and Shoulders," were from the *Post*. The literary reviewers who had not known of Fitzgerald's commercial career knew it then, and their reaction was one of displeased surprise.

"What has happened to Mr. Fitzgerald?" *The Nation* asked. "The Offshore Pirate is on the level of a musical comedy 'book'; The Ice Palace and Benediction are falsely effective bits of sentimentality; Head and Shoulders is sheer trickery—a prestidigitator's 'stunt' in writing. The Cut Glass Bowl and Bernice Bobs Her Hair touch human nature and the course of life more closely. But both share the ugly hardness of the book's title.... In 'This Side of Paradise' there was both gold and dross. Instead of wringing his art, in Mr. Hergesheimer's fine expression, free of all dross, Mr. Fitzgerald proceeded to cultivate it and sell it to *The Saturday Evening Post*. Why write good books? You have to sell something like five thousand copies to earn the price of one story. *Sic transit gloria artis.*" [26] *The Literary Review* of the *New York Evening Post* said the stories were "without the native originality and unfailing inspiration that made 'This Side of Paradise' the most promising American first novel in recent years." [27] Mencken in *The Smart Set* was even more blunt. "Here is thin and obvious stuff, cheap stuff—in brief, atrociously bad stuff," he wrote. "Let us marvel at the sagacity of a publisher who lets a young author print 'Flappers and Philosophers' after 'This Side of Paradise.' If it were not two years too late I'd almost suspect a German plot." [28]

If it were anyone's plot, it was a genteel American plot. For there was an audience which, as it delighted in the stories when they appeared in magazines, delighted in the book. "The best are stories of youth," said *The Booklist* of the American Library Association, "clever, witty, with interesting plots and amazing young characters." [29] For if it was the triumph of youth that Fitzgerald heralded, the stories proclaimed it in so much more pleasant and mellow a tone than the novel. Even *The Catholic World,* as if to contradict Fitzgerald's claim to Shane Leslie that " 'Benediction' ... has come in for the most terrible lashing from the American Catholic intelligentsia," [30] praised the book of stories: "The eight tales which form this collection mark an advance upon the author's novel.... here are to be found originality and variety, with imaginativeness of the exceptional order that needs not to seek remote, untrodden paths, but plays upon scenes and people within the radius of ordinary life.

... The book offers to busy readers entertainment that can be enjoyed with no aftermath of self-reproach for having wasted time." [31] By the winter of 1920-21, as Fitzgerald was binding himself to the literary and intellectual values of *The Smart Set* group around Mencken and George Jean Nathan, as he was writing a novel that he hoped would make the bourgeoisie stare, it was to the busy readers who took pleasure in amazing young characters that he had committed his reputation.

The success of a best-selling novel is cumulative. Although it is not possible to know the precise chronology of sales, Fitzgerald did earn almost as much in royalties from *This Side of Paradise* in 1921 as in 1920, and nearly five times more from the book of stories.[32] He published only three new magazine stories in 1921, all of them early in the year, but the new novel began a seven-month serial run in *The Metropolitan* in September. And meanwhile literary periodicals were keeping his name before the reading public. In the April *Bookman* Sidney Howard's "Flowers That Bloom in the Spring (A Bouquet of Younger Writers)," featured a line-cut of Fitzgerald and placed him "athwart the cult of youth." To Howard, Fitzgerald was "unqualifiedly the most promising young writer in English." [33] An unsigned note in "The Gossip Shop" in the same number of *The Bookman* reported, "The most vivid personality to cross the doors of the Shop during the month is the astounding F. Scott Fitzgerald, whose next novel will strike an extremely different note from 'This Side of Paradise,' but a note that will be as daring and as impudent as his laugh." Then, the gossip went on, "we watched him wave his cigarette at an audience one night not long ago, and capture them by nervous young ramblings, until he had the room (mostly 'flappers') swaying with delight. Then, the autograph hunters! This admiration embarrassed him much—but after we had escaped into the outer darkness he acknowledged, with a grin, that he rather liked it." [34] *The Bookman's* August "gossip shop" carried a humorous letter reporting on the Fitzgeralds' spring trip to Montgomery, Alabama.[35] And in the same number appeared the first parody of Fitzgerald, Chapter Three of Donald Ogden Stewart's "An Outline of American History," entitled "The Courtship of Miles Standish, In the Manner of F. Scott Fitzgerald." As the third in his series Stewart's parody of Fitzgerald followed similar parodies of James Branch Cabell and

Sinclair Lewis, an indication that Fitzgerald had attained a position, where literature connects with popular social attitudes, second only to the authors of *Main Street* and *Jurgen*. Stewart had known Fitzgerald in St. Paul; his parody is very funny and exceptionally perceptive, and he appears to have singled out the tones of Fitzgerald's fiction that had made his work notorious. *"Enter PRISCILLA,"* reads a stage direction, *"infinitely radiant, infinitely beautiful, with a bottle of vermouth in one hand and a jug of gin in the other."* In a footnote at the end of his parody Stewart wrote, "For the further adventures of Priscilla, see F. Scott Fitzgerald's stories in the 'Girl with the Yellow Hair' series."[36] He named the two novels—from the parody it is clear that he had read the first draft of *The Beautiful and Damned*—and several stories from *Flappers and Philosophers*. But none of the heroines in those stories or in the novels, not even Gloria Gilbert, possesses together the two qualities that make this parody Priscilla so memorable—excessive drinking and implied sexual looseness.

Fitzgerald's ideas about his own literary and personal reputation, so far as they were clear to him, were dominated even before the publication of *This Side of Paradise* by H. L. Mencken's views of the American reading public. His curious Mencken-style letter to his aunt and uncle in St. Paul, late in 1920, was no doubt motivated more by a desire to impress his relatives by parroting his hero than by any interest to convey information; there his contempt for popular taste was most complete. He doubted that *The Beautiful and Damned* would have the popular success of *This Side of Paradise* and vowed that "if it's necessary to bootlick the pet delusions of the inhabitants of *Main Street* . . . to make money I'd rather live on less and preserve the one duty of a sincere writer—to set down life as he sees it as gracefully as he knows how." If *The Metropolitan Magazine* tried to serialize the new novel, he was sure its circulation would drop, and he predicted "within several years you'll probably hear that I've been hung by an earnest delegation of 100% Americans."[37] However much this echoed Mencken's disdain for the American middle class, Mencken himself, as a practicing journalist, knew the importance of communicating with an audience, of writing to be read and understood. With his sense as an entertainer and his desire to be a spokesman, Fitzgerald knew it, too. But the early twenties was a time of sudden and surprising changes in reading tastes and habits. Fitzgerald perceptively pointed this out in Mencken's case when he reviewed *Prejudices: Second Series* in *The Bookman.* "Granted ... that he has done more for the national letters than any man alive," Fitzgerald wrote, "one is yet inclined to regret a success so complete. What will he do now? ... Will he find new gods to dethrone, some eternal 'yokelry' still callous enough to pose as intelligentsia before the Menckenian pen fingers? Or will he strut among the ruins, a man beaten by his own success, as futile, in the end, as one of those Conrad characters that so tremendously enthrall him?" [38]

This remarkable speculation prefigures Mencken's career throughout the Twenties, a career of extraordinary popularity and influence, accompanied by intellectual frustrations. Mencken wanted to be the iconoclast, the Nietzschean nay-sayer; but this self-image could hardly maintain itself when every thunderous No! was eagerly devoured by his intended victims. His intellectual development in the twenties was marked by a desire to run away from the popular taste that was avidly following him; by the early thirties he had been forced to run so far that his sense of social reality had deserted him; and when popular taste shifted he was left in the mid and late thirties only with his eternal No, having lost both his acute critical sense, and his audience. The man who expects to make his living as a writer must keep a self-conception of his own intellectual and literary purposes in balance with his reputation—one now says "image"—the public conception of his work that impels readers to think they want to read his books, and editors to think their readers will want to read his articles and stories. This balance was difficult for many writers to maintain in the twenties, as difficult for Fitzgerald as for Mencken; and by adopting Mencken's views of the American reading public Fitzgerald made it even more difficult for himself.

During the twenties more good writers were financially successful than in any other period of American history. Dreiser made the bestseller list with *An American Tragedy,* Sinclair Lewis with all of his books after *Main Street,* and Hemingway at the end of the decade with *A Farewell to Arms.* Good novels were purchased and read almost as avidly, and sometimes more avidly, than bad ones. Under such circumstances of unexpected popularity the most sure and steady values a writer could command were his own; and for the man who had not yet settled his intellectual values, a firm self-definition of his professional attitude was all the more necessary. Even Emerson and Whitman, with all the opportunities for multiple interpretations they introduced into their writing, managed their reputations with steadfast and single-minded care. In the first two years of his career, however, Fitzgerald had neither felt nor been made aware of the need to keep control of his own public image in the same way. His success had been swift and comprehensive, he had charmed the reading public and the reviewers and the magazine editors and a critical group of major literary figures all at once and with the same gestures, so it should have been no surprise that he took his popularity for granted; but if he lacked a wary sense of what the public thought of him, he lacked, even more significantly, a coherent idea of what was his own public. Simultaneously he had adopted *Saturday Evening Post* standards of popularity and Mencken's much different standards of a writer's audience, without assimilating them together. Thus late in 1921, when *The Beautiful and Damned* was running serially in *The Metropolitan Magazine* prior to its book publication the following March, he could write Maxwell Perkins, "I do not expect in any event that I am to have the same person-for-person public this time that *Paradise* had. My one hope is to be endorsed by the intellectually elite and thus *forced* onto people as Conrad has," and ten days later in a completely different mood tell Perkins, "I prophesy that [*The Beautiful and Damned*] will go about 60,000 copies the first year." [39] If Fitzgerald could let his sentimental readers have it both ways, there was no reason why he shouldn't have it both ways, too.

But there was a certain disquiet in Fitzgerald's mood of late 1921. It came out in bursts of despair or of pique in his letters that winter, and it was bound to find a reflection in Fitzgerald's thoughts about his reputation. For one thing his old college friend John Peale Bishop had reviewed *The Beautiful and Damned*, prematurely, in *Vanity Fair* for October 1921. In a review called "Three Brilliant Young Novelists" Bishop considered Fitzgerald's book along with *The Beginning of Wisdom* by Stephen Vincent Benét and *Three Soldiers* by John Dos Passos. Bishop faintly praised and faintly damned

Fitzgerald's novel and then turned to the subject of Fitzgerald himself. "The most interesting thing about Mr. Fitzgerald's book is Mr. Fitzgerald. He has already created about himself a legend. In New York, I have heard hints, and from Paris, stories which it would be discourteous and useless for me to repeat. The true stories about Fitzgerald are always published under his own name. He has the rare faculty of being able to experience romantic and ingenuous emotions and a half hour later regard them with satiric detachment. He has an amazing grasp of the superficialities of the men and women about him, but he has not yet a profound understanding of their motives, either intellectual or passionate. Even with his famous flapper, he has as yet failed to show that hard intelligence, that intricate emotional equipment upon which her charm depends, so that Gloria, the beautiful and damned lady of his imaginings, remains a little inexplicable, a pretty, vulgar shadow of her prototype." Stephen Vincent Benét received equally condescending treatment at Bishop's hands, for Bishop was reserving his enthusiasm for *Three Soldiers*. "It is so good," he wrote, "that I am tempted to topple from my critical perch and go up and down the street with banners and drums." The review concluded with the words, "John Dos Passos is a genius." [40]

Fitzgerald had been the first of the young men to make a big critical and popular success, and he had withstood the challenge thereafter of Floyd Dell, Robert Nathan, and Benét. But John Dos Passos had evoked from John Peale Bishop the kind of praise Fitzgerald never had. Fitzgerald had been surpassed; moreover Bishop had displayed an attitude toward him that his friends and critics were increasingly to take, the attitude that nothing in Fitzgerald's life was too private for public discussion in a lighthearted and slightly contemptuous manner. To his own literary friends he seemed to appear more as a celebrity than as a writer; and not a celebrity to whom particular deference need be paid. Thus when Fitzgerald learned that he was to be the subject of an essay in *The Bookman's* "Literary Spotlight" series, timed to coincide with publication of the novel and written by his other close literary associate from the *Nassau Lit* days, Edmund Wilson, he wrote immediately to see a copy before it went into print. [41] When Wilson sent him a copy of the forthcoming article Fitzgerald responded to its extremely intelligent and in many ways devastating criticism with honest and gracious praise. "Like everything you write," he told Wilson, "it seems to me pretty generally true. I am guilty of its every stricture and I take an extraordinary delight in its considered approbation." But there were aspects of Wilson's article that Fitzgerald knew at once would be damaging to his reputation. "Now as to the liquor thing—it's true, but nevertheless I'm going to ask you to take it out. It leaves a loophole through which I can be attacked and discredited by every moralist who reads the article. Wasn't it Bernard Shaw who said that you've either got to be conventional in your work or in your private life or get into trouble? Anyway, the legend about my liquoring is terribly widespread and this thing would hurt me more than you could imagine—both in my contact with people with whom I'm thrown—relatives and respectable friends—and, what is much more important, financially." [42] Wilson obliged him; in the printed article the only reference to drinking in which Fitzgerald himself is implicated comes in a quotation about Irish character that Fitzgerald had approved. But Fitzgerald's objections caused a brief strain in the relations between the two men, as one can see from the injured and slightly more acerbic tone of Fitzgerald's following letter. "But I feel quite sure," he finished up the next letter, "that if Mencken in doing a 'Literary Spotlight' on Dreiser . . . had remarked that Dreiser was really the hero of all the seductions mentioned in *The Titan* I think Dreiser would have torn his hair." [43] If Fitzgerald had known the truth about Dreiser and Mencken he might have tried to find a relationship more hopefully apt. For Mencken had by then ceased to champion Dreiser and was much more likely to be found privately denigrating the novelist; and soon their friendship was to break off completely.

Wilson was trying only to be honest. His temperament was far different from Fitzgerald's, but their moral and intellectual values were remarkably close; under the circumstances there were aspects of Fitzgerald's work he could simultaneously deprecate and admire. The theme of Wilson's article was that Fitzgerald, for all his talent, lacked ideas and intellectual control; nevertheless, Wilson recognized in Fitzgerald an "intellectual nimbleness" and an "intellectual importance." [44] Wilson was too involved with the personal and emotional world that lay behind *This Side of Paradise* to see clearly the novel's particular significance; the depths of Fitzgerald's novels, such as they were, did not interest him so much as the surfaces, and the criticism of American life he found there seemed to him most important of all. In trying to be honest Wilson was in fact generous; and Fitzgerald had good reason to be as grateful as he was for such a penetrating and sympathetic study.

Fitzgerald also had reason to be grateful for the press *The Beautiful and Damned* received. It was a novel that almost no one among the reviewers liked. But he was handled gently, as a person who deserved respect, as a figure of greater symbolic or social importance even than his novels were worth. Only *The New York Times,* which by its non-literary moral standards had found *This Side of Paradise* wholesome and representative, rejected the second novel completely, and on the same grounds. "It would not be easy to find a more thoroughly depressing book," *The Times* reviewer said, a book whose characters lived "lives utterly worthless and utterly futile." [45] Elsewhere, criticism of the novel was tempered by praise for the novelist himself. "I think Mr. Fitzgerald has the gift, if he has the patience to sort it out from minor gifts and give it a chance," H. W. Boynton wrote in *The Independent.* What Boynton most liked in the novel was its "modern morality," in which Anthony and Gloria were punished for their excesses; what he least liked was its wit.[46] In *The Atlantic Monthly* Henry Beston found the novel, after the promise of *This Side of Paradise,* a disappointment; "But the picture of the time is there; a really amazing picture. It represents no mean achievement. . . . the picture and the good talk carry the reader brilliantly through to the end." [47] *The Literary Digest,* on the other hand, took pains to insist that "it is not important as a picture of to-day. . . . Our young people are not like Anthony and Gloria. . . . As a strain in the national make up nothing could be more negligible." *The Literary Digest* gave extensive praise to Fitzgerald's qualities as a writer, but insisted that he had to prove himself by writing something "more important than these clever studies of a shallow group." [48] So too *The Catholic World,* which had given favorable notices to Fitzgerald's first two books, criticized the new novel for sordidness and emptiness, but conceded to Fitzgerald "the writer's gift; . . . Nevertheless, because of affectation, his work is artificial rather than artistic." [49] Edwin F. Edgett, the perceptive reviewer for

The Boston Evening Transcript, who had given a favorable welcoming review to *This Side of Paradise,* saw in the second novel no advance. "No one can justly claim that Mr. Fitzgerald is a man of no ideas. On the contrary, it may be fairly asserted that he is a man of too many ideas or of a confusion and profusion of them. It is probably for this reason that he has so many admirers, that he is the apostle of a literary cult that seeks to exalt him at once, without giving him a due trial, to the ranks of the great." [50] He may have had in mind Mencken and *The Smart Set* group; yet the "literary cult" that had exalted Fitzgerald most assiduously was not Mencken's circle, but rather that group of genteel periodicals and conventional reviewers who had found in Fitzgerald's fiction a safely traditional attitude toward postwar youth, who had made of him their youthful chronicler of youth. This was the group who had had to evaluate *The Beautiful and Damned* with circumspection, as if to protect its favored author from his unsavory themes.

At the most lighthearted extreme the New York *Tribune,* whose columnists Heywood Broun and Franklin P. Adams had attacked *This Side of Paradise,* figuratively threw up its hands at the second novel and assigned the review to Zelda S. Fitzgerald.[51] At the other, more somber, extreme, Henry Seidel Canby, editor of *The Literary Review* of the *New York Evening Post,* put in words what lay behind the equivocations of magazines like *The Literary Digest.* This time Fitzgerald had given the news on youth, and the news was bad. "He seems to say to the older generation: 'Here we are, we youngsters, and this is how we can drink and suffer and wonder and pretend to have no hope. What do you make of us?' The reply of the older generation, as Henry Seidel Canby formulates it in the New York *Evening Post,* is: 'we are a little disgusted, a little touched, and profoundly interested.' When Mr. Fitzgerald grows up, in art as well as in philosophy, Dr. Canby goes on to comment, 'he may tell us more, and more wisely. He will write better novels, but he will probably never give us better documents of distraught and abandoned but intensely living youth.'" [52] Speaking for the older generation, Canby was wise and patient enough to know how to handle the revolt of the genteel romantic hero. The aspiring young man who begins by adhering to old standards may show his power unconventionally—"this is how we *can* drink and suffer and wonder and *pretend* to have no hope"—but in the end he will return to the tried and true conventions. The older generation would not abandon Fitzgerald prematurely.

The younger generation, however, was growing impatient with its elders' choice of Fitzgerald as a spokesman for youth. "I have a suspicion," Robert Littell began his review in *The New Republic*, ". . . that a lot of people in the kindly but cool October of life are pointing to Mr. Scott Fitzgerald as the interpreter of 'the younger generation,' and are reading him as someone who understands what they do not quite understand nor altogether like, but which fascinates them as May will, I suppose, always fascinate October." Littell correctly saw that the novel, with its heavy-handed stress on universal themes, and the lack of depth of its ironic social criticism, was not about the postwar generation as *This Side of Paradise* had been. But the strength of his opposition—"I insist that Mr. Fitzgerald is not a witness, and not an interpreter"—suggests an intellectual and emotional basis deeper than a simple desire properly to emphasize the novel's themes.[53]

In *The Dial* Gilbert Seldes made the point even more explicitly. "To his contemporaries, 'interested only in ourselves and Art,' his revelations are of quite secondary importance and he has neither the critical intelligence nor the profound vision which might make him an imposing figure. His elders, naturally, do not require these things of him, since they have other sources of supply, and they are the best judges of his immediate significance. To them he presents a picture of the world which is no longer theirs, and even when they doubt his supreme truthfulness they can safely go behind the book to the author and say that this is what the young generation would like us to think." As perceptive a reader of the novel as Littell, Seldes properly recognized that the new aspects of Fitzgerald's tone in *The Beautiful and Damned* were "his overburden of sentiment and his really alarming seriousness." But what most concerned Seldes were the novel's "pretensions as a work of art," and what he was most at pains to demonstrate were Fitzgerald's failures as an artist, his "carelessness about structure and effect."[54] For Seldes and his associates on *The Dial* were interested in defining and propagating a particular set of modern aesthetic values. Fitzgerald was an obstacle in their way; as long as he held the center they would be regarded as peripheral. *The Dial's* attack on Fitzgerald was in part strategic, a move to assert its leadership and capture the center of youthful movements in the arts.

To the tacticians of the literary world Fitzgerald had a fixed place in their political spectrum, whether he knew it or not. He was known as a member of *The Smart Set* group, and knowledgeable persons who read Carl Van Doren's remarks in *The Nation*, "He has trusted, one suspects, his doctrines rather more than his gusto," were aware than Van Doren had in mind the doctrines of H. L. Mencken. It was the nature of this identification that, the more widely it became recognized, the more it precluded multiple allegiances. In April 1922, Van Doren had published his *Contemporary American Novelists, 1900-1920*, which had given high praise to *This Side of Paradise;* his concluding remarks in his review of *The Beautiful and Damned* a month later—"Why did he have to mix good poetry with indifferent moralism? Moralists are plenty but poets few."—suggest that he was resignedly giving up Fitzgerald to the Mencken camp.[55]

How much was the Mencken camp willing to claim him? Fitzgerald's friend Burton Rascoe, a fellow-traveler of the Mencken group, in his review for *The Bookman* called *The Beautiful and Damned* "blubberingly sentimental," and blamed it on the fact that Fitzgerald took himself far too seriously as a thinker. "No one of late years has appeared on the horizon with a happier verve than Mr. Fitzgerald or with a more promising narrative talent," Rascoe wrote, "and no one ever collapsed so easily into the banal and commonplace as he has in this novel. . . . He is too richly endowed with ability not to turn that ability to permanent account." [56] Mencken himself, who was unsentimental and hardheaded about his literary friends, gave Fitzgerald rather backhanded praise.

> It must be said for Fitzgerald that he discharges his unaccustomed and difficult business with ingenuity and dignity. Opportunity beckoned him toward very facile jobs; he might have gone on rewriting the charming romance of *This Side of Paradise* for ten or fifteen years, and made a lot of money out of it, and got a great deal of uncritical praise for it. Instead, he tried something much more difficult, and if the result is not a complete success, it is nevertheless near enough to success to be worthy of respect. There is fine observation in it, and much penetrating detail, and the writing is solid and sound. After

This Side of Paradise the future of Fitzgerald seemed extremely uncertain. There was an air about that book which suggested a fortunate accident. The shabby stuff collected in *Flappers and Philosophers* converted uncertainty into something worse. But *The Beautiful and Damned* delivers the author from all those doubts. There are a hundred signs in it of serious purpose and unquestionable skill. Even in its defects there is proof of hard striving. Fitzgerald ceases to be a *Wunderkind*, and begins to come into his maturity.[57]

Could Mencken's praise have meant that with *The Beautiful and Damned* Fitzgerald had committed himself wholly to Mencken?

If Fitzgerald was truly coming into his maturity during the winter of 1921-22, maturity was a condition which hampered the writing of novels. So far as his own literary endeavors were concerned, he had been in a sour mood throughout the fall. It would be fruitless to guess at the motives behind his moods, but a number of causes had contributed to it: frustration at the inadequacies of the novel, admitted and suspected; the recognition that in *Three Soldiers* Dos Passos had truly surpassed him as an artist; continued financial pressure, despite an income from his writing in 1921 of nineteen thousand dollars. Once again he began writing short stories. "Have written two good short stories," he wrote Edmund Wilson in November 1921, "and three cheap ones." [58] The cheap ones—which were probably "Two for a Cent" and the two parts of "The Popular Girl" —were quickly sold to *The Metropolitan* and *The Saturday Evening Post*. The good ones—"The Diamond as Big as the Ritz" and "The Curious Case of Benjamin Button"—were returned, as Fitzgerald reported to Wilson in January, with "letters of praise from six editors with the addenda that 'our readers, however, would be offended.'" [59] Eventually the stories were taken, respectively, by *The Smart Set* and *Collier's;* Fitzgerald was to include both, and exclude the ones he considered cheap, in his second collection of stories.

But he was even further discouraged; by January of 1922 he had reached, so it seemed, the limits of his talent and his acceptance as a writer of prose fiction. That month he began to write a play, a project which was to occupy him for almost two full years. "I am writing a comedy—or a burlesque or something," he announced to Wilson.[60] The first draft must have gone quickly, for he was candidly informing George Jean Nathan before March, "the play is, like most of my stuff, a very bad performance full of exceedingly good things. It varies between comedy and burlesque and is composed of three intermediate fanciful scenes strung together not too securely between a very solid first and last act." [61] By May Edmund Wilson had read the first draft and had sent Fitzgerald what must have been, particularly after Wilson's *Bookman* article, astonishing encouragement: "I think that the play as a whole is marvelous—no doubt, the best American comedy ever written ... I think you have a great gift for comic dialogue—even though you never can resist a stupid gag—and should go on writing plays." [62] Whatever literary motives had inspired Fitzgerald to write a play—escape from his problems with prose and a desire to renew his fame and popularity no doubt were among them—the financial possibilities of playwriting were never far from his mind; and the familiar example of Booth Tarkington was there to guide him. Later, in August 1922, asking Maxwell Perkins for yet another advance from Scribner's, he palliated his request by adding, "After my play is produced I'll be rich forever and never have to bother you again." [63] At that moment Tarkington was combining a successful career as a novelist with an even more lucrative career as a playwright. "If he has a great talent," Fitzgerald said then of Tarkington, he "has the mind of a school boy." [64] But it was, after all, the mind of a school boy that had first formed in Fitzgerald the dramatic impulse and the desire to entertain, that had led him to write plays in St. Paul and Triangle shows at Princeton; and it was not naïveté that had made Tarkington a wealthy man. Back in September 1920, a Princeton friend, Alexander McKaig, wrote in his diary, "Fitz bemoaning fact [that he] never can make more than hundred thousand a year—to do that have to become a Tarkington." [65] Eighteen months later, taking a new tack toward the goal of a hundred thousand a year, Fitzgerald was trying to turn himself into a Tarkington. It was ironic that Edmund Wilson, who had been a stern critic of Fitzgerald's weaknesses in his *Bookman* article, and who himself was soon to join *The Dial* group of aesthetes, by his praise of the play should have given Fitzgerald a further push into the Tarkington mold.

Through the spring and summer of 1922 Fitzgerald was occupied revising his play and submitting it to Broadway producers. In the May *Bookman*, only a few pages after Burton Rascoe's review of

The Beautiful and Damned, "The Gossip Shop" was chatting about Fitzgerald's new career: "A pale young man with pale blue eyes, and pale blond hair parted in the middle; a collegiate youth in New York trying to sell a play about a flapper. . . . three guesses as to the new dramatist!" [66] The Bookman's "gossip" almost made it appear as if he were an undergraduate fresh from the Princeton campus, rather than a professional writer with two novels and two dozen stories to his credit; but elsewhere the career and the themes of the latest novel had made their mark. Fitzgerald had been successful in his request to have damaging personal references deleted from Edmund Wilson's article in The Bookman; but H. L. Mencken and Burton Rascoe were less pervious to the wishes of their protégé, and they used his private behavior—or invented it—for their own purposes. In the same month that Wilson's article appeared, without mentioning Fitzgerald's drinking, Mencken referred to the "spirituous" cordiality with which Fitzgerald had been received in New York.[67] Meanwhile Rascoe was "revealing" in his New York Tribune column that Fitzgerald, in an interview with Robert Bridges, the editor of Scribner's Magazine, had leaned over and plucked out six grey hairs from the old man's beard. Apologizing to Bridges, Fitzgerald wrote, "I can only tell you what I have long suspected—that any strange happening in the new literary generation is at once attributed to me." [68] This was only part of a celebrity he had abetted and sought; but he was learning that the literary public would not endlessly condone it. In June "The Topics of The Times" used The Beautiful and Damned as sociological evidence to demonstrate how the word "party" had come to mean drunken affair.[69] Elinor Glyn, interviewed in The Bookman's "Gossip Shop," said that "Mr. Fitzgerald is a superb artist" but that he had written a novel with a deplorable theme; the interviewer said that Fitzgerald was a representative figure of youth, and when Mrs. Glyn objected to that, he "hastened to say that F. Scott Fitzgerald is very young, that he may change his philosophy." [70]

While he revised the play during 1922, Fitzgerald was also preparing his second book of stories for the press. His first impulse was to borrow the language of the movies and call the book In One Reel. Later he settled on the title Tales of the Jazz Age, and in defending it to Perkins he embraced his role as spokesman and leader more explicitly than he ever had before. "It will be bought by *my own personal public*—that is, by the countless flappers and college kids who think I am a sort of oracle," he wrote. "The splash of the flapper movement was too big to have quite died down—the outer rings are still moving." [71] *Tales of the Jazz Age* did sell better than *Flappers and Philosophers;* but the reviewers were even less kind. The *New Republic* and *The Dial* took the book as an occasion to call Fitzgerald more of a salesman than an artist; when Mencken got around to the collection almost a year later he found it unsatisfying, marked by "heavy artificiality" and "dangerous versatility." [72] Of course Fitzgerald had invited adverse criticism by the disparaging tone of his annotated table of contents, a feature he had somehow imagined would increase the appeal of the book. The quality of his self-criticism may be judged from this remark about "The Diamond as Big as the Ritz": "One well-known critic has been pleased to like this extravaganza better than anything I have written. Personally I prefer 'The Off-Shore Pirate.' " [73]

In his table of contents Fitzgerald proffered his tales of the jazz age "into the hands of those who read as they run and run as they read." [74] If this was his way of characterizing his own personal public, it was not so imprecise an observation; but its accuracy had unpleasant implications for Fitzgerald's securely optimistic sense of his hold on his audience. Fitzgerald's "personal public" thus was interested neither in his art nor in his intellect, but was part of that public, as *The Dial* claimed, that "takes its fiction as relaxation." [75] In 1922 and 1923 Fitzgerald was in the process of losing much of his interest for that public; for he was no longer moral enough for those who wanted reassuring fiction, and he was no longer unmoral enough for those who wanted their fiction risqué. It was inevitable that the taste for fiction about the antics of youth would be satisfied by writers who lacked Fitzgerald's intellectual and moral purposes; and the older generation, whose limits at last were overstepped, would morally protest. And it was only one of the ironies of the situation that the book which brought forth the moral reaction was written pseudonymously by one of the great muckraking journalists of the progressive era, Samuel Hopkins Adams. His novel, *Flaming Youth* by "Warner Fabian," published in 1923, presented a picture of sexual freedom which Fitzgerald had permitted his heroines in theory, but had denied to them in fact. The conventional periodicals were aware of the difference. "Indubitably 'Flaming Youth,' though honest, is shocking," The Bookman's "Gossip Shop" wrote. "We do not like it. It shocks us. Mr. Fitzgerald, on the other hand, has always seemed to us straightforward, honest, and gifted with an unusual sense of seeing things as they are, and not with a somewhat unpleasant smirk." [76] But the loosening of sexual morals in fiction was bound to continue. In 1923 a college novel by Percy Marks, The Plastic Age, made the best-seller lists; and its young men and women were much more sexually experienced than Amory Blaine or Rosalind Connage. As the fiction of the younger generation grew in disrepute, Fitzgerald, as the self-proclaimed spokesman of the flapper set, fully shared in it.

One indication of Fitzgerald's vulnerable position was given when he was parodied a second time, in 1923, by Christopher Ward. The difference between Ward's parody—" 'Paradise Be Damned!' by F. Scott Fitzjazzer"—and the earlier one by Donald Ogden Stewart may be simply a difference in the quality of the parodist. Yet Stewart's parody had made Fitzgerald's point of view seem absurd and funny by taking it as a given and applying it in a ludicrously incongruous historical situation. Ward's inferior parody directly challenged Fitzgerald's point of view by treating it as absurd and foolish in its own situation; in several instances simply by quoting Fitzgerald and adding, "whatever that means." [77]

More telling indications of Fitzgerald's vulnerability were to be found closer to home. From the summer of 1922 to the fall of 1923 Fitzgerald had put most of his working time into the play. He had written only three stories during that period, and salvaged another from a short section of a novel which he began in June and July 1923 but broke off in the fall to revise the play during rehearsals. Under the title of The Vegetable, or from President to Postman, the play had been published by Scribner's in April. It received favorable reviews as a funny satire, but so much of the humor and the plot line was based in drinking and drunkenness that some reviewers, like John Farrar in The Bookman, thought it more a poignant commentary on the author than it was a funny satire on American society. The Vegetable, Farrar predicted, "is of doubtful theatrical value," and he was right.[78] At opening night in Atlantic City many in the audience walked out during the second act, and a week later the production was abandoned. It was a serious blow to Fitzgerald's ego, but an even more serious one to his pocketbook. His dreams of wealth and financial security through successful playwriting were exploded. In order to meet his back obligations and continuing expenses he turned to the one secure fortress of his reputation and value, the magazines. From November 1923 to April 1924 he turned out eleven stories and six magazine articles. The least Fitzgerald earned for any one story was one thousand dollars; and his price at *The Saturday Evening Post* had risen to $1,750; even an article entitled, "Does a Moment of Revolt Come Sometime to Every Married Man?" was worth one thousand dollars to *McCall's*.[79] As soon as the financial crisis was passed, the Fitzgeralds sailed, in April 1924, to make their future home in Europe.

It was symptomatic of the chaotic and indeterminate nature of Fitzgerald's self-evaluation and reputation that he considered only four of those eleven stories worth preserving, but Edward J. O'Brien in his annual list of best short stories singled out for distinction six; and they agreed on only one, "The Baby Party."[80] It was equally perplexing that at the moment when Fitzgerald apparently had turned himself into a writer of slick magazine fiction—and after two years during which he had given no indication that he would or could write another serious novel—three important literary journalists honored him with more serious attention than they ever had before. Their aim, however, was not primarily critical; and their desire to concentrate on the man rather than on his works may explain why they were able to treat him with such surprising respect. Even Edmund Wilson's satiric imaginary conversation between Fitzgerald and Van Wyck Brooks, in its tone of merely listening rather than evaluating, presents a more honest picture of Fitzgerald's values than *The Bookman* sketch. Fitzgerald appears in Wilson's satire both banal in his ideas and pathetically unsure of his values. But this very lack of systematic ideas and certainty of values, Wilson implies, gives Fitzgerald, rather than intellectuals like Brooks, the better opportunity truly to observe and understand American life.[81] In their essays on Fitzgerald, Ernest Boyd and Paul Rosenfeld brought out these same untapped qualities of perception and unfocussed moral seriousness, strength unused behind a mask of wild behavior

and social insecurity. "Upon the theme of marital fidelity his elo-
quence has moved me to tears," Boyd wrote, "and his stern condemnation of the *mores* of bohemia would almost persuade a radical
to become monogamous. . . . Where so many others are conscious
only of sex, he is conscious of the soul." [82] Five years had passed
since the younger generation had come upon the scene, and for all
its criticism of American life no one among the younger novelists
had yet demonstrated the values or the penetration or the literary
skill required to break beneath the surface and produce a truly lasting work of art. It was as if, casting their eyes among the books and
writers on the scene, Wilson, Boyd, and Rosenfeld had separately
but alike found in Fitzgerald the same exceptional potential, greater
in him than perhaps in any other, and the same diversion, dispersion,
unfulfillment. Fitzgerald was exemplary for the failure of the whole;
he was also exemplary for its yet unspoiled possibilities.

But as the younger generation of writers was undergoing scrutiny
from the literary journalists, the younger generation of Americans
was subjected to an equally stern evaluation by its elders. "My
slogan," the imaginary Fitzgerald said in Edmund Wilson's conversation, "is that I am the man who made America Younger-Generation-
conscious." [83] It had been a good campaign and it sold well, but now
the public was tiring of it. And as he had chosen for himself the
role of spokesman and leader for the younger generation on the rise
and in its days of power, so Fitzgerald was the exemplar for the
younger generation in its decline. "The younger generation," proclaimed "The Gossip Shop" in *The Bookman* for August 1924, "as
such has passed into oblivion. There has been a young, a younger,
and a youngest since flappers first drank their way through the
brilliant pages of 'This Side of Paradise.' We do not know whether
flappers still exist or not, or whether, if they do, they still drink
cocktails. F. Scott Fitzgerald still exists, is in Europe and is writing
another novel, a thing which he has been doing for some time now.
We should think Fitzgerald could write a magnificent play about
young people. His 'The Vegetable' was far too fantastic for the
ordinary man and we cannot see how he ever expected the general
public to be interested in delirium tremens, even though he made
them vastly entertaining. No, this was not the sort of play for F.
Scott Fitzgerald to have written. He should have attempted one in

which gay young people are as flippant as gay young people are; but under which gaiety is a purpose and a seriousness which F. Scott Fitzgerald knows only too well. This young author always seems to us like a surprised baby who has been brought into the world against his will and doesn't like it very well, yet doesn't know how to remain successfully aloof from it. Fitzgerald regards life ironically but he cannot escape from living it. His latest article, following that fascinating one 'How to Live on $36,000 a Year,' is on the bringing up of children. The time when these wild young things really become serious is, it seems, when they are forced to keep the bottle warm. One of our own friends has a new baby. He no longer comes to us, when his eyes are bleared and blinking, explaining about 'that party last night'; but his explanation is quite as satisfactory and as simple. 'The baby cried last night,' he says." [84] The younger generation was growing out of its wild antics; the older generation was growing tired of them; and in August 1924 F. Scott Fitzgerald, whose reputation was in eclipse because he had strayed from the path of conventional values on which he had so optimistically begun, who only the month before had been deeply wounded by his wife's infidelity, was finishing up the first draft of The Great Gatsby.

CHAPTER SIX

Since F. Scott Fitzgerald won a place among the major writers of his generation, many critics and interpreters have wondered how his mind and art advanced so swiftly and so far from *The Beautiful and Damned* to *The Great Gatsby*. Some have engaged so assiduously in a search for sources behind *The Great Gatsby* that their efforts have been rendered ludicrous. At worst this search has unearthed sources that could not have been. R. W. Stallman, for example, has discovered that Spengler's *Decline of the West* was a major influence on *Gatsby*. As evidence he offers Fitzgerald's remark in a letter of 1940 that "I read [Spengler] the same summer I was writing *The Great Gatsby*"; but he has not checked Fitzgerald's memory against the fact that the first volume of *The Decline of the West* was not published in English until 1926, and that Fitzgerald was not a reader of German.[1] At best the search has assumed that Fitzgerald's development between 1922 and 1924 was a result of mere borrowing, just as he had in fact borrowed ideas and phrases from H. L. Mencken before 1922. Although several of Fitzgerald's critics have written exceptionally penetrating interpretations of what Fitzgerald learned from writers like Joseph Conrad, in general the critics have lacked a sense of process; above all they have not seen that Fitzgerald's development up to *The Great Gatsby*, no matter how astonishing the improvement in his intellectual and artistic grasp of his material, retains an essential continuity, builds upon the themes and attitudes that had gone before.[2] To understand how Fitzgerald matured between *The Beautiful and Damned* and *The Great Gatsby* one must search within Fitzgerald's mind and art, not outside him; and one must assume that any development so profound as to form the background for a novel like *The Great Gatsby* cannot be traced to any single source, or be absolutely fixed in any sense. Nevertheless, there is evidence enough to suggest how *The Great Gatsby* grew out of what Fitzgerald had written and thought before; but the origins of a natural growth are necessarily more mysterious than those of a transplant.

II

For all his optimism about *The Beautiful and Damned*, both for its sales potential and as a work of art, Fitzgerald suffered from moods of disquiet about the novel from the moment he put the serial version into the hands of *The Metropolitan Magazine*. Later he was convinced that the shortened magazine serial had cut sales and prejudiced the critics against the book; for some of his friends, like James Branch Cabell, read the serial in lieu of the revised and expanded hard-cover book.[3] Yet the tone of his letters after he returned from Europe in midsummer 1921 reveals his sense that the novel in either form suffered from haste of execution and confusion both of themes and of language. In July he complained to Perkins that Scribner's had not advertised *This Side of Paradise* well enough.[4] Late in August he told Perkins that he had not worked for five months and he was in an "obnoxious and abominable gloom. My third novel, if I ever write another, will I am sure be black as death with gloom. I should like to sit down with ½ dozen chosen companions and drink myself to death but I am sick alike of life, liquor and literature. If it wasn't for Zelda I think I'd disappear out of sight for three years. Ship as a sailor or something and get hard—I'm sick of the flabby semi-intellectual softness in which I flounder with my generation."[5] But his desire to "ship as a sailor or something" was as incompatible with his character as it was with the fact that his wife was seven months' heavy with child. Two weeks later he wrote to a correspondent, in his Menckenian public voice, "There is no such thing as 'getting your values straightened out' except for third-class minds who are willing to accept the latest jitney interpretation of the universe by some Illinois or South Carolina messiah." [6] And for once his Menckenian voice spoke more perceptively than his own. His personal habits were by then set in a pattern that was not fundamentally to change, no matter where he lived, for more than a decade.

It was rather his intellectual and literary habits that had begun to oppress him. The faults of *The Beautiful and Damned* lay at the back of his mind; though he claimed, in a letter to Edmund Wilson, "I have almost completely rewritten my book," it is probable that he did little more than revise the "Symposium" scene and the ending.[7] And there was his competition. Floyd Dell, Stephen Vincent Benét, and John Dos Passos were publishing novels in the fall of 1921. Dell and Benét did not worry him; but in September he read Dos Passos' *Three Soldiers*. Reviewing *Three Soldiers* for the *St. Paul Daily News*, Fitzgerald called Dos Passos "an artist." [8] But Fitzgerald's Princeton classmate John Peale Bishop, reviewing *Three Soldiers* along with the serial version of *The Beautiful and Damned* in the October *Vanity Fair*, had called Dos Passos "a genius." [9] In his own mind—and in the mind of his friend—Dos Passos had replaced him as the most brilliant young writer of their generation. "I like *Three Soldiers* immensely," Fitzgerald told Edmund Wilson, and in the next breath: "I am tired of modern novels." Fitzgerald signed off the letter, "Yours in this hell-hole of life and time, the world." [10] The success of Dos Passos had increased his irritation at his own failure.

A few days later, when Perkins asked him to tone down a mocking reference to the Bible in *The Beautiful and Damned*, his frayed temper exploded. He accused Perkins of being intimidated and of trying to intimidate him, to force him into conformity with conventional and timid beliefs. He called up "Galileo and Mencken, Samuel Butler and Anatole France, Voltaire and Bernard Shaw," among others, as precedent for his attitude. "It's the sort of thing you find continually in Anatole France's *The Revolt of the Angels*—as well as in *Jurgen* and Mark Twain's *Mysterious Stranger*. The idea, refusing homage to the Bible and its God, runs thru many of Mark Twain's essays and all through Paine's biography. *In fact, Van Wyck Brooks,* in *The Ordeal* criticizes Clemens for allowing many of his statements to be toned down at the request of William Dean Howells or Mrs. Clemens." [11] Perkins immediately wrote back, "I should hate to play . . . the W. D. Howells to your Mark Twain." [12] In the aftermath Fitzgerald apologized for his letter and made the changes Perkins asked. But the exchange had opened up issues in Fitzgerald's career that were not so easily smoothed over. In the fall of 1921 Fitzgerald had been reading and thinking about the career of Mark Twain; and if Perkins was not playing Willian Dean Howells—the limiting voice of conventional values—to his Mark Twain, the feeling still lingered that somebody was.

The affinities between Fitzgerald's fiction and Mark Twain's fiction had always been strong. In Tom Sawyer, Mark Twain had created the archetypal figure of the genteel romantic hero, the basic fictional character Fitzgerald had developed from his own observations and attitudes toward life. And in the unlikely case that Fitzgerald had not read either *Tom Sawyer* or *Huckleberry Finn*, he most certainly had studied the genteel romantic hero Booth Tarkington had copied from Tom Sawyer, Penrod Schofield. When H. L. Mencken reviewed *This Side of Paradise* he made a flattering, if not so favorable, comparison between Fitzgerald and Mark Twain. This remark may have been in the back of Fitzgerald's mind when, after returning to St. Paul in the fall of 1921, he began once more to read extensively. He went through *Brass*, by Charles G. Norris, and *Three Soldiers* at the request, presumably, of editors who sent them for review. When these two obligations were completed he turned to Albert B. Paine's three-volume biography of Clemens.[13] Thereafter he read Van Wyck Brooks's *The Ordeal of Mark Twain*, which forms an interpretative guide and critical commentary to the facts in Paine's authorized biography. Fitzgerald extensively underlined and annotated his copy of Brooks's *Ordeal;* his response to the book may be measured also by his angry letter to Perkins. With all his awareness of the similarities between his fiction and Mark Twain's, Fitzgerald could not help but recognize how much his own personality and career were shaped to fit the tragic mold that Brooks had cast for Mark Twain.

The resemblance between Mark Twain, as drawn by Brooks, and Fitzgerald is uncanny. Fitzgerald came from the same Midwestern provincial background as had Clemens. He too had been the pampered son of a strong-willed mother and a weak father. He had developed the same deference, the same almost religious awe, toward great wealth. His character too was similar. He shared with Mark Twain a certain insecurity and lack of self-assurance; and he possessed with Mark Twain an exceptional capacity for prankishness and wild gaiety. He held the same racial prejudices; he too maintained, in the midst of his literary work, an extraordinary enthusiasm for advertising and sales promotion stunts. Mark Twain had attained the status of a spokesman for his generation that Fitzgerald aspired to for his own. But as Brooks interpreted Mark Twain, Fitzgerald learned the tragic cost in frustration and self-defeat that lay behind Mark Twain's success and popularity. Brooks's *Ordeal* must have come to Fitzgerald almost as a seer or a fortune-teller might, to tell a moral tale through the mirror image of a personality, living in another age, but thinking the same thoughts and nursing the same desires; a tale that foretold for Fitzgerald the life of outward success and inner failure that had, it seemed by the fall of 1921, already been shaped for him. Fitzgerald learned more than one lesson from *The Ordeal of Mark Twain*, and the results of those lessons are striking.

The most obvious connection between Fitzgerald's reading about Mark Twain, and his own development, may be observed in the stories Fitzgerald wrote in the winter of 1921-22. "Two for a Cent" carries the echoes of Mark Twain's bitter pessimism, his belief that blind fate and chance determine men's lives. The story turns on a single penny. An ambitious boy loses it, and condemns himself to a life of poverty; a lazy boy picks it up, and it propels him to a career of wealth and international fame. There is an intensely felt descriptive realism in the story, though it is weakened by the contrivance of its plot and the implicit anti-human irony of the title.

"The Curious Case of Benjamin Button," the story of a man who was born old and grew younger the longer he lived, "was inspired," as Fitzgerald said in his table of contents to *Tales of the Jazz Age*, "by a remark of Mark Twain's to the effect that it was a pity that the best part of life came at the beginning and the worst part at the end." [14] The story reflects how closely Fitzgerald's concern with time mirrored Mark Twain's lifelong obsession with time and history. It also gave him a chance to satirize the conformity and conventionality, the business ethos, the fear of what was not ordinary, that Van Wyck Brooks had criticized again and again in his portrait of the Gilded Age; but the gimmick, as with the gimmick in "Two for a Cent" and the gimmick in so many of Mark Twain's stories, was slight. The place to look for the major implications of Mark Twain's effect on Fitzgerald's development is the novella "The Diamond as Big as the Ritz," which Fitzgerald also wrote in the early winter of 1921-22.

" 'The Diamond as Big as the Ritz,' " Fitzgerald said in his table of contents to *Tales of the Jazz Age*, "was designed utterly for my own amusement. I was in that familiar mood characterized by a perfect craving for luxury, and the story began as an attempt to feed that craving on imaginary foods." [15] Fitzgerald's critics have found it difficult to interpret these remarks; but it is quite probable that they are related to Brooks's emphasis in *The Ordeal* that Mark Twain wrote his books for money, for newspapers, for his wife, for Howells, for any reason but that he wanted to; and he placed an inordinate emphasis on the work, good or bad, that he wrote for himself alone. It was part of the role Fitzgerald was playing in that table of contents—a role of self-denigration not unfamiliar to Mark Twain—that he should go on to say, "One well-known critic has been pleased to like this extravaganza better than anything I have written. Personally I prefer 'The Offshore Pirate' "; just as Twain might have said he preferred *The Prince and the Pauper* to *Huckleberry Finn.* Fitzgerald's private opinion on "The Diamond as Big as the Ritz," which was his real opinion, was that it was "the best thing I've ever done—something really remarkable." [16] And it is remarkable, not only as a story but as an act of self-understanding and of self-creation. For if Fitzgerald had seen in Brooks's portrait of Mark Twain a mirror image of his own personality and a forecast of his potential failure and frustration, "The Diamond as Big as the Ritz" takes that nearly identical picture of himself as an opportunity to objectify his faults outside himself, and to exorcise them by recreating them as art. The story is an "exquisite novelette," as Fitzgerald called it, both as satire and as creative self-satire.[17]

Fitzgerald had read Mark Twain's "The Mysterious Stranger" presumably in the previous winter of 1920-21. If it had affected him then in any direct way, it could only have contributed to the bleak, inartistic atmosphere of pessimism that pervades *The Beautiful and Damned*. Reading Brooks's *Ordeal*, Fitzgerald found an explanation for the failure of Mark Twain's satire. "One may say," Brooks wrote, "that a man in whom the continuity of racial experience is cut as sharply as ... it was cut in Mark Twain is headed straight for an inferior cynicism. But what is almost destiny for the ordinary man is the satirist's opportunity; if he can recover himself quickly, if he can substitute a new and personal ideal for the racial ideal he has abandoned, that solution of continuity is the making of him." Later Brooks concluded, "The true satirist, however futile he may make life seem, never really believes it futile; his interest in its futility is itself a desperate registration of some instinctive belief that it might be, that it could be, full of significance, that, in fact, it *is* full of significance; to him what makes things petty is an ever-present sense of their latent grandeur." [18] These words were of extraordinary relevance to the author of *The Beautiful and Damned*, a novel that in its inferior cynicism and sense of futility had failed as much of Mark Twain's work had failed; and there is good reason to believe that they suggested to Fitzgerald a path out of his dilemma, on which "The Diamond as Big as the Ritz" represents the first steps. For Brooks himself—as Edmund Wilson was to suggest when he so presciently made Van Wyck Brooks and F. Scott Fitzgerald partners in an "imaginary conversation"—had fallen into the trap with Mark Twain; he too had abandoned the racial ideal and replaced it with no personal idea; he too had succumbed to a sense of futility about American life, with no redeeming sense of latent grandeur.[19] Reading *The Ordeal* Fitzgerald found in Brooks a cynicism equal in strength to his own; yet a cynicism directed, not to the rootless lives of New York hotel society, but rather to the conditions of life and the values that had shaped Fitzgerald's youth. In "The Diamond as Big as the Ritz" Fitzgerald was thus able to use the details of Brooks's cynicism as the basic grounds for his detached satirical tone; and since he had no need to create a cynicism of his own, he could begin to create out of the same subject matter a sense of its latent grandeur, a personal ideal of his own.

In a remarkable way, then "The Diamond as Big as the Ritz" creates satire out of Brooks's criticism of American life. In *The Ordeal* life in a provincial Mississippi river village is regarded as no better than life in hell—or rather "hell's back-yard"; John T. Unger in Fitzgerald's novella comes from Hades, "a small town on the Mississippi River." [20] Brooks portrays the American business elite as a dull crowd utterly lacking in originality and imagination; John T. Unger goes to St. Midas's School. "The fathers of all the boys were money-kings and John spent his summers visiting at fashionable resorts. While he was very fond of all the boys he visited, their fathers struck him as being much of a piece, and in his boyish way he often wondered at their exceeding sameness. When he told them where his home was they would ask jovially, 'Pretty hot down there?' and John would muster a faint smile and answer, 'It certainly is.' His response would have been heartier had they not all made this joke—at the best varying it with, 'Is it hot enough for you down there?' which he hated just as much" (76). During the Gilded Age, Brooks said, "wealth meant to Americans something else than mere material possession. ... the pursuit of it was nothing less than a sacred duty." [21] "The simple piety prevalent in Hades," Fitzgerald wrote, "has the earnest worship of and respect for riches as the first article of its creed— had John felt otherwise than radiantly humble before them, his parents would have turned away in horror at the blasphemy" (80). Brooks presented a picture of frontier life pervaded by brutality and frequent murders; Fitzgerald's creative satire made something of far greater originality out of this suggestion. He alluded to murder and brutality in the bland evasive prose of official business histories. "From 1870 until his death in 1900, the history of Fitz-Norman Washington was a long epic in gold. There were side issues, of course— he evaded the surveys, he married a Virginia lady, by whom he had a single son, and he was compelled, due to a series of unfortunate complications, to murder his brother, whose unfortunate habit of drinking himself into an indiscreet stupor had several times endangered their safety. But very few other murders stained these happy years of progress and expansion" (88). Mark Twain wrote a novel, Fitzgerald learned from Brooks, where the hero finds a mountain full of coal; Fitzgerald thereupon wrote a novella in which a Civil War veteran, prospecting in the West at exactly the same time as Mark Twain's hero, came upon a mountain full of diamonds.[22]

"The Diamond as Big as the Ritz" begins in the laconic, matter-of-fact tones that Van Wyck Brooks associated with the straight-faced Western humorists of the Gilded Age. The style and the point of view of the novella are rendered so simply and conventionally that the satire on values arises not so much from exaggeration as from a bland openness. " 'He must be very rich,' said John simply. 'I'm glad. I like very rich people. The richer a fella is, the better I like him.' There was a look of passionate frankness upon his dark face" (77). As Brooks described the Western humorists, one of their most important qualities was their ability to please both frontier and genteel audiences by a complex interconnection of two sets of values. The frontiersmen laughed at themselves; genteel Eastern audiences laughed at the frontiersmen. However much his satire implied a criticism of genteel conventions, the Western humorist rarely took a position directly opposed to dominant Eastern values. The violence and fantasy exaggeration of his stories were aspects of the failure and impotence of frontier lawlessness and disorder. The importance of "The Diamond as Big as the Ritz," as it relates to this frontier tradition, is that it operates by the same style and form, but that its values are radically altered. The frontier setting and the conventions of the Western tall tale are retained, but they are used as a grounds for satiric criticism of genteel Eastern values; the twelve pathetic men of Fish, the one element of actual frontier life in the story, are quickly passed over. The violence and fantasy exaggeration in "The Diamond as Big as the Ritz" are the aspects of success, and of the power of success, to create a lawlessness and disorder of its own; they are aspects of an apotheosis of success, the logical outcome of desires unexpectedly fulfilled. The two sets of values in complex interconnection—and in conflict—in "The Diamond as Big as the Ritz" are the American dream, and the American dream come true.

When Fitz-Norman Culpepper Washington discovered the diamond mountain in Montana after the Civil War, his act led naturally to what Nietzsche had called a transvaluation of values. Washington's diamond was so valuable, by old standards, that it was worth more than all the previously known wealth and property in the world. But since its value was so unprecedented, perhaps it could command no price, and thus be worth nothing at all. Washington was in the extraordinary position of having to protect the entire worldwide capitalist system, "lest in the possible panic attendant on its discovery he should be reduced with all the propertyholders in the world to utter poverty" (89). Moreover, he had to fear a government attempt to take control, which would also render him propertyless and penniless. Washington was responsible for the preservation of the economic and social values of all Americans; and therefore he had to exercise his power against the United States, in fact to remove his property from the United States entirely. By bribery, he corrupted government. By altering surveying instruments, he corrupted science. By deflecting the course of a river, he corrupted nature itself. But the progress of man's ingenuity had leaped beyond him, and in his son's generation the airplane was to pose a new and even more dangerous threat.

Yet their power and responsibility, and their ruthless protection of their secret, had not made the Washingtons any different in their personal habits from other wealthy Americans. Even amid the "honeyed luxury" of the Washington dining room, John T. Unger from Hades had to reply, "Yes . . . it certainly is hot enough for me down there" (83). The golf course was "all a green . . . no fairway, no rough, no hazards" (93). As for the décor of the Washington château, Braddock Washington had "caused to be kidnapped" a landscape gardener, an architect, a designer of stage settings, and a French decadent poet. None proved capable of rising to the opportunity. The "honeyed luxury" of the Washington estate was designed by "I blush to tell you, but it was a moving-picture fella. He was the only man we found who was used to playing with an unlimited amount of money, though he did tuck his napkin in his collar and couldn't read or write" (98). The Washingtons were the wealthiest family in the world, but they had not attained the status of an aristocracy; Fitzgerald no longer was mistaking plutocracy for aristocracy, as he had in *The Beautiful and Damned*. Nothing in the Washington style of life—not even their Negro slaves—cut them off from the aspirations or expectations of other enterprising Americans.

As a result the Washington redoubt was continually penetrated by daring and intrepid American fortune-hunters. Those whom Braddock Washington had captured were imprisoned in a pit. "These are some adventurous mariners who had the misfortune to discover El Dorado," Washington told John when he showed him the prisoners. "It was too dark to see clearly into the pit below, but John could tell from the coarse optimism and rugged vitality of the remarks and voices that they proceeded from middle-class Americans of the more spirited type" (94). Neither Braddock Washington's power nor his responsibilities had daunted their ambition or their irreverence. In fact, they regarded him as a tyrant in the same simple-minded, super-patriotic way Americans had looked upon Wilhelm II as a tyrant during the First World War. As aviators, the men no doubt had been trained in the war; and when Washington tells them that one of their number—a man who was taken out to teach Washington's daughter Italian—has escaped, they burst into cheers and yodels and then into a First World War song,

"Oh, we'll hang the Kaiser
On a sour apple tree——" (96)

By his own super-American success, Braddock Washington has paradoxically turned himself into an enemy of America. A squadron of planes, directed by the escaped Italian, soon comes to attack the Washington kingdom. When the Negro quarters are blown up by a bomb, Kismine Washington cries, "there go fifty thousand dollars' worth of slaves, . . . at pre-war prices. So few Americans have any respect for property" (105).

Who in the world remains with any respect for Braddock Washington's property? As dawn comes up on the morning after the attack, John sees Braddock Washington standing on a mountaintop, silhouetted against the sky. "'You out there——' Washington cried, 'You—— there——'" (108). Braddock Washington was making a bribe to God; to protect his precious domain he was not beyond this supreme corruption. All nature grew silent, then burst out with joyous sound and light; for God refused the bribe. Fitzgerald so loads his language in this section of the story that the reader cannot fail to recognize Washington's overweening pride and blasphemy. "A quality of monstrous condescension" was in his voice (108). "God has His price, of course. God was made in man's image, so it has been said: He must have His price" (109). The laconic tone of the early satire shifts to a heavily didactic moralizing style. Yet Fitzgerald's loss of control over the prose mitigates his condemnation of Braddock Washington. For Fitzgerald begins Washington's bribery speech to

God by calling him "Prometheus Enriched" (108). And to readers familiar with the classical myth of Prometheus that reference will bring to mind complexities of which Fitzgerald, with his newly moral tones, seems unaware. In his defiance of Zeus, Prometheus was a friend and benefactor to mankind. By his responsibility to capitalism Braddock Washington is also, like Prometheus, chained to a rock. And when God refuses his bribe—Prometheus too had not been above blackmail—Washington, like Prometheus, brings about a cataclysm. The symbolism Fitzgerald invokes, then, makes Braddock Washington a figure almost of tragedy, rather than of satire or moral condemnation. Washington believes he bears a responsibility to a social and economic system which paradoxically makes him an enemy of his own country; and Americans, pursuing the dream that Washington himself had fulfilled, threaten ironically to destroy the foundation of all wealth. God refuses to intervene; and Washington, in tragic recognition of his responsibility, destroys himself and his diamond mountain to protect the property-holders of the world.

In his satire on American respect for wealth and desire for riches, Fitzgerald reversed the forms of the Western tall tale by criticizing, not the unsuccessful, but the successful. And in the process he discovered, perhaps despite his own intentions, that wealth carries with itself not only banalities and absurdities, but also a heavy burden of responsibility. When the bombs begin to fall, Kismine Washington cries, "We'll be poor, won't we? Like people in books. And I'll be an orphan and utterly free. Free and poor! What fun!" John answers grimly, "It's impossible to be both together. People have found that out. And I should choose to be free as preferable of the two" (106). But to be the opposite of poor is not to be free either, as Kismine knew. Fitzgerald had taken the Western humorist's contrast of failure and success and turned it into an opposition between aspiration and an apotheosized fulfillment. The American dream, he was implying, could not survive its own extraordinary success; but neither could it accept failure. This is the burden of the sentimental and evasive conclusion, a sudden touch of Mark Twain pessimism, in which wealth becomes an illusion of youth, and youth itself a dream. " 'His was a great sin who first invented consciousness. Let us lose it for a few hours,' " John T. Unger says, falling off to sleep

(113). In "The Diamond as Big as the Ritz," Fitzgerald deepened his perception of ambition and possession of wealth in America.

III

After completing "The Diamond as Big as the Ritz"—and calling it "the best thing I've ever done—something remarkable"—Fitzgerald wrote two slick magazine stories and then almost completely turned his back on prose fiction for more than a year and a half. From January 1922 to November 1923, he devoted himself primarily to the play, *The Vegetable,* until it failed in its pre-Broadway tryouts, leaving him deeply in debt. *The Vegetable* represented a gamble for Fitzgerald, a gamble on a second quick and overwhelming success, which he would manage more astutely than the first; but *The Vegetable* was neither original nor timely, as *This Side of Paradise* had been, and though it contains clever lines and subtle insights into lower-middle-class American life, as a whole the play was derivative and clichéd. What is interesting in *The Vegetable* are Fitzgerald's obsessions, pervasive but not quite coherent, confusing and diffusing the main lines of the play—age and time, boredom and restlessness, movies and popular delusions. After his fine achievement in "The Diamond as Big as the Ritz," what reason, other than hope of large financial returns, could Fitzgerald have had for raising his questions in such a compromised, inadequate form?

There are interesting clues to an answer in Van Wyck Brooks's *Ordeal of Mark Twain.* In Edmund Wilson's *Bookman* sketch—which Fitzgerald read at precisely the moment he was starting to write *The Vegetable*—Wilson portrayed Fitzgerald as a writer who has "the desire for beauty without an aesthetic ideal"; and it was also by the standards of an aesthetic ideal that Van Wyck Brooks judged and condemned Mark Twain's literary career.[23] Mark Twain's ambition for popularity and wealth, his eclectic interest in mechanical devices, his deference to the tastes of his wife and Howells, Brooks criticized as ambitions and interests and deferences no true artist ever would have entertained. Though Mark Twain undoubtedly possessed the soul of an artist, Brooks said, that soul had been crushed beneath the external pressures of gentility and social approval; and in "blind, indirect, extravagant, wasteful ways, the creative self in Mark Twain constantly strove to break through the censorship his own will had accepted, to cross the threshold of the unconscious." [24]

Yet one of the surprising inadequacies of Brooks's argument was his inability to specify what his aesthetic standards were. Nowhere in *The Ordeal* does Brooks make clear how Mark Twain might have liberated his creative self in direct, useful, or economical ways. Brooks does profess an obvious allegiance to a vague and undefined high art ideal, to which all true artists presumably dedicate themselves; but when he refers to Mark Twain's actual circumstances, he seems to suggest that Mark Twain's creative self would have found fulfillment best by giving up literature entirely. "The life of a Mississippi pilot," Brooks wrote, "had, in some special way, satisfied the instinct of the artist in him; in quite this way, the instinct of the artist had never been satisfied again." [25] Mark Twain, Brooks implies, should have remained always a riverboat pilot; what counts most is "the happiness of the soul in process of delivering itself," and from that criterion Samuel L. Clemens should not have written a word of prose.[26] Fitzgerald possessed no coherent aesthetic values against which to judge the contradictions and evasions in Brooks's argument; and it may be that, so identifying himself with Mark Twain's personal and artistic dilemmas, he grasped at the solution Brooks offered, and turned to playwriting for more than its potential financial rewards; for the Elizabethan Drama group and the Triangle Club had first stimulated his artistic impulse in his boyhood, and he may have hoped the stage would satisfy his instinct of the artist once again.

But for the development of Fitzgerald's mind and art, 1922 and 1923 were not wasted years. For one thing, his editor Maxwell Perkins often stimulated him to read books of social interpretation and criticism. During the winter of 1921-22 Fitzgerald read Upton Sinclair's *The Brass Check* and *The Mind in the Making* by the historian James Harvey Robinson, both presumably at Perkins's urging.[27] Fitzgerald told Perkins in March 1922,

> When I wrote you about *The Mind in the Making*, I'd only read two chapters. I have finished it and entirely changed my views on its importance. I think it's a thoroughly excellent book. It states the entire case for modernity's lingering hope of progress. It is a depressing book, I think, as are Wells' and Shaw's late things, and all those of that brave

company who started out in the '90's so full of hope and joy in life and faith in science and reason. Thomas Hardy survives them all. I think when I read Upton Sinclair's *The Brass Check* I made my final decision about America—that freedom has produced the greatest tyranny under the sun. I'm still a socialist but sometimes I dread that things will grow worse and worse the more the people nominally rule. The strong are too strong for us and the weak too weak.[28]

It was perceptive of Fitzgerald to sense Robinson's relation to Wells and Shaw, and to see, beneath the crisis tone on the surface of *The Mind in the Making,* Robinson's optimism about applied scientific knowledge. When Fitzgerald spoke of himself as a socialist, he was acknowledging little more than his own affinities with Shaw and Wells, but even in his fears about nominal popular rule he was responding to a serious concern of intellectuals in the early twenties, how popular democracy could know enough to control increasingly complex and technical economic and political decisions. Both *The Brass Check* and *The Mind in the Making* are, in their own ways, about the problem of knowledge. Robinson believed that advances in scientific knowledge could be put to use in improving society, but he also implied—in a way Thorstein Veblen was to make explicit—that only scientific experts knew enough to make the decisions. Sinclair's study of the distortions and omissions in news-reporting suggested that it was impossible, under the then present state of American journalism, for the public to learn enough facts on which to base coherent decision. After his remarks to Perkins about popular rule, Fitzgerald added, "I shall not write another novel for a year but when I do it will not be a realistic one. At least I don't think it will." [29] Undoubtedly Fitzgerald considered both *This Side of Paradise* and *The Beautiful and Damned* realistic novels; and it may be that his concern with the problem of knowledge had made him feel that the realistic novel, like the novels of Wells and the plays of Shaw, was too optimistic about the future and too sure it knew all the answers. Already in "The Diamond as Big as the Ritz" he had suggested that Braddock Washington held responsibilities of which the aspiring middle-class Americans who destroyed him could not know; and it is not too much to say that in *The Great Gatsby* some of the mystery of Gatsby's past life and business affairs derives from this concern with the problem of knowledge.

There was another unresolved problem in Fitzgerald's mind on which, at the same time, Perkins helped him to focus his thinking. After Fitzgerald had written angrily accusing Perkins of trying to censor *The Beautiful and Damned,* Perkins in his reply made an effort to show Fitzgerald the distinction between contempt and pity. "The Old Testament," Perkins wrote, "ought not to be treated in a way which suggests a failure to realize its tremendous significance in the recent history of man, as if it could simply be puffed away with a breath of contempt; it is so trivial. . . . You speak of Galileo; he and Bruno showed themselves to have a genuine sense of the religious significance of the theories they broke down. They were not in a state of mind to treat the erroneous beliefs of man with a light contempt. France [the author Anatole France, whom Fitzgerald had cited in his own defense] does not so treat Christ in that story of Pilate in his old age. And 'Whited Sepulchre' is an expression of a high contempt, although applied to an object which has no such quality of significance as the Bible. My point is that you impair the effectiveness of the passage—of the very purpose you use it for— by giving it that quality of contempt." [30] Fitzgerald's contempt for his characters, for their behavior, and for their values, pervades *The Beautiful and Damned* and stories like "The Jelly Bean." In "The Diamond as Big as the Ritz" the satire attains an uneasy balance between contempt and sympathy, both for Braddock Washington and for his antagonists. By February 1922, Fitzgerald was writing to Perkins, "I found that thing by Anatole France very interesting. It's the same thing that Mencken says about Hardy and Conrad and Dreiser, the thing that lifts them above the 'cerebral' novelists like Wells—the profound gesture of pity." [31] Fitzgerald was beginning to grow out of that mood of contempt that had dominated much of his writing since *This Side of Paradise;* it was in March that he told Perkins his next novel would not be "realistic," and his rejection of realism stems not only from his belief that it was an inadequate form to cope with his intellectual problems, but also from a feeling that realism was associated with contempt. Later, when he was discussing the title for the *Tales of the Jazz Age* collection, he half-jokingly, half-seriously suggested to Perkins, "I might possibly call my book *Nine Humans and Fourteen Dummies* if you'd permit such a long title (in this case I'd have to figure out how many humans and how many dummies there are in the collection)." [32] But he assumed, off the cuff, that there were more dummies than humans in the stories; and the implication was that in the future humans would predominate.

Perkins had brought into the open the weaknesses of Fitzgerald's attitude toward his characters, but once again it was Fitzgerald's own reading and thinking that gave him the foundation for his development. As his remarks to Perkins suggest, Fitzgerald continued to be influenced by Mencken's philosophy and criticism; but now, after completing *The Beautiful and Damned,* he began to read for the first time those names he had found so prominent in Mencken's books and which he had previously adopted, on Mencken's authority alone, as his mentors. From the available evidence, it was in the winter of 1921-22 that Fitzgerald read Nietzsche's *The Genealogy of Morals,* and it was then that he first began to read the novels of Joseph Conrad. Fitzgerald's interpreters have correctly traced many of the qualities in *The Great Gatsby* to the influence of Conrad; yet in the case of the novels and tales they claim to be the sources for *The Great Gatsby—Chance, Lord Jim,* "Heart of Darkness"—no evidence exists that Fitzgerald read them until much later.[33] By stressing affinities between form and technique in *The Great Gatsby* and in some of Conrad's novels, these interpretations have obscured more interesting and important connections between Fitzgerald and Conrad in the realm of attitudes and ideas. In *The Genealogy of Morals* Fitzgerald had read Nietzsche's assertion, "An artist must resist the temptation to 'analogy by contiguity,' which would persuade him that he, himself, *is* what he imagines and expresses. The truth of the matter is that if he *were* that thing, he would be unable to imagine or express it. Homer would not have created Achilles, nor Goethe Faust, if Homer had been an Achilles or Goethe a Faust. An artist worth his salt is permanently separated from ordinary reality." [34] It was in his reading of Conrad that Fitzgerald found, not merely method, but a philosophy of life that raised Fitzgerald's own concerns to a higher, calmer, more understanding, and more generous plane.

Before *The Great Gatsby* Fitzgerald seems to have read two novels, *Nostromo* and *Victory;* the tales "Youth" and "The Nigger of the Narcissus"—at least the preface to it; and a personal memoir, *The Mirror of the Sea.* Of this list only "Youth" was written with the character Marlow as a narrative device, and in this case Marlow is telling his own story rather than the story of someone else. "The Nigger of the Narcissus" and *The Mirror of the Sea* are basically conventional third-person narratives, while the two novels are narrated in the conventional third-person authorial voice. There are techniques in these works that Fitzgerald was to adopt for himself, particularly the shift away from chronological time sequence in *Nostromo;* but what was of greatest interest to him was not so much Conrad's devices—these after all are of little value without a story compelling and complex enough to require them—as Conrad's attitude toward human hopes and human destiny. In his one substantive reference to Conrad before *The Great Gatsby,* Fitzgerald wrote— quoting himself in a letter to Edmund Wilson—" 'See here,' he said, 'I want some new way of using the great Conradian vitality, the legend that the sea exists without Polish eyes to see it. Masefield has spread it on iambics and downed it; O'Neill has sprinkled it on Broadway; McFee has added an Evenrude motor—' But I could think of no new art form in which to fit him." [35] At about the same time Fitzgerald put *Nostromo* sixth on his list of "the ten books I have enjoyed most," calling it "the great novel of the past fifty years" —a comment that anticipates the consensus of Conrad's critics, that *Nostromo* is his greatest book.[36]

What Fitzgerald meant when he said he wanted to use "the legend that the sea exists without Polish eyes to see it" was not that he wanted, with Masefield, O'Neill, and McFee to write about the sea, but that he wanted to emulate Conrad's success in making life on the sea symbolic of human desires and human fate. The sea was a subject and a setting commensurate with the moral and philosophical seriousness Fitzgerald had tried to bring to his fiction, with little success. The sea, Conrad said, was life itself; and as Marlow began his story in "Youth," "You fellows know there are those voyages that seem ordered for the illustration of life, that might stand for a symbol of existence." [37] What Fitzgerald wanted to take from Conrad was not a feeling of anger and impotence in the face of defeat, decay, and time—that after all was what he rejected when he turned his back on realism—but a feeling of romance and power that was even enhanced, rather than destroyed, by inevitable loss. "I did not know how good a man I was till then"—this was the quote from "Youth" that Fitzgerald in 1923 put at the head of a review— ". . . . I remember my youth and the feeling that will never come back any more—the feeling that I could last forever, outlast the sea, the earth, and all men . . . the triumphant conviction of strength, the heat of life in the handful of dust, the glow in the heart that with every year grows dim, grows cold, grows small, and expires—and expires, too soon, too soon—before life itself." [38] In the poignance of "Youth" Fitzgerald found the "profound gesture of pity" Mencken had described. In *Nostromo* he found—here the thematic parallels between Fitzgerald and Conrad are more suggestive than those of technique—a vague, mysterious figure, "Nostromo," romantically risen from the lower class and endowed with legendary power, "enormous vanity," "absurd fidelity"; corrupted and betrayed by a material symbol that had become enmeshed with his romantic ideals; fatally shot in error. [39] The style and form of *Nostromo* conveyed a unified visual and moral experience, romanticism and corruption side by side, and told the story with pity and dignity, despite the failure of all human desires in the end. Conrad showed Fitzgerald what it was to be an artist who had truly risen into Nietzsche's aristocratic class; who had turned away from judgment, resentment, revenge, those attitudes and motives Nietzsche had called slavish; who had thus attained the Apollonian power, as Nietzsche described it in *The Birth of Tragedy*, to control Dionysian vitality and to turn it into art. But Fitzgerald could not learn from Conrad how to do it for himself; that was the meaning of his confession to Edmund Wilson that he "could think of no new art form in which to fit him." [40] For that Fitzgerald needed a writer whose subject matter was closer to his own; and by the summer of 1922 Wilson had already supplied him.

Wilson apparently brought *Ulysses* to Fitzgerald's attention in May of 1922. Fitzgerald was obviously replying to remarks Wilson had made when he wrote, "I have not read *Ulysses* but I'm wild to—especially now that you mention some coincidence. Do you know where I can get it at any price?" [41] A month later Fitzgerald reported to Wilson, "I have *Ulysses* from the Brick Row Bookshop and am starting it. I wish it was laid in America—there is something about middle-class Ireland that depresses me inordinately—I mean, gives me a sort of hollow, cheerless pain. Half of my ancestors came from just such an Irish stratum, or perhaps a lower one. This book makes me feel appallingly naked." [42] Fitzgerald's feelings about middle-class Ireland suggest the reason why his interest in James Joyce had earlier been so slight. Fitzgerald had read *A Portrait of the Artist* before he wrote *This Side of Paradise;* but his attitudes toward Ireland and his Celtic heritage had been shaped by two genteel Catholic aristocrats, Father Fay and Shane Leslie. Amory Blaine in *This Side of Paradise* "was rather skeptical about being an Irish patriot—he suspected that being Irish was being somewhat common—but Monsignor assured him that Ireland was a romantic lost cause and Irish people quite charming, and that it should, by all means, be one of his principal biasses." [43] The Monsignor's interest in Ireland, nevertheless, like Father Fay's and Leslie's, was primarily aesthetic, if not politically reactionary; later he is reported as "having a frightful time" about the Irish Republic: "He thinks it lacks dignity." [44] Into this atmosphere the fiction of James Joyce could only enter as a jarring note; Amory Blaine is said to have been "puzzled and depressed" by *A Portrait of the Artist,* a judgment that has less to do with style and technique than with the Irish life and aspirations it depicts.[45] Fitzgerald's feelings toward Joyce were much more bluntly laid down in October 1919, when he wrote Robert Bridges, the editor of *Scribner's Magazine,* about his short-lived project to write a "diary of a literary failure." "It will be bound to have that streak of coarseness that both Wells and Butler have," Fitzgerald wrote, "but there won't be any James Joyce flavor to it." [46] Fitzgerald had been brought up to believe that James Joyce was a common Irishman, outside the bounds of literary taste.

But Wilson was teaching him something different. Early in his career Wilson had dedicated himself to enlightening the reading public, as he later said, "to the understanding of the most recent literary events in the larger international world—Joyce, Eliot, Proust, etc."; and 1922 was the decisive year, when both *Ulysses* and *The Waste Land* appeared, changing the course of English and American poetry and fiction ever thereafter.[47] It was Wilson's good luck to get *The Dial*'s assignment to write the first criticism of *The Waste Land,* in connection with the presentation of the 1922 *Dial* Award to Eliot.[48] Earlier he had reviewed *Ulysses* for *The New Republic.* These reviews were only the beginning for Wilson of a ten-year task which was to culminate in 1931 with *Axel's Castle.* Yet in 1922 Fitzgerald was only one among many whose ideas about literature were drastically revised because Wilson had guided them to the meanings in *Ulysses* and *The Waste Land.* "I read your article on *Ulysses,* the only criticism yet I could make head or tail of," Fitzgerald wrote Wilson in July 1922; and to ascertain the impact of *Ulysses* on Fitzgerald, one must first turn to Wilson's review.[49]

Fitzgerald had heard from Wilson that there was "some coincidence" between him and Joyce; for Fitzgerald a most interesting coincidence may have been the fact that Wilson devoted more than half his review to finding fault with *Ulysses,* that Joyce fell below Wilson's critical standards almost as often as Fitzgerald had in the earlier *Bookman* article. The more obvious coincidence between Joyce and Fitzgerald lay in the consequences of their lapsed Catholicism. "I feel that though [Joyce's] taste for symbolism is closely allied with his extraordinary poetic faculty for investing particular incidents with universal significance," Wilson wrote, "nevertheless—because it is the homeless symbolism of a Catholic who has renounced the faith—it sometimes overruns the bounds of art into an arid ingenuity which would make a mystic correspondence do duty for an artistic reason." Wilson had made very clear the conscious parallels between *Ulysses* and *The Odyssey,* a connection between modern life and ancient mythology which, since the reference to Prometheus in "The Diamond as Big as the Ritz," may also have been in Fitzgerald's mind; but Wilson's criticism of the symbolism in *Ulysses* was based on Joyce's too literal adherence to the structure of *The Odyssey.* And this fault, according to Wilson, led Joyce to extend his style beyond the limits of his strength. "You cannot inflate such a style or splash it about," Wilson wrote. "Mr. Joyce's native temperament and the method which it has naturally chosen have no room for superabundance or extravagant fancy. It is the method of Flaubert—and of Turgenev and de Maupassant: You set down with the most careful accuracy and the most scrupulous economy of detail exactly what happened to your characters, and merely from the way the thing is told—not from any comment of the narrator—the reader draws his ironic inference. In this genre—which has probably brought novel-writing to its highest dignity as an art—Mr. Joyce has long proved himself a master." But where Joyce had truly risen above Flaubert, Wilson said, was in his capacity to tell the truth about human ignobilities, and yet to make "his bourgeois figures command our sympathy and respect by letting us see in them the throes of the human mind straining always to perpetuate and perfect itself and of the body always laboring and throbbing to throw up some beauty from its darkness." [50] This was the quality that had "depressed" Fitzgerald and made him feel "appallingly naked," and yet it was the quality that Wilson and Joyce had forced Fitzgerald to face.[51] "Am undecided about *Ulysses* application to me," Fitzgerald wrote Wilson in August, "—which is as near as I ever come to forming an impersonal judgment." [52] It would be difficult to divine a meaning from these words, unless they are meant as a clever equivocation; for *Ulysses'* application to Fitzgerald must by nature be personal; and a personal judgment would be decisive. But perhaps one who wished for an immediate conversion experience would have asked for too much; for *Ulysses,* as Wilson said, had set "the standards of the novel so high that it need not be ashamed to take its place beside poetry and drama." [53] Fitzgerald had put off his third novel, hoping to find "a new art form" that would reshape his style and themes.[54] James Joyce confronted him with a new art form, and Wilson had made plain to him the close connection between *Ulysses* and Fitzgerald's Irish Catholic social and religious background, his poetic style, and his universal themes. "Who else has had the supreme devotion," Wilson asked rhetorically at the end of his review, "and accomplished the definitive beauty?" [55] If *Ulysses* had any application to Fitzgerald, it must have seemed this question was addressed to him.

What Wilson accomplished, in fact, by his persistent interest in Fitzgerald during 1922—by his *Bookman* article, his extravagant praise for the play, his calling Fitzgerald's attention to his connections with Joyce—was to close the gap between Fitzgerald and modern movements in the arts. The climax came in November 1922, the month *The Waste Land* was published in *The Dial* and T. S. Eliot was awarded the *Dial* Award for 1922. In an article on modern art and literature, "The Rag-Bag of the Soul," that Wilson wrote for *The Literary Review* of the *New York Evening Post,* he linked Fitzgerald's name with that of Eliot. "It is no longer a question," Wilson wrote, "as it once was, of man in relation to God, or man in relation to society, or man in relation to his neighbor. Let us merely explore a single human consciousness and make a record of what we find there without venturing even the most rudimentary ideas as to what their significance may be or as to which of them may be considered the most valuable." Quoting from *The Waste Land*, Wilson went on, "T. S. Eliot's lines . . . furnish an apt description of the situation, and a quotation from a more conventional author who has yet caught something of the spirit of the time puts it even more clearly and briefly. 'I know myself but that is all,' cries one of Scott Fitzgerald's heroes, who has 'grown up to find all gods dead, all wars fought, all faiths in men shaken.' And that is precisely the point of view of the modern novelist or poet: 'I know myself but that is all.'"

It was Wilson's purpose to say that this alone was not enough, that unchecked consciousness was an inadequate literary form to express what positive values his generation would devise. "When we do become capable again of believing in something," he wrote, "we shall probably begin to censor the record of our consciousness in the interests of our faith. . . . in a genuinely vigorous society some selection will have to be made among the instincts which make a menagerie of every human being—that certain impulses and ideas will have consistently to be suppressed while certain others are cultivated with a superlative intensity—if man is to have even the illusion of controlling his own fate." [56] This remark, too, made a peculiar appeal to Fitzgerald's stylistic and thematic needs. For the first time since the earliest moments of his career Fitzgerald could feel that his interests and his talents were in tune with the advance guard in the arts, and perhaps that he possessed a foundation in values even more firm. By the winter of 1922-23—a year after the winter of his doubts—Fitzgerald was speaking in a new voice of leadership, conveying a sense that he was on the brink of coming into his own. Reviewing one more realistic novel, he showed that he knew what was to come after realism. "And, when our Conrad or Joyce or Anatole France comes," he wrote, "such books as this will have cleared his way. Out of these enormous and often muddy lakes of sincere and sophisticated observation will flow the clear stream—if there is to be a clear stream at all." [57] There can hardly be a doubt that the American "Conrad or Joyce or Anatole France" whom Fitzgerald envisioned was to be himself.

But of course at that moment Fitzgerald was busy getting his comedy ready for the stage. Between the winter of 1921-22 and the brief start he made on a novel in the summer of 1923, Fitzgerald wrote only three stories; of these the first, "Winter Dreams," is of particular interest, for it was written in September 1922, just after Fitzgerald read *Ulysses,* and it marks the first attempt Fitzgerald made to assimilate what he learned from Conrad and Joyce into his own art. "Winter Dreams" is not an entirely successful story, it never quite brings its separate parts into a focused unity; but the development it represents in Fitzgerald's mind and art are of great significance. For the first time Fitzgerald chose as his hero a lower-middle-class figure out of his boyhood observation and experience. Dexter Green, to be sure, ends up with fabulous wealth and power; but neither his temperament nor his circumstances prepare him to be the typical upper-middle-class genteel romantic hero of Fitzgerald's slick magazine stories. "He knew that to be careless in dress and manner required more confidence than to be careful. But carelessness was for his children. His mother's name had been Krimplich. She was a Bohemian of the peasant class and she had talked broken English until the end of her days. Her son must keep to the set patterns." [58] And so for the first time—first time at least since Fitzgerald's prewar collegiate stories—the hero does not win the girl. There are no substitute genteel romantic values in "Winter Dreams" either, such as Amory Blaine devised for himself when he lost the girl in *This Side of Paradise;* despite Dexter Green's financial success, "Winter Dreams" is a story of inevitable loss.

It does not seem, though, that the loss of Miss Judy Jones is worth crying over. Her power over Dexter Green is real enough, over and over again "her casual whim gave a new direction to his life" (122). In her willfulness Judy Jones resembles the genteel romantic heroines of Fitzgerald's collegiate stories, in her mysterious wild moods she recalls the "Caroline" who beguiled Merlin Grainger in "O Russet Witch!," the earlier story which dealt more crudely with similar themes; but Judy Jones does not seem at all a realized or a created character, commensurate with her role as the embodiment of the story's idealism. Perhaps, after all, this was Fitzgerald's intention— to make Judy Jones the accidental catalyst, and thus the unworthy object, for Dexter's general romantic readiness: "It was a mood of intense appreciation, a sense that, for once, he was magnificently

attuned to life and that everything about him was radiating a bright-
ness and a glamour he might never know again" (121). So Dexter
"surrendered a part of himself to the most direct and unprincipled
personality with which he had ever come in contact" (125). It was
this yielding that Dexter was to mourn when he learned that Judy
Jones had lost her beauty, this commitment of his dreams to a mortal
object that time must destroy. For with the end of his dream he could
not escape his own imprisonment in time. "The gates were closed,
the sun was gone down. . . . 'long ago, there was something in me,
but now that thing is gone' " (135). Youth was ended; and he, too,
was mortal.

The other important story in which, before *The Great Gatsby*,
Fitzgerald put his intellectual development to artistic use, was
"Absolution." It was in fact salvaged from the novel Fitzgerald began
in July and August 1923 and broke off to revise *The Vegetable* during
rehearsals. As a story in itself "Absolution" is among Fitzgerald's
best; its significance for *The Great Gatsby* lies in its skillful fusion
of Fitzgerald's old theme of the genteel romantic hero with his new
capacity to write with feeling and penetration about lower-class lives
and aspirations. Rudolph Miller, Fitzgerald's little-boy hero, with
his romantic other self, "Blatchford Sarnemington," with his sin of
not believing he was the son of his parents, with the "honesty of
his imagination" that made him plan too cleverly and betrayed him,
is the imaginative romantic hero imprisoned within the circumstances
of his poverty; Fitzgerald at last had learned, from the characters of
Nostromo and Leopold Bloom, how truly to create his own Huckleberry Finn.[59] Fitzgerald no longer needed the rich and well-born
as characters to fit his major themes; in "The Rag-Bag of the Soul"
Edmund Wilson explained how modern literature had grown out
of the chaos of status and values, "all established society in flux, all
institutions imperilled, the gentleman among the gallipots and the
underling on the throne," and in "Absolution" Rudolph Miller, "like
the commoner in the king's chair . . . tasted the pride of the situation." [60] But unlike Fitzgerald's old upper-middle-class genteel hero,
Rudolph is too far removed from power and status for his inner consciousness to conceive of its own objects. Thus for the first time in
Fitzgerald's fiction the conventional goals of romantic imagination,
money and the girl, are missing.

The major symbol of power in the story is the Roman Catholic Church. And it was Fitzgerald's brilliant stroke to counterpoint Rudolph's imagination with that of the priest, Father Schwartz, whose diseased imagination conjures up images of magic places mingled with sexual desire. Rudolph's growth into the isolation of adolescence is also, of course, partly shaped by the awaking of his sexual desire; but by the extraordinary device of bringing the two imaginations together in the confessional, where the man of God exposed his wild dreams, Fitzgerald enabled Rudolph's romantic imagination to soar even higher than God. "There was something ineffably gorgeous somewhere that had nothing to do with God. He no longer thought that God was angry at him about the original lie, because He must have understood that Rudolph had done it to make things finer in the confessional, brightening up the dinginess of his admissions by saying a thing radiant and proud." [61] Rudolph could believe that his romantic imagination might entertain God Himself. This was a pride and a responsibility that might raise him above mortality to the status of a Prometheus, of a Braddock Washington—and which could only end as Prometheus and Braddock Washington had ended, in a cataclysm, that would destroy him and with him, man's hopes. In outline most of *The Great Gatsby* is there.

Fitzgerald put away the novel of which "Absolution" was a part to revise *The Vegetable*. When the play failed in November 1923, he was deeply in debt. He had exhausted his advances on the novel from Scribner's, and the rest of its potential earnings lay far in the future. His one recourse was the magazine market, where his name was powerful and his price was on the rise. The novel was put aside, and for the next half year Fitzgerald wrote full-time for the magazines. He turned out eleven stories in that period and almost as many articles and reviews. He accomplished what he had set out to do, clear off his debt. It would be simple to say that the stories that poured regularly, one every two weeks, from his pen, were trash, as Fitzgerald himself was later to say. More than half, it is true, were variations on the conventional formula of the genteel romantic hero—upperclass boy loses upper-class girl, boy does something outrageously clever, boy wins girl and fortune. Most of the others, it is also true, were sentimental domestic tales. Fitzgerald knew the needs of the magazine market well enough to give editors what they wanted; for what other reason were they paying him over one thousand dollars for each story? Yet his mind and his art had reached a stage of maturity that made several of these stories far more interesting than their outward shell suggests. That six months' output was, as Fitzgerald had written earlier about *The Vegetable*, "like most of my stuff, a very bad performance full of exceedingly good things." [62] Fitzgerald had important questions on his mind, questions of time, of youth, of mystery, and power. These themes crop up at the beginning of almost every story; then, at the end, typically, the action of the story suddenly speeds up, so the characters may be hurried back into line for a sentimental happy ending. But the questions remain, unanswered. In " 'The Sensible Thing' " George O'Kelly "knew that the past sometimes comes back," and he wins the girl, though their new love is different from their lost youthful love. [63] John M. Chestnut in "Rags Martin-Jones and the Pr-nce of W-les" controls a mysterious worldwide network of power to entertain the girl he wants to marry. [64] Cyrus Girard in "The Third Casket," "who filled the position of Telamonian Ajax among the Homeric characters of Wall Street," is giving away in a kind of knightly tournament "about everything they used to give away in the fairy tales—half of my kingdom and, if she wants him, my daughter's hand." [65] In "The Unspeakable Egg" there is a "Society for the Preservation of Large Fortunes" which, when an engagement between two wealthy young people was announced, arranged to have the newspapers print a "picture of a cross-eyed young lady holding the hand of a savage gentleman with four rows of teeth. . . . the public was pleased to know that they were ugly monsters for all their money, and everyone was satisfied all around." [66]

The last story of these eleven, "John Jackson's Arcady," was different. It was a rare story for Fitzgerald, a story about an older man. John Jackson was wealthy and powerful, but unhappy in his inner life. His wife had deserted him, and his son had grown up to be bad. One day he ran away from his wealth and power to the small town where he grew up. There he found the sweetheart of his youth, who was the wife of a garage owner, and still lived in the poverty from which John Jackson had long ago escaped. Alice still loved him, he still loved her. He asked her to run away with him, and she accepted. John Jackson at last was happy again. "He felt that he had established dominance over time itself, so that it rolled away for him, yielding up one vanished springtime after another to the mastery of his overwhelming emotion."[67] But when he went to take Alice away, she told him she could not desert her children. John Jackson returned alone to his wealth and power, ready to accept it as his lot in life. The story ends with a rapid burst of sentimentality. Time had conquered John Jackson after all, but it had left him with a happy ending. Take away this *Saturday Evening Post* requirement, and the movement toward *The Great Gatsby* is complete. From the fall of 1921 to the summer of 1924, a period dominated by an unsuccessful play and concluded by a dozen conventional slick magazine stories, Fitzgerald had nevertheless rediscovered the values of his intellect and the value of his art. The preparations for *The Great Gatsby* were over; all that remained for him was to write it.

CHAPTER SEVEN

Sometime in his last two years of life F. Scott Fitzgerald wrote down, on the inside back cover of André Malraux's *Man's Hope*, the sources in his own experience for chapters of *The Great Gatsby*.[1] Under Roman numerals I through IX he marked down names and places; and though he added no heading or identifying title, their meaning cannot be mistaken. Why Fitzgerald should have put down this list, however, at so late a date, unidentified, and particularly in so obscure a place, is much less clear. Perhaps, reading the novel which had grown so obviously out of Malraux's experience in the Spanish Civil War, he was moved suddenly to record how deeply the roots of *The Great Gatsby* were laid in his own experience. For the opening chapter's scene in Tom Buchanan's East Egg mansion, Fitzgerald recalled the "glamor of Rumsies and Hitchcocks"; Tommy Hitchcock was a wealthy polo player whom the Fitzgeralds met on Long Island. Gatsby's first party in Chapter III was drawn, he wrote, from "Goddards, Dwans, Swopes." Herbert Bayard Swope was a well-known journalist, Allen Dwan a movie director, who lived at Great Neck in the early twenties. Jordan Baker's story of Daisy's wedding, in Chapter IV, came from Fitzgerald's "memory of Ginevra [King]'s wedding"; and the details of Gatsby's career, as their mystery unfolded in Chapter VI, were taken from a story told to Fitzgerald by a man named Bob Kerr. The desolate setting of Wilson's garage, and

163

Myrtle Wilson's secret apartment, in Chapter II, were places recalled: "Ash heaps, memory of 125th, Great Neck." Fitzgerald remembered 125th Street from his four unhappy months in New York during the spring of 1919; and he lived to see the ash heaps bulldozed for the Flushing Meadows site of the New York World's Fair. Carraway's drive with Gatsby to New York, and their lunch with Meyer Wolfsheim in Chapter IV, came from broader recollections of Fitzgerald's "Vegetable Days in New York." The second party in Chapter VI, and the climactic events of Chapter VII, in New York and returning, Fitzgerald listed without comment, for he had already accounted for their setting and their mood.

Yet Fitzgerald took pains also to show that much of the novel had not been drawn from parallel moments in his own life. The meeting between Gatsby and Daisy in Chapter V, the murder of Gatsby by Wilson in Chapter VIII, and Gatsby's funeral in Chapter IX, he listed explicitly as his own "invention"; and thus he laid claim to the structure, the conclusion, and the ultimate meanings of *The Great Gatsby* as original creations of his own mind and art. *The Great Gatsby* has undergone exceptionally intensive and quite informative criticism in recent years, yet of the many valid ways the novel has been interpreted, none provides so solid a foundation for its meanings as Fitzgerald's own. For all his extraordinary success in creating *The Great Gatsby* as a unified emotional and artistic gesture, Fitzgerald conceived the novel, not as a solid artifact, but as an act; and its fullest meanings may be most completely uncovered by approaching the novel as a process—a process whereby Fitzgerald transformed old values and experience in the crucible of his developing art and ideas.

II

To list the parallels between *The Great Gatsby* and Fitzgerald's earlier fiction would be to catalogue extensively the themes and issues of two novels, more than three dozen short stories, and a play. It was Fitzgerald's new intellectual and artistic maturity, stimulated by his sense of connection and participation in the modern movement of the arts, that made possible his capacity to understand and recast old themes in *The Great Gatsby*'s unforgettable form. For Fitzgerald *The Great Gatsby* was not a novel of new ideas, but of new insights into old ideas. The act of re-creation is more important than the substance thus reshaped, the process more necessary to understand than the material it reworked. Yet it is not possible simply to say, here then is Fitzgerald's stock of themes and problems. As Mencken warned, Fitzgerald was supplied with so much versatility as to be a danger to himself; and though his supply of issues may have been small, he was capable of many different emphases and resolutions, depending on his form, his audience, or his moods.[2] There is no clear formula of progression in Fitzgerald's fiction before *The Great Gatsby*, as we have seen, and thus it is difficult to ascertain in what form the problems rested when *The Great Gatsby* was begun. The one certainty about the material Fitzgerald brought to *The Great Gatsby* was that Fitzgerald had his problems with it, problems to which he had not yet found any lasting satisfactory solution.

But if there was a single, most pervasive theme that connected *The Great Gatsby* to Fitzgerald's earlier fiction, it was the problem of sudden and unmerited wealth. Fitzgerald struggled with the issue first in *This Side of Paradise*, through the character of Dick Humbird. Amory Blaine had looked on Humbird as "a perfect type of aristocrat."[3] But in fact Humbird turned out to be the son of a grocery clerk, who had struck it rich by speculation in land. So Humbird suffered a violent and ugly death, almost as a punishment for Amory's self-deception. It was as if Fitzgerald regarded the Humbirds' financial success, and their rise to social status and power, as a crime; yet Amory Blaine, whose need to expunge Humbird's appeal went so far as to see a vision of him burning in hell, was himself an admirer of successful criminals. "It seemed to him that life and history were rife with the strong criminal, keen, but often self-deluding; in politics and business one found him and among the old statesmen and kings and generals."[4]

Wealth and class, formal categories and real distinctions—these were the issues which Fitzgerald in his early fiction sought to clarify. In stories like "The Four Fists" the answers seemed to lie in morality; in stories like "Two for a Cent," in fate. Sometimes he seemed to find solutions in realism, and sometimes in fantasy. But no resolution was more than temporary, for even the terms of the issue were not yet clear. If Humbird had looked and acted like an aristocrat, but had to be punished because he was not, what then was an aristocrat?

Mencken's aristocrats formed a class of birth, fortune, and intellect, along the lines of eighteenth-century Virginia. Nietzsche limited his aristocracy to artists and philosophers alone. Fitzgerald pondered their ideas and even borrowed the language of their concepts, but he resisted their meanings.[5] When he used the term "aristocrat" he meant the man of wealth alone—the "plutocrat." In *The Beautiful and Damned* Fitzgerald also claimed Anthony Patch as an aristocrat; and Anthony was punished, not by death, but by degradation and insanity.[6] But Fitzgerald's animus against aristocrats was in truth directed against plutocrats in masquerade.

Rich young men with unearned wealth could bring out in Fitzgerald this confused instinct for punishment; poor young men who desired wealth were something else. In one of the stories he wrote right after *This Side of Paradise*, "Dalrymple Goes Wrong," Fitzgerald endowed Bryan Dalrymple with the criminal strength and will Amory Blaine had admired. Dalrymple won his success in the material world by a secret life of crime. But whatever the implications of this character, Fitzgerald could not maintain them. Thereafter his ambitious poor boys who became criminals in their quest for wealth —the most important is Curtis Carlyle in "The Offshore Pirate"— were in fact upper-class genteel heroes, acting out a romantic role to win the hearts of their upper-class girls.

The hero in criminal disguise—"The Unspeakable Egg," written in 1924 just before *The Great Gatsby*, provides a cruder example—was Fitzgerald's most significant variation on the genteel romantic formula. In the course of this study the conventional genteel romantic hero, whom Fitzgerald inherited from one aspect of nineteenth-century American fiction, has been a prominent figure. He was a young man who demonstrated the power of his independent will to prove a moral point, and thereby win fortune and the girl. His task was to perform unconventionally, though without breaking any of the moral or social conventions; his best means were cleverness and imagination, the capacity to do accepted tasks in humorous and entertaining ways. Fitzgerald's truly original contribution to this genre of American fiction was to prolong its life by shifting the focus from the young man to the young woman. He created the genteel romantic heroine, and thus, partly by accident and partly by design, was made the chronicler of the age of the flapper. In all the conventional genteel romantic stories he wrote for the popular magazines before *The Great Gatsby*—the two criminal disguise stories are the only exceptions—the power of independent will rests in the hands not of the male, but of the female. No matter how daring and arduous the task performed by the hero, control over his destiny remains with the girl. As a result the young men in Fitzgerald's conventional genteel stories are vague, rather shadowy figures, even if they always win the girl's love; what interest and excitement there is in the stories is always generated by the flapper heroine.

But for all her independent willfulness the flapper heroine does not break the genteel conventions any more than the romantic hero does. As Gloria Gilbert in *The Beautiful and Damned* insisted, she was free to do anything she pleased, but sexual promiscuity did not please her. Gloria, it is true, drank far too much, but she was punished for it by her loss of beauty. Nancy Lamar in "The Jelly-Bean," who drank and gambled, was the wildest of Fitzgerald's flappers, and she too was punished, by marriage to a man she did not love. The punishment of both girls was lightened, to be sure, by the fact that both their husbands were multi-millionaires. Despite occasional innuendo and a bit of innocent necking in parked cars, Fitzgerald's willful heroines kept themselves remarkably pure.

Thus in his conventional fiction Fitzgerald gave new life to an outmoded formula by shifting the focus of attention within it. It was in his novels that he confronted the implications of the formula's true obsolescence; for he argued in *This Side of Paradise* that the economic and social foundations for genteel romantic heroism were shattered in the First World War. The heroes of his novels, Amory Blaine in *This Side of Paradise* and Anthony Patch in *The Beautiful and Damned*, shared with the old nineteenth-century genteel romantic heroes—once again Tom Sawyer is the best example—an interesting mixture of romantic ideology and sentimental emotion in one mind. In the conventions of the genteel American tradition, as we have seen, romanticism gave power to the deed, and sentiment held the results within socially acceptable bounds. Fitzgerald's significant effort in *This Side of Paradise* to provide an alternative to the genteel hero, through Amory Blaine's constructive individualism, reversed the process. Only sentiment held Amory's loyalty to a social system which had deserted him; but romantic ideology was to shape a new meaning for his sentimentally inspired acts. By the time of *The Beautiful and Damned,* however, romantic ideology had seemed to have proven itself incapable of providing any new meanings. The pathetic Anthony Patch was thus, like Amory Blaine, sentimental in his emotions, but capable only of regarding himself through a veil of romantic despair. Romantic meaning had given way to romantic meaninglessness, optimism and constructive power had been converted to pessimism and helplessness.

The genteel romantic hero, who formed the backbone of Fitzgerald's best fiction as well as his worst, of his most original work as well as his most conventional, was never to fall lower. The process of recovery and growth that began after *The Beautiful and Damned* retained this hero, with his mingled romantic dreams and sentimental feelings. But as the conventional resolution of romance and sentiment had been rendered impossible by the war, so too were Fitzgerald's postwar alternatives—romantic meaning or romantic meaninglessness—outmoded by his maturing insight. The possibility of a resolution within society no longer mattered, for he had discovered a different realm whereby social failure or social success could be judged. Henceforth the genteel romantic hero would be a flawed superman, a man who, merely by his belief that the impossible was still possible, that sentiment and romance could still be resolved, placed himself beyond the safety, and beyond the comprehension, of conventional society. Society would judge him, to be sure, but so long as Fitzgerald through his art could provide another mode of judgment, the genteel hero's fate might be raised to the stature of a national tragedy.

This structure emerges only imperfectly from "The Diamond as Big as the Ritz," for Fitzgerald was torn between punishing Braddock Washington and exalting him. Yet the novella marks the single most important turning point, before *The Great Gatsby,* in Fitzgerald's mind and art. While turning "The Romantic Egotist" into *This Side of Paradise* the author had discovered that the genteel romantic hero was a victim of the First World War, and ever since he had been faced with a dilemma. He could please his slick magazine readers by writing as if the wealthy and clever old hero was still as lively as ever; or he could try in his novels to create new values in place of the moribund old, or coherently to portray the decadence of youth without values. No alternative had satisfied him, for the values of the genteel romantic hero were his own values, and the problem was to combine genteel romantic values with his own true perceptions of society. Of all Fitzgerald's early fiction "The Offshore Pirate" was the most cogent statement of his dilemma. There he had fused the conventional genteel romantic hero to his own conception of the unconventional, self-created individual, in the person of the ambitious, class-conscious, criminal band-leader, Curtis Carlyle, only to destroy his creation by a sentimental ending. By "The Diamond as Big as the Ritz" Fitzgerald had discovered new means in his maturing intelligence and artistry to re-create the fusion, and to make it stick. With "The Diamond as Big as the Ritz" the major dilemma affecting Fitzgerald's themes and values had been solved, and the first block in the foundation of *The Great Gatsby* was laid.

III

Yet as the themes Fitzgerald recast in *The Great Gatsby* had already been his concerns in his earliest fiction, so too the means whereby he achieved his maturity—at least in the basic tones and gestures he brought, almost unconsciously, to the art of fiction—had been in his hands from the very first. One of the major thrusts in the modern movement of the arts was the desire to regain a sense of connection with the past and the eternities; and Fitzgerald, whose religious and literary backgrounds particularly endowed him with a sense of time and the supernatural, whose intellectual energy was devoted to relating values and tradition in conflict, was as well prepared as any to participate creatively.

The past and the eternities, a sense of universal patterns in human behavior, appear from the start in Fitzgerald's fiction. Sources of influence are not difficult to trace, even though it is impossible precisely to determine the nature of their use. Fitzgerald's Roman Catholic background, in its non-liturgical forms at least, provided him with a philosophy of history and a feeling for the supernatural. Shane Leslie's primers on the First World War taught him two different, but not contradictory, historical perspectives on his own experience; on the one hand the war marked a definite and conclusive break with Victorian civilization, on the other it was simply a phase, though a major one, of world-historical movements centuries old and with centuries yet to run. From Monsignor Robert Hugh Benson's Catholic novels Fitzgerald probably derived his sense for the presence of supernatural forces in natural events, which expressed itself most obviously in "The Devil" episode of *This Side of Paradise*. Benson was a convert from Anglicanism to Catholicism, as was Fitzgerald's friend and mentor, Father Sigourney Webster Fay, a convert in America from the Episcopal Church to Catholicism. In both conversions a common factor may have been a feeling that the Roman Catholic faith gave greater scope to the aesthetic and mystical sides of their natures; at the end of the nineteenth century, after decades of hostility, many genteel American Protestants were attracted to the beauty and serenity of Roman Catholic ritual and art. Leslie and Father Fay had both been intimates of Henry Adams; Leslie had learned his philosophy of history from Adams, and Father Fay had collaborated with Adams on an article about the German threat to religion. For Fitzgerald, then, the gap between specifically American and specifically Catholic views was never difficult to close.

Yet after *This Side of Paradise* Fitzgerald's preoccupations in his fiction reflect little Roman Catholic influence. Though a sense of time and a sense of universal patterns continue to pervade his work, their conscious intellectual source, where they had one, was the poetry of English Romanticism. Keats and the Romantics taught Fitzgerald that truth was beauty and beauty was eternal, a faith that gave as coherent a meaning to life as any more formal theology; but he also learned from the poets that life must be lived for the moment only, for nothing mortal, and especially neither youth nor beauty, could be made to last. In *This Side of Paradise* Fitzgerald had tried to cope with the complications of these conflicting doctrines, retaining the Romantic sense of immediacy and rejecting the truth of beauty; in *The Beautiful and Damned* he tried unsuccessfully to encompass all Romantic contradictions and to rise above them with a negative faith of his own, the belief that life was meaningless. But in his magazine stories he could pick and choose with equanimity, for the power of sentiment could rise above any inconsistency. In "The Offshore Pirate," remarkable for knitting together his most original insights and his sentimental evasions into one whole, Fitzgerald let Ardita Farnham proclaim the Romantic belief in personal courage: "A sort of insistence on the value of life and the worth of transient things. . . . My courage is faith—faith in the eternal resilience of me." But her faith was not his own. "To me the interesting thing about Ardita," he interpolated, "is the courage that will tarnish with her beauty and youth." Fitzgerald sensed the dramatic pathos in his heroine's belief in the eternal strength of mortal qualities, but in "The Offshore Pirate" he preferred to gloss it over. She marries a wealthy genteel romantic hero who would lie to her "just as sweetly as you know how for the rest of my life" and illusion would never be disturbed.[7]

Elsewhere Fitzgerald's sense of time and the eternities came from even less precise and conscious sources. From his experiences in Montgomery, Alabama, the home of his wife, he developed a feeling for the Southern view of time and the past, a feeling expressed in "The Jelly-Bean" and "Two for a Cent" and especially in "The Ice Palace," where Sally Carrol Happer loves to visit cemeteries and tries to keep "that old time" alive within her. What took Sally temporarily away from her drowsy South was her conflicting desire "to live where things happen on a big scale"—a desire, not merely to make money, but, in the modern idiom, to be a part of the action.[8] Thus, in the attitudes derived from his own experience, there was a conflict between ambition and tradition equally as significant as the conflict in his Romantic influence between the eternity and the transiency of beauty. Though the Romantic contradiction, for the time being, had to be avoided, the contradiction in his social inheritance between permanence and change could easily be resolved in the convention of the genteel romantic hero, a convention that gave assurance of permanence in change in a form as ritually precise as any primitive culture's rite of passage to maturity. And so the genteel romantic hero became an element of escape from Fitzgerald's problems with time and the eternities as well as from his problems of theme and value.

But where the genteel romantic hero did not avail—particularly in *The Beautiful and Damned* and in the stories written under the influence of a realism which explicitly denied the genteel conventions—Fitzgerald's concern with time and with universal patterns created more problems than solutions. Time was a villain, a despoiler, an enemy to be met and conquered; universal patterns stole originality from human life and even cheated individuals of their significance. This was the impasse which confronted Fitzgerald in the winter of 1921-22—an impasse which, coupled with his dilemmas over character and social theme, led him temporarily to give up fiction in favor of stage comedy; but which also provided him with the opportunity to read and to think his way free. For he had already, early in that winter, hit upon the germ of his solution. Though *The Beautiful and Damned* represents the nadir of Fitzgerald's capacity to comprehend and control his material, he had already, before his slight effort to revise the novel, begun to write "The Diamond as Big as the Ritz." He had never before felt such artistic despair and intellectual confusion; and yet at that moment his dangerous versatility, combined with the exceptional resilience of his talent, came up with a combination of elements almost perfectly right.

By writing the novella "utterly for my own amusement" Fitzgerald excused himself from the responsibility of either criticizing conventional forms or adhering to them, and gave license to his fancy to play freely on ideas of wealth.[9] The fusion of his fantasy, completely unfettered for the first time from genteel formulas, with a not unfamiliar craving for luxury, gave birth to the diamond mountain and the man of wealth raised to the status of a god. Braddock Washington, the Prometheus Enriched who destroyed himself and his fortune instead of destroying human hopes and values, retained greater dignity than Fitzgerald had meant for him to have; thereafter it remained only for Fitzgerald to create a character adequate to his conception of greatness and of tragic plight.

The conception, then, was originally Fitzgerald's; the process whereby it attained *The Great Gatsby's* perfection of form, as we have seen, began with his reading and reflection on the fiction of Joseph Conrad and James Joyce. From his reading of Conrad's "Youth" and *Nostromo* Fitzgerald grasped what he had not learned from the Romantic poets, that, as his favorite Keats had written, "the excellence of every Art is its intensity, capable of making all disagreeables evaporate, from their being in close relationship with Beauty & Truth." [10] The loss of youth and beauty, even the loss of life, could be overcome by an art which was intense enough to preserve the quality of romance and power, even though their substance must disappear; time, though it still conquered, might nevertheless lose its terror. Thus it was that Conrad gave to Fitzgerald his first insight into what Keats had stated as his doctrine of negative capability: "That is," Keats wrote, "when man is capable of being in uncertainties, Mysteries, doubts, without any irritable reaching after fact & reason—Coleridge, for instance, would let go by a fine isolated verisimilitude caught from the Penetralium of mystery, from being incapable of remaining content with half knowledge. This pursued through Volumes would perhaps take us no further than this, that with a great poet the sense of Beauty overcomes every other consideration, or rather obliterates all consideration." [11] In his reading of *Ulysses* Fitzgerald had been led to discern the same principles in a more familiar setting and a more accessible form. Fitzgerald's short story "Winter Dreams," written right after he read *Ulysses*, demonstrated how Joyce had helped him shift his focus to a lower-class character whose yearning for beauty, though expressed still in conventional terms, was surrounded by a new sense of mystery. Finally, in the short story "Absolution," the romantic imagination of Rudolph Miller discovers that it is capable of conceiving a beauty, and sustaining its mystery, separate from an idea of God. Fitzgerald's imaginative hero thus possessed the means, not to defy God, but to entertain Him. Neither God's wrath nor didactic social morality could account, thereafter, for the downfall of such a grand, creative figure.

IV

In April 1924, Fitzgerald sailed with his family to Europe, where he planned immediately to begin his third novel. Just before his departure he wrote a long, confessional letter to Maxwell Perkins, as if to dredge up and leave all his feelings of guilt and regret behind him. One need not agree with the precise nature of his own self-condemnation—he had a tendency to dramatize and exaggerate there as elsewhere—to recognize its therapeutic value. "I feel I have an enormous power in me now," he concluded, ". . . . in my new novel I'm thrown directly on purely creative work—not trashy imaginings as in my stories but the sustained imagination of a sincere yet radiant world. . . . This book will be a consciously artistic achievement and must depend on that as the first books did not." [12]

The full nature of Fitzgerald's conscious artistry, however, is not easily uncovered. No indications exist but the text itself, and a few suggestive hints in letters Fitzgerald wrote during the composition of *The Great Gatsby*. "Absolution," he told Perkins, "was to have been the prologue to the novel but it interfered with the neatness of the plan"; so there was a plan, and its form required that the hero's origins remain mysterious to the end.[13] As soon as they settled on the French Riviera he read biographies of Byron and Shelley; near the end of his work he promised Perkins that changes in the proof would make it "one of the most expensive affairs since *Madame Bovary*." [14] At times he wanted to call the novel *Trimalchio* or *Trimalchio in West Egg*, so Gatsby must have been consciously modeled, at least in part, on the vulgar parvenu of Petronius's Roman satire, *The Satyricon*; and *The Satyricon* is regarded as a mock-heroic version of *The Odyssey*, with Encolpius, the narrator, a comic Ulysses.[15] Even personal remarks seem to have a bearing on the issues of the novel; twice, once frivolously and the other time seriously, he expressed the wish "to start over," to begin life anew.[16]

But there is evidence also that Fitzgerald was not conscious of the form taking shape under his hand. When he received Perkins' reaction to the first draft—an extraordinary letter of praise, tempered by the criticism that "Gatsby is somewhat vague"—Fitzgerald's "first instinct," as he reported to Perkins, "was to let [Gatsby] go and have Tom Buchanan dominate the book." Parenthetically he added, "(I suppose he's the best character I've ever done—I think he and the brother in *Salt* and Hurstwood in *Sister Carrie* are the three best characters in American fiction in the last twenty years, perhaps and perhaps not)," a curious insight into the uncertainty of purpose and the uncertainty of taste that still lay below the surface of Fitzgerald's exceptional confidence of direction and judgment during the writing of *Gatsby*. "But Gatsby sticks in my heart," he said. "I had him for a while, then lost him, and now I know I have him again." His energies during the revision went into sharpening and deepening the portrait of Gatsby, and when it was done he told Perkins, "I know Gatsby better than I know my own child." [17]

There is no doubt, then, that *The Great Gatsby* is a work of conscious artistry, in its language, in its structure, and in its themes; but it is also fair to say that the process whereby *The Great Gatsby* attained its ultimate form was a process in which Fitzgerald's mind did not play a wholly conscious part. As Thomas Mann said of criticism on *The Magic Mountain*, "One always needs to be reminded; one is by no means always in possession of one's whole self. Our consciousness is feeble; only in moments of unusual clarity and vision do we really know about ourselves. As for me, I am glad to be instructed by critics about myself, to learn from them about my past works and go back to them in my mind. My regular formula of thanks for such refreshment of my consciousness is: 'I am most grateful to you for having so kindly recalled me to myself.'" [18] An interpretation of *The Great Gatsby* poses, as it were, a similar responsibility and opportunity.

V

The greatness of Jay Gatsby, in *The Great Gatsby*, is created in Nick Carraway's vision, out of himself. Nick is the narrator of the novel and also its seer, the man of two parts, the participant and the observer. "I was within and without," Nick says, at once the man behind the yellow window of the city flat, yet placing himself down below with the casual watcher, looking up and wondering—"simultaneously enchanted and repelled by the inexhaustible variety of life." [19] It is this special trait, this doubleness, that enables Nick to encompass all the novel's life within his values and his understanding, to create the frame in which the reader may see even more. For even as he observes the natures and the motives of the novel's characters his own heart harbors their same emotions and desires. And thus he is able to appreciate, as he tells us at the start, before he is called upon to judge. The end is in the beginning of *The Great Gatsby*, and Nick came home from that summer on Long Island wanting "the world to be in uniform and at a sort of moral attention forever" (2); but we learn first that his capacity for "infinite hope" has not been lost. "I am still a little afraid of missing something" (1). Gatsby's "extraordinary gift for hope," his "romantic readiness," had exempted him from Nick's moral revulsion, and as the end is in the beginning, so Nick keeps himself open to find a new beginning in the end. A phenomenon as great and grandiose as Gatsby may yet come again to strain his capacity for wonder.

The frame that Nick creates is a circle, a circle that begins as it ends, in the West. "I see now," Nick says near the end, "that this has been a story of the West after all—Tom and Gatsby, Daisy and Jordan and I, were all Westerners" (177). And as Nick contains within himself the natures and motives of the others, so the emotions and desires that send him on his journey East, that shape his vision of the East, are Western—and stand for them all. After the First World War Nick had come home restless. "Instead of being the warm center of the world, the Middle West now seemed like the ragged edge of the universe—so I decided," Nick said, "to go East and learn the bond business" (3). Settled on Long Island, "with the sunshine and the great bursts of leaves growing on the trees, just as things grow in fast movies," Nick felt "that familiar conviction that life was beginning over again with the summer" (4). Nick's sense of the movement of life was thus tied to the natural flux of the seasons. Nature was to provide him as well with the images that built his vision of the new scene. And Nick sees the city, the new "warm center of the world," in images of wonder and felicity borrowed from the Western country and frontier. With Tom Buchanan and Myrtle Wilson, Fifth Avenue on a summer Sunday afternoon was "so warm and soft, almost pastoral, . . . that I wouldn't have been surprised to see a great flock of white sheep turn the corner" (28). Later, driving with Gatsby across the Queensboro Bridge, Nick feels that he is seeing the city again for the first time, "in its first wild promise of all the mystery and the beauty of the world. . . . 'Anything can happen now that we've slid over this bridge,' I thought, 'anything at all. . . .' Even Gatsby could happen, without any particular wonder" (69). Anything at all—"I liked to walk up Fifth Avenue and pick out romantic women from the crowd," Nick says, "and imagine that in a few minutes I was going to enter into their lives, and no one would ever know or disapprove. Sometimes, in my mind, I followed them to their apartments on the corners of hidden streets, and they turned and smiled back at me before they faded through a door into warm darkness" (57). For Nick, as for Tom and Myrtle, Gatsby and Daisy, summer in the center of the world is a season for fulfilling dreams of love. The circle of Nick's frame is a voyage from the old center of the world to the new, and a returning homeward; and within that circle is the circle of nature, the life-giving and life-ending cycle of the seasons. Nick's narrative voice and his vision make *The Great Gatsby* a novel of patterns, within the characters and without, separate and finally together.

Nick's introduction to the new center of the world is a slow and at first reluctant one. For nature as he encounters it on Long Island in the beginning is neither the pastoral nor the wild nature of his familiar West. Nature in those communities of "natural curiosities," East and West Egg, is an entertainer—a creator of trick images, making "great bursts of leaves" grow "on the trees, just as things grow in fast movies" (4); a provider of stage masks, like the "thin beard of raw ivy" that added a touch of nature to diminish the falsity of Gatsby's "spanking new" imitation French villa (5); an acrobat, as was the lawn at Tom Buchanan's house—"The lawn started at the beach and ran toward the front door for a quarter of a mile, jumping over sun-dials and brick walks and burning gardens—finally when it reached the house drifting up the side in bright vines as though from the momentum of its run" (6-7). Nick's sense of nature's playfulness around the houses of the rich—almost nature's mockery—quickens his feelings for both the magic possibilities of wealth and the certainties of his own moral standard. It was as if nature's giddiness at the Buchanans' house—the breeze blowing through the living room, rippling and fluttering the white dresses of Daisy and Jordan Baker "as if they had just been blown back in after a short flight around the house" (8)—makes Nick all the more careful to preserve his own sense of right. He is aware then only of the sharp difference between the Buchanans' way of living and the manners of the West. His moralistic response to the revelation of Tom's adultery, with its melodramatic appeal for the police and its sentimental picture of Daisy rushing out of the house, child in arms, conveys the conventional judgment of the West—a standard that remains intact, no matter how greatly Nick's vision may grow. His feeling of disgust on leaving the Buchanans' shapes the tone for his first unexpected encounter with Gatsby back home. The wind, the same wind that had blown Daisy's and Jordan's dresses, "had blown off, leaving a loud, bright night, with wings beating in the trees and a persistent organ sound as the full bellows of the earth blew the frogs full of life." Nature is playing a solemn, mocking, frog-voiced song to accompany Gatsby's long vigil; and Nick's feeling that Gatsby had "come out to determine what share was his of our local heavens" bears the same double sense as at the Buchanans', mingled awe and disgust at the power and the pride of wealth (21). Then he sees that Gatsby's gesture encompassed nothing more tangible than "a single green light, minute and far away, that might have been the end of a dock" (22).

The alternative to nature's mockery, among the homes of the novel's protagonists on Long Island, is nature's absence. The valley of ashes next to the garage where Myrtle Wilson, Tom's mistress, lives with her husband, is a desolate area, a "waste land" (24). Rather *it* mocks nature; Nick pictures it as "a fantastic farm where ashes grow like wheat into ridges and hills and grotesque gardens"; and it mocks the endeavors of men as well, for as Nick envisions it the ashes take the forms of houses and even, "with a transcendent effort, of ash-grey men who move dimly and already crumbling through the powdery air" (23). George Wilson is like one of those ash-grey figures, spiritless and anaemic, so covered with dust that he seems to fade into the cement color of his garage walls. Only Myrtle Wilson possessed the immense natural vitality temporarily to escape, repeating to herself, the first day Tom took her, the liturgy of the waste land's death in life, "you can't live forever; you can't live forever" (36). Where nature is absent, the power that reigns is the inscrutable power resident in the brooding, persistently staring eyes of Dr. T. J. Eckleburg in the faded advertisement that overlooks the scene.

Nick had been forced to accompany Tom and Myrtle in their rendezvous, and he washed down his reluctance with the whiskey Tom produced. It was the second time, he said, he had been drunk in his life, and his drinking was the source of his new and broader perspective, the feeling that he was "within and without, simultaneously enchanted and repelled by the inexhaustible variety of life" (36). Yet his perspective was not so broad that it lost its geographical basis. "When they do get married," Myrtle's sister says, speaking of Myrtle and Tom, "they're going West to live for a while until it blows over." And Nick replies, "It'd be more discreet to go to Europe" (34).

Nick gets drunk for a third time when he attends one of Gatsby's parties. Through the summer nights he had listened to the "music from my neighbor's house," (39) watched the immense effort of caterers, fruiterers, servants, gardeners that went on behind the scenes to produce Gatsby's festive setting; the magic power of wealth so pervades Gatsby's parties that even "the premature moon" was "produced like the supper, no doubt, out of a caterer's basket" (43). To his first party Nick had been invited, but most of the guests, he said, were not."People went there "and after that they conducted themselves according to the rules of behavior associated with amusement parks. Sometimes they came and went without having met Gatsby at all, came for the party with a simplicity of heart that was its own ticket of admission" (41). They paid him tribute by romantic speculation; his mystery was so grand it inspired "whispers about him from those who had found little that it was necessary to whisper about in this world"(44). Myrtle Wilson's sister Catherine, who had once been an uninvited guest, had already speculated he was a nephew or cousin of Kaiser Wilhelm. Others heard that he had killed a man; or that he had been a German spy. In their rumors the source of his wealth lay not only in criminal behavior, but in treason, or hostility to the United States. It was the nature of their simple hearts to take their pleasure more easily without knowledge, holding action and judgment in easier balance, than can Nick with his greater perception. Yet one of the uninvited guests is capable of insight into Gatsby's nature even before Nick. He was the stout middle-aged man, with enormous owl-eyed spectacles, who excitedly informed Nick and Jordan Baker that the books in Gatsby's library were real. " 'See!' he cried triumphantly. 'It's a bona-fide piece of printed matter. It fooled me. This fella's a regular Belasco. It's a triumph. What thoroughness! What realism! Knew when to stop, too—didn't cut the pages. But what do you want? What did you expect?' " Owl Eyes's wonder is directed not at the possible origins—his tone implies his judgment of the parvenu—but at the achievement; not at the mystery, but at the spectacle itself. Owl Eyes's vision is on a different plane from Nick's, then, not so deep, yet undivided. His admiration puts on Gatsby's showmanship, whatever its motives or consequences, the seal of professional success. Then he snatched the book from Nick's hands "and replaced it hastily on its shelf, muttering that if one brick was removed the whole library was liable to collapse" (46) —recognizing its precariousness too.

At Gatsby's party as at Myrtle's apartment, Nick's drinking deepens his vision of reality. "I was enjoying myself now. I had taken two finger-bowls of champagne, and the scene had changed before my eyes into something significant, elemental, and profound" (47). It is then that he encounters Gatsby, and is prepared to see beyond the others into Gatsby's visionary world. "He smiled understandingly —much more than understandingly. It was one of those rare smiles with a quality of eternal reassurance in it, that you may come across four or five times in life. It faced—or seemed to face—the whole external world for an instant, and then concentrated on *you* with an irresistible prejudice in your favor. It understood you just as far as you wanted to be understood, believed in you as you would like to believe in yourself, and assured you that it had precisely the impression of you that, at your best, you hoped to convey. Precisely at that point it vanished—and I was looking at an elegant young roughneck, a year or two over thirty, whose elaborate formality of speech just missed being absurd" (48). As Owl Eyes sees none of the mystery and only the showmanship, Nick can see beyond the fact of mystery to the value it contains—the possibility and the reality of personal self-creation. And between them, sensing neither the one nor the other, the guests at Gatsby's party fell even more deeply under the influence of his music. Fitzgerald presents Gatsby's party in a style dominated by aural imagery, the language of sound and of song— the musical motif and the novel's larger, universal themes come together in the playing of "Vladimir Tostoff's *Jazz History of the World*" (50).

Leaving the party Nick encounters Owl Eyes again, recognizing him first by his "unusual quality of wonder" (54). Owl Eyes had just gotten out of an automobile which had lost a wheel and gone into a ditch, and his attitude toward the accident was a direct parallel to his appreciation of Gatsby's showmanship—"the fact was infinitely astonishing to him," but he had no interest in the causes behind it. " 'Don't ask me,' said Owl Eyes, washing his hands of the whole matter. 'I know very little about driving—next to nothing. It happened, and that's all I know' " (54). Owl Eyes's wonder at the fact is strangely complemented by the driver's insistence that nothing unusual had happened at all. Owl Eyes's accident was the first of several accidents in *The Great Gatsby*, each of which sends out ripples, as from a stone dropped in a pond, across the novel's images and themes—the imagery of cycle and circle, through the wheel of the tire and the steering wheel; the language of movement, of social mobility, and of restlessness; and of economic and social dreams.

To Nick at first the automobile had been linked with natural beauty and romance—"Already it was deep summer on roadhouse roofs and in front of wayside garages, where new red gas-pumps sat out in pools of light" (21)—and with possibilities of sexual licentiousness; even George Wilson's garage, that most dismal of settings, had made Nick suspect, in Tom Buchanan's presence, "that this shadow of a garage must be a blind, and that sumptuous and romantic apartments were concealed overhead" (25). The automobile can remain a symbol of beauty and romance for New York's Eastern Europeans and aspiring Negroes (69), but after Owl Eyes's accident Nick sees it for himself in a different light. Later on he learns that Tom Buchanan's first adultery was revealed when he "ran into a wagon on the Ventura road one night, and ripped a front wheel off his car," breaking the arm of the hotel chambermaid who was with him (78). And even more immediately came Nick's argument with Jordan Baker about driving.

> It started because she passed so close to some workmen that our fender flicked a button on one man's coat.
> "You're a rotten driver," I protested. "Either you ought to be more careful, or you oughtn't to drive at all."
> "I am careful."
> "No, you're not."
> "Well, other people are," she said lightly.
> "What's that got to do with it?"
> "They'll keep out of my way," she insisted. "It takes two to make an accident."
> "Suppose you met somebody just as careless as yourself."
> "I hope I never will," she answered. "I hate careless people. That's why I like you." (59)

After that conversation Nick thought he loved Jordan; but at the end of the novel Jordan uses it for self-justification in breaking off with Nick. " 'Oh, and do you remember'—she added—'a conversation we had once about driving a car? ... You said a bad driver was only safe until she met another bad driver? Well, I met another bad driver, didn't I? I mean it was careless of me to make such a wrong guess. I thought you were rather an honest, straightforward person. I thought it was your secret pride" (179). Jordan's recollection was not the true parallel, however, for her argument with Nick; the careless driver who met someone as careless as herself was Daisy, and that someone was Myrtle Wilson.

Nick's next vision of Gatsby comes on the momentous day when he meets Meyer Wolfsheim and hears Jordan Baker's story of Gatsby and Daisy. Gatsby calls for Nick in his fabulous car, a car that with its melodic three-noted horn, its "labyrinth of wind-shields that mirrored a dozen suns," its interior like "a sort of green leather conservatory," appears almost as a satiric symbol of the novel's musical, universal, and natural themes (64). On the drive Gatsby tries to dispel some of the mystery that surrounds him. " 'I'll tell you God's truth.' His right hand suddenly ordered divine retribution to stand by" (65). God's truth is only half-truth, a mixture of reality, the Montenegran medal and the Oxford photo, with the gross sentimentality of, "After that I lived like a young rajah in all the capitals of Europe—Paris, Venice, Rome—collecting jewels, chiefly rubies, hunting big game, painting a little, things for myself only, and trying to forget something very sad that happened to me long ago" (66). At lunch Gatsby's associate Wolfsheim, with his sad memories of "the night they shot Rosy Rosenthal" in the Old Metropole, and his tremulous apologies for belonging to an older generation, waxes even more sentimental—so sentimental that even Gatsby can notice it (70, 73).

Nick is staggered when Gatsby tells him that Wolfsheim was the gambler "who fixed the World's Series back in 1919." Nick remembers the incident, "but if I had thought of it at all I would have thought of it as a thing that merely *happened,* the end of some inevitable chain. It never occurred to me that one man could start to play with the faith of fifty million people—with the single-mindedness of a burglar blowing a safe." Asking, then, how it happened, Nick is told by Gatsby: "He just saw the opportunity" (74). Gatsby's bland business-lunch answer brings together, in incongruous conjunction, enormous, criminal power and the most simple and normal of motives: and it fills in the patterns of Gatsby's character just at the moment when Jordan Baker is to lift the first veil from his mystery. Wolfsheim's state of mind is the analogy for Gatsby's, at least for that part of Gatsby's inner life which corresponds with Owl Eyes's perception of the outer, the mere upstart who nevertheless was putting on a perfect show. Gatsby's burst of mingled earnestness and sentiment appears side by side with Wolfsheim's similar effusion; and in Gatsby's momentary absence Wolfsheim confides to Nick how seriously he applies conventional moral standards to his prospective associates. Though a Jew, Wolfsheim thus is portrayed as a man with attitudes and values common to the conventional American business class. Only Nick is not able to rest contented, as Owl Eyes was, with the mere fact of a happening; he must get behind it to its source. He is incredulous because so grand and heinous a crime should have as its source so banal and so conventional a motive; but what is more important is his discovery that so enormous a deed—a deed he suggests, however ironically, that tampers with the very foundation of social beliefs—should have as its source the power and the will of a single individual. So the simplicity of Wolfsheim's heart, and the terrifying enormity of its reach, prepares Nick for Jordan's story of Gatsby and Daisy.

Her story removes only one of the veils from Gatsby's mystery, the veil that covered his immediate purpose and goal. Gatsby's background stands otherwise no more revealed than from the information that he was an Oxford man, or even the possibility that he had been a German spy. The striking image of Jordan Baker's opening paragraph, that when her new plaid skirt blew a little in the wind "the red, white and blue banners in front of all the houses stretched out stiff and said *tut-tut-tut-tut,* in a disapproving way," brilliantly conveys the mingled patriotism and prudery of that wartime American society—a society into which, ironically, Jay Gatsby's officer uniform was a sufficient ticket of admission. For Nick this new knowledge deepens his vision of reality even more. The magic possibilities of wealth had appeared to him in the setting of a mocking nature; the elemental and profound qualities of Gatsby's personality had been sensed only in a vague and drunken way. Now the glimpse of truth that reduces Gatsby to the level of other men paradoxically enhances his special stature all the more. "Then it had not been merely the stars to which he had aspired on that June night," Nick says. "He came alive to me, delivered suddenly from the womb of his purposeless splendor" (79). Nick's "merely" conveys a double meaning. It suggests that Gatsby's significance as a symbol grows as his object appears more limited and also, in the conventionality and sentimentality of his motives, more universal. Yet it implies too that so grand a power and so intense a dream have reshaped the commonplace into something elemental and profound, have so enhanced his desire that its object has in fact been turned into a goal greater and less accessible even than the stars. After Jordan's story Nick sees the world as if bathed in a new light from the revelation of Gatsby's desire. There in the city, the new, warm center of the world, the powers of nature and the promise of sensuality seem to fuse. "The sun had gone down behind the tall apartments of the movie stars in the West Fifties, and the clear voices of little girls, already gathered like crickets on the grass, rose through the hot twilight:

> "I'm the Sheik of Araby
> Your love belongs to me.
> At night when you're asleep
> Into your tent I'll creep——" (79)

Nick learns that he is to arrange the meeting between Gatsby and Daisy.

The meeting is brought to fruition through an extraordinarily rich and complex patterning of Fitzgerald's themes. It marks the completion of a cycle within the novel's larger cycle, a moment of regeneration, of beginning again, portended by a natural symbol of fertility, the pouring rain. The moment of Gatsby's and Daisy's reunion is symbolized in a comic scene that marks the death of time. Gatsby's "head leaned back so far that it rested against the face of a defunct mantelpiece clock.... 'We've met before,' muttered Gatsby.... Luckily the clock took this moment to tilt dangerously at the pressure of his head.... 'I'm sorry about the clock,' he said.... 'It's an old clock,' I told them idiotically. I think we all believed for a moment that it had smashed in pieces on the floor" (87-8). Gatsby himself had made the symbolic gesture of a "nervous circuit of the house" (89), and when Nick leaves Gatsby and Daisy alone he goes out into the "small muddy swamps and prehistoric marshes" of his inundated lawn, a scene which suggests the chaos to which men symbolically return, in primitive rites, at the moment of regeneration of time (89). Here Fitzgerald added one of his most imaginative touches, associating Nick, the visionary who sees a new reality beyond the common-place reality, with the philosopher Immanuel Kant. "There was noth-ing to look at from under the tree except Gatsby's enormous house, so I stared at it, like Kant at his church steeple, for half an hour" (89). It was Kant's habit to stare at a church steeple through his window while he mulled over his philosophical concerns. A neighbor's trees grew so tall, however, they hid the steeple from Kant's view. But at Kant's request their tops were cut, and he was able to resume his contemplation. Nature resists man's efforts to find transcendent real-ity behind its earthly face.[20]

The imagery of nature and the imagery of sound play together through the scene, shaped specifically by references to flowers and to Daisy's voice. Floral imagery entered the novel in Daisy's and Myrtle's names; earlier flowers had linked nature with Gatsby's magic powers and with his mystery: " 'He's a bootlegger,' said the young ladies, moving somewhere between his cocktails and his flowers. 'One time he killed a man who had found out that he was nephew to Von Hindenburg and second cousin to the devil. Reach me a rose, honey, and pour me a last drop into that there crystal glass' " (61). Nick had heard the "excitement" in Daisy's voice when he met her earlier at the Buchanans' (9-10), and Jordan recognized too that "there's something in that voice of hers . . ." (79). Nature enters into Nick's house, where Gatsby and Daisy met, through the green-house of flowers that Gatsby had sent over, and through Daisy's voice, whose "exhilarating ripple . . . was a wild tonic in the rain" (86). From outside the house Nick thought the rain had sounded "like the murmur of their voices, rising and swelling a little now and then with gusts of emotion" (89-90). Gatsby's house too was "vivid with new flowers," but though Daisy had admired the gardens outside, her awe gave way inside before the even more vivid display of Gatsby's shirts, a display so overwhelming that it could strain and muffle her remarkable voice (92-4). Although Daisy's voice could mingle with and enhance the natural beauty of the scene, it faded to silence before Gatsby's power to create an even greater beauty, even to reshape the beauty of nature itself; he was "an ecstatic patron of recurrent light," a creator of life, a power comparable to the sun (90).

The success of the scene depends as well on its mundane aspects—

Nick's worries about his hospitality; the half-sinister, half-ludicrous glimpses into Gatsby's business affairs; Nick's reflections on the social history of Gatsby's mansion, brought to a succinct completion by a demonstration of the relation between the inner workings and the outer appearance of such an establishment: "A maid began opening the upper windows of his house, appeared momentarily in each, and, leaning from a large central bay, spat meditatively into the garden" (89). The end of the scene brings to one memorable focus all the patterned themes: the theme of the cycle, of the end and the beginning of time, of death and of rebirth; the significance of Gatsby's dreams and of his magic powers, of his parties and his music; the imagery of nature and the imagery of sound. Klipspringer is playing a popular tune on the piano. Gatsby and Daisy are seated together on a couch. "As I watched him," Nick says, "he adjusted himself a little, visibly. His hand took hold of hers, and as she said something low in his ear he turned toward her with a rush of emotion. I think that voice held him most, with its fluctuating, feverish warmth, because it couldn't be over-dreamed—that voice was a deathless song" (97).

The veil that lifts next from Gatsby's mystery reveals, not only the object, but the source—and the language hints that the object and the source must be linked inevitably together. "Jay Gatsby" is revealed as the invention of James Gatz, as "Blatchford Sarnemington" was the creation of Rudolph Miller in "Absolution." Like Rudolph, Gatz was a lower-class young man whose imagination was so powerful that it leapt beyond his social and economic circumstances. Beyond, in origins, was "his Platonic conception of himself," a self-creative power that made him more powerful in his way than God, equal to a god, responsible to God—"he must be about His Father's business, the service of a vast, vulgar, and meretricious beauty" (99). He was the impresario whose imagination could put on a show entertaining to God Himself. But beyond, in practical expectations, were the only goals of the genteel American hero at the end of the nineteenth century, wealth, the girl, and social standing. For the aspiring lower-class genteel hero, like Dexter Green in "Winter Dreams" or John Jackson in "John Jackson's Arcady," wealth and social standing were easy to obtain, yet the girl was unattainable. James Gatz's dreams were unmistakably erotic, were for the girl.

186

"The grotesque and fantastic conceits haunted him in his bed at night. A universe of ineffable gaudiness spun itself out in his brain while the clock ticked on the wash-stand and the moon soaked with wet light his tangled clothes upon the floor. Each night he added to the pattern of his fancies until drowsiness closed down upon some vivid scene with an oblivious embrace. For a while these reveries provided an outlet for his imagination; they were a satisfactory hint of the unreality of reality, a promise that the rock of the world was founded securely on a fairy's wing" (99-100). James Gatz met his destiny, transformed himself into Gatsby, when Dan Cody's yacht appeared in Little Girl Bay.

This revelation, interjected by Nick at the start of Chapter VI, begins in a sense the second movement of the novel, a movement that comes eventually to focus on the economic and social aspects of Gatsby's dream as the first movement had emphasized the mysterious, the romantic, and the universal. Now Gatsby's dream and his creation are seen momentarily through the eyes of the wealth and standing—and of the girl—to which he aspires. "By God, I may be old-fashioned in my ideas," says Tom to Nick, discovering that Gatsby knows Daisy, "but women run around too much these days to suit me. They meet all kinds of crazy fish" (104). And Daisy herself was appalled and offended by Gatsby's parties, by the "raw vigor" of his guests and also by the romantic possibilities in the setting and the songs, the possibility of "some authentically radiant young girl who with one fresh glance at Gatsby, one moment of magical encounter, would blot out those five years of unwavering devotion" (108, 110). Yet it was she for whom the songs were meant, she who when she sang them made them live as they were meant to. "Daisy began to sing with the music in a husky, rhythmic whisper, bringing out a meaning in each word that it had never had before and would never have again. When the melody rose, her voice broke up sweetly, following it, in a way contralto voices have, and each change tipped out a little of her warm human magic upon the air" (109). After Daisy leaves the party Gatsby makes clear to Nick how well he understood this; but he also reveals that his songs were a means to an end infinitely more grand. "He wanted nothing less of Daisy than that she should go to Tom and say: 'I never loved you.' After she had obliterated four years with that sentence they could decide upon the more practical measures to be taken. One of them was that, after she was free, they were to go back to Louisville and be married from her house—just as if it were five years ago." "'You can't repeat the past,'" Nick says. "'Can't repeat the past?' he cried incredulously. 'Why of course you can!'" (111).

Gatsby, the man with the smile of eternal reassurance, the ecstatic patron of recurrent light, wants not merely to represent the patterns of renewal and recurrence, not merely to demonstrate them by his reunion with Daisy, but literally to re-enact them. Until he could destroy the present and return to the beginning, his world was still in chaos, a chaos symbolized by the "desolate path of fruit rinds and discarded favors and crushed flowers" (111) he walked up and down. "He talked a lot about the past, and I gathered that he wanted to recover something, some idea of himself perhaps, that had gone into loving Daisy. His life had been confused and disordered since then, but if he could once return to a certain starting place and go over it all slowly, he could find out what that thing was. . . ." That love had been born at the end of a season, "one autumn night . . . when the leaves were falling . . . a cool night with that mysterious excitement in it which comes at the two changes of the year. . . . Out of the corner of his eye Gatsby saw that the blocks of the sidewalks really formed a ladder and mounted to a secret place above the trees—he could climb to it, if he climbed alone, and once there he could suck on the pap of life, gulp down the incomparable milk of wonder. His heart beat faster and faster as Daisy's white face came up to his own. He knew that when he kissed this girl, and forever wed his unutterable visions to her perishable breath, his mind would never romp again like the mind of God. So he waited, listening for a moment longer to the tuning-fork that had been struck upon a star. Then he kissed her. At his lips' touch she blossomed for him like a flower and the incarnation was complete" (112). It had occurred at the death of the year and was an act that gave him a glimpse of his own mortality. So Gatsby's quest was a double quest, a quest to recover the object of his vision and a quest to recover the vision in its godlike, imperishable form. It was yet one more version of the cycle; but in Gatsby's imagination the past had died five years before and the new life had not yet been born. To Gatsby, then, all the intervening years, the war, the career, the house and the parties, all belonged

188

to the "wasteland" as much as the ash heaps and the Wilsons. Despising his role as a creator of romantic revelry, he wanted to attain for himself what he had provided so well for others. Gatsby would no longer play the vulgar, newly rich entertainer, like the parvenu in Petronius's *Satyricon*. "His career as Trimalchio," Nick says, "was over" (113).

Daisy was coming over to Gatsby's house quietly in the afternoons. "The whole caravansary had fallen in like a card house at the disapproval in her eyes" (114). As Fitzgerald had seen long before in a collegiate story. "The Pierian Springs and the Last Straw," men became creative, like Philoctetes in the myth, because of a wound. Heal the wound and the Pierian Springs of the Muses dry up. Gatsby's reunion with Daisy had healed his wound and put to an end his creative imagination. To Gatsby of course the wound would not be healed until he could turn back the clock to a new beginning. But though he continued his quest it had lost the mysterious beauty his imagination had once imparted to it. As Daisy's love had spurred on his desires it had ironically deprived him of the power to envision them in the old way. Without the magic significance of his old vision Gatsby's desire to begin again was simply a quest for the social status that the winning of wealth and the girl had not yet given him.

> Then wear the gold hat, if that will move her;
> If you can bounce high, bounce for her too,
> Till she cry, "Lover, gold-hatted, high-bouncing lover,
> I must have you!"

That was Fitzgerald's epigraph, attributed to Amory Blaine's poet friend from *This Side of Paradise*. Gold-hatted Gatsby—Fitzgerald had once thought of giving the novel that title, and also considered *The High-Bouncing Lover*—had bounced high enough to win the girl.[21] " 'She's got an indiscreet voice,' " Nick says to Gatsby. " 'It's full of ——' I hesitated. 'Her voice is full of money,' [Gatsby] said suddenly. That was it. I'd never understood it before. It was full of money—that was the inexhaustible charm that rose and fell in it, the jingle of it, the cymbal's song of it. . . . High in a white palace the king's daughter, the golden girl . . ." (120). Gatsby's discovery comes after the destruction of his creative imagination. Nick's feeling for the song of it and the fairy-tale quality of it is retained from his own past vision of Gatsby's magical dreams. For Gatsby the realization can mean only that he had won the money and won the girl but had yet to win the sense of status and security with which the voice spoke. All that he seemed to possess fortified him in his resolution—but he was leading from his own weakness into Tom Buchanan's strength.

On the day of the confrontation the weather symbolized the change. It was hot, it was broiling, "almost the last, certainly the warmest," day of the summer, a day heralding the death of a season, but holding out no promise of a new beginning (114). "What'll we do with ourselves this afternoon?' cried Daisy, 'and the day after that, and the next thirty years?' 'Don't be morbid,' Jordan said, 'Life starts all over again when it gets crisp in the fall' " (118). "In this heat every extra gesture was an affront to the common store of life," but it was Daisy's voice, the voice full of money, that got them to their feet and on their way into New York (115, 119). It is an ominous sign that Fitzgerald gives Jordan the task of expressing the reassuring symbols of the cycle, and rising to the romantic possibilities of the city: "I love New York on summer afternoons when everyone's away. There's something very sensuous about it—overripe, as if all sorts of funny fruits were going to fall into your hands" (125). Nick's feeling for the sensuous possibilities of the city had been expressed in pastoral and floral images of life. Jordan's suggests an image of nature abundant and strange—past the point of natural growth and ready to burst. But Nick's sense of the city has been altered too; the girders of the elevated tracks, which he once described as pillars, now call to his mind the image of a spider's web (68, 125).

Tom Buchanan's strength had been up to now physical strength, the power of the body that had enabled him to break Myrtle Wilson's nose with a short, deft movement of his open hand (37). But Tom's real strength, his imperishable strength, lies in the power of his social standing. "His family were enormously wealthy," Nick had said, and coming East from Chicago "he'd brought down a string of polo ponies," displaying his wealth "in a fashion that rather took your breath away" (6). Tom Buchanan's social standing came from his wealth; his wealth *was* his social standing. Fitzgerald had at last come to realize that the upper-class figures whom he had described and analyzed and criticized and punished in his fiction were not aristocrats, but men of wealth alone. Tom Buchanan was a plutocrat. There were no redeeming qualities in his personality. As Maxwell Perkins, truly an aristocrat, wrote Fitzgerald, "I would know Tom Buchanan if I met him on the street and would avoid him." [22] In Tom Buchanan, Fitzgerald created a character equally impossible to like or to respect. But in drawing him truly he endowed Tom with social strengths that were comprehensible and not to be despised.

An upper class based solely in plutocratic wealth is an upper class, almost by its very origins and composition, without morality. Certainly its enormous financial powers place it far above common morality. Yet middle-class Americans refuse to accept the upper class as different from themselves in kind; and so, partly by necessity and partly by willed choice, the American upper class assumes responsibility for the values of the whole. Nick is tempted to laugh at Tom for his "transition from libertine to prig," yet the two poles well define the plutocrat's freedom and his duty—he *can* be both, he *must* be the latter. " 'Nowadays people begin by sneering at family life and family institutions,' " Tom avers, " 'and next they'll throw everything overboard and have intermarriage between black and white' " (130). Tom's ranting about race and science is ludicrous, but it also arises from a true responsibility, a responsibility that Gatsby, significantly, recognizes for its power. Tom's investigations into Gatsby's "drug-store" business reveal that Gatsby is a bootlegger. When Gatsby is confronted with the accusations by the man he regards as his rival for Daisy's love, the man who represents the social standing he aspires to, Gatsby's face twice takes on an "unfamiliar yet recognizable look" (121, 135). This look, which makes him appear to Nick indeed as if he had killed a man, is a look of shame. The moment when Daisy sees it on Gatsby's face, he has lost her. Gatsby feels shame because his ambition respects the ends of Tom's responsibility and power more than it condones his own means. What defeats Gatsby is not his lack of magic power, but his embarrassment before social power. "Flushed with his impassioned gibberish," Nick said of Tom, "he saw himself standing alone on the last barrier of civilization" (130). This remark renders Tom ludicrous too, but it is not without its positive thematic importance. American society does not die with Gatsby but lives on with Tom; and so long as that last barrier of civilization does not fall, the cyclical patterns of the novel suggest that there will be others like Gatsby who arise to test their hopes against it. Tom's survival as the last barrier of civilization is a paradoxical indication that the American dream lives on beyond the death of Gatsby.

The patterns of the novel move swiftly thereafter to a close. It is, of course, one aspect of the novel's fine-spun patterns that, to paraphrase Mencken's review, the wife, at the wheel of her lover's car, runs down and kills the lover of her husband.[23] But the death of Myrtle Wilson affects more significantly the patterns of the novel's themes and universal implications. The "death car" was the car the interior of which had seemed to Nick a "green leather conservatory" (64), and the girl who had blossomed for Gatsby like a flower sat at the wheel. For Gatsby she had finally become just another aspect of nature's mockery. And as the magic aura departed from Gatsby's quest, similarities between Gatsby and Myrtle emerge more clearly —two careless, immoral lower-class figures destroyed by their own too great determination, destroyed by the greater power of the careless and immoral rich. Shorn of his powers Gatsby even resembles the pathetic George Wilson, who "borrowed somebody's best suit to get married in" (35) just as Gatsby courted Daisy in the borrowed dignity of his Army uniform; who also had his woman taken from him by Tom Buchanan; who seems, alone with Gatsby, to take seriously the idea of God. Myrtle knew about her husband what Tom knew about Gatsby, that both men lacked the power to sustain the objects of their wills. By the standards of sheer physical vitality Myrtle shared with Tom, both men were cowards. "You dirty little coward," Myrtle screamed as her last words to her husband (138). Tom's final judgment on Gatsby was, "The God damned coward!" (142).

On the night of the accident the remaining veils come off Gatsby's mystery, came off "because 'Jay Gatsby' had broken up like glass against Tom's hard malice, and the long secret extravaganza was played out" (148). Nick's vision of this final revelation is changed to reflect the altered circumstances of Gatsby's quest. He perceives, not the magic possibilities of Gatsby's dream, but the social and economic facts from which they grew. When Gatsby first met Daisy the disparity between his status and hers paradoxically could only make her more attainable; for the gap was so great there was no midway point between seizing nothing and seizing all he could. "He took what he could get, ravenously and unscrupulously—eventually he took Daisy one still October night, took her because he had no real right to touch her hand." From this relation it was not Daisy who felt compromised, even more paradoxically, but Gatsby. Daisy after all was a plutocrat like Tom, powerful enough to rise above mere morality. But Gatsby, once he had been given a taste of the favors riches can bestow, and looking on their experience no doubt in the portentous light of middle-class morality, could not take so casual a view. "He felt married to her, that was all." And so "he found that he had committed himself to the following of a grail" (149). But Gatsby's grail, in this version of Nick's vision, seems far more specific than the wondrous possibility of self-fulfillment and self-creation Nick had seen before. "Gatsby was overwhelmingly aware of the youth and mystery that wealth imprisons and preserves, of the freshness of many clothes, and of Daisy, gleaming like silver, safe and proud above the hot struggles of the poor" (150). Gatsby's grail thus represented nothing more than the security and wealth and power of the plutocratic American upper class. Only when Gatsby comes out with his "curious remark" about Daisy's love for Tom— " 'In any case,' he said, 'it was just personal' "—is Nick reminded that beyond the mere social and economic goals there was "some intensity in his conception of the affair that couldn't be measured" (152).

"The night," the night during which Gatsby poured out his whole story to Nick, "had made a sharp difference in the weather and there was an autumn flavor in the air" (153). The end of Gatsby's quest coincides with the end of the season of life; the cycles had made their revolution and come back again to the point where the end meets the beginning. The man who had lived by the waste land comes to bring desolation to another for whom the world of love and dreams was dead. Gatsby "must have felt that he had lost the old warm world, paid a high price for living too long with a single dream. He must have looked up at an unfamiliar sky through frightening leaves and shivered as he found what a grotesque thing a rose is and how raw the sunlight was upon the scarcely created grass. A new world, material without being real, where poor ghosts, breathing dreams like air, drifted fortuitously about . . . like that ashen, fantastic figure gliding towards him through the amorphous trees" (162). Gatsby's body was found on an air mattress in his pool. "The touch of a cluster of leaves revolved it slowly, tracing, like the leg of a transit, a thin red circle in the water." Nature no longer mocks, but provides with its own dead leaves the proper symbol. Wilson, the murderer, had come to believe he was carrying out God's vengeance, and Gatsby had immersed himself in water as if in preparation for his meeting with the God whose vision he had almost overreached. "It was after we started with Gatsby toward the house," Nick said, "that the gardener saw Wilson's body a little way off in the grass, and the holocaust was complete" (163). The fire of old dreams is fully extinguished, so the fire of new dreams can be lit.

The final patterns are drawn in the account of Gatsby's funeral. Only Nick, the seer, can remember Gatsby for his magical qualities. "It grew upon me," Nick says, "that I was responsible, because no one else was interested—interested, I mean, with that intense personal interest to which everyone has some vague right at the end" (165); and Nick begins to have "a feeling of defiance, of scornful solidarity between Gatsby and me against them all" (166). Yet Nick is not the only one with memories. There are others who complete their own insight into Gatsby's life. Gatsby's father comes for the funeral, bringing his simple faith that the Poor Richard precepts on the way to wealth his son had once practiced were sufficient explanation for the riches he attained. "If he'd of lived," the father says, "he'd of been a great man. A man like James J. Hill. He'd of helped build up the country" (169). For all his naïveté there is a grain of truth in the father's admiration, a recognition that for better or for worse men like James J. Hill did build the country, which carries the implication that without these men the country would not have been built. Nick settles Gatsby's father, appropriately, in the music room. Wolfsheim's reluctance to attend the funeral expresses in part his extraordinary sentimentality: "I hardly know where I am when I hear about a thing like this and am completely knocked down and out" (167). Wolfsheim is filled in fact with sentimental memories of the past—memories which show more precisely than ever the criminal sources of Gatsby's wealth—but there too Wolfsheim's reluctance expresses another grain of wisdom. " 'Let us learn to show our friendship for a man when he is alive and not after he is dead,' he suggested. 'After that, my own rule is to let everything alone' " (173). At the funeral, finally, Owl Eyes shows up, and Fitzgerald's language suggests more clearly than before a possible connection between the eyes of Dr. T. J. Eckleburg, Owl Eyes, and God. "The rain poured down his thick glasses, and he took them off and wiped them to see the protecting canvas unrolled from Gatsby's grave. . . . Dimly I heard someone murmur 'blessed are the dead that the rain falls on,' and then the owl-eyed man said, 'Amen to that,' in a brave voice" (176). If Owl Eyes speaks for God, then God *had* been entertained, did approve of Gatsby's showmanship. And the rain suggests God's blessing, a symbol of the fertility of human imagination, of other Gatsbys to be born. Perhaps it is relevant to add that Owl Eyes was brought to Gatsby's party by a Roosevelt, a name suggesting his connection to an American family which by birth, fortune, and intellect, had the right truly to call itself an aristocracy.

/At the novel's end Nick withdraws to the West. He expresses his final vision in images of order. The moment of self-knowledge and judgment is at hand, and Tom and Daisy, Jordan, all the East, fall short of Nick's reiterated sense of right. But the moment for appreciation had not yet passed. In the famous final passages of the novel Nick reassumes the role of the visionary seer. All at once the whole of American experience takes on the character of Gatsby's romantic quest and tragic failure; the history of a continent finds expression in the transcendent images of felicity man made from the beauty of its mocking nature./"Gatsby believed in the green light, the orgiastic future that year by year recedes before us. It eluded us then, but that's no matter—tomorrow we will run faster, stretch out our arms farther. . . . And one fine morning——So we beat on, boats against the current, borne back ceaselessly into the past" (182). The hope shall always be, its fulfillment shall never be. Men die, but their dreams are imperishable, renewed again and again at the fountain of nature—or of art.

With *The Great Gatsby* F. Scott Fitzgerald created his own vision of national tragedy and of high art, created a novel which with every passing year more clearly assumes a place among the imperishable works of American fiction. He had come a long way since the early moment in his career when he denied Keats's poetic statement that beauty was truth, and truth beauty. In *This Side of Paradise* and *The Beautiful and Damned* the beauty he rejected and the beauty that proved false was the beauty of a woman; in *The Great Gatsby* he found truth in the beauty of art, and beauty in its truths. With *The Great Gatsby* he found self-fulfillment and self-creation as an artist— and yet, as with Gatsby, a tragic fall was to follow closely upon his success.

CHAPTER EIGHT

With *The Great Gatsby* F. Scott Fitzgerald knew he had come into his own at last as an artist. In the midst of composition, from the French Riviera in August 1924, he wrote Maxwell Perkins, "I think my novel is about the best American novel ever written. . . . It's been a fair summer. I've been unhappy but my work hasn't suffered from it. I am grown at last." [1] When it was almost done he proclaimed to Edmund Wilson, "My book is wonderful, so is the air and the sea." [2] The excess of bravado he put into these remarks was justified when Perkins responded generously and perceptively to the manuscript. "Thanks and thanks and thanks for your letters," Fitzgerald wrote back. "I'd rather have you and Bunny [Edmund Wilson] like it than anyone I know. And I'd rather have you like it than Bunny. If it's as good as you say, when I finish with the proof it'll be perfect." [3] During the winter Fitzgerald polished the proofs in Rome and Capri, and indeed he came close to accomplishing what he had promised. He knew he had written an important novel and once again he began to rate himself against his competition. "Is Lewis' book any good?" he wrote John Peale Bishop in March. "I imagine that mine is infinitely better—." [4] Again to Bishop, calling up the moment nearly four years before when his classmate had slighted him in a review: "Do you still think Dos Passos is a genius? My faith in him is somehow weakened. There's so little time for faith these days." He was putting all his faith into himself. "The cheerfulest things in my life," he told Bishop, "are, first, Zelda, and second, the hope that my book has something extraordinary about it. I want to be extravagantly admired again." [5] Now he hoped to reap the public rewards of his personal success.

As the date of publication approached, April 10, 1925, he was worried. There was the ever-present problem of money, of course. With his back debts taken care of by the stories he had written in the previous winter, he had lived while in Europe on advance royalties from *Gatsby*. Unless the novel was an extraordinary best-seller, he could expect to earn nothing more in royalties. Simply to meet current expenses he wrote a story for *The Saturday Evening Post* in November and another for *Redbook* in December, even before the revision of proofs was completed. "I've got a new novel to write," he told Perkins from Rome before Christmas 1924, "—title and all— that'll take about a year. Meanwhile, I don't want to start it until this is out and meanwhile I'll do short stories for money (I now get $2000 a story but I hate worse than hell to do them), and there's the never-dying lure of another play." What kind of success he was hoping for from *The Great Gatsby* was indicated later in the same letter: "If my book is a big success or a great failure (financial—no other sort can be imagined, I hope) I *don't* want to publish stories in the fall"—meaning a book of stories to follow the novel. "If it goes between 25,000 and 50,000, I have an excellent collection for you." [6] Great failure was under 25,000 copies, then, and big success was over 50,000. Elsewhere he predicted to Perkins sales of 80,000 copies. What he appeared to want was financial freedom, a position of security where, as he wrote John Peale Bishop, "I need write no more but only novels." [7] Yet this position had been his from the start if he had wanted it, and if he had squandered his chance before 1925, the movie and dramatic rights to *The Great Gatsby* brought him more than enough to write as he pleased. The deeper, more important worry on Fitzgerald's mind was about *The Great Gatsby*'s critical reception.

For he had written a novel that resembled his earlier work in subject and theme, but in its quality and significance was like nothing he had done before it. "This time I don't want any signed blurbs on the jacket," he told Perkins even before his editor had seen the novel, "—not Mencken's or Lewis' or Howard's or anyone's. I'm tired of being the author of *This Side of Paradise* and I want to start over." [8] This after all was a central theme of the novel, the idea of regeneration, the hope of beginning anew. But it was a difficult trick under any circumstances for a commercial writer, one whose steady readership was predicated on a continuity of expectations. Fitzgerald recognized this in a humorous way when he wrote to Edmund Wilson, "I will now give you the Fitz touch without which this letter would fail to conform to your conception of my character," and began to talk about money.[9] And though writers have successfully begun again with subjects and treatments completely new, how could Fitzgerald expect to succeed with a subject and theme so familiar? A fortnight before publication Fitzgerald heard how his uncle had responded to a preliminary announcement of the book. "He said: 'It sounded as if it were very much like his others.'" "I wondered," he told Perkins, "if we could think of some way to advertise it so that people who are perhaps weary of assertive jazz and society novels might not dismiss it as 'just another book like his others.' I confess that today the problem baffles me—all I can think of is to say in general to avoid such phrases, 'a picture of New York life,' or 'modern society'—though, as that is exactly what the book is, it's hard to avoid them. The trouble is so much superficial trash has sailed under those banners." [10] A part of it, he knew, had been his own.

"I want to be extravagantly admired again," he had told Bishop. If ever he had a sense of who his readers were and why they read him, it had slipped away during his year in France; or he had been simply too out of touch to catch the shifts in literary taste ominously exemplified by "The Gossip Shop's" slighting remarks about him in the August 1924 *Bookman*.[11] If he expected critics to explain for readers the nature of his new artistry, as Mencken had done for Dreiser and Wilson for Joyce—as he long ago asserted to Maxwell Perkins, in the dubious context of *The Beautiful and Damned*, "My one hope is to be endorsed by the intellectually elite and thus be *forced* onto people as Conrad has" [12]—his memory of the book reviewing trade had also failed him. The reception of *The Great Gatsby* marked one of those rare moments in American literary history when a novel later recognized as a masterpiece was given over to its contemporaries for judgment.

Overwhelmingly the reviews were favorable. *The Great Gatsby* was liked, it was praised, it was recommended. "An Admirable Novel," *The Saturday Review of Literature* titled its review; "Fitzgerald on the March," proclaimed *The Nation*.[13] Yet there were disturbing signs that Fitzgerald had fallen further in esteem since *Tales of the Jazz Age* and *The Vegetable* than he possibly could have imagined. Most of the reviews were displayed less prominently than in the past; *The New Republic* ignored the book entirely. Implicitly many of the reviewers assumed that he had far to go to redeem his past, and *The Great Gatsby* was only a partial beginning. *The Independent's* completely hostile review, which by professing to like *This Side of Paradise* better demonstrated once more the conventional viewpoint that had largely established Fitzgerald's reputation in the beginning, conceded *The Great Gatsby* "may prove that he can still be effective—outside the field of sophisticated juveniles." [14] And this tentative sense of incomplete redemption was repeated at nearly every point along the spectrum of literary taste. *The Bookman,* which had always taken Fitzgerald too seriously as a philosopher, only to shake its head at his philosophy, fell back on the bromide it had used for five years, "a brilliant young man, immensely puzzled by life and disturbed by shifting values in his own scheme." [15] Even Fitzgerald's friend Carl Van Vechten, *The Nation's* reviewer, proclaimed that Fitzgerald had come to resemble Booth Tarkington, and concluded equivocally with, "What Mr. Fitzgerald may do in the future, therefore, I am convinced, depends to an embarrassing extent on the nature of his own ambitions." [16] Many of the reviewers who wrote favorably of *The Great Gatsby* still seemed to have adopted an implicit point of view which John M. Kenny, Jr., in *The Commonweal* made explicit: "Taken alone, *The Great Gatsby* is a mediocre novel. In the light of his former books, it marks an important stepping-stone toward a literary excellence which Scott Fitzgerald ought some day to achieve." [17]

Even reviewers who unequivocally liked *The Great Gatsby,* with none of the future strings attached, were hard put to say exactly why. They confessed that the novel was far better than a simple summary of the plot would suggest, that there were patterns and mysteries they had not pierced at all. William Rose Benét in *The Saturday Review of Literature*, after displaying his confusion for most of the review, had to point out to his readers at the end that his confusion did not imply a lessening of his admiration, that he really did recommend the book.[18] Among the most favorable reviews there was as much evidence of hasty reading, failure of comprehension, and slipshod writing, as among the least favorable. Their paraphrases of the plot and themes were woefully inadequate; Thomas Caldecott Chubb, whose review in *The Forum* was the most perceptive about Fitzgerald's themes and intentions, referred to Tom and Daisy Buchanan as Dorothy and Ted.[19] Mencken, whose review in the *Baltimore Evening Sun* was a significant tribute to Fitzgerald's artistry, was completely unsympathetic to Fitzgerald's themes and treatment. Curiously, from his primary interest in novels as social documents, he preferred *This Side of Paradise* quite as much as the conservative and conventional reviewers did.[20]

As publication day passed for *The Great Gatsby* Fitzgerald was on his way from Capri to Paris, where his rented car had to be returned before a deadline. Ernest Hemingway, who took part in the last leg of the trip, has described it for us in *A Moveable Feast* with malicious glee; but part of Fitzgerald's behavior enroute to Paris may be explained by the news about *Gatsby* that reached him in Marseilles.[21] Perkins' cable set the tone for Fitzgerald's first response to the reception of the novel. He had described the reviews as excellent and the sales picture as cloudy, and Fitzgerald's business-like reply was undoubtedly founded on the assumption that the novel was a critical success and a commercial failure. "Your telegram depressed me. . . . ," he wrote from Marseilles. "If the book fails commercially it will be from one of two reasons or both. First, the title is only fair, rather bad than good. Second, *and most important*, the book contains no important woman character, and women control the fiction market at present. I don't think the unhappy ending matters particularly." With the realization that *The Great Gatsby* would not be a best seller all his literary and financial hopes for the future vanished in a moment. Bitterly he pictured his circumstances. "In all events I have a book of good stories for the fall. Now I shall write some cheap ones until I've accumulated enough for my next novel. When that is finished and published I'll wait and see. If it will support me with no more intervals of trash, I'll go on as a novelist. If not, I'm going to quit, come home, go to Hollywood and learn the movie business. I can't reduce our scale of living and I can't stand this financial insecurity. Anyhow, there's no point in trying to be an artist if you can't do your best. I had my chance back in 1920 to start my life on a sensible scale and I lost it, and so I'll have to pay the penalty. Then perhaps at 40 I can start writing again without this constant worry and interruption." [22] The desperate tone of this declaration may in part be attributed to the first shock of financial disappointment; unfortunately there were further disappointments to come.

In Paris Fitzgerald saw the first reviews. Immediately he recognized what Perkins had not seen, or had preferred in his cable not to reveal. "Most of the reviewers floundered around in a piece of work that obviously they completely failed to understand," Fitzgerald wrote Perkins, "and tried to give it reviews that committed them neither pro nor con until someone of culture had spoken." [23] Letters of praise from H. L. Mencken and Edmund Wilson cheered him, but as the review picture filled out it only confirmed his first impressions—and there was a low blow to take from his old acquaintance Burton Rascoe, book editor of the *New York Tribune,* who compared *Gatsby* to the titillating novels of high society romance Robert W. Chambers wrote as entertainment for shopgirls. "I think all the reviews I've seen, except two, have been absolutely stupid and lousy," he wrote again to Perkins. "Someday they'll eat grass, by God! This thing, both the effort and the result, have hardened me and I think now that I'm much better than any of the young Americans *without exception.*" [24]

But if Fitzgerald was hardened by his disappointment at the reviews and sales of *The Great Gatsby,* he was simply hardened into old and unchanged attitudes, as a remark in a letter to Edmund Wilson jokingly made clear: "There's no news except that Zelda and I think we're pretty good, as usual, only more so." Mainly what had made him hard also made him bitter, bitter against traveling Americans in Paris—"If I had anything to do with creating the manners of the contemporary American girl," he told Wilson, "I certainly made a botch of the job"; bitter at the "boob critics" and at writers like his old friend Thomas Boyd, who seemed to pander to their taste for naturalistic novels on American farm life; and bitter at himself.[25] "I have all the money I need and was growing rather tired of being a popular author," he wrote Mencken, who unfortunately could not have been prepared to appreciate Fitzgerald's irony. "My trash for the *Post* grows worse and worse as there is less and less heart in it. Strange to say, my whole heart was in my first trash. I thought that 'The Offshore Pirate' was quite as good as 'Benediction.' I never really 'wrote down' until after the failure of *The Vegetable* and that was to make this book possible. I would have written down long ago if it had been profitable—I tried it unsuccessfully for the movies. People don't seem to realize that for an intelligent man, writing down is about the hardest thing in the world." [26]

Since completing the first draft of *The Great Gatsby* he had already written down on three separate occasions—one of the stories, "Love in the Night," had actually appeared in *The Saturday Evening Post* just before *Gatsby* was published, a coincidence that must have undercut any impression that Fitzgerald was making a fresh start. "Love in the Night" was Fitzgerald's first story set in Europe, though it was written in the familiar genteel romantic mode. In Cannes, during the summer of 1914, Val Rostoff, son of a Russian prince and a wealthy Chicago beauty, anonymously woos an American girl. The Russian Revolution turns Val into a Riviera cab driver, but the girl returns in the early twenties and finds her anonymous romancer. (Can't repeat the past? Why of course you can!) She also happens to be wealthy, and they will no doubt live happily ever after. [27] The next story, "The Adjuster," is significant because it marks Fitzgerald's first explicit exorcising of his flapper creation, the genteel romantic heroine, the beautiful, young, willful girl. Luella Hemple's selfishness had caused her husband's breakdown and her child's death. A mysterious psychiatrist, Doctor Moon, tells her, "We make an agreement with children that they can sit in the audience without helping to make the play, but if they still sit in the audience after they're grown, somebody's got to work double time for them, so that they can enjoy the light and glitter of the world. . . . It's your turn to be the centre, to give others what was given to you for so long." The story ends with a glimpse of a happy future. [28] In the third story, "Not in the Guidebook," a lower-class wife is enabled to begin life over by an improbable coincidence. Milly Cooley is deserted by her unemployed husband, First World War hero Jim Cooley, as they arrive in France, ostensibly en route to a job. In Paris Milly is be-friended by William Driscoll, an impresario-type who runs an amus-ing tour of the Paris sights. It turns out that Jim Cooley is nothing but a bum who stole the medals rightfully belonging to none other than Driscoll. With Driscoll, Milly finds her true love.[29] By now Fitz-gerald was earning two thousand dollars a story. If "writing down" was difficult, these stories show how well he had mastered the art.

These were the stories Fitzgerald wrote, paradoxically, while wait-ing for the reception of *Gatsby* to prove him an artist. Yet after his disappointment over *The Great Gatsby* he immediately began one of his finest works of fiction, the novella "The Rich Boy." As time went on during the late spring and early summer of 1925, moreover, the support and encouragement he had hoped for from *The Great Gatsby* began to come through. By June he had received the remark-able letter of congratulation on *The Great Gatsby* from Gertrude Stein, and letters from Edith Wharton, James Branch Cabell, Van Wyck Brooks and others.[30] If the "cheap reviewers" failed to appre-ciate the novel, his fellow artists recognized its merits without quali-fication. *The Bookman*, whose reviewer had equivocated in so agonized a way over *The Great Gatsby* in June, ran this comment from the novelist Louis Bromfield in August: "[F. Scott Fitzgerald], over whom there has been much head shaking among our more sober reviewers, emerges as a fine, objective novelist freed of the excesses of youth." [31] And by August Fitzgerald had found the critic capable of playing the Mencken to his Dreiser or the Wilson to his Joyce.

Gilbert Seldes reviewed *The Great Gatsby* in the August number of *The Dial*. As managing editor of *The Dial* three years earlier he had written—under the pseudonym Vivian Shaw—an attack on Fitz-gerald from the viewpoint of the modern movement in literature and art. Later he resigned from *The Dial* to write a book on American popular culture, published in 1924 as *The Seven Lively Arts*. On the Riviera in 1924, before the completion of *Gatsby*, he and Fitzgerald became friends. Fitzgerald gave Seldes credit for writing the first intelligent reviews of Ring Lardner's work. His review in *The Dial* was, equally, the first intelligent criticism of *Gatsby*. What mattered most to Seldes was the novel's "artistic structure" and the evidence it gave of Fitzgerald's artistic vision; it was from the point of view of artistic standards that Seldes had attacked Fitzgerald's reputation back in 1922. Seldes saw the patterns of the novel, the concentration of style and the austere composition of the scenes, the justness of the detail and the structured movement of the whole. "The plot works out," he wrote, "not like a puzzle with odd bits falling into place, but like a tragedy, with every part functioning in the completed organism." And the meanings of the tragedy were also clear to him. "[Fitzgerald's] tactile apprehension remains so fine that his people and his settings are specifically of Long Island; but now he meditates upon their fate, and they become universal also. He has now something of extreme importance to say; and it is good fortune for us that he knows how to say it." Seldes called *The Great Gatsby* one of the finest of contemporary novels. "Fitzgerald has more than matured," he wrote, "he has mastered his talents and gone soaring in a beautiful flight, leaving behind him everything dubious and tricky in his earlier work, and leaving even farther behind all the men of his own generation and most of his elders." [32]

Seldes wrote another favorable appraisal of the novel—and Fitzgerald's whole career as well—in his "New York Chronicle" for T. S. Eliot's London quarterly, *The New Criterion*. "Fitzgerald ... has certainly the best chance, at this moment, of becoming our finest artist in fiction," Seldes wrote there, but he explained also that *The Great Gatsby* had not received a good press. "I am not concerned with Fitzgerald's royalties," he concluded, "but he stands at this time desperately in need of critical encouragement." [33] Seldes had given him the most perceptive kind of encouragement twice over, and in the two periodicals which more than any others spoke to and for avant-garde writers in England and America. It is possible that Seldes's remarks in *The New Criterion* prompted T. S. Eliot's famous letter on *The Great Gatsby*. "It has interested and excited me more than any other new novel I have seen, either English or American, for a number of years. . . . ," Eliot wrote Fitzgerald. "In fact it seems to me to be the first step that American fiction has taken since Henry James. . . ." [34] Fitzgerald prized Eliot's critical encouragement over any other he received.

Fitzgerald *was* concerned with his royalties. But as early as June 1925, he had word that dramatic rights to *Gatsby* would be sold, and that his immediate financial worries, at least the worries that forced him to write the trash he so abhorred, would soon be over. At the end of May he had received Gertrude Stein's letter on *The Great Gatsby*, in which she praised the way he wrote naturally in sentences and told him, "You are creating the contemporary world much as Thackeray did his in *Pendennis* and *Vanity Fair* and this isn't a bad compliment." [35] By midsummer of 1925, then, by the time Miss Stein's letter and one from Edith Wharton and the proofs of Seldes's *Dial* review were in his hands, Fitzgerald had every reason to be satisfied with what *The Great Gatsby* had accomplished. He was extravagantly admired again, admired by those who counted most, the important American writers and critics of his time. But it seems clear that this kind of admiration, alone, would not satisfy him.

If one recalls Van Wyck Brooks's *Ordeal of Mark Twain*, Fitzgerald was in the position of a Mark Twain who had succeeded where Brooks's Mark Twain had failed. He had brought out the latent artistry that was in him, and he had created a work of art that explored as deeply as he knew how the values of his own society. No William Dean Howells or Mrs. Clemens had held him back. But Fitzgerald had never been so opposed to the values of Mrs. Clemens or Howells as Brooks was, nor so opposed as he had appeared when he attacked the American bourgeois mentality in language borrowed from H. L. Mencken. At the start of his career he had immediately become both a popular writer and a spokesman for his generation. These were roles from the beginning of his literary awareness he had wished for, and when they came he had embraced them without reserve. To learn suddenly that his best novel, his extraordinary achievement, was neither popular nor representative was a shock the depths of which his new supporters could hardly fathom. Miss Stein and Mrs. Wharton, Seldes, Hemingway, and the others had formed their artistic values apart from public standards and public taste. Whether by accident or design Fitzgerald's literary values had always been entwined with the values of the reading public. Now his main pillar of support—for the work that mattered—had been knocked out from under him, and his instincts hesitated between two poles of safety open to him, "pure" artistry on the one hand and the most popular of art forms—the movies—on the other. In one mood he could boast to Perkins, "the happiest thought I have is of my new novel—it is something really NEW in form, idea, structure—the model for the age that Joyce and Stein are searching for, that Conrad didn't find"; in another he could pessimistically inform Seldes, in the letter thanking him for the *Dial* review, "My new novel may be my last for ten years or so—that is, if it sells no better than *Gatsby* (which has only gone a little over 20,000 copies), for I may go to Hollywood and try to learn the moving picture business from the bottom up." [36]

He was outsprinting Joyce and Stein at one moment, quitting the field in the next. This hestitation and indecision between two sets of values is an important facet of Fitzgerald's behavior in the months and years after *The Great Gatsby*. One can hardly explain Fitzgerald's personal life on the basis of his literary frustrations, to be sure. The most traumatic of his drunken exploits occurred in Rome in the winter of 1924-25, at the very time when he was polishing *The Great Gatsby*'s proofs to such perfection; in an argument over a taxi fare he hit a policeman, and then he was beaten up and thrown in jail. [37] Fitzgerald's drinking escapades were to continue at a high pace through all of 1925 and 1926, until he returned to the United States in December of that year. His biographers have fully described them, and one may guess as one chooses whether they were caused by his wife, his companions, the flaws in his own character, or some other source. What concerns this study of his mind and art is the relation of his intellectual and imaginative life to the personal affairs which shaped the course of his career. And it does seem certain that the lack of focus in Fitzgerald's literary self-awareness did play a part in his personal behavior.

For he was living in the center of the American expatriate colony of writers. "I have met most of the American literary world here (the crowd that centers about Pound)," he told Mencken, "and find them mostly junk-dealers; except for a few like Hemingway who are doing rather more thinking and working than the young men around New York." [38] Perhaps the intellectual and imaginative center of Fitzgerald's problems comes down, after all, to Hemingway. The intensity of feeling between Fitzgerald and Hemingway has recently been brought to life in Morley Callaghan's and Hemingway's own memoirs; an intensity that lives for us because it was still alive for Callaghan and Hemingway nearly forty years after the events. [39] Fitzgerald first mentions Hemingway in a letter to Perkins in October 1924, one of his characteristically generous gestures to help other writers he admired; he tried as well to make Perkins take an interest in the work of Gertrude Stein.[40] In 1925 the friendship between Fitzgerald and Hemingway grew close. Both men were intensely competitive. Hemingway no doubt recognized, after *The Great Gatsby*, that Fitzgerald was the man he had to beat; Fitzgerald had had the popular success and financial rewards that Hemingway wanted, though he was in a position openly to disdain them. To Fitzgerald, Hemingway was what he had never been and had often wished to be—the artist of complete integrity, the artist who was also a man of action; and there was no way Fitzgerald could put a mask of disdain on that. He must have felt himself inferior to Hemingway almost from the start, a feeling that Hemingway must also have exploited as soon as it was clear to him. Perhaps it was Hemingway's presence that made it impossible for the extraordinary praise Fitzgerald received for *Gatsby* really to take hold. Fitzgerald had outdistanced all his known competitors, only to feel beaten by a dark horse, younger than he, who had hardly published a word. When Fitzgerald wrote self-deprecatingly to Gertrude Stein, in answer to her congratulatory letter, "You see, I am content to let you, and the one or two like you who are acutely sensitive, think or fail to think for me and my kind artistically . . . much as the man of 1901, say, would let Nietzsche . . . think for him intellectually. I am a very second-rate person compared to first-rate people," he was rating himself the loser.[41]

The nature of Fitzgerald's patronage of Hemingway is rendered in its amusing and curious light by an incident recorded neither by Callaghan nor by Hemingway, but by the writer who had served so often as a symbol and analogue in Fitzgerald's career, Booth Tarkington. When Tarkington was in Paris in 1925 Fitzgerald brought Hemingway around to meet him. "My impression" of Hemingway, Tarkington later recalled, "was of a Kansas University football beef; but I rather liked him. Fitzgerald [a fellow Princetonian] brought him up and was a little tight—took him away because Hemingway was to have a fight that afternoon at three o'clock, though I gathered they'd both been up all night." [42] Fitzgerald's chief service to Hemingway, of course, lay in the aid he rendered in Hemingway's shift away from the publishers Boni & Liveright to Scribner's. And the most public of his efforts in Hemingway's behalf was the important article he wrote for the May 1926 number of *The Bookman*, "How To Waste Material: A Note on My Generation."

"How To Waste Material" was far more than a boost to Hemingway. It was Fitzgerald's critical and intellectual rendering of his perceptions about American literature that had emerged in the wake of *The Great Gatsby's* popular failure. It states in a generalized and ordered way the viewpoint of the half-anguished, half-satiric outbursts in his earlier letters to Perkins; and as such it belongs among the most important documents on American literature in the twenties. "How To Waste Material" marks, in a sense, Fitzgerald's formal severance from the "schools" of criticism and fiction that inflated his reputation, only to let out the air at his moment of artistic self-mastery. He had discovered that they had all along demanded a kind of subject matter and treatment marked, in their writers and their products, "by the insincere compulsion to write 'significantly' about America"—"insincere because it is not a compulsion found in themselves." To represent these separate "schools" he wisely singled out their strongest figures, respectively, H. L. Mencken and Sherwood Anderson. Mencken's idea, he wrote, "had always been ethical rather than aesthetic"—an insight proved, if proof were needed, by Mencken's review of *The Great Gatsby*. Anderson, of whom reviewers spoke "as an inarticulate, fumbling man, bursting with ideas," was, on the contrary, Fitzgerald said, "the possessor of a brilliant and almost inimitable prose style, and of scarcely any ideas at all." Though their own pioneering work was exempt from Fitzgerald's criticism—Mencken "has yet done more for American letters than any man alive," he wrote—he saw them as the instigators of doctrines and forms that their followers and imitators had debased. Out of the mass of fiction produced in "what was to have been a golden age," Fitzgerald wrote, only one book survived—*The Enormous Room* by E. E. Cummings. "Some of the late brilliant boys are on lecture tours (a circular informs me that most of them are to speak upon 'the literary revolution!'), some are writing pot boilers, a few have definitely abandoned the literary life—they were never sufficiently aware that material, however closely observed, is as elusive as the moment in which it has its existence unless it is purified by an incorruptible style and by the catharsis of a passionate emotion." [43] This was the nature of art as Fitzgerald had learned it, as every page of *The Great Gatsby* demonstrated it; but for his object lesson Fitzgerald chose not his own novel, but the stories of Ernest Hemingway.

How seriously Fitzgerald adhered to his standards for the art of fiction was demonstrated by "The Rich Boy," the long story he started as the first disappointing reviews of *The Great Gatsby* were coming in. "Begin with an individual," the story opens, "and before you know it you find that you have created a type; begin with a type, and you find that you have created—nothing." [44] As "The Adjuster" had been written as if to exorcise the genteel romantic "flapper" heroine, "The Rich Boy" was an effort to repudiate the whole structure of genteel romantic formulas as Fitzgerald had inherited them from the nineteenth century. "If I wrote about his brothers," the narrative voice goes on, "I should have to begin by attacking all the lies that the poor have told about the rich and the rich have told about themselves—such a wild structure they have erected that when we pick up a book about the rich, some instinct prepares us for unreality. Even the intelligent and impassioned reporters of life have made the country of the rich as unreal as fairy-land" (152). One may suspect that Fitzgerald in revulsion at the lack of understanding for his novel was rejecting *The Great Gatsby*'s mood and setting out of hand; rather his target was more precisely the old-fashioned genteel romantic hero—the upper-class young man of will and playful imagination, the twentieth-century Tom Sawyer, who had formed part of the foundation for Gatsby's character, but was seen most clearly in Fitzgerald's conventional slick magazine stories. Far from turning his back on *The Great Gatsby*, Fitzgerald in "The Rich Boy" was building on the novel—building, specifically, on the novel's insight into the American plutocracy, and its responsibility to protect the forms and values of American society as a whole. Anson Hunter of "The Rich Boy" is a decent and likeable version of Tom Buchanan, a Tom Buchanan dispassionately observed through the lens of a cleansed and simple style.

Anson Hunter lacks neither will nor playful imagination; what he lacks is will and playful imagination as expressions of a young man's aspirations, whether in conventional or creative form, for there was nothing beyond him unexplored and unattained to excite his will and imagination. "His aspirations were conventional enough—they included even the irreproachable shadow he would some day marry, but they differed from the aspirations of the majority of young men in that there was no mist over them, none of the quality which is variously known as 'idealism' or 'illusion.' Anson accepted without reservation the world of high finance and high extravagance, of divorce and dissipation, of snobbery and of privilege. Most of our lives end as a compromise—it was as a compromise that his life began" (154). Anson Hunter grows out of Tom Buchanan, but he also marks an interesting return to the old concept of the "personage" that played so important a part in Fitzgerald's early fiction. Amory Blaine in *This Side of Paradise* was the product of Fitzgerald's new self-creative, socially reconstructive definition of a "personage." Anson resembles the old definition that Amory reinterpreted, the definition expressed in the novel by Monsignor Darcy: "He is never thought of apart from what he's done. He's a bar on which a thousand things have been hung—glittering things sometimes, as ours are, but he uses those things with a cold mentality back of them." [45]

Anson Hunter of "The Rich Boy" is the man on whom glittering things are hung. He gives others the feeling that they are "preeminently safe and taken care of" (156), and he took "pleasure in helping people and arranging their affairs. . . . He had an instinctive and rather charitable knowledge of the weaknesses of men and women, and, like a priest, it made him the more concerned for the maintenance of outward forms. . . . His day was never too full nor his mind too weary to give any sort of aid to any one who asked it. What had been done at first through pride and superiority had become a habit and a passion" (161, 164, 172). His only passion. For ironically Anson Hunter, the man who began life having everything, could expend his will and imagination with the firmest sense of social right, the sense—similar to the sense Lambert Strether expresses at the end of Henry James's novel *The Ambassadors*—of getting nothing for himself. Anson can succeed in breaking up his Aunt Edna's extramarital affair by the power of "his main weapon, which was his own true emotion" (175), the desire to maintain the forms. But in the end his old friends drift away from him, occupied with emotions more subjective and less lofty than his own. Anson is left at the end the cold and impotent observer of the simple domestic pleasures enjoyed by the only girl he ever loved, whom he lost by the power-lessness of his will to take her for himself; his repeated "yes" to her demands for affirmations to her happiness conveys so much of his weakness and his bitter strengths (185-6). "The Rich Boy," in the purity of its style and conception, is one of Fitzgerald's finest stories, marred only by an occasional lapse into sentimentality or into the melodramatic realism of his past, as in the suicide of Edna's lover. But the spare, dry nature of Fitzgerald's tone and treatment recalls not so much *This Side of Paradise* as the prose style of Ernest Hem-ingway. And before he was able to finish "The Rich Boy," Fitz-gerald had to take time out to write a shorter story; it was "A Penny Spent," one of his weakest, written in the old conventional genteel romantic way.[46] There seemed no escape from his dilemma, not from either of its horns.

The dilemma was posed by his own adherence to high standards for the art of fiction. One horn of the dilemma was that he took the standards too seriously, the other that he did not take them seriously enough. Though these seem opposing points of view, they are not necessarily contradictory. In the background lay the depressing fact that *The Great Gatsby* had not attained a reputation commensurate with its qualities. To meet his own standards—and also to vindicate his reputation—he should have to write a work of art greater even than *The Great Gatsby*. But he felt himself inferior as an artist to writers like Gertrude Stein and especially Hemingway, and that feeling made him question his ability to write anything good at all. He wanted all, it seemed, wanted to write a work of incomparable artistry—or he wanted nothing. This is not a full explanation of his behavior in the nine years from the publication of *The Great Gatsby* to the publication of *Tender Is the Night* in 1934, but it is the main explanation that emerges from a consideration of Fitzgerald's mind and art.

Fitzgerald's new novel—the novel that was to provide "the model for the age that Joyce and Stein are searching for, that Conrad didn't find"—was begun late in 1925.[47] He worked on it through 1926, until in December of that year—still held fast by the two horns of his dilemma—he returned to the United States to try a stint as a screen-writer in Hollywood. He was offered $3500 in advance to write a screenplay for the actress Constance Talmadge. If his story was accepted he would receive over twelve thousand dollars in all. The Fitzgeralds stayed in Hollywood two months, conducting their lives on the same plane as they had in Paris and on the Riviera. Before they left, his completed screenplay, a "flapper" romance in a college setting, was rejected. In the absence of concrete evidence one may yet assume that the dilemma of his career he had left Europe to escape had pursued him even to Hollywood. Perhaps his sense of his own capacities as a writer of prose fiction inhibited him from adhering fully to the standards of motion-picture writing. Perhaps it was a question of technical competence; he had made himself a professional writer by close attention to the needs and techniques of the slick magazine market, a form of attention he could not possibly have given screenwriting in the circumstances of his visit. One suspects he saw too many possibilities in his material, was personally too close to it—or even that he was simply too much an artist—ruthlessly to shape his story to movie stereotypes. What he lacked most of all was a sense of purpose, or a need. He did not need the money that much, he did not want that much to put himself in a position where he could not go on with the new novel. For all the talk of Fitzgerald's modeling his characters on himself, this was a case where he seemed to model himself on one of his characters: Anthony Patch from *The Beautiful and Damned,* the man who would not limit himself, who considered his possibilities so great he could bring himself to strive for no one thing at all. In the literary world Fitzgerald was blocked by a vision of a perfection he could not reach, in the film world by the cold facts of a perfection he had not trained himself to reach. From the present perspective, no matter how living an alternative screenwriting had seemed for him, it appears that he never had a chance to succeed. Fitzgerald rented "Ellerslie," a house in Edgemoor, Delaware, outside Wilmington, and went back to work on his novel.

What matters for the present discussion is not what *Tender Is the Night* was about, but that he had so many difficulties with it, difficulties which made a great impact on his own self-awareness as a writer. During 1925 and 1926 he had completed no more than two or three chapters, though he sold the serial rights to *Liberty* magazine and even while in Hollywood promised to deliver the manuscript in June. Eighteen months later he had made almost no progress. In 1929 he did some work on a new version of the novel, and in 1930 he made one more attempt to salvage something out of his original conception. For all that went into *Tender Is the Night* from these five years of intermittent writing, the published book is essentially a new novel in form and conception, begun in 1932 while Fitzgerald was living at La Paix, outside Baltimore, and completed there in March of 1934.[48] The nine-year gap between *The Great Gatsby* and *Tender Is the Night* has often been considered a costly lapse and an ignominious failure, yet in the history of American literature great writers have not uncommonly taken nearly a decade between novels. Dreiser published no novel between *The "Genius"* in 1916 and *An American Tragedy* in 1925, Hemingway none between *A Farewell to Arms* in 1929 and *To Have and Have Not* in 1937. The important question is not why he failed to complete a novel more rapidly between 1925 and 1934, but how it affected his self-regard and his reputation as a writer.

In 1926 Fitzgerald's reputation was higher than it had ever been before, higher than it was ever to be again within his lifetime. *The Great Gatsby* had already brought him praise and admiration from the important writers and critics of his era; and when his third collection of stories was published early in 1926 the newspaper and magazine reviewers belatedly joined them. Fitzgerald had preferred not to bring out a book of stories if *The Great Gatsby* had been a popular success. But when *Gatsby's* commercial failure forced him to put together *All the Sad Young Men* the reviewers ironically had a chance to give Fitzgerald the acclaim they had earlier withheld from the novel. "With *The Great Gatsby*, it is generally agreed, Mr. Fitzgerald came into his full maturity as a novelist," William Rose Benét stated in *The Saturday Review of Literature*, although he had not really joined this consensus in his favorable but equivocating review of the novel.[49] "It becomes apparent that he is head and shoulders better than any other writer of his generation," *The Bookman* at last proclaimed—a proclamation given a special kind of irony for the fact that it appeared in the same number with "How To Waste Material," Fitzgerald's introduction of Hemingway to *The Bookman's* readers.[50] Other reviewers, if not so obviously making up for their failure to appreciate *The Great Gatsby*, were almost as favorable to the book of stories. *All the Sad Young Men* contained four of the eleven stories Fitzgerald wrote in the winter of 1923-24 to clear himself from debt; three earlier stories, including "Absolution"; and "The Adjuster" and "The Rich Boy" from his recent work. Out of this somewhat uneven collection each reviewer found one or two stories he especially liked, and each of the nine stories was picked by one or another reviewer as a favorite. In *The Dial* "The Baby Party" and "Hot and Cold Blood" were singled out for "sureness and insight," a judgment—made without tongue in cheek—almost indistinguishable from *The Outlook's*, at the opposite end of the literary spectrum.[51] The reader who looked for artistry could find it in *All the Sad Young Men*, and so could the reader who wanted morality; there was realism in it as well as romance, sentiment as well as irony. Once more Fitzgerald was all things to all people, as he had been when *This Side of Paradise* started his career so successfully. For a brief time he was universally admired again.

All the Sad Young Men sold over fourteen thousand copies, a far larger sale than Fitzgerald had expected, and it pulled Fitzgerald clear of his debt to Scribner's for the first time in four years. When the news of the first critical and commercial response came through, Fitzgerald was obviously delighted. "In fact, with the play [the dramatization of *Gatsby*] going well and my new novel growing absorbing," he wrote Maxwell Perkins, "and with our being back in a nice villa on my beloved Riviera (between Cannes and Nice), I'm happier than I've been for years. It's one of the strange, precious, and all too transitory moments when everything in one's life seems to be going well."[52] At that happy moment, out of debt at last, and with over thirty thousand dollars coming in from the dramatic and film rights to *Gatsby*, Fitzgerald gave up the short-story writing that had become so distasteful to him. After February 1926 he was to write no stories for the next fifteen months.

The four stories he wrote in the fall and winter of 1925-26, after completing "The Rich Boy," demonstrate his impatience with the form. Having to put his matured art and intellectual perception into the requirements of slick magazine stories was as if he were an adolescent boy forced to wear short pants. You couldn't do or say what you wanted; it was all a little foolish and uncomfortable. "Presumption" was a sentimental rewrite of *Gatsby*, with all the mystery left out and all the mechanics of wealth—respectable wealth, this time—put in. A "poor young man" seems to have ended up a failure in his struggle for romance "against a snobbish, purse-proud world." "It was all a preposterous joke on him, played by those to whom the business of life had been such jokes from the beginning. He realized now that fundamentally they were all akin . . . affirming the prerogative of the rich to marry always within their class, to erect artificial barriers and standards against those who could presume upon a summer's philandering. The scales fell from his eyes and he saw his year and a half struggle and effort not as progress toward a goal but only as a little race he had run by himself, outside, with no one to beat except himself—no one who cared." [53] Yet after this tragic insight the young man learns in the last sentence that he has won the girl.

"The Adolescent Marriage" is told partly from the point of view of a sixty-eight-year-old architect and partly from the point of view of a young architect in his employ. The young man has eloped with a rich young girl. But his poverty quickly destroys their marriage. The girl's parents have it annulled and the girl is protectively absorbed back into the social life of the rich. " 'So that's that,' [the young man] said finally in a new hard voice. 'I realize now that from beginning to end I was the only one who had any conscience in this affair after all.' " [54] He devotes himself to architecture, brilliantly designs a suburban cottage that wins a prize. A career of devotion to his art opens up before him, he passionately embraces it. But when he enters his newly constructed prize cottage he finds the rich young girl waiting for him inside. She loved him all the time. Anyway, she is pregnant by him. Sentiment and realism march hand in hand to the altar.

For "The Dance" Fitzgerald used as his narrator a young New York girl, who speaks in Conradian tones of "the unknown depths, the incalculable ebb and flow, the secret shapes of things that drift through opaque darkness under the surface of the sea." [55] She is referring to the atmosphere of violence and passion compressed beneath the quiet life of a small Southern town, where the story takes place. But "The Dance" does not succeed in uniting the tragic melodrama of one plot with the sentimental romance of the other. The last of the four stories, "Your Way and Mine," possesses an even more obviously broken back. It contains two business plots, one that abruptly stops in the middle without finishing, the other that abruptly stops at the end without finishing. "This is one of the lousiest stories I've ever written," Fitzgerald told his agent Harold Ober. "Just terrible . . . It hasn't *one redeeming touch* of my usual spirit in it." He asked Ober not to send it either to the *Post* or to *Redbook*, but promised for the future "two of the best stories I've ever done in my life." [56] This last was a falsehood to mitigate "Your Way and Mine." Early in 1926 Fitzgerald had come to a dead end as a short-story writer.

Yet for the next eight years Fitzgerald was known to the reading public chiefly as a writer of popular stories. With his inability to progress during 1926 on the novel, and the failure of his experiment as a screenwriter, he was forced to turn back to short stories. Writing stories was his way, at first, of keeping up an extravagant social life at Ellerslie and in France. Then, after April 1930, it became his way of providing the expensive psychiatric care for his wife. Though the novel was interrupted by drinking, by travel, by family tensions, then finally completely dropped after Zelda's mental breakdown, Fitzgerald wrote his stories anytime, anywhere, like the professional writer he was. He turned out five in the last half of 1927, seven in 1928, seven in 1929, eight in 1930, nine in 1931, four more in the first five months of 1932, until he began seriously to work on *Tender Is the Night*—forty stories in all over a period of almost exactly five years. With his rate per story climbing to a high of four thousand dollars, Fitzgerald earned over one hundred thousand dollars—almost exclusively from *The Saturday Evening Post*—in the three years 1929-31. In "How To Waste Material" he had described the ways some writers of his generation had given up or lost their artistry. As if by self-fulfilling prophecy he had become his own best, or worst, example. No one else seemed to be wasting material so prodigally as he.

The strains of his life as an artist and an intellectual over the years from 1926 to 1932—to say nothing of his personal and social life—were exceptionally intense. His aims were unrealistically high. He had undertaken to write a novel better than Conrad, better than Joyce, better than Stein—better, more appropriately, than *The Great Gatsby*. But he was caught in a cross-fire of conflicting intentions. He had no real conception of what such a novel would be like, only feelings of how it ought to be. At the same time he had conceived a plot but he had not brought to it that "passionate emotion" that made *The Great Gatsby* so memorable. Thus his beautiful prose passages never quite lived up to the conception he had not clearly formulated; and none of his ideas took on quite the tone of feeling he wanted them to have. Fitzgerald had wanted to begin anew—to repeat the past as Gatsby had wanted to—and he succeeded and failed in quite the same manner as Gatsby. It was as if he had gone back to where he was just after writing *This Side of Paradise*. He was plunging ahead on as ambitiously projected and as artistically and intellectually flawed a novel as *The Beautiful and Damned* had been. But you can't repeat the past; he was now far too mature an artist and intellectual ever to bring another *Beautiful and Damned* to completion. Meanwhile there were his ever-present insecurities. In the back of his mind he believed that "the critics" were still hostile to him, were hoping that he would really prove to be a wash-out; and there was the star of Ernest Hemingway, rising in popularity, with *A Farewell to Arms* in 1929, to heights Fitzgerald had never reached.

A Farewell to Arms marked a turning point for Fitzgerald's self-respect. When he had begun his new novel back in 1925 it was easy to believe, as he had written Perkins then, that he was the best American novelist, that the new work would remove all remaining doubts and hesitations. By 1929 it was impossible to believe so confidently in himself any longer. Since 1926 Hemingway had produced an impressive book of short stories and an immensely successful novel; Fitzgerald had produced nothing permanent at all. Hemingway's manner toward Fitzgerald changed, in keeping with his conviction that he had proved himself far superior as a man and as a writer. He ridiculed Fitzgerald's claim to work eight hours a day on his writing; even Zelda Fitzgerald, whose habits had often hindered her husband's writing in the past, revolted against their waste and dissipation. She became obsessed with the need to work, to accomplish something. Surrounded in his professional and family life by persons apparently far more serious and dedicated than he, Fitzgerald was thrown on the defensive. He began to excuse himself. He became more and more touchy.

"Your analysis of my inability to get my serious work done is too kind," he wrote Hemingway in September 1929, "in that it leaves out the dissipation, but amongst acts of God it is possible that the five years between my leaving the Army and finishing *Gatsby* (1919-1924) which included 3 novels, about 50 popular stories and a play and numerous articles and movies may have taken all I had to say too early, adding that all the time we were living at top speed in the gayest worlds we could find." [57] To an admiring correspondent he explained, "About five years ago I became, unfortunately, interested in the insoluble problems of personal charm and have spent the intervening time on a novel that's going to interest nobody.... Unfortunately my sense of material is much superior to my mind or my talent and if I ever survive this damned thing I shall devote my life to musical comedy librettos or become swimming instructor to the young Mikadesses of Japan." [58] When his agent Ober prodded him on the novel exactly at the moment of Zelda's breakdown, Fitzgerald exploded: "I know you're losing faith in me, and Max too, but God knows one has to rely in the end on one's own judgment. I could have published four lousy, half-baked books in the last five years and people would have thought I was at least a worthy young man not drinking myself to pieces in the South Seas—but I'd be dead as Michael Arlen, Bromfield, Tom Boyd, Callaghan and the others who think they can trick the world with the hurried and the second-rate." [59] On the same day he wrote almost the same words to Perkins. "I wrote young and I wrote a lot and the pot takes longer to fill up now, but the novel, my novel, is a different matter than if I'd hurriedly finished it up a year and a half ago.... *I know what I'm doing* —honestly, Max.... 'He's through' is an easy cry to raise but it's safer for the critics to raise it at the evidence in print than at a long silence." [60]

Throughout his life Fitzgerald retained a bit of pseudo-scientific folk wisdom he had picked up in his youth, the "fact" that the body's cells completely renew themselves every seven years. Technically, so his version went, after seven years an entirely new person comes into being; he used this idea as a gimmick in a 1932 *Post* story, "On Schedule." [61] You can't repeat the past; yet with the exception that Fitzgerald did not publish a novel as confused and hurried as was *The Beautiful and Damned*, the years 1929-31 in his career bear an uncanny resemblance to the years 1922-24. Seven years after that early nadir in his career he was acting it out, almost step by step, all over again. There were the same angry and self-despairing letters, the same excessive drinking, the same sense of falling behind his competitors—even the same curious revival of critical comment at the lowest point of his depression. Just as Edmund Wilson, Paul Rosenfeld, and Ernest Boyd had revived interest in Fitzgerald in 1924, so Gorham Munson and Lawrence Leighton brought him new consideration in 1931 and 1932. Both Munson and Leighton—like the three literary journalists seven years before them—were critical of the novelists of the twenties. In his survey of "Our Post-War Novel" for *The Bookman* Munson found Fitzgerald the only signifi-cant novelist whose work was not marred by naturalism. "Mr. Fitz-gerald seems to me more radiant with promise than any other younger novelist we have," Munson wrote. "Fired by Mr. Fitzgerald's example, young American writers might have broken free of the canons of naturalistic and realistic fiction (canons that in reality are stultifying to art) and the course of our post-war novel might have been from documentary fiction toward poetic fiction. . . . This was not to be. Mr. Fitzgerald has not published a novel since 1925 and his vogue has been succeeded by the vogue of Mr. Ernest Heming-way." [62] Writing in Harvard's journal of the new criticism, *Hound & Horn*, Leighton found Hemingway, Fitzgerald, and Dos Passos, his three American subjects, all inferior writers, though of the three he called Fitzgerald the best.[63]

Yet the minor similarities between the two stages of Fitzgerald's career become merely coincidence beside their larger connection. During both periods Fitzgerald's difficulties masked the fact that he was struggling to work out a new conception of his material, that he was going through a painful process of growth. For all the pride and egotism that made him want to outdo *The Great Gatsby* in his new novel, to outdo Joyce and Conrad and Stein as well, there was a sounder principle behind his ambition, too. He wanted not merely to succeed more greatly, but also to do better. He did not want his mind and art to rest. The qualities of mind that had enabled him— had forced him—to grow beyond *This Side of Paradise* and *The Beautiful and Damned* now pushed him to grow beyond *The Great Gatsby*. "It was always the becoming he dreamed of, never the being," Fitzgerald had written of Amory Blaine so long ago.[64] The personal sadness and the professional frustrations of Fitzgerald's life between 1926 and 1932 ought not to obscure the process of becoming that he was meanwhile working through; for as difficulties now were permanent characteristics of his personal life, so too were new possibilities now a permanent characteristic of his mind and art.

CHAPTER NINE

A process of becoming, a principle of growth in intellect and art, creates the form for F. Scott Fitzgerald's development from *The Great Gatsby* to *Tender Is the Night;* and the process of becoming, in its most cosmic sense, was on Fitzgerald's mind when he returned east from Hollywood early in 1927 to take up the task once more of writing fiction. In Hollywood he had begun to read *The Decline of the West* by Oswald Spengler. Maxwell Perkins had recommended Spengler to him, and whether from Perkins's suggestion or from another, Fitzgerald bought Spengler's first volume on his way to Hollywood or shortly thereafter.[1] How much attention he was able to give Spengler's arduous prose, while preparing a movie script and leading his own strenuous social life in Hollywood, is an open question; but he absorbed enough so that when he was interviewed in New York on his return from the west it was Spengler about whom he wished to talk. "Here was I," his interviewer wrote, "interviewing the author of 'This Side of Paradise,' the voice and embodiment of the jazz age, its product and its beneficiary, a popular novelist, a movie scenarist, a dweller in the gilded palaces, a master of servants, only to find F. Scott Fitzgerald, himself, shorn of these associations, forecasting doom, death, and damnation to his generation, in the spirit, if not in the rhetoric, of your typical spittoon philosopher."[2] For his first public appearance in New York—his first performance before the New York literary world since the spring of 1924, when he had gone abroad to write *Gatsby*, Fitzgerald portrayed himself in an old familiar role, the philosopher of the jazz age.

Fitzgerald's interviewer hardly took him seriously; and there is no reason why anyone who had grown cynical toward stories "about flappers for philosophers" should look upon "Fitzgerald, Spenglerian" as anything new. Fitzgerald's sudden interest in historical prophecy is yet one more aspect of his curious reversion to the moods and attitudes that shaped his intellect and art at the very start of his career. For at Princeton he had been deeply influenced by the Celtic world-historical pessimism expressed in the war books of Shane Leslie, and more distantly by his mentor Father Fay and by Henry Adams; and later his acquaintance with Mencken's criticism and the novels of Frank Norris had briefly built this world-weariness into a naturalistic mood of despair. With *The Great Gatsby* and "The Rich Boy" Fitzgerald's art and intellect had mastered the doubts and questions of his early career. Now, by his reading of Spengler at a time of new doubt and hesitation, Fitzgerald brought one period of his career, the period that *Gatsby* and "The Rich Boy" had completed, to a final close. Spengler gave Fitzgerald the chance to begin again; and it was Spengler who revived Fitzgerald's fascination with the First World War, for *The Decline of the West* had opened all the old questions and issues of the war once more. Yet it was not necessary for Fitzgerald to begin again totally. New answers had to be sought to old questions, but the answers he had already painfully attained were not wiped out. "Spengler stands on the shoulders of Nietzsche," Fitzgerald said in his interview, "and Nietzsche on those of Goethe." In the same way Fitzgerald was able, in his new effort, to stand on the shoulders of all he had thought and created before.

In his interview Fitzgerald called *The Decline of the West* his "bed-book," a warning against overestimating his grasp of Spengler's thought. But he need not have read beyond the introduction to have been challenged fundamentally. Fitzgerald's development before *The Great Gatsby* had been shaped by a gradual abandonment of a historical perspective; or rather by the growth of a universal framework over an already well-developed historical point of view. In 1923 he had begun *The Great Gatsby* as a historical novel, but in the following year he put aside that manuscript, salvaging from it only the short story "Absolution." He had decided to make Gatsby's origins more mysterious; to show, ultimately, how Gatsby "sprang from his Platonic conception of himself." [3] *The Great Gatsby* became a novel about the nature of America, but it carried its social values and historical perspective into a realm of universal symbols and suprahistorical myths. Gatsby stands for essential qualities of America; and so he stands above time and history, a symbol of eternally recurring hopes and dreams. For all its insights into history, *The Great Gatsby* is basically an ahistorical novel.

Fitzgerald's strategic withdrawal from history took a different form in "The Rich Boy." That long story was deeply historical in its feeling for the relations among class and wealth and personal values. But in his complex effort to create social depth for his story, while at the same time shaking the reader loose from stereotyped ideas about the rich, Fitzgerald tactically began by denying the story's social breadth. "There are no types, no plurals. There is a rich boy, and this is his and not his brothers' story." After that forewarning Fitzgerald felt able to switch in the next paragraph from singular to plural: "Let me tell you about the very rich. They are different from you and me." [4] For "The Rich Boy" the device was an exceptionally effective one, providing a dramatic tension for the reader between the claims of uniqueness and an obvious movement toward wider social significance. But in 1926 it was a device Fitzgerald would not and could not repeat.

By reading Spengler, at his moment of impasse early in 1927, Fitzgerald was drawn back once more to think about the possibilities of historical perspective; indeed, if he had fallen as deeply under Spengler's spell as his interview suggests, he might have been convinced that no other perspective than the historical was appropriate for him to use. For Spengler insisted from the start of *The Decline of the West* that only a historical point of view was available to Western man. "Thus our theme," Spengler wrote, "which originally comprised only the limited problem of present-day civilization, broadens itself into a new philosophy—*the* philosophy of the future, so far as the metaphysically-exhausted soil of the West can bear such, and in any case the only philosophy which is within the *possibilities* of the West-European mind in its next stages. It expands into the conception of a *morphology of world history,* of the world-as-history in contrast to the morphology of the world-as-nature that hitherto has been almost the only theme of philosophy." To Spengler the most effective comparison between world-as-nature and world-as-history lay in the contrast between Classical and Western man. "In the world-consciousness of the Hellenes," he continued, "all experience, not merely the personal but the common past, was immediately transmuted into a timeless, immobile, mythically-fashioned background for the particular momentary present. . . . the Classical culture possessed no *memory*, no organ of history in this special sense. The memory of the Classical man—so to call it, though it is somewhat arbitrary to apply to alien souls a notion derived from our own—is something different, since past and future, as arraying perspectives in the working consciousness, are absent and the 'pure Present' . . . fills that life with an intensity that to us is perfectly unknown." Spengler's Classical man obviously resembles Fitzgerald's Jay Gatsby and, to a slightly lesser degree, Anson Hunter of "The Rich Boy"; and *The Great Gatsby*, with its remarkably deep and complex natural imagery, locates the significance of America more properly in a world of nature than in a world of history. But Spengler, rejecting the "innocent relativism" that enabled modern writers to draw parallels between past types and contemporary characters, focused Fitzgerald's attention instead on the forms and psychological insights of history.[5]

For Spengler the most significant concept in historical studies was "destiny." In order to discover the destiny of his own culture, the culture he called "West-European-American," Spengler drew a fundamental distinction between two terms often used interchangeably, *civilization* and *culture*. "In this work," he explained, "for the first time the two words, hitherto used to express an indefinite, more or less ethical, distinction, are used in a *periodic* sense to express a strict and necessary *organic succession*. The Civilization is the inevitable *destiny* of the Culture, and in this principle we obtain the viewpoint from which the deepest and gravest problems of historical morphology become capable of solution. Civilizations are the most external and artificial states of which a species of developed humanity is capable. They are a conclusion, the thing-become succeeding the thing-becoming, death following life, rigidity following expansion, intellectual age and the stone-built, petrifying world-city following mother-earth and the spiritual childhood of Doric and Gothic." Thus he made the meaning of his title clear: "The 'Decline of the West' comprises nothing less than the problem of *Civilization.*" For the culture of the West had already passed into the state of civilization. "The transition from Culture to Civilization," according to Spengler, "was accomplished for the Classical world in the 4th, for the Western in the 19th Century." And he went on: "What is the hall-mark of a politic of Civilization to-day, in contrast to a politic of Culture yesterday? It is, for the Classical rhetoric, and for the Western journalism, both serving that abstract which represents the power of Civilization—*money.*" [6] It is hard to see how Fitzgerald could not have been deeply affected by a point of view which added a philosophical foundation to the values he had expressed in his art from the earliest days of his career.

Scepticism, Spengler wrote, was the only philosophical position left open to the West. "Scepticism is the expression of a pure Civilization; and it dissipates the world-picture of the Culture that has gone before. For us, its success will lie in resolving all the older problems into one, the genetic. The conviction that what *is* also *has become*, that the natural and cognizable is rooted in the historic, that the World as the actual is founded on an Ego as the potential actualized, that the 'when' and the 'how long' hold as deep a secret as the 'what,' leads directly to the fact that everything, whatever else it may be, must at any rate be *the expression of something living.* Cognitions and judgments too are acts of living men. The thinkers of the past conceived external actuality as produced by cognition and motivating ethical judgments, but to the thought of the future they are above all *expressions and symbols. The Morphology of world-history becomes inevitably a universal symbolism.*" [7] To Spengler, in other words, it was possible to create a far more profound universal symbolism through the forms of history than through the forms of myth. It was this conception Fitzgerald took with him to Ellerslie in April, 1927—and reinforced by reading Spengler's second volume late in 1928—that lies at the heart of his process of becoming from *The Great Gatsby* to *Tender Is the Night.*

II

The slick magazine stories of the years 1927-32, the so-called potboilers that Fitzgerald churned out so regularly in all kinds of psychic and emotional weather, surprisingly provide greater insight into the nature of that process than any other aspect of his work—more than the truncated and discarded manuscripts of the uncompleted novel, more than his sometimes less than candid and sometimes overly dramatized professional correspondence, far more than has heretofore been supposed. No aspect of his fiction has been treated less as literature and more as autobiography than this group of stories; and Fitzgerald's own later treatment of them has helped to obscure their values. When he began *Tender Is the Night* he went through the *Post* stories and "stripped" them of paragraphs, phrases, characters, incidents, points of view, whatever seemed potentially useful for the novel. Those stories he "stripped" were "permanently buried." [8] When he came after *Tender Is the Night* to put together a new collection of stories, the "stripped and permanently buried" group were unavailable. *Taps at Reveille*, the collection published in 1935, therefore contains primarily those stories irrelevant to the main lines of Fitzgerald's intellectual and artistic development between 1927 and 1932. A chronological approach to the stories presents a rather different picture.

Yet the path of an artist's growth is no more smooth than the path of any other interior development. To the dilemmas that impeded his way unexpectedly Fitzgerald added dilemmas of his own making, right from the start. When he was writing two short stories in a season and earning $30,000 from them over a year he had no more respect for the short story form than in those fifteen months of 1926-27 when he wrote no short stories at all. It pleased his vanity, yet it embarrassed his literary values, to be paid so much by *The Saturday Evening Post;* and if financial necessity forced him to work out his new ideas through the short story, he could never take the form seriously enough to give either his conception or his art full justice. The dilemma was his own creation far more than has been recognized by those who put down Fitzgerald's *Post* stories as "potboilers" turned out for money. The *Post* was a guardian of middle-class values, to be sure, but its editor, George Horace Lorimer, was a man, as Fitzgerald knew, with his own high literary tastes and standards. The *Post* printed a great deal of conventional fiction but very little fiction of poor quality; Fitzgerald knew the distinction and he worked by it. Yet he also knew that the *Post* would take the best he could give, no matter how far from the conventional he strayed. During these years the *Post* published "Babylon Revisited," "Magnetism," "The Rough Crossing," "Two Wrongs," and "One Trip Abroad," all far from conventional stories; "Crazy Sunday" appeared in *The American Mercury*, but there is evidence it was rejected by a popular magazine other than the *Post*. The conditions of magazine publishing in the late twenties were far less a factor in shaping Fitzgerald's short fiction than his own moods and circumstances. Like Coleridge in Keats's letter about negative capability, Fitzgerald as a short-story writer would let go by more than one "fine isolated verisimilitude caught from the Penetralium of mystery," not so much from being incapable of remaining content with half knowledge—though that too—as from incapacity or unwillingness to hold on to it within the form.[9]

The difficulties of Fitzgerald's personal life are well known, but there is one relevant minor incident that serves as prologue to his years as a short-story writer, and provides their beginning with the proper tone of pathos—with perhaps a little of parody. While in Hollywood Fitzgerald was briefly infatuated with a seventeen-year-old actress, Lois Moran. As if to illustrate perfectly Fitzgerald's folklore about seven-year cycles, Miss Moran bore the same name as the heroine of Fitzgerald's short story "Benediction," written almost exactly seven years earlier. "They do say," *The Bookman*'s "Gossip Shop" reported in April 1927, "that [Fitzgerald] is taking screen tests and wishes to try out for leading man to Lois Moran."[10] But by April, of course, he had already retreated from Hollywood to Ellerslie. And by June he had completed his first short story in sixteen months, "Jacob's Ladder," a story about a seventeen-year-old Hollywood actress and a disappointed lover twice her age. But "Jacob's Ladder" is a powerful and sensitive short story that proves again how Fitzgerald's artistry created fiction far different from and far more significant than the personal experience on which it may have been based.

Jacob Booth in "Jacob's Ladder" is a wealthy New York investor, who, like Maury Noble in *The Beautiful and Damned* and Anson Hunter in "The Rich Boy," was a little too apathetic. "Like so many Americans he valued things rather than cared about them. His apathy was neither fear of life nor was it an affectation; it was the racial

228

violence grown tired. It was a humorous apathy." But when he met Jenny Delahanty, sixteen, a beautiful department store clerk, "he knelt suddenly at the heart of freshness." Jacob wanted to awaken Jenny, to help her grow from a physical beauty to a beautiful person. He arranges a screen test for her, and when she succeeds he lives "more deeply in her youth and future than he had lived in himself for years." But Jacob, curiously, was as much Gatsby as Anson Hunter, as ideologically romantic as he was apathetic. "She did not know yet," he thought, "that splendor was something in the heart; at the moment when she should realize that and melt into the passion of the universe he could take her without question or regret." Jacob is not in love with Jenny so much as he is in love with an image of love. And Jenny, now Jenny Prince, a professional actress, a girl grown into distinction and good manners as Jacob had planned, cannot love him. They separate at the end of the story, and Jacob, distraught, sees Jenny's name on a movie marquee. " 'Come and rest upon my loveliness,' " Jenny's name said. " 'Fulfill your secret dreams in wedding me for an hour.' " Jacob enters the theater. "She was there! All of her, the best of her—the effort, the power, the triumph, the beauty. Jacob moved forward with a group and bought a ticket at the window. Confused, he stared around the great lobby. Then he saw an entrance and walking in, found himself a place in the fast-throbbing darkness." [11] Jacob Booth, with his apathy that was "the racial violence grown tired," with his romantic love of the image of love, is Fitzgerald's old hero in a new form; in a remarkable way he sets a *leitmotif* for the next seven years of Fitzgerald's fiction, culminating in *Tender Is the Night*.

"Jacob's Ladder" began Fitzgerald's new career as a professional writer of short stories; thereafter he was to turn out one about every five weeks for five full years. But it also squandered, by its very quality and breadth, nearly all of his newly acquired material. He followed it with "The Love Boat," another good story of a wealthy man's "restless longing after fleeing youth." [12] In "The Love Boat" the man returns after many years to visit the lower-class girl he had once courted in his youth. The visit, conveyed in a sinister atmosphere of drinking, violence, possible adultery, and the break-up of a marriage, disillusions him; and disaster is implicit in the story's resolution. "Jacob's Ladder" and "The Love Boat," both uncollected, belong among Fitzgerald's best short stories; but they set a standard of quality and thematic depth that Fitzgerald could hardly expect to maintain. In his next story, "A Short Trip Home," he did not even try. It is a curious reversion to the mood and setting of *This Side of Paradise*, and the story's structure is built upon the sense of immanent supernatural evil that played so large a part in Fitzgerald's first novel.[13] His next story, "The Bowl," was about college football, but it was written from Fitzgerald's mature perspective. The theme of "The Bowl" was the nature of achievement: "All achievement was a placing of emphasis—a molding of the confusion of life into forms." Dolly Harlan, a college football hero, becomes involved with a society girl, Vienna Thorne. The tone that prevails in her social group is apathy; one does nothing that is not "worth doing." And being a football hero is obviously not worth doing; so Dolly apathetically breaks a leg. The rest of the story is the story of Dolly's comeback, his discovery that one must do what one can do; that there is a quality and style to achievement infinitely superior to the quality and style of fashionable disdain. Dolly throws over Vienna Thorne and wins the heart of Daisy Cary, a movie actress. "They understood each other. They were both workers; sick or well, there were things that Daisy also had to do. She spoke of how, with a vile cold, she had had to fall into an open-air lagoon the winter before. . . . She was eighteen and I compared her background of courage and independence and achievement, of politeness based upon realities of cooperation, with that of most society girls I had known. There was no way in which she wasn't inestimably their superior." [14]

For the last story he wrote in 1927, "Magnetism," Fitzgerald went back to Hollywood for his setting. The central character of "Magnetism" is not a beautiful young actress, but an actor with whom a beautiful young actress, among others, falls in love. George Hannaford, the actor, was "simple and dignified" in his taste, "instinctively gentle" in manner; and he was well and happily married. But George possessed something he could not control. "You were so brave about people, George," one of his disappointed admirers tells him. "Whoever it was, you walked right up to them and tore something aside as if it was in your way and began to know them. . . . You can't control charm. It's simply got to be used. You've got to keep your hand in if you have it, and go through life attracting people to you that you don't want." And that is the cross George is doomed to bear, condemned by his smile that withdraws the veil between him and every woman, "unconsciously promising her a possible admission to the thousand delights and wonders that only he knew and could command." [15] George Hannaford is another new version of Fitzgerald's old romantic hero, a simple and dignified figure rather than a clever, showy one, but a man who even despite himself creates romantic dreams of love. In four of the five short stories of his new professional work—putting aside the anachronistic "A Short Trip Home"—Fitzgerald had sustained a level of quality in his short fiction in a way that he had never done before. He had imagined a number of new insights into his material—insights into the nature of achievement and the meaning of professionalism, into the love of age for youth, into the value of manners, into new aspects of the romantic hero. But by the nature of the form he worked in, his insights could be no more than fragmentary and partial, shaped more for him than by him by the limitations of his material, and lacking still a coherent structure of purpose and direction. The inherent insufficiency of even his best efforts at short fiction may have been in his mind when, after two months of no writing at all, he began the series of Basil Duke Lee stories that was to occupy him almost exclusively for a year.

Why at this particular moment Fitzgerald should turn back to his adolescence for a subject is a matter open obviously to more than one conjecture. In each of the five stories he had written in 1927 after resuming his career as a magazine writer he had created girls of eighteen or younger as significant characters. It may have been his calculated professional judgment that the teen-age crowd was where his primary audience lay; or he may simply have given in to his personal obsession with youth and and the terrors of growing old. Since his new material and new insights did not appear capable of infinitely producing new short-story situations, he may have returned to a subject with which he could feel more secure. Certainly, for all his concern with adolescence, his own early youth was material that he had hardly mined. Most of what he had written of adolescence in the early, unpublished novel, "The Romantic Egotist," had been cut or greatly condensed when he turned it into *This Side of Paradise*. The Basil Duke Lee stories may simply be read then as a belated revision of "The Romantic Egotist" by an author who had turned into a mature professional writer—a portrait of the artist as a young man presented as dramatized fiction, rather than as autobiographical self-interrogation.

But the Basil Duke Lee stories possess an even more central point of continuity with Fitzgerald's earlier career, one that brings together in a more unified way Fitzgerald's obviously disparate motives: they linked Fitzgerald's fiction once again with the stories and novels of Booth Tarkington. In the commercial literary world Fitzgerald's name naturally went together with Tarkington's. Just as reviewers in 1920 had praised *This Side of Paradise* as the work of a new Tarkington, so five years later Fitzgerald's friend, Carl Van Vechten, could say blandly in his review of *The Great Gatsby* that Fitzgerald resembled Tarkington more than anyone else.[16] So much for Fitzgerald's pretensions to be the American Conrad or the American Joyce; Van Vechten could hardly have known that Fitzgerald looked on Tarkington with open disdain. Fitzgerald envied Tarkington his success, and in moments of weakness it was easy for him to fall back into the Tarkington pattern, but fundamentally from an early point in his career he had known that his growth as an artist depended upon his overcoming Tarkington's compromise with gentility. "My contempt for Tarkington," he wrote Julian Street in July 1928, when he was midway in the Basil Duke Lee series, "extends only to his character of being ashamed of his early sins and thus cutting out of his experience about one half of life. He woke up one morning sober and 40, and thought that no one had ever been lascivious or drunk or vain except himself, and turned deliberately back to the illusions of his boyhood." [17] Fitzgerald had in mind the kind of response Tarkington gave when critics attacked his novel, *Seventeen,* for its suppression of adolescent sexual awakening. "I don't see it," Tarkington had replied. "I never knew a youth who had that sense of torment under the circumstances depicted in 'Seventeen.'" His adolescent hero, William, "didn't recognize anything." [18] In the Basil Duke Lee stories Fitzgerald's adolescent heroes recognized a lot. It seems clear that Fitzgerald wrote the series as an experiment with the genre of genteel romantic boys' stories, to see how they turned out when that missing half of life was added. Fitzgerald cut the stories straight from the Tarkington mold. But he put in what Tarkington had left out, adolescent awareness of sex.

Yet the Basil Duke Lee stories were an experiment that did not wholly succeed. For a time Fitzgerald planned to make a book of them—a book that might restore his old appeal to the popular audience who had been indifferent to *Gatsby* and who seemed certain to respond with equal coolness to his novel in progress. But again his own peculiar dilemma rose up to plague him. "The Basil Lee stories were a mistake," he wrote late in 1929 to an admirer who had praised them, "—it was too much good material being shoved into a lousy form." Still he thanked her for liking them. "I thought they were rather better," he wrote, "than the response they had." [19] At heart he believed his popular fiction could be good fiction, and he resented criticism that he was wasting his talents by writing down to the popular taste; yet even more deeply in his artistic consciousness he felt the weakness and inadequacy of his popular work. Not that the Basil Duke Lee stories were trash, conceived either in ignorance or deliberate waste; they were good but he knew simply that they were not good enough. After *The Great Gatsby* Fitzgerald had tried to reconcile his artistry with his popular work, and he had failed. After *Gatsby* his new novel had not lived up to his own impossibly high standards of artistry, and so, out of despair and out of need, he put it aside and turned to magazine stories. Though he tried to keep separate his two realms of fiction, in a showdown it was by his standards of art that all his work was judged. None of his short stories, by their very nature, could clear that difficult test. Here, in the gap between his daily creative endeavor and his underlying disdain for it, lay one source of the tension that exploded in anger when Harold Ober raised again in 1930 the old idea of putting together the Basil stories in a book.

In all Fitzgerald wrote nine Basil Lee stories, carrying Basil into his freshman year at Yale, where continuing would have meant rewriting *This Side of Paradise*—or writing a New Haven version. The Basil stories were not wholly out of character with the short stories that precede and follow them; they may be read as much as the others for evidence of maturing perceptions and new insights. But if the insights possessed any power, the Basil stories, as Fitzgerald retrospectively saw, were even less capable than the other stories of carrying their weight. Late in 1928, with seven Basil stories done and two more still to be written, Fitzgerald broke into the series to write a different kind of story, "The Last of the Belles." [20] But "The Last of the Belles" was hardly an improvement on the form of the Basil stories. It went back for its setting and themes to Fitzgerald's First World War experience at Southern Army posts, back to the atmosphere of a Southern romantic way of life that he had re-created in *The Beautiful and Damned* and several earlier short stories. As he had done before in his Southern stories he even used some of the old characters, notably Sally Carrol Happer from "The Ice Palace" and Nancy Lamar from "The Jelly Bean." "The Last of the Belles" was the work of a fine professional magazine writer, precise in its language, quiet and self-assured in tone; but it is a curiously flat and empty story, written out of old emotions and old perceptions. As with "A Short Trip Home," Fitzgerald in this story was merely reusing the past, rather than re-creating it. The Basil Duke Lee stories, for all their inadequacies, were founded at least on a reinterpretation of experience, not simply a recollection.

Fitzgerald had lived a year at Ellerslie from the spring of 1927; in April 1928, he went back to France for a long spring and summer abroad, returning in September. One attraction of the Basil Duke Lee series, no doubt, was that it provided him a form and a subject he could write about on the run; at least four of the nine stories, and perhaps another, were written while Fitzgerald was abroad or traveling. For the fall and winter of 1928-29 the Fitzgeralds returned to Ellerslie. In February he wrote the last Basil story, "Basil and Cleopatra," and in March they sailed again for Europe, this time expecting to stay. Just as he was in process of transferring his life and his work back to France, Fitzgerald wrote a short story, "The Rough Crossing," about a crisis in a marriage. No one has ever precisely established the story's chronological relation to Fitzgerald's movements, but the matter does possess a certain significance. Some critics have read it as a direct autobiographical account of the Fitzgeralds' passage to Genoa in 1929.[21] Yet it seems quite unlikely that Fitzgerald would have been able to turn so deep a personal issue so quickly into fiction. The story was completed sometime in March, the same month the Fitzgeralds crossed, and published in the *Post* early in June. One may as plausibly believe that Fitzgerald planned and perhaps even wrote it before sailing; he could have drawn his material from two Atlantic crossings he made in 1928. Once again the issue is autobiography and art in Fitzgerald's fiction. At Ellerslie the Fitzgeralds' relationship had visibly deteriorated; his stories of marital difficulties could hardly not relate at all to his own problems. Yet so often have critics interpreted his work as if it transformed fact directly into fiction, one may usefully recall once more that art and life are separate realms.

Marriage problems, and adultery, had been muted but not insignificant subjects in Fitzgerald's earlier fiction. So long as he aspired to realism he could not have overlooked them; but still his genteel formulas provided a cloak of innocence and inevitably a happy ending. Gloria in *The Beautiful and Damned* had felt no constraints against adultery except that she lacked the desire; in such stories as "Gretchen's Forty Winks," "One of My Oldest Friends," and "John Jackson's Arcady," real or potential marital difficulties were raised and then glossed over, here by a twist of plot, there by a retreat to conventions. One aspect of Fitzgerald's triumph in *The Great Gatsby* lay in his subordinating the obvious fact of adultery to the artistic themes and values of the novel as a whole. After *Gatsby,* marital troubles were raised in "The Adjuster," only to be solved by a *deus ex machina* in the person of a mysterious psychiatrist; and in "The Rich Boy," adultery was portrayed as a rather sordid thing in the eyes of the central figure, Anson Hunter. When his long holiday from fiction had ended, Fitzgerald took up the theme again in "The Love Boat," where marital difficulties formed a forboding undertone, and in "Magnetism," where George Hannaford's marriage momentarily tottered because of his unwilled attractiveness to other women. But "The Rough Crossing" was Fitzgerald's first short story where husband and wife both played a leading role, and where the crisis in their marriage was the principal event.

Yet "The Rough Crossing," for all its thematic importance, did not provide an entirely satisfactory treatment. Fitzgerald cared more for creating symbols than characters; his husband and wife, Adrian and Eva Smith, are archetypically named, and the story ends, "There are so many Smiths in this world." Fitzgerald opened by drawing their ship at sea as a separate world—"certainly not a boat, but rather a human idea, a frame of mind"—and then he threw the ship into an ocean storm, a symbolic parallel for Adrian and Eva's inner turmoil.[22] Symbolic forms and schematic action dominate. Character and motivation are thin. Confronting a marital crisis directly for the first time in his short fiction, Fitzgerald was able only to skate along the surface, describing its outer aspects but hardly creating it from within. Yet beneath the surface, beyond the partly ironical and partly soothing happy end, lies an undertone of emotional conflicts and tensions sounding only as distant echoes.

After "The Rough Crossing" Fitzgerald wrote two minor stories in old conventional patterns. They are interesting only because, even in his inconsequential work, Fitzgerald could not escape the themes and qualities of mind that shaped his growth. "Majesty," a flapper-style story about a debutante who ends up as an Eastern European queen, opens with the lines, "The extraordinary thing is not that people in a lifetime turn out worse or better than we had prophesied; particularly in America that is to be expected. The extraordinary thing is how people keep their levels, fulfill their promises, seem actually buoyed up by an inevitable destiny." [23] "At Your Age," another youth-and-age love story with an eternal recurrence motif—when the hero reached age fifty the "wheel of his life had revolved again"—ends with a different type of insight into character and destiny: "But he could not have walked down wasted into the darkness without being used up a little; what he had wanted, after all, was only to break his strong old heart. Conflict itself had a value beyond victory and defeat, and those three months—he had them forever." [24] Then, during two summer months in Cannes, while also trying to reshape and salvage the long-postponed novel, Fitzgerald turned again to the theme of marital crisis in a neglected, undervalued story, "The Swimmers."

Fitzgerald created his structure for "The Swimmers" out of historical perspectives he had learned in Spengler's *Decline of the West*. Spengler's conception that history possessed a living genetic form provided the form of the fiction. Fitzgerald was concerned less with Spengler's "world history" than with the history of America; the nature and meaning of American history were as important as—and quite inseparable from—the nature and destiny of his characters. "The Swimmers" was the first of Fitzgerald's stories in which the basic symbolism grew out of a feeling for historical form—as, in a different context, Spengler said it must.

Henry Clay Marston is an American expatriate in Paris, no artist but an intellectual businessman who had left the "moral confusion" of his "ever-new, ever-changing country" when it appeared that the questions life posed could only be answered in France. After eight years abroad, with a French wife and two sons, Henry refuses to go back, even when a lucrative business offer is made. But when he discovers his wife's infidelity, his well-ordered life collapses into chaos and despair. He becomes ill, and takes his family to a French sea resort for a rest cure. There he tries to rescue an endangered swimmer, though he is himself unable to swim. The person whom he bravely aids turns out to be an eighteen-year-old American girl, another of Fitzgerald's teen-age heroines, but one who for the first time carries a significance greater than simply her physical youth: "In her grace, at once exquisite and hardy, she was that perfect type of American girl that makes one wonder if the male is not being sacrificed to it, much as, in the last century, the lower strata in England were sacrificed to produce the governing class." Except for her one dangerous moment she is normally a good swimmer who spends, so it seems, all her time swimming. Henry asks her why. "To get clean," she answers. At once this motive reveals to Henry a larger national purpose. "I mean we've got too fastidious even to clean up our messes," he responds. Inspired by this vision, Henry learns to swim and brings about his own recovery.

Henry had not married a perfect American type, but still he sensed that he was being sacrificed as well to whatever type his French wife represented. "American men," he says, "are incomplete without money"; so to make himself more complete he returns to America and takes up his lucrative job. But if money makes completion, the more a man has the more complete he is; thus, apparently, Choupette Marston reasons, for in America she begins an affair with Henry's wealthy backer, Charles Wiese. Henry, fortunately, can rely on different values. "Henry Clay Marston was a Virginian of the kind who are prouder of being Virginians than of being Americans. That mighty word printed across a continent was less to him than the memory of his grandfather, who freed his slaves in '58, fought from Manassas to Appomattox, knew Huxley and Spencer as light reading, and believed in caste only when it expressed the best of race." Henry thinks often about such things as race and manners, and he knows his Virginia heritage gave him a "quality of detachment peculiar to old stock" and in manners "a good form devoid of forms . . . based on kindness and consideration." With his wife's second infidelity he knew too that "he possessed again the masculine self he had handed over" to her. The question remained how to clean up the mess, particularly to retain custody of the two boys for himself. In his grandfather's time "the matter would have been simpler. Dueling pistols in the old Wharton meadow at dawn. It would be to Henry's advantage if things were like that today."

Still Henry had his own advantage. On a warm summer night the three figures in the love triangle agree to have their confrontation in Wiese's motorboat out on the quiet bay. Wiese pilots the boat out into the water, feeling fully in control. He is wealthy and possesses Choupette. He shuts off the motor and turns to Henry, forcefully demanding his capitulation. "Money is power," he says. "Money made this country, built its great and glorious cities, created its industries, covered it with an iron network of railroads. It's money that harnesses the forces of Nature, creates the machine and makes it go when money says go, and stop when money says stop." But out on the cool calm waters Nature mocks Wiese's money power. As he spoke, the "boat meandered in a placid little circle." Feeling victorious, Wiese tries to restart the motor, but he fails. "Without will or direction" the boat drifts rapidly out toward sea. Nature has them in its grip; and of the three Henry alone is in tune with Nature, for only he can swim. He offers to swim for aid if they give him custody of the children, and they capitulate to him. They do not know, as he knew, that a crosscurrent would soon have washed them safely to a shore. Henry's control over nature gives him greater power than mere money. Money, as Spengler said, represents the power of civilization, the strongest force within a culture in decline. But Henry Marston, with his manners and values derived from the past, his sense of rapport with the forces of Nature, can draw upon the power of an earlier American culture that in him still survived.

Again Henry leaves America for Europe, but he feels differently about his country now. He had found the answers to life's questions, after all, at home, and it was as if by his own hand he had made the power and the beauty of the old America come alive once more. "Watching the fading city, the fading shore, from the deck of the *Majestic,* he had a sense of overwhelming gratitude and of gladness that America was there, that under the ugly debris of industry, the rich land still pushed up, incorrigibly lavish and fertile, and that in the heart of the leaderless people the old generosities and devotions fought on, breaking out sometimes in fanaticism and excess, but indomitable and undefeated. There was a lost generation in the saddle at the moment, but it seemed to him that the men coming on, the men of the war, were better; and all his old feeling that America was a bizarre accident, a sort of historical sport, had gone forever. The best of America was the best of the world. . . . France was a land, England was a people, but America, having about it still that quality of the idea, was harder to utter—it was the graves at Shiloh and the tired, drawn, nervous faces of its great men, and the country boys dying in the Argonne for a phrase that was empty before their bodies withered. It was a willingness of the heart." [25]

Aboard his ship Henry encounters the eighteen-year-old girl he had met at the sea resort in France. She too is a Virginian; and together, no doubt, youth and maturity shall share their common sense of the past and knowledge of Nature. For the significance of its themes and the nature of its imagery "The Swimmers," among all the stories Fitzgerald wrote from 1927 to 1932, is the most important precursor to *Tender Is the Night.* In relation to Dick Diver's story it stands as "John Jackson's Arcady" stood to Gatsby's—so soon as Fitzgerald could conceive a tragic ending for "a willingness of the heart," his material for *Tender Is the Night* would be complete.

But tragedy came first to Fitzgerald in social and personal forms rather than in the forms of art. "The Swimmers" appeared in the *Post* on October 19, 1929. Four days later the New York stock market broke, and within a fortnight the great crash had wiped out the boom of the twenties. Far off in Paris, wrapped up in the problems of his novel and of his marriage, Fitzgerald gave no overt sign of recognition; but later stories showed how much, with his remarkable sensitivity to social moods, he was aware. When the crash came, however, he was completing yet another story of marital difficulties, "Two Wrongs." Fitzgerald's purpose in writing "Two Wrongs" can hardly be examined without stumbling once more into the autobiographical trap. For itself "Two Wrongs" is hardly of primary interest. But more than any other story Fitzgerald wrote about marriage it draws on the circumstances of his own. "Character is the greatest thing in the world," Bill McChesney says, but he possesses little and his wife Emmy possesses much.[26] A successful theatrical producer, McChesney ruins himself by drink and too much social climbing. At his most degraded moment, Emmy suffers a miscarriage. When she recovers she takes up ballet dancing as feverishly as Zelda Fitzgerald was even then pursuing it. Unable to rely on her husband, she assumes the dominant role. She succeeds as a dancer; he falls seriously ill with tuberculosis. She allows him to go west alone, and he gives himself up to die. Her wrong cancels out his earlier one; but his sad end calls forth little more than the moralistic pity of sentimental realism. Those who read fiction as autobiography may decide whether "Two Wrongs" is self-condemnation or self-pity; in any case it carried sadness and pessimism about marital problems as far as they could tolerably go. As the conditions of his own marriage grew worse at the end of 1929, Fitzgerald sought a different subject for the stories he was still regularly turning out.

In the first month of 1930 he dipped again into the genteel romantic past and came up with his answer. He created Josephine Perry, a female Basil Duke Lee, and she served him through five short stories that form a series bearing her name. "First Blood," the opening story, takes place in 1914 when Josephine is sixteen, "an unconscious pioneer of the generation that was destined to 'get out of hand.'"[27] The last story leaves Josephine in the midst of the First World War. The Josephine series may thus be considered a belated introduction to the postwar "flapper" stories, as the Basil Lee stories were a mature prologue to *This Side of Paradise*. But from the start the Josephine stories lacked the originality and distinctive tone that were the Basil stories' saving features. Though Josephine's adventures take place before the war and are meant to have a certain historical value, she is no more than another one of Fitzgerald's genteel romantic heroines, the rich, young, willful girls who populated his conventional magazine fiction of the early twenties. And while her series treated sex more openly than the earlier genteel stories, alongside teen-aged girls like Jenny Prince in "Jacob's Ladder" or Betsy D'Amido in "The Rough Crossing," Josephine looks pale. Moreover, Fitzgerald lost interest in Josephine long before he dropped her. After a North African vacation in February 1930, he wrote the second story, "A Nice Quiet Place," in March. The third, "A Woman with a Past," written in June, was balanced delicately between tolerant sympathy for Josephine and a cynical new note. For the two remaining the balance fell heavily on the caustic side. In "A Snobbish Story," written in September, Josephine is one of "the rich and powerful of the world," undermining art and creative promise; but the bohemian writers who represent the prewar "Chicago Renaissance" in arts and letters are mocked even more than she.[28] The last story, "Emotional Bankruptcy," was written nearly a year later, at a time when Fitzgerald's attitude toward his heroine had turned to open scorn. The phrase that later became famous almost as a personal symbol was coined not in self-analysis but as a farewell to Josephine. It is she who is emotionally bankrupt, all her love used up at eighteen, left only with "her vast, tragic apathy." [29] Rather than a historical introduction to the genteel romantic heroine, the Josephine stories, whatever Fitzgerald's original intention, ended up as a goodbye to all that.

On April 23, 1930, the day exactly six months after the New York stock market broke, Zelda Fitzgerald suffered a mental breakdown. But even her illness did not put an end to Fitzgerald's regular production of short stories; rather, the resulting medical expenses made it imperative for him to write more. During her fifteen months in a Swiss sanitarium, from June 1930 to August 1931, Fitzgerald wrote a dozen stories—a rate exceeded only in the first happy weeks after *This Side of Paradise* was accepted, and in the debt-ridden winter of 1922-23. Obviously his fiction suffered the effects of haste and of competing demands for his energy and concentration; but Zelda Fitzgerald's illness also must have struck him deeply. A new tough and cynical tone entered Fitzgerald's fiction; the old romantic promise remained, as a theme and as a plot line, but fulfillment as a possibility was gone. Even the happy endings he devised, falling back more and more on conventional formulas, were marred by a new harsh element. Good and bad stories alike became blurred, for the old and the new tones coming together in Fitzgerald's fiction did not mix effectively. As disorder reached a new extreme in Fitzgerald's life, disorder gradually became not only a theme of his fiction but also a problem in its form.

Following the April breakdown, Fitzgerald wrote "The Bridal Party" in May, a Josephine story in June, "One Trip Abroad" in August, and another Josephine story in September. "The Bridal Party" and "One Trip Abroad" are both better than average; they demonstrate quite clearly the direction Fitzgerald was moving and the problems he encountered. Written so soon after Zelda Fitzgerald's breakdown "The Bridal Party" poses a curious challenge for interpreters of Fitzgerald who look for autobiographical messages. For it replays once more the poor boy–rich girl love story, the story Fitzgerald wrote so often so many ways. This time the poor boy who lost the rich girl suddenly falls into wealth, and the rich boy who won the rich girl suddenly goes broke. But still the rich girl marries her newly poor fiancé; and the newly rich boy regards his loss less with bitterness and grief than detachment and relief. In tone the story is uncertain, lacking a single emotional thrust. Fitzgerald clearly wrote it with the feeling that the twenties were over, and it shows his first sense of disillusion with the twenties atmosphere. Yet still, in the newly poor boy's audacious spirit, he conveyed a certain grace —"This is our way of doing things. . . . Generous and fresh and free; a sort of Virginia-plantation hospitality, but at a different pace now, nervous as a ticker tape." [30]

As in "The Bridal Party," "One Trip Abroad" far more effectively sets a mood than portrays character. Put briefly, it is the story of an attractive young American couple who come into money, go to Europe, and fall victim to moral and physical decay. Through a series of set scenes—one step after another, as it were, on the way down—decline is created as an atmosphere; but Nicole and Nelson Kelly are not developed fully enough to give it substance. "They found, as so many have found, that the charm of idyllic interludes depends upon one person's 'giving the party'—which is to say, furnishing the background, the experience, the patience, against which the other seems to enjoy again the spells of pastoral tranquility recollected from childhood." Fitzgerald was to do far more with this observation; but, lacking personalities to fill it out, it slips on stage in "One Trip Abroad" only as a brief aside. The Kellys end up convalescing in Switzerland, where they see another couple who had shadowed them through each step of their fall. "It seemed like destiny that at last here in this desolate place they should know them, and watching, they saw other couples eyeing them in the same tentative way." [31] A flash of lightning strikes, and the Kellys see that the other couple, so attractive at the start and at the end so repulsive, are really themselves. Strangely, then, the others vanish. Fitzgerald had been unable to create characters commensurate with his sense of destiny, so he fell back instead on his old feeling for the supernatural.

Fitzgerald wrote two more stories in 1930. The first, "The Hotel Child," displays his new cynicism by mocking European sham nobility.[32] It was a third-rate effort of a kind he had not perpetrated since "Your Way and Mine" back in 1926. Yet he followed it with "Babylon Revisited," the story most readers consider his best. The creative process is still far too much a mystery for us to know how in the half year since Zelda Fitzgerald's breakdown he had moved from "The Bridal Party" to a Josephine story, "One Trip Abroad" to another Josephine story, and from the third-rate "Hotel Child" to the extraordinary "Babylon Revisited." Perhaps the obvious pique in "A Snobbish Story" and "The Hotel Child," their half-serious anger at Josephine and at the rich, at writers, at sham nobility, and at social climbers, cleansed his fiction momentarily of its conventional and genteel dross. In simplicity of style and in freedom from trickery— trickery like the grandfather's bequest of $250,000 in "The Bridal Party" or the supernaturalism of "One Trip Abroad"—"Babylon Revisited" was unlike any story Fitzgerald had written since "Jacob's Ladder" more than three years before. And yet it follows "The Bridal Party" and "One Trip Abroad" as a certain kind of culmination.

Together the three stories make up a three-act domestic tragedy. "The Bridal Party" sets in motion a marriage; "One Trip Abroad" conveys its decline; "Babylon Revisited" provides moral and dramatic resolution. As the last story opens Charlie Wales recalls a bachelor's party at the Ritz bar like the one Hamilton Rutherford threw in "The Bridal Party." Charlie and his wife Helen had quarreled like Nicole and Nelson Kelly, thrown away their money as freely as the Kellys, and Charlie, like Nelson, must convalesce in Switzerland. But if the three stories progressively develop the same material, still "Babylon Revisited" exists in a different realm of fiction from the other two. In "Babylon Revisited" Fitzgerald fused two qualities—a sense of the past and a passion for love—that had not come together since *The Great Gatsby*.

"Babylon Revisited" rests on a sense of historical process, on change, on the irrevocable passage of time: specifically on the deep gap already opened up between the feeling of the twenties and the new mood after the crash. Charlie Wales is himself a chronicler of time and change—the story opens with his inquiries, "And where's Mr. Campbell? . . . and George Hardt?" Yet most of all he chronicles his own past—the rich and drunken days when he had lost his wife to death and his daughter to Helen's sister as a ward. Then, he had spent his money "as an offering to destiny that he might not remember the things most worth remembering, the things that now he would always remember—his child taken from his control, his wife escaped to a grave in Vermont." Now, "he believed in character; he wanted to jump back a whole generation and trust in character again as the eternally valuable element." Then, he had wanted to run away from his own destiny; now, he would embrace it fully. But first he had to trace his way back through the recent past. "Babylon Revisited" takes shape through Charlie's deepening self-discovery.

But the lesson of his past was neither moralistic nor profound. He had spent too much, had used his head too little. He had been one of those "men who locked their wives out in the snow, because the snow of twenty-nine wasn't real snow. If you didn't want it to be snow, you just paid some money." At last he learns that no matter how much he lost in the crash, he "lost everything I wanted in the boom." So he had found out his own past; but nothing in the past can be recovered, and the movement of passion in "Babylon Revisited" comes from the counterpoint to Charlie's self-discovery, from a movement toward a new and open future. Charles wants Honoria, his daughter, back; the passion of his parental love for her provides the depth of meaning and moral focus. For Charlie is capable of comprehending his own past; but understanding only allows him to know why he is unable to control his present and his future. Knowledge and helplessness, together mingled, give the last line its great pathos: "He was absolutely sure Helen wouldn't have wanted him to be so alone." [33] "Babylon Revisited" is a beautiful story, that by simplicity and clarity of tone achieves in its form what *The Great*

Gatsby attained in the form of the novel—perpetual freshness, a richness enough to satisfy all.

Yet as 1931 opened "Babylon Revisited" was just another ripple in a seemingly unending stream of stories. During that year, when Fitzgerald three times crossed the Atlantic and twice the American continent, he wrote nine stories. No one, least of all Fitzgerald, has ever resurrected any from back numbers of the *Post* and *Redbook*, and no injustice has been done. In those days Fitzgerald lived in Lausanne while Zelda Fitzgerald was undergoing treatment not far away. By his own account he wrote then more in haste than he had for years, since the hectic early months of 1924 when he was struggling to clear away debts and get to Europe with write *Gatsby*. As a short-story writer he was far more competent in 1931 than he had been in 1924; nothing he wrote in the later year was quite so meretricious as several stories he had written earlier. But the line between good work and trash was no less clear. Except for the last and most caustic of Josephine stories, Fitzgerald's cynicism of 1930 was washed away in the artistic and emotional resolution of "Babylon Revisited." But the uncertainty that had first appeared in "The Bridal Party" and "One Trip Abroad" had grown into a dominant note that sounds through the serious stories Fitzgerald wrote in 1931.

"Indecision," the first story of that year, appropriately named the problem. Tommy McLane is a man who cannot decide between two women; but the story seems as evasive as Tommy McLane's firm choice. "A New Leaf" tells the story of an attractive drunk who can or will not reform himself. "What makes you think that people change their courses?" one character asks. "Sometimes they dry up or even flow into a parallel channel, but I've never known anybody to change." Dick Ragland breaks rather than bends—he dies at sea by falling overboard, perhaps a willed suicide, perhaps a drunken accident. Fitzgerald leaves it unclear, to the story's detriment. "Flight and Pursuit" is a realistic story about an emotionally bruised woman, but it marks the beginning of a falling back into the modes of conventional genteel fiction. Thereafter Fitzgerald wrote two inferior stories about the Depression. "Between Three and Four" opens significantly: "This happened nowadays, with everyone somewhat discouraged. A lot of less fortunate spirits cracked when money troubles came to be added to all the nervous troubles accumulated in the prosperity—

neurosis being a privilege of people with a lot of extra money. And some cracked merely because it was in the air, or because they were used to the great, golden figure of plenty standing behind them, as the idea of prudence and glory stands behind the French, and the idea of 'the thing to do' used to stand behind the English. Almost everyone cracked a little." But it ends up as a melodramatically moralistic story about a business suicide. "A Change of Class" is a conservative, sentimental story about a barber who goes from rags to riches in the boom and back again to rags; poor, he is happier.[34]

Fitzgerald wrote one more story on European soil, a story that holds up to judgment a decade and a generation, as if he knew it marked an end. "Six of One—" is indifferent art, but significant for its feelings and ideas. It is more an essay than a story, with an inadequate plot devised to carry along the more important thrust of meaning. The story opens in 1920. Barnes, a wealthy, older man, meets at a friend's house half a dozen young, rich boys about to enter Yale. "They left Barnes with a sense of having . . . gained a sharp impression of a whole style, a whole mode of youth, something different from his own less assured, less graceful generation, something unified by standards that he didn't know. He wondered vaguely what the standards of 1920 were, and whether they were worth anything—had a sense of waste, of much effort for a purely esthetic achievement. . . . He felt a sudden premonition that his generation in its years of effort had made possible a Periclean age, but had evolved no prospective Pericles. They had set the scene: was the cast adequate?" Barnes decides to run a test against this aristocracy of "young knights." He seeks out six outstanding seniors from the local public high school and arranges to pay their way through college, in an experiment to see how the naturally talented fare in competition with the richly endowed. The story ends a decade later. Only one of the rich boys has come through well, but Barnes was not willing to crow over it. "After all, any given moment has its value; it can be questioned in the light of after-events, but the moment remains. The young princes in velvet gathered in lovely domesticity around the queen amid the hush of rich draperies may presently grow up to be Pedro the Cruel or Charles the Mad, but the moment of beauty was there. Back there ten years, Schofield had seen his sons and their friends as samurai, as something shining and glorious and young, perhaps as something he had missed from his own youth. There was later a price to be paid by those boys, all too fulfilled, with the whole balance of their life pulled forward into their youth so that everything afterward would inevitably be anti-climax; these boys brought up as princes with none of the responsibilities of princes! Barnes didn't know how much their mothers might have had to do with it, what their mothers may have lacked." Of his own half-dozen the results had been more mixed, befitting their more varied backgrounds. "His own experiment—he didn't regret it, but he wouldn't have done it again. Probably it proved something, but he wasn't quite sure what. Perhaps that life is constantly renewed, and glamour and beauty make way for it; and he was glad that he was able to feel that the republic could survive the mistakes of a whole generation, pushing the waste aside, sending ahead the vital and the strong. Only it was too bad and very American that there should be all that waste at the top; and he felt that he would not live long enough to see it end, to see great seriousness in the same skin with great opportunity—to see the race achieve itself at last." [35] For all its inadequacies, "Six of One—" stands as one of Fitzgerald's significant forward steps—as "The Swimmers" had newly perceived his country, and "Babylon Revisited" the decade past, so "Six of One—" achieved a new perspective on his own generation's destiny, the downward curve of its flight from youth into maturity. More than ever, *Tender Is the Night* was in his grasp.

In September 1931, Fitzgerald returned home for good. Still he continued to write, almost as if short stories were a medieval religious mania, a perverted form of worship to his art. Early in the fall, back in America, he wrote two more. "The Freeze-Out" was a good story in the traditional genteel romantic mode, a serious story about generations: "None of the men of father's age have any principles"; "Diagnosis" was a weak one built around psychoanalysis. Five November and December weeks he worked in Hollywood, again without success. Returning to Montgomery, he re-created Hollywood's atmosphere and personalities in "Crazy Sunday," a story about a screenwriter's relations with a brilliant producer and his actress wife. In April 1932 he wrote two more. "Family in the Wind," set in Alabama, recounts how a tornado helps an alcoholic doctor give up the bottle and begin again. "What a Handsome Pair!" tells the sad story of a husband and wife who have similar skills and interests, and compete. Each story weakly treats a familiar theme. But in May, the month Fitzgerald moved to Baltimore, he dipped too deeply into the old formulas at last. That month he wrote "The Rubber Check," a conventional genteel story, with overtones of bitterness, that was his poorest story in half a decade. "Five years have rolled away from me," he wrote Maxwell Perkins in May, "and I can't decide exactly who I am, if anyone. . . ." [36] After an even two-score stories since June of 1927, after personal and artistic crises that had deepened his perception of his material even as they had largely frustrated his capacity to use it fully, Fitzgerald as a professional short-story writer had hit rock bottom. In June 1932, he began *Tender Is the Night.*

CHAPTER TEN

In the spring of 1932 F. Scott Fitzgerald prepared a long preliminary sketch for *Tender Is the Night*. "The novel should do this . . . ," he began his "General Plan," and though he borrowed the language of this self-injunction from another writer's book, in the context its imperative tone was wholly new and all his own.[1] He had been working on the novel, after all, for almost seven years. Back in 1925 he had proclaimed it would be "something really NEW in form, idea, structure—the model for the age that Joyce and Stein are searching for, that Conrad didn't find"; and thereafter this boast and this desire had weighed like a false crown upon his mind.[2] His conception of what he ought to write—a model for the age, yes, and also a work to vindicate himself after *The Great Gatsby*'s disappointing popular reception—held him like an anchor to plans and ambitions that were far removed from his own talent and inclination. He thought he would write a profound social novel, like *Crime and Punishment* or *An American Tragedy* built upon a murder; better yet, a matricide. In seven years he produced a string of sketches on American expatriate life in Europe in the twenties. As the gap widened between ambition and idea, between idea and accomplishment, as Ernest Hemingway grew in critical reputation and popular appeal far to overshadow him, Fitzgerald's novel faded more and more out of the realm of possibility. He worked on it during infrequent spurts, a little in 1925 and 1926, a brief flurry in 1929, a last effort in 1930 to salvage perhaps something from the hopes of half a decade. Six separate versions of the novel have been counted through these years before Fitzgerald wrote his "General Plan"; hundreds of discarded manuscript pages survive from these early drafts. Yet with all this effort and frustration, *Tender Is the Night* was not truly begun until Fitzgerald cut loose from his grand conceptions and vanished hopes and specified "The novel should do this."

After seven years of difficulties, Fitzgerald at last committed himself in the "General Plan" to ground his novel, not on ambition, but on emotion. "Whether it's something that happened twenty years ago or only yesterday," Fitzgerald in an essay explained the lesson of those years, "I must start out with an emotion—one that's close to me and that I can understand." [3] To approach the fullest meanings of *The Great Gatsby* it had been necessary to recognize its long foreground of development in Fitzgerald's mind and art. But for *Tender Is the Night* one must rather lay aside the long years of occasional labor and dwindling hopes that comprise the history of the novel from 1925 to 1932. Sitting down in 1932 to write his "General Plan," the author freshly conceived his novel, and prepared to write a work of art completely new.

II

"The novel should do this," Fitzgerald began his sketch: "Show a man who is a natural idealist, a spoiled priest, giving in for various causes to the ideas of the haute bourgeoisie, and in his rise to the top of the social world losing his idealism, his talent and turning to drink and dissipation. Background one in which the leisure class is at their truly most brilliant and glamorous such as Murphys." [4] It is difficult now to read these lines as Fitzgerald meant them, for "spoiled priest" so long has served as metaphor and touchstone for his own career. In its application to Fitzgerald, though, "spoiled priest" has lost its precise meaning as the term describing a candidate for the priesthood who failed to take his vows. Rather it has taken on a sentimental aura, as if it described a Roman Catholic moralist more moral than the Church, a holy renegade, the sinner so much sweeter than the saint. Of course, as Fitzgerald used the term in his sketch—and even more as he created the character of Richard Diver for *Tender Is the Night*—it does quite clearly suggest all that and more. But Fitzgerald also called his character a "natural idealist," a phrase far less suggestive and therefore far more useful for an understanding of his intentions in the new novel. For Richard Diver turned out to be the son of a Protestant clergyman; and in his character as a "natural idealist" he is less a "spoiled priest," an Irish romantic like Joyce's Stephen Daedalus, than he is that central figure from Fitzgerald's youth and from his fiction, the genteel American romantic hero.

From the beginning of his career Fitzgerald had used the genteel romantic hero almost as his mannequin, a figure he could dress up in each of the literary and intellectual styles he tried. In most of his popular short stories he took the figure as he came, fully clothed in the moral and social values of late-nineteenth-century genteel America. There he was the deserving young man who by his strong will and clever imagination nicely preserves social stability while he fulfills romantic dreams. But in his novels Fitzgerald tried to replace the genteel modes with more modern styles of life. Amory Blaine of *This Side of Paradise* broke with genteel society in order to commit himself to a constructive individualism; Anthony Patch of *The Beautiful and Damned* found nothing to commit himself to and fell victim to fashionable indifference. At that point Fitzgerald had stripped himself of either negative or positive alternatives to the genteel romantic hero; and it was then that he was able to work his way through to a conception in *The Great Gatsby* of the genteel romantic hero as a creative, tragic figure. With Jay Gatsby the genteel romantic hero attained his apotheosis. No wonder Fitzgerald was anxious thereafter to free himself from a stereotype he had explored and re-created seemingly to its artistic limits. He had not completely turned his back on stereotypes, though, as his prologue to "The Rich Boy"—"There are no types, no plurals"—might have indicated.[5] For even before he had completed "The Rich Boy," he had given his new novel the tentative title *Our Type*. But if he planned to create stereotypes in his novel at least he was working with new ones.

Over the five years he worked on the novel, however, Fitzgerald was never able to bring his new type precisely into focus. What emerges from the discarded manuscripts is a figure who suggests a modern counterpart to the myth of Edgar Allan Poe. Francis Melarky, the central character of *Our Type*, was a Southerner who had been dismissed from West Point, then worked as a technician in Hollywood. Traveling abroad with his mother, Francis first is beaten up during a drunken brawl in Rome, then falls in with an American social set on the Riviera where, unable to work, he dips deeper into habits of waste and dissipation. He falls in love with the wife of a man whose social manner he greatly admires. At that point the manuscript ends. According to Fitzgerald's plans, Francis would then have suffered a nervous breakdown, and, taunted into rage by his domineering mother, he would have killed her. The new type, from this account, was to have been a temperamental, frustrated artist (or pseudo-artist, or technician of the arts), wasted by drink and sloth, mentally broken and a little mad, until finally he became a matricide.[6]

But a precise characterization of Francis Melarky—that curious name, combining autobiography with Irish nonsense—was hardly ever Fitzgerald's major interest in his work in progress. "*Our Type* is about several things," Fitzgerald wrote in August 1925 to Maxwell Perkins, "one of which is an intellectual murder on the Leopold-Loeb idea. Incidentally it is about Zelda and me and the hysteria of last May and June in Paris."[7] From the first, then, Fitzgerald planned to combine his story of a murder with a picture of a social setting and atmosphere. A few weeks later he received a jolt that, from our retrospective knowledge of his failure to complete the novel, could only have placed the entire conception of a murder-matricide novel in doubt. In December 1925, Theodore Dreiser published *An American Tragedy*. Within two weeks the novel had sold more than 13,000 copies, and reviewers were greeting it as the greatest American novel of the decade. Dreiser's popular and critical success with a murder novel on a social theme left Fitzgerald holding an empty bag of expectations he may well have suspected could never now be filled. "In a certain sense," he wrote Perkins in February 1926, "my plot is not unlike Dreiser's in the American Tragedy. At first this worried me but now it doesn't for our minds are so different."[8] No matter how much his plot resembled Dreiser's, Fitzgerald knew his hero would be a far different type from Dreiser's Clyde Griffith. Clyde rather was much closer in character to James Gatz–Jay Gatsby, aspiring young men who shared the same poor, Midwestern background. But even as he defended his conception against competition from Dreiser, Fitzgerald was slowly letting it slip away. Early in 1926 he came up with an alternative title, *The World's Fair*, suggesting an emphasis on the place and the atmosphere far more than on character. And in what he actually wrote on the novel, mood and setting play far more important roles than does the character Francis Melarky. Fitzgerald apparently never wrote the scenes in which Melarky was to be mad or murderous, and in the scenes he did write Melarky appears primarily as a bystander and observer of a wider social scene. After he had just completed a novel that T. S. Eliot called "the first step that American fiction has taken since Henry James," Fitzgerald seemed on his way to writing a novel about Americans abroad, filtered through the eyes of an involved observer, much as James had done in *Roderick Hudson* and in *Daisy Miller*.[9] Though the idea of a matricide remained until Fitzgerald discarded the entire project, the concept of a new character had long since disappeared. From the early manuscripts to the "General Plan" for *Tender Is the Night*, Fitzgerald shifted from a novel essentially about American expatriate life to a novel about the genteel American hero abroad. *Our Type* had never really been his type.

The genteel romantic hero in one of his disguises played a supporting role in the new novel almost from its conception; and true to his type he seemed to liven up his part and dominate the scene. For a month in the late summer of 1925 Fitzgerald had stayed with Gerald and Sara Murphy at their Villa America near Antibes, which they had established as a social center for expatriate American writers, musicians, and artists. When Fitzgerald had informed Perkins in August of his plans for the new novel, his vision of the American expatriate atmosphere was "Zelda and me and the hysteria of last May and June in Paris." [10] But by the time he actually began to write he had shifted the scene to a Riviera setting modeled on the Murphys'. In the novel the Murphys were re-created first as the Rorebacks and then as Seth and Dinah Piper—like Henry James before him Fitzgerald was now more openly than ever trying out symbolic names. Seth and Dinah were to be throwbacks or "roarbacks" to an earlier, more graceful world of manners in America, or "pipers" leading the American expatriate colony back to that lost lovely world;

and as Fitzgerald had conceived his work as a novel of manners, the Pipers more and more engrossed his creative interest and attention. In his novel he was never willing completely to grant the validity of their style or their world, though Francis Melarky fell deeply under their spell and as a principal character faded slowly into their shadow. He appears in the discarded manuscripts less as a character in his own right and more as an observing chorus, a Nick Carraway to their Gatsby. He was in love with Dinah Piper and wholly an admirer of Seth, whose step in Melarky's eyes "was quick and alert as if he had just come from some great doings and was hurrying on toward others, organizer of gaiety, master of a richly encrusted, eso- teric happiness. His hat was a grand hat and he carried a heavy stick and thin yellow gloves. Francis thought what a good time everyone would have who was with him tonight, and the aura of Seth's good taste cooled his blood for a moment. 'Yes,' he said to himself, 'they're the most attractive people in the world. Absolutely perfect.' " [11] Yet Fitzgerald did not want the reader to take Melarky's point of view for granted. In another portion of the manuscript Abe Grant says to Francis, "Young man, don't get the idea that Seth asks so little. He's lived all his life on better minds than himself. There's not an idea or an attitude of his that you can't trace to somebody or some- thing—the St. Marks School–Harvard–Porcellian attitude, Legendre the painter, and Parkinson, the works of Coué which is probably the only book he ever read, my ideas about music until somebody put him on to Antheil." [12] Neither man was to be accepted completely at face value; each had particular needs and motives which limited his personal point of view. But Fitzgerald was never able in the early manuscripts to go deeper into the strengths and weaknesses of the Pipers' social style. Toward the Pipers he lacked at this point his own organizing point of view; and his conception of the novel, tugged at on one side by the requirements of the matricide plot and on the other by his growing interest in the characters of Seth and Dinah Piper, gradually was pulled to pieces. The blame rests squarely on the shoulders of Seth Piper, the genteel romantic hero in a new incarnation.

For more than five years Seth Piper was a dead end, a character whose immense significance Fitzgerald could intuit but not yet grasp. But his conventional short fiction, which he began writing again in the summer of 1927, provided him surprisingly with a multiplicity of open ends, and there he experimented with the genteel romantic hero in a variety of roles. As variations on the old and ever-present theme of the genteel romantic hero, where the relative success or failure of one story matters less than the shape of styles and meanings in the stories as a group, Fitzgerald's short fiction from *The Great Gatsby* to *Tender Is the Night* falls into strikingly new and different patterns. It was as if, after creating in *The Great Gatsby* his tragic vision of the genteel romantic hero, Fitzgerald had to break it up into its parts and test the parts again before he would try to put it together once more in *Tender Is the Night*. Two stereotypes of his hero dominate the stories, stereotypes divided perfectly, in the stories that matter, along chronological lines. The first stereotype takes shape like a hemisphere around the pole of Gatsby, the second is formed, from this perspective, as a hemisphere around the pole of Richard Diver; on either side of the equatorial line stand "The Swimmers" and "Two Wrongs," two stories Fitzgerald wrote during the summer and fall of 1929.

The genteel romantic stereotype that formed around the pole of Gatsby was a man who had attained prominence and power in life, who had succeeded, moreover, as a businessman or a football hero, as a movie star or a playwright, because he possessed exceptional qualities of stability and self-control. But as he comes alive in Fitzgerald's fictional world a woman also enters his life, a woman who by design or not upsets its careful balance. Passion flares up, and threatens disorder to the whole organized social and moral structure of the hero's life. Passion passes, or is unfulfilled, and he is left to restore his order as best he can. Each of the seven versions of this figure manages one way or another to repair the rent and survive the crisis. In the most memorable of the stories, "Jacob's Ladder," Jacob Booth substitutes the synthetic passion of the movies for the real passion of which life has frustrated him. Two other single men, Dolly Harlan in "The Bowl" and Tom Squires in "At Your Age," reassert stability respectively by two different forms of the conventional happy ending, one by replacing a false woman with a true one, the other by a sentimental renunciation. Three others, Bill Frothingham in "The Love Boat," George Hannaford in "Magnetism," and Adrian Smith in "The Rough Crossing," all married men whose marriages seem momentarily at the breaking point, restore an equilibrium that seems no more than fragile and temporary. The last of these figures, Henry Marston in "The Swimmers," brings this genteel romantic stereotype to a climax and slightly alters it. By solving the crisis in his life Henry does not simply restore his old order, he builds a new one. All seven of his figures are men of will and creative imagination, in conformity with Fitzgerald's older stereotype of the genteel romantic hero; but they imagine love as a means to some more remote and essential end, unlike the earlier conventional heroes who looked upon love as an end in itself, a reward for success in their clever maneuvers. In these seven stories imagination creates disorder, and the power of the will must be used to paste order together again. Only Henry Marston of these seven has at his disposal the natural and social resources to create a brand new order; and "The Swimmers" was the last of Fitzgerald's short stories in which the hero was a man of will.

The second genteel romantic stereotype, in the stories after "The Swimmers," was a man who either lacked will or had lost it. "Two Wrongs," the story Fitzgerald wrote right after "The Swimmers," represents the transition. Bill McChesney begins as a man of will, but his imagination—which took specific form as excessive drinking and social climbing—brings about a family tragedy. Thereafter he renounces his will and resigns himself to approaching death. This new stereotype portrays a figure who either is unable to exercise will, or fails when he tries to do so. What frustrates him is the past—past attitudes, past habits, past misdeeds. Gatsby wanted to repeat the past but could not; now it is as if the hero *must* repeat the past because he is powerless to alter its consequences. Michael Curley of "The Bridal Party," though he became rich, seemed to prefer the attitudes he had formed in his days of poverty. Tommy McLane of "Indecision" cannot choose between a young girl and an older woman with a past. Nelson Kelly of "One Trip Abroad" and Dick Ragland of "A New Leaf" were trapped by habits they had formed and could not break; there was no such thing as a "new leaf." Charlie Wales of "Babylon Revisited" had succeeded in reforming himself; but past misdeeds still exerted control over his will. The past triumphed completely in "Crazy Sunday," where Joel Coles is frustrated not by his own past but by memories of other pasts; the willful hero was the victim, finally, of history.

In "The Swimmers," in which the last of the willful heroes appeared, history had come to his aid as a guide and a resource; in "Crazy Sunday," where Joel Coles was a man unable to act by his own will, history proved his undoing. Fitzgerald's attitude toward history in the stories he wrote after 1927 was shaped by his reading of Oswald Spengler's *Decline of the West*. Spengler provided a historical and philosophical underpinning for Fitzgerald's pervasive concern with money; it was the emphasis on money, Spengler said, that gave contemporary civilization its distinctive character, and made it different from the culture of the past. Henry Marston in "The Swimmers" had drawn on the past for his powers of will; in his person historical culture overcame the money values of the new civilization.

But curiously Fitzgerald could not envision Henry carrying on this unity of power and value in the country where it was forged. Understanding and loving his country as never before, Henry nevertheless at the end of the story returns to Europe. Though his victory had been real, a triumph of culture over money-oriented civilization, the future that Fitzgerald created for him was evasively sentimental: so much insight gained, so much power expended, for the possibility of romance with an eighteen-year-old girl. In "The Swimmers" Fitzgerald had seen a way for the willful hero to overcome the power of money, but he had not been able to envision a social setting in which the genteel hero effectively could live. Henry Marston's new order was real, but irrelevant. Thereafter in Fitzgerald's stories the genteel romantic hero hardly put up a fight against money, even when the money was his own. He had succumbed at last to the forces of history.

In "Six of One—," the last story Fitzgerald wrote in Europe, he stood back as it were and looked down on his generation from the long, historical view. They had had to pay a price, the older man muses. Youth gave them too much. But though it gave them great opportunities it gave them no responsibilities, and so in later life they lacked the seriousness to accomplish much. They had been wasted; yet the old man still feels that the republic can push them aside and go on. From Fitzgerald's first response to Spengler early in 1927 to the last story he wrote before ending his expatriation, the feeling had grown in him not that America had failed the genteel romantic hero, but that in some way the genteel romantic hero had failed his own American race. Yet as the old man in "Six of One—" said, "After all, any given moment has its value; it can be questioned in the light of after-events, but the moment remains. . . . the moment of beauty was there."[13] As his concentration shifted between the glamor of Seth Piper's life in the uncompleted novel and the failures of the genteel heroes in his stories, Fitzgerald gradually was becoming aware of a way to bring the two, the beauty and the failure, together in one social and individual unity. But the path was opened for him, not by his renewed interest in history, but by a newly developed interest in the literary psychology of D. H. Lawrence and the abnormal psychology of Carl Gustav Jung.

Spengler's historical perspective, after all, could give Fitzgerald a context for the decline of the genteel romantic hero but could tell him little about the content, the manner, and the movement of the fall. "He's lived all his life on better minds than himself," as Abe Grant said of Seth Piper in *The World's Fair*, trying to puncture Francis Melarky's inflated vision of the genteel hero. "There's not an idea or an attitude of his that you can't trace to somebody or something." Had Fitzgerald been satisfied with Henry Marston's triumph in "The Swimmers" he could have fused it with the expatriate social setting of the novel and permitted Henry and his girl to live there on the Riviera, happily ever after. Dick Diver in *Tender Is the Night* may be recognized, in his personal qualities, as a combination of Henry Marston's rapport with the past and with nature, and of Seth Piper's social grace and skill. But Dick Diver does not live on the Riviera happily ever after. For an understanding of the internal flaws of his genteel romantic hero, Fitzgerald had to look, not to history, but to studies of individual minds and emotions.

The circumstances of Fitzgerald's new interest in psychology are obviously connected with Zelda Fitzgerald's mental breakdown and with his subsequent effort to understand her difficulties and to assist in her cure. But though his interests came eventually to focus on Zelda's illness it is not quite clear whether they originated with it. "Then Powell Fowler and his wedding party arrived," Fitzgerald wrote to Maxwell Perkins in May 1930, "and I got unfortunately involved in dinners and nightclubs and drinking; then Zelda got a sort of nervous breakdown from overwork and consequently I haven't done a line of work or written a letter for twenty-one days." But apparently he had found time to read. "Have you read *The Story of San Michele* and D. H. Lawrence's *Fantasia of the Unconscious?*" he immediately went on. "Don't miss either of them." [14] There is sufficient evidence that Fitzgerald read both these books and that they were as important in his development toward *Tender Is the Night* as was his concern over his wife's illness.

The Story of San Michele hardly ranks in importance with Lawrence's *Fantasia*, or with Fitzgerald's later reading of Jung, yet it may have provided Fitzgerald with a point of view he might not have attained otherwise. *The Story of San Michele* was the autobiography of a Swedish doctor, Alex Munthe, who practiced on a fashionable clientele in Paris and later founded a clinic on Capri.[15] On its publication in 1929 the book became an astonishing best-seller in England and America, and with hindsight one can readily recognize the qualities that made it popular: Munthe's courage and his modesty, his adventures and his love of animals, his mysticism and his form of popular psychology. Perhaps more important, he was also a talented spinner of yarns. Fitzgerald apparently read the book early in 1930, but in April 1931, in a letter to John Peale Bishop, he compared one of Bishop's stories unfavorably to Munthe's autobiography, " 'Death and Young Desire' doesn't come off," he wrote, "—as for instance the handling of the same theme in *The Story of San Michele*." [16] For Fitzgerald then, *The Story of San Michele* possessed at least some of the qualities of art. But what may have mattered more to him about Munthe's story was that a book about a doctor could be so immensely popular. In the classic American novels, medical men had been villains and destroyers. Chillingworth in Hawthorne's *Scarlet Letter* and Sloper in Henry James's *Washington Square* were cast as cold-hearted men of science, insensitive to human values. Sinclair Lewis's *Arrowsmith* had broken through this stereotype in 1925; but *Arrowsmith* was published a month before *Gatsby*, and for competitive reasons, as well as for reasons of literary taste, Fitzgerald regarded it with disdain.[17] In the course of Zelda's illness, Fitzgerald came to know many physicians, and it was this firsthand experience which underlay his portrait of Dick Diver as a medical man. Yet Munthe's book, more than any other, had shown him that a well-told story about a doctor could be enormously popular, and it may have been with Munthe's success in mind that he made his hero in the new novel a physician, and called the book at one point in its composition, *Doctor Diver's Holiday.*

How Fitzgerald came, early in 1930, to read D. H. Lawrence is far less clear. *Fantasia of the Unconscious,* published originally in 1922, was neither recent nor popular. It is unlikely that Fitzgerald had previously read much, if any, of Lawrence's fiction, and a single reference to Lawrence in his letters of the twenties suggested that he knew Lawrence only as an influence on Sherwood Anderson, as the romantic naturalist of *Sons and Lovers.*[18] Yet whether he was led to the *Fantasia* by chance or by someone's suggestion, the choice was one of extraordinary importance for the development of *Tender Is the Night.* Lawrence and Fitzgerald were never so far apart in their fundamental views—particularly as critics of Victorian values —as their styles of life and the nature of their fiction might suggest; and *Fantasia of the Unconscious* focused even more than *Studies in Classic American Literature* on the psychological and moral issues in American culture which at the beginning of 1930 Fitzgerald himself was striving to master.

From Fitzgerald's perspective, *Fantasia of the Unconscious* was most significantly a study of the relationship between creativity and sex. To Lawrence, Freud's emphasis on sex as the root of human behavior was a fine attack on orthodox religious idealism, but to raise sex, through scientific logic, to the status of a first cause seemed to Lawrence equally as foolish as orthodox religion. There was a motive in human behavior, Lawrence said, more important and more dynamic than sex.

> And what is this other, greater impulse? It is the desire of the human male to build a world: not "to build a world for you, dear"; but to build up out of his own self and his own belief and his own effort something wonderful. Not merely something useful. Something wonderful. Even the Panama Canal would never have been built *simply* to let ships through. It is the pure disinterested craving of the human male to make something wonderful, out of his own head and his own self, and his own soul's faith and delight, which starts everything going. This is the prime motivity. And the motivity of sex is subsidiary to this: often directly antagonistic.

So for Lawrence "the essentially religious or creative motive is the first motive for all human activity." The aim of Lawrence's psychological theory was to find a synthesis for creative idealism and the sex drive. The trouble with modern society was that it held sex and idealism separate at two poles.

> Sex as an end in itself is a disaster: a vice. But an ideal purpose which has no roots in the deep sea of passionate sex is a greater disaster still. And now we have only these two things: sex as a fatal goal, which is the essential theme of modern tragedy: or ideal purpose as a deadly parasite. Sex passion as a goal in itself always leads to tragedy. There must be the great purposive inspiration always present. But the automatic ideal-purpose is not even a tragedy, it is a slow humiliation and sterility.[19]

For Lawrence the consequences of this tragic situation were directly felt in the relations between the sexes. In his polar theory the normal poles of action and emotion had been in modern life reversed. "In fulfilling the Christian love ideal . . . Man has assumed the gentle, all-sympathetic role, and woman has become the energetic party, with the authority in her hands. The male is the sensitive, sympathetic nature, the woman the active, effective, authoritative. So that the male acts as the passive, or recipient pole of attraction, the female as the active, positive, exertive pole, in human relations." Though man remains the doer and thinker, Lawrence maintains, "he is so only in the service of emotional and procreative woman. His highest moment is now the emotional moment when he gives himself up to the woman, when he forms the perfect answer for her great emotional and procreative asking. . . . Man becomes the emotional party, woman the positive and active. Man begins to show strong signs of the peculiarly strong passive sex desire, the desire to be taken, which is considered characteristic of woman." And nowhere is this crisis more acute than in America, which lacks an organic class structure to protect against the social anarchy caused by this reversal of polar roles. "Americans must make a choice," Lawrence wrote. "It is a choice between belief in man's creative, spontaneous soul, and man's automatic power of production and reproduction. It is a choice between serving *man,* or woman. It is a choice between yielding the soul to a leader, leaders, or yielding only to the woman, wife, mistress, or mother." [20]

Lawrence's description of modern sexual relations corresponds closely with the conventional patterns of genteel romantic behavior that Fitzgerald followed in his popular stories and re-created in *The Great Gatsby* as national myth and tragedy. Though the genteel formula emphasized male willfulness, Lawrence made clear that its form of willfulness was simply one aspect of the man's more fundamental subjugation by the woman; and it may have been that Lawrence's emphasis on the male's passive role influenced Fitzgerald in his stories between 1930 and 1932 to deny the genteel romantic hero the powers of his independent will. Lawrence sharpened and reinforced Fitzgerald's perception of the nature of the situation. But Fitzgerald had supplied his own social explanation, and Lawrence provided him with no additional psychological explanation for it. Even after reading Lawrence, Fitzgerald had yet to find a firm psychological foundation for the treatment of the genteel romantic hero he had been moving toward in his art. It remained for the tragedy of Zelda Fitzgerald's mental illness to put him in contact with the psychological theories of Carl Gustav Jung.

Jung was in the American air in the twenties as Freud was, and Fitzgerald had not been unaware of either. But his relationship to the psychoanalytic fad among literary intellectuals suggests once more how deep his roots were in the past, how closely he stood, in the decade he was supposed to have symbolized, to conservative, old-fashioned values. In one of his stories that best represents conventional genteel formulas, "The Unspeakable Egg," written in 1924, a New York psychoanalyst is satirized as a pompously ineffectual figure. In "The Adjuster" the psychiatrist Doctor Moon reminds the heroine of her human and social responsibilities, and thus serves as an instrument of conventional social control. Yet Fitzgerald's unwillingness to adopt the modish uses of psychoanalytic theory implies neither indifference nor lack of awareness. Just as Fitzgerald came belatedly to the modern movement in the arts, approaching it from his own perspective to serve his own artistic purposes, so he came later than others to grasp the significance of psychoanalysis, but he grasped it significantly on his own terms and with his own aims firmly in mind.

In Fitzgerald's preference for Jung over Freud there is an internal consistency that hindsight may explain—Jung's emphasis on the col-

lective unconscious, on the social rather than the biological foundations of human behavior, corresponds both with Fitzgerald's social
awareness and with the historical view of human cultures Fitzgerald
had learned from Oswald Spengler. But at that time Fitzgerald's
interest in Jung developed more likely by chance. From Paris, where
Zelda Fitzgerald suffered her mental breakdown, she was moved to
a clinic in Switzerland. When her case was diagnosed as schizophrenia, she was admitted to a sanitarium at Prangins, near Geneva.
At Prangins she was under the care of Dr. Oscar Forel, a psycho-
therapist closely connected with the Zurich school of psychiatry, of
which Jung was the leader. At one point Forel called in for con-
sultations the psychiatrist Eugen Bleuler, the second most important
figure of the Zurich school and one of the pioneers in the diagnosis
of schizophrenia. Moreover, Bleuler had been one of the founders
of the Swiss movement for clinical treatment of alcoholism, a type
of therapy that the Kellys experienced in "One Trip Abroad" and
Charlie Wales in "Babylon Revisited," both written after Zelda entered Prangins. During the fifteen months his wife remained at
Prangins, Fitzgerald lived mainly in Lausanne, where he occasionally met people who were studying with the Zurich school of psy-
chiatrists. In Lausanne, sometime in 1931, Fitzgerald obtained a
copy of Jung's *Psychological Types*. He also came to own Jung's
Psychology of the Unconscious.[21]
    What Fitzgerald learned from his reading in the works of Jung
and in his conversations with Jung's students is a matter open only
to speculation. Possibly his own interest in social types—his search
for "Our Type" that had eluded his reach for nearly five years—led
him to Jung's general descriptions in *Psychological Types*. There
Jung makes his famous distinction between extraverted and intro-
verted types and describes their various forms and characteristics.
To claim that the character of Dick Diver was drawn out of Jung's
typology obviously distorts Fitzgerald's mode of artistic creation.
And yet it is difficult not to believe that he gained from Jung organizing and shaping insights into the psychology of his genteel romantic hero. "Hysteria is, in my view," Jung wrote, "by far the most
frequent neurosis with the extraverted type. The classical example
of hysteria is always characterized by an exaggerated rapport with
the members of his circle, and a frankly imitatory accommodation

to surrounding conditions. A constant tendency to appeal for interest and to produce impressions upon his milieu is a basic trait of the hysterical nature. A correlate to this is his proverbial suggestibility, his pliability to another person's influence." [22] Fitzgerald was forced to take an interest in abnormal psychology in an effort to understand his wife's illness and his own relation to it; but he was able also to deepen his perceptions on psychological types and to see their connection with the social types whose nature he was striving to grasp in his new novel. Nothing better demonstrates Fitzgerald's developed perception than his readiness, in the "General Plan" he wrote for the novel in 1932, to take on for the first time as his subject the psychological disintegration of the genteel romantic hero.

"I believe that if one is interested in the world into which willy-nilly one's children will grow up," Fitzgerald wrote to Margaret Turnbull in September 1932, as he was beginning *Tender Is the Night,* "the most accurate data can be found in the European leaders, such as Lawrence, Jung, and Spengler, and after that in the very sincere young Americans emerging one by one. . . ." [23] Fitzgerald had found in Lawrence, Jung, and Spengler the "data" for a deeper understanding of his own social and fictional world; and at last, with his new novel under way, he was once again placing himself among the very sincere young American writers whose insight into the future world he considered second almost to none.

III

The novel Fitzgerald outlined early in 1932 contained one intellectual element that is difficult to find in the completed version of *Tender Is the Night.* The hero was to have been a "communist-liberal-idealist, a moralist in revolt." [24] After himself succumbing to the old order, he was as a final gesture to have sent his son to the Soviet Union for his education. Like so many other American writers of his generation, Fitzgerald, in the aftermath of the Great Depression, discovered Karl Marx. "Scott reads Marx," Zelda Fitzgerald wrote to John Peale Bishop while Fitzgerald was writing *Tender Is the Night,* "—I read the cosmological philosophers. The brightest moments of our day are when we get them mixed up." [25] Fitzgerald read at least *The Communist Manifesto,* in which he marked passages relating to the bourgeois class.[26] The language of the "General Plan" quite clearly indicates that a Marxist approach to social class gave Fitzgerald his final perspectives on the economic and class origins of genteel romantic heroism—his final perspectives, but hardly his full perspective.

Fitzgerald's first working title for the new novel was *The Drunkard's Holiday,* a title that bears little relation to the finished work, unless it means to suggest both the psychological flaws of the hero and the social milieu in which they were revealed—his "giving in for various causes to the ideas of the haute Bourgeoisie," before his final downfall. When his manuscript was typed up he changed the title to *Doctor Diver's Holiday: A Romance,* which seems to indicate not so much a statement of form—the form of the nineteenth-century romance, as opposed to the novel—as an assertion of mood, a claim for the beauty he had created as well as the social realism of his hero's decline. Perhaps it was this perception of beauty within or beyond his realism that led Fitzgerald back at the last moment to John Keats, the poet whom Yeats in *A Vision* used as his example of the obsessed man, the man in whose poetry there is "an exaggerated sensuousness that compels us to remember the pepper on the tongue as though that were his symbol." [27] From the "Ode to a Nightingale," where faery lands are as forlorn and sad and fraught with danger as are real lands, he took his epigraph and his title:

> Already with thee! tender is the night,
>
> . . .
>
> But here there is no light,
> Save what from heaven is with the breezes blown
> Through verdurous glooms and winding mossy ways.

Tender Is the Night is the story of a faery land like Keats's faery land, a land Fitzgerald learned at last to render with exaggerated sensuousness and with pepper on the tongue, a land created by romantic imagination, but the scene, as Lionel Trilling writes of Keats, "of an erotic fulfillment which implies castration." [28]

IV

The faery land of *Tender Is the Night* is veiled at first in mystery; only slowly it emerges as a land created by one man. Rosemary Hoyt and her mother enter it as if they entered on a silent theater stage, and the reader senses the theatrical quality of the setting before he learns that Rosemary herself is a motion-picture actress. In the first two paragraphs the scene is set—a quiet, cool, pastoral scene, against which its one significant feature is twice sharply set off: the "short dazzling beach," the "bright tan prayer rug of a beach." [29] Gausse's Hotel, set among the tall palms and dark pines and "the cupolas of a dozen old villas rotted like water lilies," forms the backdrop, the painted scene behind the stage. "Of all the region only the beach stirred with activity" (4); the beach alone was the stage. Settled in at the hotel Rosemary passes through the beach to swim in the sea and then re-enters it from the open side, from the audience side, where she can see the stage as a spectator might see it a moment before she becomes a participant.

The stage was divided between the dark people and the light, and as a light-skinned uninitiate herself Rosemary first encounters the lights—Campion and Dumphry, Mrs. Abrams, the McKiskos— who are, like her, outside the mystery, left wondering and guessing. But Rosemary yearns toward the dark group, mostly Americans but "unlike the Americans she had known of late," presided over by a "fine man in a jockey cap." Watching them she begins to sense the theatrical nature of the setting. "After a while she realized that the man in the jockey cap was giving a quiet little performance for this group; he moved gravely about with a rake, ostensibly removing gravel and meanwhile developing some esoteric burlesque held in suspension by his grave face. Its faintest ramification had become hilarious, until whatever he said released a burst of laughter" (6). The man in the jockey cap was playing the role then of a comedian —or of a clown.

Gradually under the sun all that lay offstage became unreal to her. "It seemed that there was no life anywhere in all this expanse of coast except under the filtered sunlight of those umbrellas, where something went on amid the color and the murmur" (11). Rosemary falls asleep in the sun, and wakes to find her legs burned crimson, already on her way to becoming one of the dark. She is alone on the beach with the man in the jockey cap. He is cleaning off the beach. She asks him the time, and he tells her. "They faced the seascape together momentarily. 'It's not a bad time,' said Dick Diver. 'It's not one of the worst times of the day.' He looked at her and for a moment she lived in the bright blue world of his eyes, eagerly and confidently. Then he shouldered his last piece of junk and went up to his car, and Rosemary came out of the water, shook out her peignoir and walked up to the hotel" (12). By the end of the first scene on the beach Rosemary was acting out her own part. Ceasing to be a spectator, she had also ceased to see.

Rosemary Hoyt's angle of vision dominates the first book of *Tender Is the Night,* but hers is not the only point of view, and the reader is forewarned to take it with its proper grain of salt. She is introduced as a girl "who had magic in her pink palms and her cheeks lit to a lovely flame, like the thrilling flush of children after their cold baths in the evening. Her fine forehead sloped gently up to where her hair, bordering it like an armorial shield, burst into love-locks and waves and curlicues of ash blonde and gold. Her eyes were bright, big, clear, wet, and shining, the color of her cheeks was real, breaking close to the surface from the strong young pump of her heart. Her body hovered delicately on the last edge of childhood—she was almost eighteen, nearly complete, but the dew was still on her" (3-4): a description with precisely that kind of exaggerated sensuousness that compels us to remember the pepper on the tongue, to notice how childish in fact she is. And if the reader is taken in by her beauty, Fitzgerald presses his point with perhaps an excess of admonitory caution: "her immature mind" (19), "her naïveté" (21), "as dewy with belief as a child from one of Mrs. Burnett's vicious tracts" (34), "Rosemary had never done much thinking" (40). "Rosemary was a romantic" (31), and *Tender Is the Night* is a romance about the excesses and the failures of romanticism.[30]

Rosemary had never done much thinking—"save about the illimitability of her mother's perfections" (40). The star of the movie "Daddy's Girl" is a girl without a daddy, and partly as compensation she lavishes on her mother love enough for two. But her mother is too strong to have her head turned. Mrs. Elsie Speers—a symbolic name in a novel of symbolic names—is a wholly admirable character, but the sharpness of her name, befitting the twice-widowed wife of a cavalry officer and an Army doctor, signifies her power to draw blood. As the novel opens she is ready at last to sever Rosemary's umbilical cord (40). "By not sparing Rosemary she had made her hard—by not sparing her own labor and devotion she had cultivated an idealism in Rosemary, which at present was directed toward herself and saw the world through her eyes. So that while Rosemary was a 'simple' child she was protected by a double sheath of her mother's armor and her own—she had a mature distrust of the trivial, the facile, and the vulgar. However, with Rosemary's sudden success in pictures Mrs. Speers felt that it was time she were spiritually weaned; it would please rather than pain her if this somewhat bouncing, breathless and exigent idealism would focus on something except herself" (13). Thus it pleased her when Rosemary announced that she had fallen in love with Dick Diver that moment on the beach; but it is clear that her love for Dick is a kind of transference of parental love, that "Daddy's Girl" at last had found her daddy. Much of Rosemary's love for Dick thus takes on the quality of the relationship in the movie, "a father complex so apparent that Dick winced for all psychologists at the vicious sentimentality" (69). Dick himself recognized "the nursery footing upon which Rosemary persistently established" their affair (84-5)—recognized it the moment he wanted to sweep the nursery footing away and push their affair forward into maturity.

For Rosemary, falling in love with Dick was falling in love also with an atmosphere, a setting, and a time. She had come to the Riviera after all out of season, in the summer, and she "became a little self-conscious, as though she were displaying an unhealthy taste for the moribund; as though people were wondering why she was here in the lull between the gaiety of last winter and next winter, while up north the true world thundered by" (14). Sitting in the green twilight of a café in Cannes, she found "the dim conversations of the nineties realer and nearer than the headlines of the French paper" (15). This sense of slipping away from present time back into past time prepares her—as her immaturity and her naïveté and her romanticism also prepare her—to enter Dick Diver's theater stage, his artificial world. Fitzgerald wants us to know that Rosemary's unqualified admiration for Dick is a product of her own inexperience

and susceptibility. "He seemed kind and charming—his voice promised that he would take care of her, and that a little later he would
open up whole new worlds for her, unroll an endless succession of
magnificent possibilities" (16)—only a young girl's imagination could
create a romantic vision so incommensurate with the act that called
it forth. And yet Fitzgerald also is at pains to let us know that Rosemary's vision has glimpsed, at least in part, the truth.

"Do you like it here—this place?" Rosemary asks. " 'They have
to like it,' said Abe North slowly. 'They invented it' " (17). The
Divers' world is their own created world—"*our* beach," as Nicole
says, "that Dick made out of a pebble pile" (20)—a world out of
season in the Nietzschean sense, a world built in criticism of and
competition with the "true world" that was thundering by up north.
"The Divers' day was spaced like the day of the older civilizations
to yield the utmost from the materials at hand" (21), and the Divers'
way of life re-created the dream of a civilization where each individual might fulfill his own selfhood, find his own identity, live at the
furthest range of his promise. "To be included in Dick Diver's world
for a while was a remarkable experience: people believed he made
special reservations about them, recognizing the proud uniqueness
of their destinies, buried under the compromises of how many years.
He won everyone quickly with an exquisite consideration and a
politeness that moved so fast and intuitively that it could be examined only in its effect. Then, without caution, lest the first bloom
of the relation wither, he opened the gate to his amusing world. So
long as they subscribed to it completely, their happiness was his
preoccupation, but at the first flicker of doubt as to its all-inclusive-
ness he evaporated before their eyes, leaving little communicable
memory of what he had said or done" (27-8). When Rosemary
arrives at last at the Divers' villa—named for Diana, goddess of the
moon and of hunting, protectress of women—"Rosemary was thinking that the Villa Diana was the centre of the world" (29), as Nick
Carraway in *The Great Gatsby* had felt New York to be the new,
warm center of the world. But Rosemary did not know that "the
lush midsummer moment outside of time" (163) was almost over,
and that the center of the world was ripe—overripe—and ready to
plunge into chaos.

There was much Rosemary did not know, and her ignorance presented Fitzgerald with a problem of form in *Tender Is the Night* he was never wholly able to overcome. The first scene of the novel, chapters one and two of Book One, establishes the narrative point of view: by leaving the audience and entering the stage Rosemary gives up the role of the soliloquist and begins to speak in the voice of the dramatic monologuist; by faling in love with Dick she abandons the general social perspective and assumes a highly personal point of view. Fitzgerald wanted to present Rosemary's point of view for its own significant value, while enabling the reader to judge her limitations and distortions, to understand something other than what Rosemary understood. Therein lay his problem, for he was unable within the dramatic structure of the narrative to provide the materials for an alternative perspective; the character Abe North partly fulfills the need for a different point of view, but Fitzgerald could not develop his angle of vision as fully as was required.

Fitzgerald therefore found it necessary not only repeatedly to warn the reader against Rosemary's perspective—stressing her naïveté, her romanticism, her lack of thought—but also to enter the narrative as a soliloquist, speaking in the authorial voice for a general social perspective he was unable to introduce in any other way. Rosemary's "naïveté responded whole-heartedly to the expensive simplicity of the Divers, unaware of its complexity and lack of innocence, unaware that it was all a selection of quality rather than quantity from the run of the world's bazaar; and that the simplicity of behavior also, the nursery-like peace and good will, the emphasis on the simpler virtues, was part of a desperate bargain with the gods and had been attained through struggles she could not have guessed at. At that moment the Divers represented externally the exact furthermost evolution of a class, so that most people seemed awkward beside them—in reality a qualitative change had already set in that was not at all apparent to Rosemary" (21-2). One need not be opposed to the authorial voice in fiction to recognize how intrusions of this sort created difficulties for Fitzgerald. Through Rosemary's eyes the reader is led to see the romantic beauty and even the social radicalism of Dick Diver's utopian world, a world we are to recognize as a true and possible world, and not wholly spurious. And yet Fitzgerald must undercut Rosemary's vision in order to make us see the economic and moral weaknesses which doom Dick Diver's world to failure. His inability to present both points of view within the dramatic form of the narrative creates a certain ambiguity in Book One of *Tender Is the Night*, an ambiguity that is not fully resolved. The problem persisted in Fitzgerald's mind long after publication of the novel, until finally he planned a new edition with the structure drastically revised.

For there is at stake in this problem of narrative form nothing less than the nature and destiny of Doctor Richard Diver. He appears in the opening pages of *Tender Is the Night* in roles successively exalted. As the man in the jockey cap, he entertains, he performs on a stage. But he has also created that stage world, created it physically in the past with his own hands, and still creates its living structure in the present. To Rosemary Hoyt, naïve and romantic, Dick Diver's world takes on the aura of a mystic, magical place—from a pebble pile he had made a "bright tan prayer rug of a beach" (3), and, when she ascends to the Villa Diana above, Rosemary feels she has reached the center of the world. Dick is capable not only of making one magic world, but she feels he can take care of her and take care of all the others, too (27). Dick Diver is a hero of extraordinary powers; through his manners he creates a world of romantic dreams, just as Gatsby had done through his parties. Yet this magical, romantic role, real and important as it is, is no more the sum of Richard Diver than it was of Jay Gatsby. Alongside Gatsby, Fitzgerald created in Nick Carraway a seer who could find the beauty behind the crassness; with Diver, Fitzgerald let the beauty overflow, and then he had to find a way to make the pain be known. Unlike Gatsby, Dick Diver is conscious of his contraries, aware of the dissimulation behind his magical, creative role. But neither Dick's consciousness nor his dialogue quite sufficed Fitzgerald in his effort, early in the novel, to counterpoint Rosemary's romantic view. Once more to make his point he was forced to intrude his authorial voice into what he had unsuccessfully tried to maintain as a dramatic narrative. Dick's "excitement about things reached an intensity out of proportion to their importance, generating a really extraordinary virtuosity with people. Save among a few of the tough-minded and perennially suspicious, he had the power of arousing a fascinated and uncritical love. The reaction came when he realized the waste and the extravagance involved. He sometimes looked back with awe at the carnivals of affection he had given, as a general might gaze upon a massacre he had ordered to satisfy an impersonal blood lust" (27). The faery land of *Tender Is the Night,* Fitzgerald makes clear, is a faery land where love is fulfilled, not only through Rosemary's romantic vision of "infinite and unknown possibilities," but equally in images of blood and battle.

The military analogy becomes explicit later when Dick Diver's career is linked with that of U. S. Grant, but all through Book One, Rosemary's book, the military imagery is taking form. The party Dick gave at the Villa Diana, the party through which Rosemary found a romantic fulfillment, Dick planned as "a really *bad* party." "I want to give a party," he told Nicole, "where there's a brawl and seductions and people going home with their feelings hurt and women passed out in the cabinet de toilette. You wait and see" (27). And in the middle of the party he contrasts his attitude directly with Rosemary's by telling her that he wants the summer "to die violently instead of fading out sentimentally" (37-8). Later, after their trip to Paris, Dick guides his group on a tour of a First World War battle-field, "simplifying it always until it bore a faint resemblance to one of his own parties" (59). Here one of the most significant dialogues of the novel takes place, linking the military imagery to the theme of romantic love and also to the sense of time.

" 'This took religion and years of plenty and tremendous sureties and the exact relation that existed between the classes,' " Dick says. " 'The Russians and Italians weren't any good on this front. You had to have a whole-souled sentimental equipment going back further than you can remember. You had to remember Christmas, and post-cards of the Crown Prince and his fiancée, and little cafés in Valence and beer gardens in Unter den Linden and weddings at the mairie, and going to the Derby, and your grandfather's whiskers.' "

" 'General Grant invented this kind of battle at Petersburg in sixty-five,' " Abe North suggests.

" 'No, he didn't,' " Dick answers, revealing his own view of the general to whom he is linked, " '—he just invented mass butchery. This kind of battle was invented by Lewis Carroll and Jules Verne and whoever wrote Undine, and country deacons bowling and mar-raines in Marseilles and girls seduced in the back lanes of Württem-berg and Westphalia. Why, this was a love battle—there was a century of middle-class love spent here. This was the last love battle.' "

" 'You want to hand over this battle to D. H. Lawrence,' said Abe"
—Lawrence who had written in *Fantasia of the Unconscious*, "And
instead of this gnawing, gnawing disease of mental consciousness
and awful, unhealthy craving for stimulus and for action, we must
substitute genuine action. The war was really not a bad beginning." [31]

" 'All my beautiful lovely safe world blew itself up here with a
great gust of high explosive love,' Dick mourned persistently....
The silver cord is cut and the golden bowl is broken and all that,
but an old romantic like me can't do anything about it.' "

" 'I'm romantic too' " (57-8). Rosemary has the last word, a
fine touch of exaggerated sensuousness, a subtle irony that here as
elsewhere in the novel lightly deflates Dick's values even as it insists
upon them.

So, too, in Abe North's caustic observations there is a grain of
truth that Dick may not necessarily see. On the occasion of another
party, Rosemary observes Dick, and his "enthusiasm, the selflessness
behind the whole performance ravished her, the technic of moving
many varied types, each as immobile, as dependent on supplies of
affection as an infantry battalion is dependent on rations, appeared
so effortless that he still had pieces of his own most personal self
for everyone" (77). Fitzgerald did not place together "ravished" and
"infantry" by chance. Grant may have invented no more than mass
butchery, but at least he fought to preserve the Union. But his successor, General Diver, stages his love battles, his carnivals of affection, for no other reason seemingly than "to satisfy an impersonal
blood lust" (27). His own role as a military commander comes clear
to him in the moment in a Paris restaurant when Nicole and Rosemary and Dick learn that the party beside them is composed of Gold
Star mothers and widows of dead soldiers. "Over his wine Dick
looked at them again; in their happy faces, the dignity that surrounded and pervaded the party, he perceived all the maturity of
an older America. For a while the sobered women who had came to
mourn for their dead, for something they could not repair, made
the room beautiful. Momentarily, he sat again on his father's knee,
riding with [Mosby] while the old loyalties and devotions fought on
around him. Almost with an effort he turned back to his two women
at the table and faced the whole new world in which he believed"

(100-101). Dick was reaching back to a lost past within a past, to the romantic gallantry of Confederate cavalry raiders; a lost past that his own military leadership—a leadership that gave Rosemary "a conviction of homecoming, of a return from the derisive and salacious improvisations of the frontier" (34)—could only, like Grant's, destroy. What is significant about Dick's recollection is that it reaches back to a past not his own; it was something he, too, could not repair.

For Dick Diver's past is neither the ante-bellum South nor the frontier West but rather the genteel middle-class America of the late nineteenth century, the "whole-souled sentimental" America similar to the German and English and French societies that went to war in 1914 and blew themselves up "with a great gust of high explosive love" (57). Dick's past is the world of "religion and years of plenty and tremendous sureties and the exact relation that existed between the classes," the world the war destroyed, as Amory Blaine learned in *This Side of Paradise,* as Dick Diver mourns. Dick's past is the world of genteel romantic love, a world of romantic imagination, where neither love nor imagination steps outside the bounds of social convention. Dick Diver is yet one more version of the conventional genteel romantic hero; but like all of Fitzgerald's genteel heroes he is also something more—like Gatsby a creative figure, in Dick's case a re-creative figure, who restores the lost utopia of the past. "Their own party was overwhelmingly American and sometimes scarcely American at all. It was themselves he gave back to them, blurred by the compromises of how many years" (52). He brought the past to life again, the utopian American past, the imaginary American past; as Gatsby believes you really might repeat the past, so Dick believed you really might return to it. But on returning, the past can only be what it was before, the conventional, late-nineteenth-century, genteel America. As a genteel hero, Dick can imagine romantic dreams of love and magic possibilities; as a creator, he can build those dreams into a living world; yet he suffers still as does any genteel hero who sees through or beyond the conventions, and his carnivals of affection that make a new romantic world for others serve for him only as massacres he had seemingly ordered to satisfy an impersonal blood lust.

But his blood lust in fact is not at all impersonal. As the soldiers of World War One had fought and died for love, so too Dick stages his massacres for love, for personal love. Rosemary's love for him brings out his motive through Book One. " 'You're the only girl I've seen for a long time,' " Dick says to her back on the beach, " 'that actually did look like something blooming' " (22). She blooms for him, as her name signifies, as a symbol of remembrance, literally as the dew from the sea. She brings to him youthfulness and memories of his own youth—his own equivocal, genteel youth. It is her presence that compels him to give a "really *bad* party" (27), to invite the light-skinned crowd, the climbers and the outcasts, as a way of showing off the virtuosity of his playful imagination. Rosemary has just come to feel that the Villa Diana was the center of the world when to her chagrin the outcasts enter through the gate. "Rosemary had a sharp feeling of disappointment—she looked quickly at Dick, as though to ask an explanation of this incongruous mingling. But there was nothing unusual in his expression. He greeted his new guests with a proud bearing and an obvious deference to their infinite and unknown possibilities. She believed in him so much that presently she accepted the rightness of the McKiskos' presence as if she had expected to meet them all along" (29). It is Rosemary's naïveté and romanticism that eventually overcome the incongruity of the scene, but despite the light touch of irony in these sentences Dick's utopian powers are at work, however incommensurate with their objects. Dick is showing off his cleverness and Rosemary is won over. The violence that follows is violence that Dick had desired —as a consequence of his impersonal blood lust, and as a foretaste of the personal blood lust that drives him. The military analogy holds: genteel romantic love finds its fulfillment, here as in the First World War, in violence and destruction. Dick's dilemma after his "really *bad* party" lies in his effort to turn genteel romantic love into something else.

The party in the Villa Diana is the first skirmish in the love affair between Dick and Rosemary. It develops through their trip to Paris, the visit to the battlefield, their kiss in the taxicab, to the moment when Dick realizes that "the nursery footing upon which Rosemary persistently established it" annoyed him, and that she "had her hand on the lever more authoritatively than he" (84-5). From that moment on Dick can no longer be the genteel romantic hero; he was "too shaken by the impetus of his newly recognized emotion to resolve things into the pattern of the holiday, so the women, missing something, lapsed into a vague unhappiness" (85). For Dick now explicitly recognizes what the genteel romantic conventions were invented to hide, his sexual desire for Rosemary.

And so the past to which Rosemary returns Dick is the past of the adolescent boy in Victorian America, the genteel hero driven to sexual dreams and fantasies by the constraints and evasions of his society. The Yale boy casually tells Dick of Rosemary's adventures in a Pullman compartment—a scene Fitzgerald borrowed, significantly, from the last of the Basil Duke Lee stories [32]—and "with every detail imagined, with even envy for the pair's community of misfortune in the vestibule, Dick felt a change taking place within him. Only the image of the third person, even a vanished one, entering into his relation with Rosemary was needed to throw him off his balance and send through him waves of pain, misery, desire, desperation" (88). Dick rushes out to Rosemary's studio on the outskirts of Paris. "Dignified in his fine clothes, with their fine accessories, he was yet swayed and driven as an animal. Dignity could come only with an overthrowing of his past, of the effort of the last six years. He went briskly around the block with the fatuousness of one of Tarkington's adolescents. . . . Dick's necessity of behaving as he did was a projection of some submerged reality: he was compelled to walk there, or stand there, his shirtsleeve fitting his wrist and his coat sleeve encasing his shirtsleeve like a sleeve valve, his collar molded plastically to his neck, his red hair cut exactly, his hand holding his small briefcase like a dandy—just as another man once found it necessary to stand in front of a church in Ferrara, in sackcloth and ashes. Dick was paying some tribute to things unforgotten, unshriven, unexpurgated" (91).

As a symbol of remembrance Rosemary recalls Dick to his youth, makes him see how false his present life is. Ironically she sees his present life as a re-creation of the past, of the true, romantic past; but through Dick's eyes we know his created world is a stage world where the actors play their parts only so long as he directs and plays the lead. But if he will not keep up the play, where can he turn for release? One alternative to his stage direction—to the beach umbrella which Rosemary felt shading her even in Paris—is the true present. The true present has its own stage life, the life of the movie studio that Fitzgerald draws in a brilliant paragraph as a scene from a purgatorial underworld; and when its theatrical props are removed, the present is still a purgatory, inhabited paradoxically by the light-skinned people, the McKiskos, Mrs. Abrams, Campion and Dumphry, suffering through their ambitions and desires. Dick's "really *bad* party" already intrudes the present into the created past—both Brady, the movie director, and the light-skinned group are there—and the mixture is one that produces violence Dick can neither direct nor control, in the duel and again in the shooting scene at the railroad station. The house hewn from the frame of Cardinal de Retz's palace, meanwhile, contains "nothing of the past, nor of any present that Rosemary knew," but "seemed rather to enclose the future so that it was an electric-like shock" (71). The future is a stage-set, too, but a monstrous one, a "Frankenstein" world made up of the dissipated and the exploiters, and after their brief encounter with the "terrible" future Rosemary and Dick are thrown into each other's arms, escaping back to their separate romantic pasts. But for Dick the past is after all no more than a *cul de sac,* a return to the "unforgotten, unshriven, unexpurgated" genteel romantic fantasies, to the fatuousness of a Tarkington adolescent and the jealous pain of youthful desire without the exquisite manners and the charm that make him creative, and make him loved. Dick's dilemma is complete, and he knows it: he cannot be satisfied unless he sexually fulfills the love his genteel romantic heroism earns him; he cannot seek sexual gratification without throwing off his genteel romantic mask; yet without the mask he would no longer be so loved. The genteel romantic personality with which he is blessed and cursed provides no satisfaction, except for others. For Dick Diver there is no dimension of time in which he can find release; more significantly than ever his infatuation with Rosemary takes place in a "lush midsummer moment outside of time."

Dick's dilemma is presented in a sense even more succinctly in the case of Abe North, whose role as Dick's counterpart is one of the most intriguing and perplexing aspects of Book One of the novel. Once the parallel between Dick and U. S. Grant is made explicit, one cannot but suspect that the name Abe North is also meant to have symbolic significance, particularly when Abe is first described, "His voice was slow and shy; he had one of the saddest faces Rosemary had ever seen, the high cheek-bones of an Indian, a long upper lip, and enormous deep-set dark golden eyes" (9). It is difficult to escape the implication that Abe North is Abe Lincoln, as Dick Diver is U. S. Grant; that Abe, with "the solemn dignity that flowed from him," with "his achievement, fragmentary, suggestive, and surpassed," his "will to live, now become a will to die" (83), dies symbolically as Lincoln did, his work unfinished, before the spirit of the Gilded Age took command, while Grant lived on ineffectually to preside over the rapacious capitalism that demeaned the idealism of the war. The Lincoln-Grant relationship between Abe and Dick is strengthened by the sense Book One conveys that Abe is even more of a creative figure than Dick, or at least a different kind of creative figure, and of a higher order—an original mind, where Dick at his best is a synthesizer and classifier.

Early in the novel Abe is described as a composer "who after a brilliant and precocious start had composed nothing for seven years" (34). His dilemma in time is as great as Dick's, if not greater. Abe is returning to America to resume his composing, but neither his wife nor his friends harbor any hope that Abe will actually fulfill his plan. " 'I can't see why you've given up about everything,' " Nicole Diver challenges him, and Abe replies, " 'I suppose I got bored; and then it was such a long way to go back in order to get anywhere' " (81). The only way Abe can rediscover his past is through his drinking. "The drink made past happy things contemporary with the present, as if they were still going on, contemporary even with the future as if they were about to happen again" (103). Preferring to go back to his past by drinking, rather than by returning to America, Abe leaves the boat-train and doubles back to Paris. Abe's mode of recovering the past, however, is a sign not of personal rebirth but of personal disintegration—a personal disintegration which can only destroy the meaning of the past as it recaptures it. Drunk in a bar, Abe accuses a Negro of stealing money from him; but the circumstances are clouded by "the alcoholic fog"; an innocent man is accused, and yet another innocent man is arrested. A Negro named Peterson supports Abe. He follows Abe to the Divers' hotel, and there he is shot and left to die on Rosemary Hoyt's bed. Abe North's personal disintegration spreads out into a social catastrophe for the expatriate

Negroes in Paris: the arrested man's name is Freeman. To this the Great Emancipator has fallen.

And by so falling Abe North leaves his legacy of disintegration to Dick. His last words in the novel mean nothing except as a suggestion of Dick's future drinking and bad manners, a prefiguring of Dick's decline. " 'But remember what George the Third said,' " he says reproachfully to Dick, " 'that if Grant was drunk he wished he would bite the other generals' " (108). Abe leaves, and already his legacy is at work. Rosemary discovers the bleeding body of Jules Peterson on her bed. Dick, to protect Rosemary, carries the body into the hall and passes the bloody blanket and sheets across to Nicole in their own room. And Nicole, recognizing the sexual implications of the blood-stained sheets from Rosemary's bed, relapses into madness in the bathroom.

V

The moment before Abe North intruded his premonitions of destiny into Dick Diver's and Rosemary Hoyt's developing affair, Rosemary had "stood up and leaned down and said her most sincere thing" to Dick: " 'Oh, we're such actors—you and I' " (105). With her words the movement of Book One of Tender Is the Night reaches its climax. For she had entered into the action of the novel by appearing on Dick Diver's stage; gradually by capturing Dick's love she had taken the direction of the scene away from him, as he well knew; and her linking them together both as actors is a sign that she, too, has come to recognize her domination. A similar movement shapes Book Two of the novel, a movement from Dick's power and control at the beginning of Book Two to his weakness and dependence at the end. In the second book Dick's loss of control takes place in relation not to Rosemary but to the Warren family, and the themes of the book are not love and sex and manners, but rather love and sex and money.

As Book One opens out into Dick Diver's created world, so Book Two begins by placing Dick Diver in a world he had not made: Book One takes place in the faery land of creative imagination, Book Two in the vast and solid world of history. Fitzgerald's sense of history, so long cultivated but so much more difficult to render in his art, attained its artistic fulfillment in a remarkable passage at the opening of Book Two. Beginning with the metaphor of Switzerland as an island in the First World War, "washed on one side by the waves of thunder around Gorizia and on the other by the cataracts along the Somme and the Aisne," it moves on to juxtapose the "intriguing strangers" in the cafés of Berne and Geneva with the "blinded or one-legged men, or dying trunks," crossing in trains between the bright lakes, the bright posters of 1914 with inspiringly ferocious men and the withered posters of 1917 after three years of massacre—"and no country was more surprised than its sister republic when the United States bungled its way into the war." Few passages in Fitz-gerald's fiction present so complex a setting and emotion with such simplicity and economy and beauty. And Dick Diver, even in war-time, "was already too valuable, too much of a capital investment to be shot off in a gun" (115). His country could not yet afford to lose him, not for love nor money.

Book Two opens in the year 1917, with Doctor Richard Diver twenty-six years old, a former Rhodes Scholar from Yale, a student of psychiatry in Vienna. This is the "heroic period" in Dick Diver's life, but it it is one of the weak points of *Tender Is the Night* that this brief chapter describing Dick as he was before his intricate des-tiny began—"like Grant, lolling in his general store in Galena" (118) —is so sketchy and vague. Lucky Dick he was called at New Haven, and he reasons to himself, "Lucky Dick can't be one of these clever men; he must be less intact, even faintly destroyed. If life won't do it for him it's not a substitute to get a disease or a broken heart, or an inferiority complex, though it'd be nice to build out some broken side till it was better than the original structure" (116). This is the conventional view of the sources of creativity, the view that Fitz-gerald had presented as far back as his college days in "The Pierian Springs and the Last Straw," the view that Edmund Wilson de-scribed in the title essay of his collection, *The Wound and the Bow*. Dick has no wound and thus it seems he has no bow: "He knew . . . that the price of his intactness was incompleteness. 'The best I can wish you, my child,' so said the Fairy Blackstick in Thackeray's *The Rose and the Ring*, 'is a little misfortune.' " Dick argues the point with a Rumanian intellectual who reassures him that he is not a romantic philosopher, only a scientist. And yet Dick's intactness is itself a wound, for it is the intactness of a self-deceived American.

"Dick got up to Zurich on less Achilles' heels than would be required to equip a centipede, but with plenty—the illusions of eternal strength and health, and of the essential goodness of people; illusions of a nation, the lies of generations of frontier mothers who had to croon falsely, that there were no wolves outside the cabin door" (117). The price of this form of intactness is incompleteness, but Fitzgerald does not make clear that Dick may complete himself in two possible ways, as a creative scientist, or as a genteel romantic hero. So long as Dick is intact he is incomplete, and the natural way for an American of Dick's generation to complete himself is through genteel romantic heroism. "His voice . . . wooed the world" (19), Rosemary had thought, but the world far more wooed him, and true to D. H. Lawrence's claim in the *Fantasia of the Unconscious*, he was the submissive one while the world—the woman's world—was the initiator. When the world made love to him, Dick Diver could not say no, and instead of gaining a bow because of his wound, his American wound had made him, as he whispered to himself, "Lucky Dick, you big stiff" (116). But the genteel romantic hero's love-making with the world provided no completion either.

The world first made love to Dick Diver in the person of Nicole Warren, an American mental patient at a clinic in Switzerland. During the war they had accidentally met and her attitude toward him had become, as Dr. Gregorovius said, "a transference of the most fortuitous kind" (120). His therapeutic influence was worked through the form of letters. "If you come here again with that attitude base and criminal and not even faintly what I had been taught to associate with the rôle of gentleman then heaven help you," Nicole wrote him early in the correspondence. "However, you seem quieter than the others, all soft like a big cat. I have only gotten to like boys who are rather sissies. Are you a sissy? There were some somewhere." And again, "Last year or whenever it was in Chicago when I got so I couldn't speak to servants or walk in the street I kept waiting for someone to tell me. It was the duty of someone who understood. The blind must be led. Only no one would tell me everything—they would just tell me half and I was already too muddled to put two and two together." And again, "Here I am in what appears to be a semi-insane asylum, all because nobody saw fit to tell me the truth about anything. If I had only known what was going on like I know

now I could have stood it I guess for I am pretty strong, but those who should have, did not see fit to enlighten me. And now, when I know and have paid such a price for knowing, they sit there with their dogs lives and say I should believe what I did believe. Especially one but I know now" (121-3). Nicole Warren sounds like a sheltered girl who is shattered by discovering the reality of sex beneath the appearance of romantic love. But her case is rather more complicated than that: the problem involves not only sex and love, but also the Warren family money.

The particular nature of genteel romantic conventions as they developed in post–Civil War America took form not only from religious or literary or cultural values, but even more significantly from a social and economic setting. The genteel romantic conventions were a way of assuring social control in a society that was highly mobile and yet was stratifying swiftly, especially at the top. They were a means for a predominantly middle-class society to control through cultural standards both the lower strata striving for improvement, and the higher strata whose economic success had created a new kind of unbounded power. Genteel romantic formulas worked as long and as well as they did partly because the highest economic groups had emerged so recently from the middle classes that they were not yet able to throw off middle-class habits of mind, even when they had ceased to observe the injunctions, and partly because genteel romantic formulas often enough provided real rewards. But genteel romanticism as a cultural norm was doomed when the upper strata became so much richer and more powerful than the middle class and when, after a time, they no longer cared to profess middle-class values, except when threatened. It was the First World War, as Dick Diver said, that expended a century of middle-class love, and laid bare for the twenties the hollow wreckage of genteel values. From the start of his career, Fitzgerald had sensed the change, and in his best fiction—in "The Diamond as Big as the Ritz," *The Great Gatsby*, "The Rich Boy," and *Tender Is the Night*—he explored the ambiguous relationship between wealth and genteel values. But as the war had demonstrated the weakness of genteel romanticism and proclaimed the triumph of the rich, so a decade later the Great Crash exposed the weaknesses of capitalism: *Tender Is the Night* is Fitzgerald's first major work of art written after the crash, and though the novel takes place when capitalism is at the height of its powers—summer 1925 to summer 1929—Fitzgerald is judging it from the perspective of its fall.

The extraordinary power of the Divers' wealth is apparent in Book One:

> Nicole was the product of much ingenuity and toil. For her sake trains began their run at Chicago and traversed the round belly of the continent to California; chicle factories fumed and link belts grew link by link in factories; men mixed toothpaste in vats and drew mouthwash out of copper hogsheads; girls canned tomatoes quickly in August or worked rudely at the Five-and-Tens on Christmas Eve; half-breed Indians toiled on Brazilian coffee plantations and dreamers were muscled out of patent rights in new tractors—these were some of the people who gave a tithe to Nicole, and as the whole system swayed and thundered onward it lent a feverish bloom to such processes of hers as wholesale buying, like the flush of a fireman's face holding his post before a spreading blaze. She illustrated very simple principles, containing in herself her own doom, but illustrated them so accurately that there was grace in the procedure. (55)

But not until Book Two is its source made clear. Nicole belongs to a great feudal family of Chicago, whose power is so vast that it can command a United States cruiser to carry her through the submarine blockade, a family for whom "money is no object" and, therefore, nothing else is either—rules or standards or values or whatever else the middle class builds up to protect itself. And yet it must profess the middle-class ethic because an ostensibly democratic society would not tolerate an articulated feudal system of values—part of Braddock Washington's dilemma in "The Diamond as Big as the Ritz"—and because it lacks the imagination to fashion an ethic wholly new. "His fine shoulders shaking with awful sobs inside his easy-fitting coat" (129), Devereux Warren confesses how in all innocence and ignorance and self-deception the idealized love between father and daughter turned suddenly to incest. If behind the façade of filial sentiment lurks such a thing, no wonder Nicole came to believe that the façade of genteel romantic conventions conceals similar sexual desires.

The precise purpose of the genteel romantic hero in nineteenth-century America was to serve as a smokescreen to cover up the truth Nicole so tragically discovered, to divert energies and desires into

283

harmless pursuits through the power of his romantic imagination. This was a secret of success for the poor but presentable young man of talent, the true nature of whom Fitzgerald laid bare by exaggeration, by endowing his genteel heroes with extraordinary powers. In 1917 Dick Diver had seemed to possess no special powers—except the ambition to be as powerful a psychologist as Jung or Freud—and he seemed also successfully to have escaped the wealthy society that might want to use his genteel romantic talents. "Men and women had made much of him, and perhaps what had brought him back to the centre of the great Swiss watch, was an intuition that this was not too good for a serious man . . . he used to think that he wanted to be good, he wanted to be kind, he wanted to be brave and wise, but it was all pretty difficult. He wanted to be loved, too, if he could fit it in" (133). Franz Gregorovius says, "You are attractive to women, Dick," and Dick replies, "Then God help me!" (131). In a half-dozen remarkable short chapters—remarkable for passages of poetic prose of great beauty and romantic suggestiveness, counterpointed by the scientific candor of the clinical point of view and the crass hardness of Baby Warren—Dick Diver against his will falls in love and marries Nicole Warren. "On the centre of the lake, cooled by the piercing currents of the Rhone, lay the true centre of the Western World" (147), and in the center of the Western world Doctor Diver, the ambitious young psychologist, finds his true destiny as the genteel romantic hero.

With chapter eleven of Book Two the novel resumes the present action of Book One. "The lush midsummer moment outside of time was already over," and Dick Diver's faery land of Book One lies revealed as nothing more than a combination of therapy and high society—paraphrasing one of Dick's remarks, a "meeting of Sigmund Freud with Ward McAllister" (169). With chapter eleven, Dick is seen wholly through his own eyes; and his exquisite manners, that to Rosemary created a world and restored people to themselves, seem to Dick no more than "a trick of the heart." Dick knows perfectly well the genteel origins of his manners, their source in an exaggeration of a certain style, born of defeat. "From his father Dick had learned the somewhat conscious good manners of the young Southerner coming north after the Civil War. Often he used them and just as often he despised them because they were not a protest against how unpleasant selfishness was but against how unpleasant it looked" (164). Now he was discovering how much his manners had been used to hide the selfishness of others, how much his own self had been trapped in the net of Nicole's wealth and Nicole's illness. Yet to break away from the manners he despises would be to break away as well from his most essential self: this is the tragic dilemma of the genteel hero.

For Dick "time stood still and then every few years accelerated in a rush, like the quick re-wind of a film" (180). Time had stood still for him in the summer on the beach, but now it was moving fast, away from his intellectual ambitions, from his career, and from his youth, and the road back was blocked by the nature of his past. The only way out lay in "an overthrowing of his past" (91), a dropping of the pretense of good manners and the sentimental lies about romantic love. But to overturn his past would court destruction of his self. "Somehow Dick and Nicole had become one and equal, not apposite and complementary; she was Dick too, the drought in the marrow of his bones. He could not watch her disintegrations without participating in them" (190-91) because the source of her disintegration lies in the same dissimulation which his social role was made to bolster. But where her disintegration arose from one ugly incident, his disintegration stems from the very core of his personal identity. The true neurotic in *Tender Is the Night* is not Nicole Diver, but her husband.

> He had lost himself—he could not tell the hour when, or the day or the week, the month or the year. Once he had cut through things, solving the most complicated equations as the simplest problems of his simplest patients. Between the time he found Nicole flowering under a stone on the Zürichsee and the moment of his meeting with Rosemary the spear had been blunted. Watching his father's struggles in poor parishes had wedded a desire for money to an essentially unacquisitive nature. It was not a healthy necessity for security—he had never felt more sure of himself, more thoroughly his own man, than at the time of his marriage to Nicole. Yet he had been swallowed up like a gigolo, and somehow permitted his arsenal to be locked up in the Warren safety-deposit vaults. (201)

Dick Diver, the successful genteel romantic hero, had attained an erotic fulfillment which implied castration. The only way back now to his own selfhood and separate identity lay in a new demonstration of his sexual potency: "He was in love with every pretty woman he saw now, their forms at a distance, their shadows on a wall" (201). Yet his genteel romantic being still rested on Victorian prudery. Like his patients Dick Diver was a divided personality, stretched out on the rack of genteel culture, pulled apart by sexual dreams on one hand and social sublimation on the other—torn apart between potency and castration.

Fitzgerald brilliantly portrays the widening breach between Dick's separate selves in Book Two by his treatment of Dick's relations, not with Nicole, but with her sister, Baby Warren, and her rival, Rosemary Hoyt. They matched the two poles of his divided personality, Baby the extreme of social conventionality and sexlessness, Rosemary the other extreme of sentimental romanticism and erotic desire. To reinforce his themes of sexual potency and castration Fitzgerald turned to a common sexual metaphor. Baby Warren was "both formidable and vulnerable, he decided, remembering other women with flowerlike mouths grooved for bits" (150); Rosemary "was a young mustang" (164), and when Dick meets her in Rome her beauty was "all groomed, like a young horse dosed with Black-seed oil" (207). Rosemary first came upon Dick, of course, when he was wearing a jockey cap.

"Baby Warren wanted to talk to Dick, wanted to talk to him with the impetus that sent her out vaguely toward all new men, as though she were on an inelastic tether and considered that she might as well get to the end of it as soon as possible. She crossed and re-crossed her knees frequently in the manner of tall restless virgins" (151). Fitzgerald brutally puts her down with a single adjective: "onanistic" (152). Nicknamed "Baby," she is also immature emotionally and socially, strung together by her naïve Anglophilism and her genteel American sentimentality; and Dick's mounting impatience with genteel evasions leads him three times to contradict her: when he mocks his own good manners (177-8), when he denies her praise for the English (214), and when, to her compliment, " 'You can keep a party going by just a little sentence or a saying here or there. I think that's a wonderful talent,' " he replies, " 'It's a trick' " (216). Dick can afford gently to disagree with Baby Warren so long as he maintains his moral superiority over her. But one false step will expose him to the full weight of the power that the Warren money wields; and it is his effort to recover his sexual potency, already taken from him by the power of the Warren money, that drives him on to that false step.

In Rome, returning from his father's funeral, Dick encounters Rosemary. At last they make love together; but Dick, recognizing that he does not love her nor she him, directs his sexual passion for her into prurient curiosity about her sex life. He was potent after all, and yet in regaining his sexual prowess he is still unable to separate it from genteel premises: Knowing that she has been promiscuous, he wants out of pride and jealousy fully to know it all. "He felt increasingly Victorian" (217). His probing reduces her to despairing tears, and she cries out, "I feel as if I'd quarreled with Mother" (219). So Dick is still the missing father figure in her life, even after they have consummated their affair. That night Dick avoids returning to her, drinks too much and gets involved in a drunken brawl—once more ravishment and bloody battle go hand in hand. Dick is arrested and beaten at the jail. Baby Warren is called to rescue him, and with "the clean-sweeping irrational temper that had broken the moral back of a race and made a nursery out of a continent" (232), she succeeds. Warren money saves him, and "she had the satisfaction of feeling that, whatever Dick's previous record was, they now possessed a moral superiority over him for as long as he proved of any use" (235). But the moral superiority of Warren money is a subject of high irony. Leaving the jail Dick cries, "I want to make a speech. . . . I want to explain to these people how I raped a five-year-old girl. Maybe I did—" (235). It seems clear that in Dick's eyes his copulation with "Daddy's Girl" was the same as Devereux Warren's copulation with his daughter: an act of incest. Dick and the Warrens are therefore morally equal: their domination over him is not a result of their moral superiority, whatever Baby thinks, but of their economic power.

VI

"Men and women had made much of him, and perhaps what had brought him back to the centre of the great Swiss watch"—in the spring of 1919—"was an intuition that this was not too good for a serious man" (133). Nearly a decade later, Dick Diver returns again to the center of the Western world, marking an end that bears no promise of a new beginning. "Dick," Kaethe Gregorovius proclaims, "is no longer a serious man" (241). The scene in Lausanne serves as a symbol of his decay. Dick goes there to see about the case of a young homosexual, a person whose "very charm made it possible for [him] to perpetrate his outrages" (245)—an odd parallel to Dick's own character; later this professional encounter would provide a pretext for a slanderous accusation against Dick, an ironic parody of his true sexual role in the novel, and an indication that his role was finished. Moreover, in Lausanne Dick comes upon Nicole's father, who seems to be dying, but who suddenly gets up from his death bed, pays his bill with a thousand dollar note, and takes off for Paris. Dick Diver and Devereux Warren may now be morally equals, but money is a stronger source of energy than manners.

The energy of money had been spending and sapping the energy of manners through the Divers' marriage, and now the energy of manners is gone. Book Three of *Tender Is the Night* is Nicole's book, an account of Nicole's recovery of herself, of herself as Nicole Warren, a creation of money, rather than Nicole Diver, a creation of manners. Nicole's self-recovery takes place as Dick's character disintegrates, but in the context also of styles of life which enormous wealth has made "fabulous." Mary North, widow of the composer whose name and manner symbolized so much, had married an Asian nobleman who "was not quite light enough to travel in a pullman south of Mason-Dixon"(258). The actual moment of separation for Dick and Nicole—who had been so long one personality that they signed their names "Dicole"—comes, in April 1929, on a yacht named the "Margin." "If she need not, in her spirit, be forever one with Dick as he had appeared last night, she must be something in addition, not just an image on his mind, condemned to endless parades around the circumference of a medal" (277). Beneath Nicole Diver lay another person, Nicole Warren of Chicago, temporarily injured by an incestuous act, but slowly recovering inside her. "Nicole had been designed for change, for flight, with money as fins and wings. The new state of things would be no more than if a racing chassis, concealed for years under the body of a family limousine, should be stripped to its original self" (280).

It is with Tommy Barban that Nicole's true being is at last stripped bare. "When did you begin to have white crook's eyes?" he asks her, and she answers, "If my eyes have changed it's because I'm well again. And being well perhaps I've gone back to my true self—I suppose my grandfather was a crook and I'm a crook by heritage, so there we are" (292). Together they go to a hotel in Nice, where they make love. Afterward, Tommy "inspected the oblong white torso joined abruptly to the brown limbs and head, and said, laughing gravely: 'You are all new like a baby'" (295). White-eyed, white-skinned, Nicole is no longer one of the dark-skinned actors on Dick Diver's stage.

Dick's little drama is over: "His beach, perverted now to the tastes of the tasteless; he could search it for a day and find no stone of the Chinese Wall he had once erected around it, no footprint of an old friend" (280). One old friend has returned, though, Rosemary Hoyt, and in a discussion of her acting Dick reveals how he staged the scene he had dominated so long: "On the stage you're trying to entertain. . . . You do the unexpected thing until you've maneuvered the audience back from the objective fact to yourself. *Then* you slide back into character again" (288). Succinctly put, this is the method of the genteel romantic hero, the clever entertainer who paints a pretty gloss over the objective facts of life. But the genteel romantic hero's days are over.

Almost over. Dick performs one last act in his genteel romantic show. Mary North and Lady Caroline Sibley-Biers, dressed as sailors, pick up two French girls, a scene ensues, and they are arrested. Dick is called to get them out. "'Dick, you can always arrange things,'" Mary cries out, "'—you always could'" (304). In his last genteel romantic act, performed for French police, Dick makes an ironic fantasy out of the fabulous wealth that has used him up. "'The Italian Countess . . . is the grand-daughter . . . of John D. Rockefeller Mellon. . . . In addition she is the niece of Lord Henry Ford'" (305). And this one last call for his imaginative talents gives rise to one last effort by Fitzgerald to explain the ultimate cause of Dick's collapse —an effort ascribed to Dick's self-knowledge, but so out of character for Dick Diver in Book Three that it reads far more as one of the obvious authorial intrusions:

He got up and, as he absorbed the situation, his self-knowledge assured him that he would undertake to deal with it—the old fatal pleasingness, the old forceful charm, swept back with its cry of "Use me!" He would have to go fix this thing that he didn't care a damn about, because it had early become a habit to be loved, perhaps from the moment when he had realized that he was the last hope of a decaying clan. On an almost parallel occasion, back in Dohmler's clinic on the Zürichsee, realizing this power, he had made his choice, chosen Ophelia, chosen the sweet poison and drunk it. Wanting above all to be brave and kind, he had wanted, even more than that, to be loved. So it had been. So it would ever be.... (302)

Dick's flaw, then, is in himself: his destiny of his own making. Yet his flaw is the flaw of a society: his illusions the "illusions of a nation, the lies of generations of frontier mothers who had to croon falsely, that there were no wolves outside the cabin door" (117). The novel comes to an end, in chapter twelve of Book Three, with a remarkable recapitulation of its genteel romantic themes. Dick goes to take a last look at the beach. " 'This is his place,' " Nicole says to Baby. " '—in a way he discovered it. Old Gausse always says he owes everything to Dick' " (312). But the beach no longer belongs to him now: with a white sun beating down out of a white sky, even nature denies him. Moving up on the terrace, Dick stops with Mary North. " 'I've spent most of my time defending you this summer,' " Mary says, and Dick replies, " 'That remark is one of Doctor Eliot's classics,' " a reference which calls forth the genteel culture of the Gilded Age.

" 'You're all so dull,' he said."

" 'But we're all there is!' cried Mary."

"His eyes, for the moment clear as a child's, asked her sympathy and stealing over him he felt the old necessity of convincing her that he was the last man in the world and she was the last woman . . . their glances married suddenly, bedded, strained together." For one last moment sexual desire and the genteel romantic dreams seem united: but "his blood raced slow." Dick Diver, the creator of romantic dreams who briefly built a beach into a faery-land utopia, stands up to go. "He raised his right hand and with a papal cross he blessed the beach from the high terrace" (313-14).

Dick returns to the upper–New York State country from which he had long ago set out. Nicole liked to think "his career was biding its time, again like Grant's in Galena" (315). Once more Dick Diver's career is linked with Grant's. But time does not repeat itself. Dick had had his moment of obscurity, like Grant in Galena; had become like Grant a great military commander, giving parties like love battles out of blood lust; and ended like Grant the President, a soured, ineffectual front man for immense and selfish wealth. But there were no more love battles to be fought: in the summer of 1929, when Dick Diver took leave of the beach he had created, the Gilded Age had only a few more weeks to run. The genteel middle-class American culture, which Dick Diver expressed in so remarkable a way, had lost its values in the First World War, and it was soon to lose its economic foundations as well. Dick Diver fades away into the mystery of the American heartland, which had borne him up into his destiny. But its blood, too, raced slow.

Tender Is the Night ends thus without the promise of a new beginning, slips quietly back into the unrecoverable past. Into the novel which occupied nine years of his life, Fitzgerald poured a profusion of themes and images, poured all the passion of his social discontent and his historical understanding. *Tender Is the Night* is most of all a novel of emotion, of beautiful and sad and sometimes artistically uncontrolled emotion. Through the carelessness of his publisher it was—and still is—a novel of incongruous and distracting imperfections, misspellings, repetitions, wrong words; but through Fitzgerald's own lack of artistic detachment it is also a novel of imperfect form, a novel whose dramatic structure is continually broken by the author's effort to insert a wider social perspective that he felt he had not fully made clear. It was this flaw in the novel's form that led Fitzgerald to plan a structural revision. But when the revised version was posthumously prepared and published it lost the dramatic energy of the novel without gaining the formal clarity that only a textual revision could have attained.[33]

Yet to recognize the lapses of form in *Tender Is the Night* should not detract from the novel's extraordinary achievements. In a way Fitzgerald fulfilled the ambitions with which he had begun his new novel back in 1925. *The Great Gatsby* had placed him among the leaders of the modern movement in the arts, and yet he had wanted to move beyond, to write a novel that would be "the model for the age that Joyce and Stein are searching for, that Conrad didn't find." [34] With *Tender Is the Night* he did move beyond the modern movement, moved away from universal myths and toward the pathos of history. This novel is a vision in art of an era in American history, of the failure of a society and of an individual who embodied its graces and its weaknesses. In *Tender Is the Night* Fitzgerald created a work of fiction rare in American literature, a novel uniting romantic beauty and also historical and social depth; and he proved by his creation that his art, and his identity as an artist, could survive the death of the society which had nurtured and sustained him.

CHAPTER ELEVEN

As F. Scott Fitzgerald brought *Tender Is the Night* to a close in the fall and winter months of 1933, the novel became for him more than merely a work of art, more even than the means for recovering the lost ground of his literary reputation. Rather it served as a test of his own personal strength and will, a setting for his own self-affirmation. *The Great Gatsby* had been a kind of *tour de force*, he told John Peale Bishop; *Tender Is the Night* was "a confession of faith." [1] In his art he created the beauty and weakness of an outmoded style of life; for himself he proclaimed a new mode of behavior. "For me the test of human values is conformity to the strictest and most unflinching rationality," he wrote Margaret Turnbull as he worked on the novel, "while in your case it is based on standards of conduct." [2] Between his values, and the conduct of the characters he had created in *Tender Is the Night*, a great gulf had opened up. "Work really was the best thing with which to fill a life," he wrote in a *Saturday Evening Post* story late in 1932. With his daughter and her friends he took every opportunity to impress the new philosophy. "The only thing I ever told you definitely was that popularity is not worth a damn and respect is worth everything, and what do you care about happiness—and who does except the perpetual children of this world?" he wrote Andrew Turnbull; and in his first letter to his daughter, Frances, he said, "All I believe in in life is the rewards for virtue (according to your talents) and the *punishments* for not fulfilling your duties, which are doubly costly." [3] Dick Diver was thirty-seven years old at the climax of *Tender Is the Night*, exactly Fitzgerald's age when he completed it; consciously Fitzgerald applied to himself the same standards of judgment as to his hero, and asserted to the world that he had passed where Diver failed. He had decided, as he told Maxwell Perkins, "to be a serious man." [4]

In completing *Tender Is the Night*, Fitzgerald regained his self-esteem, proclaimed his own self-mastery. But it was too late now for him to wipe the old slate clean; the waste and sadness of the past possessed him still. Zelda Fitzgerald remained seriously ill. In January 1934, she suffered her third mental breakdown, and her illness absorbed Fitzgerald's energy and concentration at a critical moment in the revision of his manuscript. Moreover, he had fallen deeply in debt to his agent and his publishers, and to meet expenses he put aside the novel five times to write short stories for the *Post*. Only one, "More than Just a Home," holds any lasting interest. Like *Tender Is the Night* it assesses the values of the genteel American past, symbolized in the story by an old Victorian house resembling the one Fitzgerald lived in at the time. At the end the house stands empty within and deteriorating outside. "Whatever its further history, the whole human effort of collaboration was done now. The purpose of the house was achieved—finished and folded—it was an effort toward some commonweal, an effort difficult to estimate, so closely does it press against us still." [5] If Fitzgerald meant to assert he had survived that vanished genteel past, with which his art and mind were bound so closely, two sentimental *Post* stories he published in the fall of 1933 belied him.

His entrapment by the past was complicated by the difficulties of preparing *Tender Is the Night* for publication. Once more, as with *The Great Gatsby*, he faced the dilemma of advertising a novel whose subject matter would not suggest the art and intelligence brought to bear on it. "*Don't* accentuate that it deals with Americans abroad —there's been too much trash under that banner," he warned Perkins, and again: "Please do not use the phrase 'Riviera' or 'gay resorts.' Not only does it sound like the triviality of which I am so often accused, but also the Riviera has been so thoroughly exploited by E. Phillips Oppenheim and a whole generation of writers and its very mention invokes a feeling of unreality and insubstantiality." [6] For publicity and exposure, moreover, as well as for more money, Fitzgerald decided to publish the novel as a serial in *Scribner's Magazine*. He wanted to bring out the novel in April 1934, in advance of the European travel season, so it was split up into four magazine installments starting in January. Fitzgerald had serialized only one previous novel, *The Beautiful and Damned*, and had hardly changed it at all in shifting it from magazine to book. With his next novel. *The Great Gatsby*, he had decided against magazine publication because he wanted time to revise and improve the text. Now for *Tender Is the Night* he wanted both serial publication and time for revising the text. But serialization doubled his work and cut in half the time he had to do it. Then he gave away a full month of working time by going on a holiday to Bermuda just before Christmas.

Inevitably the result was haste and confusion, which contributed not only to the errors and repetitions that appeared in the novel, but to the more fundamental weaknesses in the novel's form. The first serial installment went to press with almost no revision. Later installments were revised so heavily in galley proof that type had to be completely re-set. "Please do not send me any book galley for the present," he told Perkins in mid-January, "just hold it there. I am already confused by the multiplicity of irons I have in the fire and as far as possible would prefer to do the book galley in one or two long stretches." [7] But he found time to revise only the first section of the novel, the part he had failed to go over for the serial; the latter part went into print with little change from the serial version.

Fitzgerald's concern with form was conveyed in a revealing remark to Perkins early in February. In the serial version he wanted to preserve the scene where Mary North and Lady Caroline Sibley-Biers are arrested for picking up two French girls while dressed as sailors. "It is legitimate to ruin Dick but it is by no means legitimate to make him an ineffectual," he insisted. "In the proof I am pointing up the fact that his intention dominated all this last part, but it is not enough, and the foreshortening without the use of this scene . . . does not contain enough of him for the reader to reconstruct his whole personality as viewed as a unit throughout—and the reason for this is my attempt to tell the last part entirely through Nicole's eyes. I was even going to have her in on the Cannes episode but decided against it because of the necessity of seeing Dick alone." [8] Fitzgerald was not unaware of the weak points in his novel, but in the early months of 1934 he lacked time and energy to correct them; or correction may no longer have been possible for him, or even important. "The thing is perhaps too crowded for story readers to search it through for the story," he admitted to Perkins, "but it can't be helped, there are times when you have to get every edge of your fingernails on paper." [9] He had completed what he had set out to do, and he would commit it to the reviewers as it stood.

Almost a decade had gone by since Fitzgerald last offered up a book to major newspaper and magazine reviewers, and an era had passed into history. But the review pages remained calm ports in the storm, sturdy relics of continuity in an age of flux. *The New York Times Book Review* under J. Donald Adams and the *New York Herald Tribune's* daily reviews by Lewis Gannett indeed had grown more conventional and conservative than they had been a decade before. Among those who reviewed *Tender Is the Night* in April 1934 were Henry Seidel Canby and Mary M. Colum, who had reviewed *The Beautiful and Damned* twelve years previously. Legend has it that left-wing critics were lying hostilely in wait to ambush *Tender Is the Night;* instead Fitzgerald placed his last and most mature novel about the postwar period into the hands of reviewers who looked back nostalgically on *This Side of Paradise,* and who regarded him as a fair-haired college boy gone wrong.

The conventional reviewers wrote a majority of the reviews in the first week after publication, and their tone was the same one genteel reviewers had taken toward Fitzgerald ever since he strayed from their fold. "His mental nutriment seems to have been a trifle too jazzy," Miss Colum complained, "and lacking in some of those more solid vitamins which give a writer sympathy with the characters he is creating . . . he has never really mediated on life." J. Donald Adams agreed. "One looked, too, for more deepening of tone, for a firmer grasp of life," he said. "His new book is clever and brilliantly sur-faced, but it is not the work of a wise and mature novelist." John Chamberlain reviewed the novel intelligently and favorably in *The New York Times.* Horace Gregory handled the book intelligently but with less enthusiasm in the *New York Herald Tribune Books* supplement.[10] In general, though, *Tender Is the Night* failed to meet the standards of the first reviewers, not as a work of art but as a work of philosophy; and not because it lacked radicalism in radical times, but because it was not conservative enough for the conventional genteel reviewers.

C. Hartley Grattan, reviewing the novel in July for the most radical periodical that gave it space, saw the situation exactly. Dick Diver's fate, he wrote in *The Modern Monthly*, "is so close to that of unstable personalities in any place and time that it has been perversely misread by those critics anxious to avoid the implications of the whole book." More than any other reviewer Grattan caught the full implications of the novel; thus it was the most radical reviewer who saw how radical Fitzgerald's aims had been. Grattan quoted in full the passage describing how the world's economy toiled for Nicole. He grasped both the beauty and the corruption in the Divers' way of life, as Fitzgerald had intended it. He praised Fitzgerald as a novelist who "has grown steadily and now definitely promises to emerge as one of the really important interpreters of the upper middle class in our time." [11]

It was this promise, curiously, which a less radical but no less perceptive reviewer, William Troy in *The Nation*, found most disheartening. Troy related Dick Diver to Jay Gatsby, recognizing the common stereotype which underlay their characters. But "the repetition of the pattern," he said, "turns out to be merely depressing. It is time now for Mr. Fitzgerald, with his remarkable technical mastery of his craft, to give us a character who is not the victim of adolescent confusion, who is strong enough to turn deaf ears to the jingling cymbals of the golden girl." [12]

By the time the reviews by Troy and Grattan appeared, the general reception and the sales possibilities of the novel had already been settled. This time Fitzgerald had not been so naïve as to expect the acclaim and financial success that he had hoped for *Gatsby*. He knew enough about professional reviewers by now so that any intelligent reading of his work might seem a bonus, and enough about his public to be aware that book sales would not make him rich. From an artistic point of view, he had as good reason to be satisfied with his accomplishments, and firm in his resolve, as at any other time in his career. Gilbert Seldes, the critic who had sensed his intentions and recognized his achievement more than any other in the past, said of *Tender Is the Night,* as Fitzgerald told a correspondent, "that I had done completely what I started out to do and that it was worth doing." [13] His old friends Edmund Wilson, John Peale Bishop, Christian Gauss, and H. L. Mencken gave him support and appreciation. But his old dilemma returned once more to haunt him.

Fitzgerald badly needed money, and yet he wished to be an artist, like Joyce or Stein, who stood above all mundane things. His hopes, it seems clear, rested on the possibility of selling *Tender Is the Night* to the movies; but neither the reviews nor the sales made the novel an attractive commercial prospect in the eyes of Hollywood. Without a movie sale he would have to go back to popular magazine fiction just to earn a living. "I would rather be an artist than a careerist," he wrote H. L. Mencken a few days after *Tender Is the Night* was published. "I would rather impress my image (even though an image the size of a nickel) upon the soul of a people than be known except in so far as I have my natural obligation to my family —to provide for them. I would as soon be as anonymous as Rimbaud, if I could feel that I had accomplished that purpose—and that is no sentimental yapping about being disinterested. It is simply that, having once found the intensity of art, nothing else that can happen in life can ever again seem as important as the creative process." [14] Yet now he would have to descend once more to the trash he had come to despise. In the fall of 1933 he confessed to Maxwell Perkins, "What worries *me* is the possibility of being condemned to go back to *The Saturday Evening Post* grind at the exact moment when the book is finished. I suppose I could and probably will but I will need a damn good month's rest outdoors or traveling before I can even do that." [15] The victory he had gained over himself and his past was turning out to be no more than the first skirmish in a long and drawn-out war; now he should have to prove his new philosophy of virtue and work and duty, his claim to the title of "serious man," all over again. But nearly all his energy and strength had been spent in the battle to finish *Tender Is the Night.*

II

Tender Is the Night, Fitzgerald said, "completes my story of the boom years." [16] But instead of carrying his story up into the present, Fitzgerald turned next in his fiction to a setting more than a thousand years back in the past. In the month that *Tender Is the Night* was published, he wrote the first Philippe story for *Redbook Magazine.* Later in the fall he wrote three more episodes in the series about a young count in ninth-century France. "Am so fascinated with the medieval series," he wrote Maxwell Perkins in November 1934, "that my problem is making them into proper butcher's cuts for monthly consumption. I have thought of the subject so long that an actual fertility of invention has become even a liability." [17] Fitzgerald's lifelong interest in history partly explains his desire to write a series of stories set in medieval France; but his treatment of the subject makes clear that other motives were at work as well. Like Mark Twain, whom he had emulated at another critical moment in his career, Fitzgerald retreated to the past more directly to confront the present. Mark Twain turned to a medieval setting in *The Connecticut Yankee* as a way of coping with the age of machines, and in "The Mysterious Stranger" to express his cosmic despair. Fitzgerald returned to ninth-century France, in the same way, as a means of handling in his art the political and social issues of the Great Depression.

Fitzgerald's Philippe de Villefranche lives in the late ninth century, two generations after Charlemagne. When Philippe was an infant his father had been killed and he and his mother carried off to Spain. Fitzgerald's story begins twenty years later as Philippe returns to wrest back his land from the invading Normans. His effort takes place in a setting of increasing disorder, the dissolution of institutions, a rapid decline into social chaos. The young and inexperienced Philippe struggles to gain control over his father's domain and to secure the allegiance of peasants who live on his land. For what he lacks in experience, Philippe makes up by toughness and resolution, by a naïve daring tempered by sound political and strategic sense. Above all he can lead. He understands power and is capable of wielding it; in that harsh environment there is no other way to survive.

With his "Count of Darkness" Fitzgerald at last succeeded in creating a different type of hero from the genteel romantics who had dominated his fiction so long. Fitzgerald's ninth-century France bears no trace of the Victorian imagination; his Philippe is rude, and Philippe's men are cruder and crueler. Philippe and his entourage partake of a different form of romantic imagination. They resemble nothing so much as a band of lawless and yet somehow admirable gangsters, as the American imagination of the thirties envisioned such men in films like *Public Enemy*. They use contemporary American slang and gangster argot; Philippe commands the rough and biting wit of a Sam Spade. Philippe de Villefranche is one of the tough-guy heroes of the American thirties, a character one can bring to life by imagining Cagney or Bogart playing his role. Lacking the comic invention and fantasy of Mark Twain's medieval setting— aspects of Mark Twain's Victorian cast of mind that Fitzgerald now rejected—the Philippe stories became instead an incongruous mingling of historical and contemporary realism. Though Fitzgerald planned to write ten stories in the series and presumably to publish them quickly as a book, *Redbook*'s editors had second thoughts after taking three. With only four completed Fitzgerald turned in disgust to other things; the fourth story, finally accepted by *Redbook*, was published only after his death.[18]

After writing the first Philippe story in April 1934, Fitzgerald returned as he had forecast to the *Post* grind. He wrote three *Post* stories in the late spring and summer of 1934. In style and conception they rank among the weakest short stories Fitzgerald had written thus far in his career, but two make partial efforts to deal directly with the present. "No Flowers" compares three generations at their college proms, the Gilded Age of the late nineteenth century, the golden age just before 1917, and the "tin age" of the Great Depression. "New Types" even more directly carries on the effort begun in the Philippe series. Paula Tressinger is a new type: tough, ruthless, and determined. Leslie Dixon, back from long years in China, encounters this type he had not known in America before. "So with Paula now, facing her proud mask, he saw his country all over again. He felt, simultaneously, that awesome loneliness of that which had led them all here, and a pride in the fact that somehow they had done so many of the things they had promised to do in their hearts. The ambition of lonely farmers, perhaps—but the cloth of a great race cannot be made out of the frayed lint of tired princes. . . ." The story ends sentimentally and happily.[19]

Meanwhile, when Zelda Fitzgerald became ill once more, Fitzgerald polished up two of her short articles for *Esquire,* a new magazine that Arnold Gingrich had started in the autumn of 1933, and to which Ernest Hemingway was regularly contributing. "Show Mr. and Mrs. F. to Number—" appeared in the May and June numbers, "Auction—Model 1934" in July, thus beginning the magazine connection that was to sustain Fitzgerald, if not financially at least as a publishing author, for the remainder of his life. In the fall of 1934 Fitzgerald wrote two short, mediocre stories for *Esquire,* "The Fiend" and "The Night Before Chancellorsville." [20] His total production, then, in the nine months from April to December 1934, showed no diminution of energy—nine stories, revising Zelda's articles and writing several of his own, and extensive but unsuccessful efforts to sell *Tender Is the Night* and another story to the movies. Certainly Fitzgerald was not shirking his work and duty; what virtue lay in such a miscellaneous and generally inferior output is another question. But it was only half the drain on Fitzgerald's energy during this period, and the other half contained the straws that broke the camel's back.

It had been customary for Fitzgerald throughout his career to publish a collection of short stories after each novel. But never before had he faced a situation like the one that confronted him after *Tender Is the Night.* All the stories he had written since "The Rich Boy" were available—counting his new stories of 1934, more than fifty in all—but there were few he had not stripped of a character or a phrase or an incident for *Tender Is the Night.* By midsummer 1934, he was hard at work selecting and checking. "The slow thing is to look through *Tender Is the Night* and see what phrases I took out of the stories," he explained to Maxwell Perkins. "This is confused by the fact that there were so many revisions of *Tender* that I don't know what I left in it and what I didn't leave in it finally." [21] Once again he was trapped in a dilemma of his own making. Many of the good stories had been stripped. Scenes from "Jacob's Ladder," "The Bowl," and "Basil and Cleopatra" became part of Dick's love affair with Rosemary. Scenes from "One Trip Abroad" and "Indecision" went into the Swiss setting of the novel. A portion of "The Rough Crossing" was used for Dick's Atlantic voyage. But many of the stories that were still available Fitzgerald refused to reprint without extensive revision. "There are certain other stories in the collection that I couldn't possibly *think* of letting go out in their current form," he wrote angrily when Perkins suggested revisions would not be necessary. "I fully realize that this may be a very serious inconvenience to you but for me to undertake anything like that at this moment would just mean sudden death and nothing less than that." [22]

He planned to work on new material during the daytime and revise the old stories in the evenings, but this heavy burden of work soon began to wear him down. Tired and wrought up, he had trouble sleeping nights, and his work in the day became doubly difficult. He missed the deadline for publishing the story collection in the fall, but still he worked on, sleeping less, and now once again drinking more. Forced back into the past to revise the stories he had written four or six years before, he found himself, like Charlie Wales in "Babylon Revisited," prisoner of a past he was powerless to rectify. Like Dick Diver, he could neither avoid the past nor throw it over. Slowly, then with growing awareness, he discovered he could no longer maintain his belief that he was a "serious man." In the summer and fall of 1934 Scott Fitzgerald's crack-up began.

III

"Crack-up" was Fitzgerald's name for the crisis of self-confidence he passed through after the publication of *Tender Is the Night*. Outwardly he suffered poor health and insomnia. He drank more, spoke bitterly about his profession, and constantly moralized with his daughter and her friends. His physical ills of course exacerbated his sense of artistic and intellectual failure, perhaps even served as its primary cause. After all he had determined that *Tender Is the Night* should be his final word on the genteel romantic hero, should put the seal on his story of the boom. He had avoided identifying himself with the plight of his hero Doctor Diver, had even affirmed his own career and purpose by creating the genteel hero's decline in his art. Moreover, he had known not to expect popular and financial success from the novel. Yet in the months after April 1934, he suffered as hard a fall as if he had been more than ever freighted with illusions.

In the heat of his triumph in finally completing *Tender Is the Night* he did not take to heart what his artistic success and his intellectual self-mastery implied: he did not fully appreciate that with *Tender Is the Night* he was closing off a subject for his fiction and the phase of his career directed to exploiting that subject. At the moment he proclaimed himself a "serious man," asserting that virtue and work and duty were all that mattered to him in life, Fitzgerald no longer possessed a subject to be serious and virtuous and dutiful about. When at last it came clear to him, pressed upon him by the weight of a decade's dull and lifeless magazine production, his new self-affirmation crashed down like a house of cards. Lacking a subject to write about, Fitzgerald began to doubt he could go on as a writer. It was this self-doubt, replacing so swiftly the resurgence of competence and power he had felt as he finished *Tender Is the Night*, that made Fitzgerald fear he had cracked up.

The reception of *Tender Is the Night* was the first harsh blow to his self-confidence. He thought he was prepared for the worst from the reviewers, but public criticism is difficult for the healthiest of writers to take, and in Fitzgerald's case the good face he put on only briefly concealed the rankling he felt underneath. How deeply he had been hurt he made clear a few months later in an introduction to The Modern Library reissue of *The Great Gatsby*. He used the introduction as an opportunity to reply to conventional critics who had overpraised his early books and failed to understand *Gatsby* or *Tender Is the Night*. "How anybody could take up the responsibility of being a novelist without a sharp and concise attitude about life is a puzzle to me," he said, alluding to the complaints of reviewers like Mary Colum and J. Donald Adams that he lacked a firm "grasp of life." Recalling the days before he wrote *Gatsby*, he made a similar rebuttal: "I had recently been kidded half haywire by critics who felt that my material was such as to preclude all dealing with mature persons in a mature world. But, my God! it was my material, and it was all I had to deal with." Fitzgerald's tone of bitter and yet uncertain self-justification was far different from the quiet confidence of "How To Waste Material: A Note on My Generation," written after the disappointing reception of *The Great Gatsby*, or the firm conviction of Frank Norris's "The True Reward of the Novelist," which his own introduction faintly echoes. "Your pride is all you have," Fitzgerald wrote, "and if you let it be tampered with by a man who has a dozen prides to tamper with before lunch, you are promising yourself a lot of disappointments that a hard-boiled professional has learned to spare himself."[23] But after fifteen years as a professional, Fitzgerald himself had not yet learned.

Shortly after the reviews were in, Fitzgerald was jarred again by an unexpected blow from Ernest Hemingway. As far back as 1929, with *A Farewell to Arms*, Hemingway had emerged the winner in his personal competition with Fitzgerald for popularity and critical acclaim, so that Fitzgerald's continued caution in dealing with his friend seemed at times excessive almost to paranoia. But Fitzgerald's caution was justified: even twenty years after Fitzgerald's death Hemingway in *A Moveable Feast* still kept the battle going. Yet no form of caution could have prepared Fitzgerald for the cruel strike that Hemingway delivered in response to *Tender Is the Night*. Hemingway not only had reservations about the new novel; he expressed criticism of Fitzgerald's choice of a wife and deprecated *The Great Gatsby*. One need not be a partisan of either man to recognize that Hemingway no longer respected Fitzgerald, and that Fitzgerald, despite the even tone of his reply to Hemingway's "old charming frankness," knew it.[24]

Thereafter, blows came rapidly. *Tender Is the Night* failed to interest the movie studios, closing the door to a financial windfall that might have rescued the author from his debts and his indenture to the popular magazines. The *Post* meanwhile rejected a story, and *Redbook* vacillated over the medieval series. Growing physically weaker, drinking more, Fitzgerald was trapped in the fatiguing effort to put together a book from old and unsatisfactory stories. In the fall of 1934, a few installments of Edmund Wilson's *To the Finland Station* appeared in *The New Republic,* and Fitzgerald wrote Wilson "to agree passionately with an idea that you put forth in a discussion of Michelet: that conditions irretrievably change men."[25] Only a few months before, Fitzgerald had reminded H. L. Mencken that he had decided to be an artist, rather than a careerist. By late 1934 it seemed unlikely he could manage to be either.

One of the curious ironies of Fitzgerald's crack-up period was the growing gap between the person and the legend, the way Fitzgerald thought and the way that others thought of him. In a time when scores of writers were turning left, it should hardly be necessary to insist that Fitzgerald turned, too. Yet Fitzgerald is rarely mentioned among the radical writers of the thirties: the incongruity with his reputation would be too great. Nevertheless, Fitzgerald for some time considered himself a communist. Early in the fall of 1934 he wrote his cousin, Mrs. Richard Taylor, that he had given up politics. "For two years I've gone half haywire trying to reconcile my double allegiance to the class I am part of, and the Great Change I believe in. . . . I have become disgusted with the party leadership and have only health left enough for my literary work, so I'm on the sidelines. It had become a strain making speeches at 'Leagues Against Imperialist War,' and their treatment of the Negro question finished me." [26] Fitzgerald had spoken on "How the War Came to Princeton" at a meeting of the Student Congress Against War in Baltimore. But more than a year later an anti-war drama he had written was played on a radio program called "World Peaceways"; Paul Robeson and Senator Gerald P. Nye also appeared on the show.[27]

Yet in a realm far removed from pacifist politics and personal fate, a different Scott Fitzgerald ascended to a place of eminence he had hardly dared hope for. In the thirties no one had forgotten him; rather they rediscovered an earlier Fitzgerald. More precisely, they invented him. By the mid-thirties Fitzgerald already served as the symbol of the Flapper Age. All the complicated social changes of the postwar decade, the altered relationships between parents and children and the loosening of sexual mores, were simplified and condensed into one comprehensible image: the female heroine of F. Scott Fitzgerald's popular stories. Half a decade after their passage into history the twenties were recalled as "the F. Scott Fitzgerald era," and the high-living, audacious young people who had vanished into a dull and serious maturity were remembered as "the F. Scott Fitzgerald generation." For those who looked back with nostalgia and for those who looked back with derision Fitzgerald equally provided the symbols. To one his heroines were "golden girls," to the other they were "flappers who treated their elders with fine high scorn." As he passed through his crisis of self-confidence Fitzgerald meanwhile collected scores of magazine and newspaper clippings which recognized him as the creator or the spokesman for an age and a generation. Of course they gave him credit for much he had not done; inevitably the spokesman comes to stand for more than one person alone can encompass, and spokesman was a role that he had never shunned. Nevertheless, Fitzgerald was distressed to find himself called "the prophet of Flaming Youth and very little restraint." He had been out of the country a decade earlier, and thus unaware, when conventional writers began to tar the moralist of the Flapper era with its amoralities.[28]

In a newspaper interview he gave in 1935 Fitzgerald tried to restore some precision and subtlety to the legend of the generations. With his characteristic feeling for the nuances of social change he distinguished six different generations in the twenty years since the War. The prewar generation, the last generation in the Victorian tradition, he described as inhibited, and fundamentally moral in its ideas and actions. For the war generation, his own, Fitzgerald referred significantly to a novel: Hemingway's *A Farewell to Arms*. Between 1919 and 1929 Fitzgerald found two generations, neither of whom he admired. The postwar generation was essentially weak, he believed, without standards or vitality, and looked to the two earlier generations for guidance. Fitzgerald carefully dissociated himself from this generation, of whom he was thought to be the prophet. Rather he recalled the two controversial college novels of the mid-twenties, *The Plastic Age* and *Flaming Youth*, which had described the sex life of college youth with the lack of restraint of which Fitzgerald himself was accused. He carried his condemnation further toward the second generation of the twenties, the generation of the Boom, whom he called "brassy, metallic, and in their ethics unsympathetic." Their best quality, he said, was a scorn of weakness, their worst, "a sort of inhumanity." The generation of the Crash was similar to the War generation: the blow had given it dignity. Finally there came the generation of the Depression, the children of hard times. "The less the parents of today try to tell their children," Fitzgerald cautioned, "the more effective they can be in making them believe in a few old truths. This generation should be held close to whatever elements of character we have been able to find and develop in ourselves." [29]

Fitzgerald talked often of character, but now with more confidence than ever, and in a review of *Taps at Reveille*, the new collection of stories, William Troy recognized that character had all along been Fitzgerald's principal theme. *Taps at Reveille* came out finally in the spring of 1935, and most reviewers treated it as an occasion either to pan or to shake their heads over Fitzgerald once more. But Troy took it as an opportunity to talk about Fitzgerald's career as a whole, and although he was critical he gave Fitzgerald a rare kind of intelligent and sympathetic review. "If Mr. Fitzgerald could enlarge his vision to correspond to his interest," his interest, that is, in character, Troy wrote, "he would do much both for his own reputation and for the amelioration of current American fiction." [30]

By the time *Taps at Reveille* was published, the worst phase of the crack-up seemed over. Finishing the story collection and removing its burden from his shoulders helped boost Fitzgerald's spirits, and meanwhile he was trying hard to keep from drinking. Early in 1935 he wrote "The Intimate Strangers," a sentimental popular story in the old manner, but which demonstrated at least his evocative romantic prose style, unimpaired, for the first time since *Tender Is the Night*.[31] It showed that he could return to the familiar formula and do it just as well as ever, but he did not want to. The old manner and the old themes were dead, long live the new. But the new was yet to be born. "I've simply got to arrange something for this summer that will bring me to life again," he wrote Perkins in April, "but what it should be is by no means apparent." [32] Searching his resources, he found nothing but Philippe. Two days later he wrote Perkins again with a plan for turning the medieval story into a novel, whatever *Redbook* thought of its parts. "That is my only plan," he confessed. "I wish I had these great masses of manuscripts stored away like Wolfe and Hemingway but this goose is beginning to be pretty thoroughly plucked I am afraid." [33] He never carried the Philippe project further. Instead he slipped back into the conventional popular mode, but with far less success than before. The first story was fair of its type, the second mediocre. "It was easier" to write sentimental stories, he told Julian Street, who had praised one, "when I was young and believed in things and hoped that life might be a happy matter for some people. But as you learn that happiness is a prerogative of the perennial children of this world, and not too many of them, it becomes increasingly difficult." [34] In the summer of 1935 Scott Fitzgerald had recovered his health but not yet his hope: he was an archer who could find no more arrows in his quiver, a writer who apparently had nothing left to write.

IV

Fitzgerald's art had always encompassed more than simply his life transformed into fiction: his best work possesses its beauty and its value because it was formed within literary traditions and social settings that transcend an artist's personality. Fitzgerald himself knew this, but he knew as well the limits of his inspiration. "Mostly, we authors must repeat ourselves—that's the truth," he wrote not long after he returned to genteel romantic heroism as the central theme for *Tender Is the Night*. "We have two or three great and moving experiences in our lives . . . then we learn our trade, well or less well, and we tell our two or three stories—each time in a new disguise—maybe ten times, maybe a hundred, as long as people will listen." [35] His own two or three great and moving experiences took place in the realms of love and imagination: he wrote the best-seller and he won the girl. No doubt his personal success made possible the several score sentimental love stories he wrote. But he lost the girl, too—lost her momentarily to an adulterous act, and lost then, even more, the "golden girl" of his romantic imagination. This personal loss certainly must have provided some aspect of the emotional maturity and depth of understanding which shapes his best work, *The Great Gatsby* and *Tender Is the Night*. Yet Fitzgerald was an artist, and no matter how often thereafter he founded his fiction in a sense of loss, he did so as an act of artistry and not as self-confession: the sense of loss was not specifically of *his* loss. His art was different from his life, and the greater his art the less it drew overtly on his life. So in fact he did possess one last, most personal of arrows for his bow, if only he cared to use it.

The summer of 1935 Fitzgerald lived at a resort hotel in Asheville, North Carolina. There he met a young married woman, and they engaged in a brief love affair. When it was past he wrote about it to the novelist James Boyd. "I have just emerged not totally unscathed, I'm afraid, from a short violent love affair . . ." he said. "I had done much better to let it alone because this was scarcely a time in my life for one more emotion. Still it's done now and tied up in cellophane and—and maybe some day I'll get a chapter out of it. God, what a hell of a profession to be a writer. One is one simply because one can't help it." [36] Whatever else the affair meant to him it seemed to release him from the burden of holding silently within himself the act of adultery which had caused his personal loss a decade before. Returning to Baltimore in early fall he wrote "Image on the Heart," a short story quite clearly based on Zelda Fitzgerald's brief love affair with a French aviator in 1924.

A young American goes to meet his girl at a university town in southern France, where she has been studying. They are to be married there. But a week before his arrival a French aviator had come into town on leave, and the American girl had fallen in love with him. Nevertheless, the marriage goes on as planned, but it can never be the way it might have been. "When the stars were bright on the water," the story ends, "he said: 'We'll build our love up and not down.' 'I won't have to build my love up,' she said loyally. 'It's up in the skies now.' They came to the end of France at midnight and looked at each other with infinite hope as they crossed the bridge over into Italy, into the new sweet warm darkness." [37] With "Image on the Heart" Fitzgerald at last completed the past—overcame the final and most personal aspect of his past, and turned it into art. In one conquering artistic gesture "Image on the Heart" marks an end to the past and also a new beginning. As soon as "Image on the Heart" was done he began the "Crack-Up" essays. The story belongs with them as the first part of his confession—the first act in his new effort explicitly to make Scott Fitzgerald's life the central subject of his art.

In his ledger Fitzgerald put down the "Crack-Up" essays as "biography." Even if this were a slip of his pen, it conveys an essential truth: the Scott Fitzgerald who was his subject was not, or at least was no longer, himself. The "Crack-Up" essays were self-confession but they were equally self-creation, a means of drawing the line between future and past, a ritual gesture to separate a new life from the old. The old Scott Fitzgerald had withered away late in 1934, his purpose in life completed; a new Scott Fitzgerald, risen in his place, through his art would give the former self a decent eulogy. The essays form a drama in three acts. Act One, "The Crack-Up," describes the destruction of the old Scott Fitzgerald, "cracked like an old plate." Act Two, "Pasting It Together," clears away the debris. Act Three, "Handle With Care," reconstructs a new Fitzgerald.[38] What makes the drama seem more real than staged is the sense that self-creation moves hand in hand with creation of the prose: the making of art and the making of biography—or autobiography—comprise in fact the very same gesture. Until he formed his story through his art, Fitzgerald did not know who he would become.

"The Crack-Up" describes Fitzgerald's loss of vitality, his feeling that life had lost its savor. "I began to realize that for two years my life had been a drawing on resources that I did not possess, that I had been mortgaging myself physically and spiritually up to the hilt. What was the small gift of life given back in comparison to that?—when there had once been a pride of direction and a confidence in enduring independence." What was to be done, he could only say with a wry effort at humor, "Will have to rest in what used to be called the 'womb of time' " (72). In "Pasting It Together" Fitzgerald gives "a cracked plate's further history" (75)—a picture of how the pieces looked when they broke apart. "A man does not recover from such jolts," Fitzgerald said, recalling the traumatic moment when he had to drop out of Princeton and thus forfeit the presidency of the Triangle Club, "—he becomes a different person and, eventually, the new person finds new things to care about" (76). Writing *This Side of Paradise* and belatedly winning the girl turned him into yet another person, one with "an abiding distrust, an animosity, toward the leisure class." This was Scott Fitzgerald the famous writer, "distrusting the rich, yet working for money with which to share their mobility and the grace that some of them brought into their lives" (77), born in 1920 and passed away by 1935. Curiously, though Fitzgerald described the core of his crack-up as a loss of physical strength and spiritual vitality, "a call upon physical resources that I did not command, like a man over-drawing at his bank" (77), his most concrete statement of what it was like came as an outburst against the movies—an expression of pique because he had lost the race for popularity.

"So there was not an 'I' any more—not a basis on which I could organize my self-respect—save my limitless capacity for toil that it seemed I possessed no more. It was strange to have no self—to be like a little boy left alone in a big house, who knew that now he could do anything he wanted to do, but found that there was nothing that he wanted to do—" (79). In the third essay, "Handle With Care," Fitzgerald proclaims his new self. His break with the past was clean. "The old dream of being an entire man in the Goethe-Byron-Shaw tradition, with an opulent American touch, a sort of combination of J. P. Morgan, Topham Beauclerk and St. Francis of Assisi, has been relegated to the junk heap" (84). No longer would he try to lead the life of the genteel romantic hero. "There was to be no more giving of myself" (82). It was a desperate kind of self-assertion, aggressive and a little petty, but finally there was nothing future or conditional about it: "I have now at last become a writer only" (83). So a new Scott Fitzgerald at last emerged; but the most severe of all his jolts lay just ahead.

V

The kind of writer Fitzgerald became after the "Crack-Up" essays was the sort "Image on the Heart" and the essays had prophesied—one who writes openly and candidly about himself. He started pleasantly enough by writing an amusing story, "Too Cute for Words," about a widower with a thirteen-year-old daughter like his own. The *Post* took the story, and Fitzgerald hoped to launch Bryan Bowers and his daughter Gwen into a series like the Basil or the Josephine stories, promising both steady subjects and steady money. But the second story was much inferior to the first, and the series was soon abandoned.[39]

For *Esquire* Fitzgerald followed the "Crack-Up" essays with a series of personal sketches which served almost as footnotes to the essays, or as experimental trials of his resolution, "I have now at last become a writer only," as if to test its strength. The first, "Three Acts of Music," is fiction, but a story less about people than about popular music. Back in his Triangle Club days at Princeton Fitzgerald had thought about becoming a song writer, and the possibility had never been forgotten over the years. Now it was as if in his story he were asking what it might have been like to give people a few lyrics to sing, instead of the "golden girl," the legend of the flapper. "We've had all that anyhow, haven't we?" a woman says in the story. "All those people—that Youmans, that Berlin, that Kern. They must have been through hell to be able to write like that. And we sort of listened to them, didn't we." [40]

Thereafter he wrote two sketches called "Author's House" and "Afternoon of an Author." The house in "Author's House" is the author's creative mind, the storehouse of experience and events that make him a writer, and the kind of writer he is. As the author and his guest move from room to room the author describes the building of his consciousness, his house of fiction. At last they reach the top, the tower from which the author had once, briefly, surveyed the entire landscape. Coming down the visitor says, "It's really just like all houses, isn't it?" The author agrees. "I didn't think it was when I built it, but in the end I suppose it's just like other houses after all." [41]

The next piece, "Afternoon of an Author," is less symbolic and more directly autobiographical, but no less an effort to review and reconsider his whole artistic life. The author goes out to the barber one afternoon for a shampoo, and as he moves through the day his mind ruminates on himself and his career.

> The shampoo ended. When he came out into the hall an orchestra had started to play in the cocktail room across the way and he stood for a moment in the door listening. So long since he had danced, perhaps two evenings in five years, yet a review of his last book had mentioned him as being fond of night clubs; the same review had also spoken of him as being indefatigible. Something in the sound of the word in his mind broke him momentarily and feeling tears of weakness behind his eyes he turned away. It was like in the beginning fifteen years ago when they said he had "fatal facility," and he labored like a slave over every sentence so as not to be like that. "I'm getting bitter again," he said to himself. "That's no good, no good —I've got to go home." [42]

But it was bitterness and self-reproach above all that marked these reminiscences. The assertion that was to mark Fitzgerald's emergence from the crack-up, "I have now at last become a writer only," was never farther from the truth.

"Never any luck with the movies," the author in "Afternoon of an Author" warned himself. "Stick to your last, boy." [43] But the last no longer produced durable goods, and the temptation of the movies was growing harder and harder to resist. Once song writing had truly been appealing, but back in 1919 popular music was a tried and tested, stereotyped form, while fiction offered new and open opportunities. Yet looking at postwar American literature in 1935, the excitement and success of fiction writing in the early twenties might have seemed a completion rather than a new beginning. Mencken's creative leadership in criticism once appeared far more stimulating than the motion picture work of D. W. Griffith, and who in the movies could compare with Lewis and Anderson, Conrad and Joyce, Stein and Dos Passos? But in 1935 the positions were reversed.

"I saw that the novel," Fitzgerald wrote in "Pasting It Together," "which at my maturity was the strongest and supplest medium for conveying thought and emotion from one human being to another, was becoming subordinated to a mechanical and communal art that, whether in the hands of Hollywood merchants or Russian idealists, was capable of reflecting only the tritest thought, the most obvious emotion. It was an art in which words were subordinated to images, where personality was worn down to the inevitable low gear of collaboration. As long past as 1930, I had a hunch that the talkies would make even the best selling novelist as archaic as silent pictures ... there was a rankling indignity, that to me had become almost an obsession, in seeing the power of the written word subordinated to another power, a more glittering, a grosser power ..." (78). But now that his own written words seemed to have completely lost their power, Fitzgerald was ready to stifle his indignation and cast his lot with the alluring new medium; after all, the desire to reach an audience had always been as strong in him as the desire to practice a pure art form, and now that his prose artistry seemed to have deserted him what else held him back? As early as December 1935, the same month he wrote the last two "Crack-Up" essays, Fitzgerald talked with his agent about signing on in Hollywood as a screenwriter. His resolution, "I have now at last become a writer only," stood then primarily in reference to his social life, and was open all along to the possibility of different tasks and different forms. By June 1936, when he wrote the last story of his career for *The Saturday Evening Post*, Hollywood was only a matter of time.

In July, diving at a hotel pool in Asheville, Fitzgerald broke his shoulder. He was laid up in bed following this accident when the

August 1936 *Esquire* arrived, containing his own sketch, "Afternoon of an Author," and Hemingway's story, "The Snows of Kilimanjaro." Reading Hemingway's story, he came across the passage, "The rich were dull and they drank too much, or they played too much backgammon. They were dull and they were repetitious. He remembered poor Scott Fitzgerald and his romantic awe of them and how he had started a story once that began, 'The very rich are different from you and me.' And how someone had said to Scott, Yes, they have more money. But that was not humorous to Scott. He thought they were a special glamorous race and when he found they weren't it wrecked him just as much as any other thing that wrecked him." [44] Fitzgerald was furious and deeply hurt. The casual reader of the August *Esquire* might have thought that Hemingway had said nothing more damaging about Fitzgerald than what Fitzgerald, in "Afternoon of an Author," had said about himself. But one man's self-reproach is different from another's cutting condemnation; and Fitzgerald had never mentioned Hemingway's name in print except to praise him. With so ugly a gesture to bear from the man he had only recently called his "artistic conscience," Fitzgerald a few weeks later was visited by a journalist for the New York *Post*, who went back and wrote an article exposing Fitzgerald in all his physical weakness and loss of pride. If that were not unhappy enough, *Time* picked up the story and gave it national exposure. All those who had wondered whatever happened to Scott Fitzgerald could now know that he had crashed as completely as the era to which the press was so fond of giving his name.[45]

Whatever depths Fitzgerald reached in the wake of Hemingway's gibe and the newspaper exposé, on the surface he was less despairing than he had been in the months after publication of *Tender Is the Night*. In the earlier period, the one he described in the "Crack-Up" essays, he had felt himself slipping, and feared the unknown abyss that suddenly lay open before him. By late 1936 he was more familiar with misfortune, and knew the contours of the chasm where he fell. Hemingway's insult he managed within a short time to shake off. "He is quite as nervously broken down as I am," he wrote of Hemingway to a friend, "but it manifests itself in different ways. His inclination is toward megalomania and mine toward melancholy." [46] Melancholy became Fitzgerald's word for his condition. Rather than the anguish he had suffered in the crack-up days, he settled into a persistent state of gloom. "This general eclipse of ambition and determination and fortitude," he told Perkins, "all of the very qualities on which I have prided myself, is ridiculous, and, I must admit, somewhat obscene." [47] His attention shifted toward the future. He did not know what he would do, but he was able to look forward to some next step, whatever it might be. He was waiting.

Fitzgerald was writing, too, but as a writer of prose fiction he had slipped more disastrously than in any other way. Between the summers of 1936 and 1937 he wrote eight short stories for *Esquire*. The best of them, "An Alcoholic Case" and "Financing Finnegan," are of interest only because they are so clearly autobiographical. Several of the others are as crudely conceived as the stories Fitzgerald wrote when he was in his teens. In a reminiscence Fitzgerald wrote early in 1937 his mind drifted back over the days of his early success, when *This Side of Paradise* was a best-seller and he wrote "The Camel's Back" in one sitting and "Bernice Bobs Her Hair" raised a storm among readers of *The Saturday Evening Post*. He re-created his own early self as a romantic hero like the romantic heroes of so many of his stories, and he allowed his readers to sense the young man's fate only by implication. "And there are still times when I creep up on him," the article ends, "surprise him on an autumn morning in New York or a spring night in Carolina, when it is so quiet that you can hear a dog barking in the next county. But never again as during that all too short period when he and I were one person, when the fulfilled future and the wistful past were mingled in a single gorgeous moment—when life was literally a dream." [48] In the final passage of "Early Success" Fitzgerald revived his romantic sensibility with the same poignancy and suggestiveness as in the last pages of *The Great Gatsby*. For part of him was like Gatsby now, the old romantic part, while part of him was Nick Carraway, surviving the magical creative figure, and judging him. The wheel of Fitzgerald's life had turned full circle, and at last he was ready to start life anew. In June 1937, a screenwriter's contract came through for him. Relieved, and once more excited, Fitzgerald left at once for Hollywood.

CHAPTER TWELVE

F. Scott Fitzgerald went out to Hollywood in the summer of 1937 with the hope that a new life and new career lay open before him. His old career and life had long since slipped away. Abruptly, when Zelda Fitzgerald suffered her first mental breakdown in 1930, Fitzgerald broke away from the literary circles in which he had lived and worked during the twenties. In Switzerland and Baltimore he made his life among doctors and nurses and a small group of friends. At first he profited from a circumscribed social setting. It provided him energy and time for writing, and withdrawn into this quiet world he succeeded at last in completing *Tender Is the Night*. But as years went by, as he retreated from Baltimore to the mountain resorts of North Carolina, as the doctors and nurses who peopled his life became his own and not his wife's, Fitzgerald fell into an isolation as morbid and as creatively stultifying as Hawthorne's years of self-seclusion in a garret. He found no way to struggle free from his morass until the Hollywood opportunity lifted him bodily out of it, carried him three thousand miles across the continent into a new job —really his first work on salary since his brief days in advertising— and a new community of artistic endeavor. "There are no second acts in American lives," Fitzgerald had put in his notebook during the dark days of his crack-up.[1] Arriving in Hollywood, he set out to prove that statement false.

316

On his way west Fitzgerald thought through his strategy. Twice before he had tested his talent in Hollywood, twice before he had failed. His first effort early in 1927 had come at a critical moment in his career. *The Great Gatsby,* published in 1925, had been recognized by fellow writers as an important work of art; with *All the Sad Young Men* in 1926 the reviewers belatedly hailed Fitzgerald as the best of the young American writers. Sales of the dramatic and film rights to *Gatsby* had freed Fitzgerald from his bondage to *The Saturday Evening Post,* and he planned to move swiftly ahead on a new novel. But at the height of his success, Fitzgerald faltered. He seemed to have convinced himself that Ernest Hemingway was a superior artist; and living in a community of expatriate writers on the Riviera, he began to lose his conception of his work as well as of his status. The year free from financial pressure was a wasted year. Fitzgerald returned from France directly to Hollywood, where his rank as the leading American writer still went unchallenged. "At that time I had been generally acknowledged for several years as the top American writer," he recalled for his daughter a decade later, "both seriously, and as far as prices went, popularly. I had been loafing for six months for the first time in my life and was confident to the point of conceit." In the back of Fitzgerald's mind lay the possibility that screenwriting might supply him with an easy source of income while he devoted his creative energies to his novel. But through overconfidence Fitzgerald muffed his opportunity. The script he wrote was rejected, and financial necessity drove him back to writing stories for the *Post.*

When he returned a second time from Europe, the new novel hardly nearer to completion than it had been five years earlier, Fitzgerald tried his luck in Hollywood once more. This time, he said, "Far from approaching it too confidently I was far too humble." He never got a chance to submit a complete script because another man changed it as he wrote. That script too was rejected, and Fitzgerald left, "disillusioned and disgusted." On his third try he was determined not to make the same mistakes. "I must be very tactful but keep my hand on the wheel from the start—find out the key man among the bosses and the most malleable among the collaborators—then fight the rest tooth and nail until, in fact or in effect, I'm alone on the picture. That's the only way I can do my best work." [2] All his energy and concentration was mustered for the effort, for this third time he could not afford to fail.

Yet no matter how great his financial need or how desperate the state of his career, there was something equivocal in Fitzgerald's approach to Hollywood in 1937. He could not start anew even if he wanted to. He had not been hired at a thousand a week because of any demonstrated proficiency as a screenwriter, but because of his success as a writer of fiction. At least until he established himself with several screen credits, his leverage lay in his status as a novelist and short-story writer. So long as his period of apprenticeship lasted, Fitzgerald was forced to keep one foot in and one foot outside Hollywood, even if he wanted to plunge in with both; for in a crisis his court of last resort remained his fiction. This form of equivocation would naturally pass away if Fitzgerald succeeded; after a year or two he could become unequivocally a screenwriter, as William Faulkner and Nathanael West had attained professional status as screenwriters, no matter what they did or said as novelists.

But there was another form of equivocation that would not pass away, an equivocation that existed in Fitzgerald's mind. In his crack-up days he may have despaired because movies had superseded fiction as mass entertainment, but he never conceived the possibility that movies might equally with fiction aspire to serious art. For Fitzgerald the novel was still the important form, the serious form, "the strongest and supplest medium for conveying thought and emotion from one human being to another"; and as he had written one of the greatest novels of his generation, no matter how enthusiastically he might throw himself into a new career in the movies, he could not but feel that the work was only second best.[3] Unlike Faulkner and West he was in too desperate a position to feel either hard-boiled or indifferent. Against his own advice he had let a few conventional book reviewers tamper with his pride, but he was determined not to extend the privilege to anyone in Hollywood.

Even before Fitzgerald began his new career, then, his venture into Hollywood gave him an unexpected chance to settle at last the central issue of the old career. Under the worst of circumstances he was able to make a choice, when under the best of circumstances a decade previously, he could not; and now he chose fiction as an art, rather than fiction as a means to popular success. Of course the decision was threadbare and theoretical. Neither alternative lay open to him: he seemed unable to produce either a work of art or a salable popular story. Nevertheless, the choice itself was of fundamental importance. By stating the old alternatives in a new way, Hollywood made it possible for Fitzgerald to solve the dilemma that had dominated his literary life ever since, with *The Great Gatsby,* he had proven to himself that he was an artist as well as a commercial story writer. After *Gatsby* he knew that the fusion of popular success with critical acclaim he had achieved with his first novel had been accidental and spurious, a lucky conjunction of the right book at the right moment to fill the right need. Yet he could not shake off that combination as a desirable and attainable goal, and intermittently thereafter he sought it, with growing vacillation between the poles of art and popularity, with increasing confusion as to his own best aims and procedures. By 1937, with both possibilities seemingly closed off, he saw that his failure was caused not only by his personal mismanagement, but also by an indecisive strategy.

Hemingway was his prime example. Back in 1925 and 1926 Hemingway had been one of the snags on which he was caught, because with Hemingway he could parade neither his commercial success nor his dedication as an artist—Hemingway made him feel inferior in both aspects of his career. Now he discovered that Hemingway, by proclaiming his adherence to the purest standards of artistry even as his writing grew more and more commercial, had achieved the fusion of critical acclaim and popular success that had eluded Fitzgerald since *This Side of Paradise.* It was the pose that counted, far more than the result, as the whole history of his reputation with the conventional reviewers and the popular press could have told him. But the issue was no longer a living one. So long as Hollywood had taken over the field of popular entertainment that Fitzgerald's sentimental *Post* stories once had dominated, Fitzgerald's choice was simple: the only way he could conceive of himself as a writer of fiction was to conceive of himself pre-eminently as an artist. The popular pole of his old dilemma thus was subsumed in his screenwriter's job; the artistic pole he retained, intact but for the moment unapproachable. If the old dilemma ever were to reassert itself, it would come as a conflict between the movies and his fiction.

II

Fitzgerald's first assignment in his new job at Metro-Goldwyn-Mayer studios was a backhanded tribute to his old reputation. He was given the task of final revision on the script of *A Yank at Oxford*, which was about to go into production as the first M-G-M movie filmed in England under a new commercial arrangement. There was a curious circumstance in the assignment that pointed up from the start the gap between Fitzgerald as a novelist and Fitzgerald as a screenwriter: Fitzgerald himself had never attended Oxford, but in his two important novels his fictional heroes, Jay Gatsby and Dick Diver, had.

The irony was extended with Fitzgerald's second assignment, one in which he came in at the beginning rather than the end. He was put to work preparing a "treatment"—a synopsis or scenario—on Erich Maria Remarque's *Three Comrades*, a novel set in Germany after the First World War and conveying the atmosphere of social and moral decay. After reading the treatment, the producer, Joseph Mankiewicz, gave the responsibility for writing the script jointly to Fitzgerald and an experienced Hollywood screenwriter, Ted Paramore. Paramore had been a friend of Edmund Wilson's, and Fitzgerald had known him back during the glorious days in New York after *This Side of Paradise* and *Flappers and Philosophers* had established Fitzgerald as a popular favorite. He had even called one of the minor characters in *The Beautiful and Damned* Fred Paramore, but if the portrait was drawn from life it was not meant to be flattering. Now Paramore stepped in and frustrated Fitzgerald's desire to work alone on the script. Fitzgerald acknowledged his own inexperience but obviously it grated on him to have a man he considered a studio hack rework his prose and ideas; he sensed, too, whether rightly or wrongly, that Paramore considered him at best an amateur and at worst a washed-up drunk, and he bridled at it. Conflict rapidly developed. Avoiding a face-to-face confrontation, Fitzgerald wrote Paramore a long letter, climaxed by an appeal which revealed his true feelings of superiority over both his material and his colleagues: "the idea of sitting by while you dredge through the book again as if it were Shakespeare—well, I didn't write four out of four best-sellers or a hundred and fifty top-price stories out of the mind of a temperamental child without taste or judgment." [4]

The battle between fiction and movies broke out almost at once, then. But it was joined not on the ground of art against entertainment, but on the seemingly lost territory of popular fiction; Fitzgerald's claims to artistry were his ultimate weapon, and using them would have closed off all opportunities for maneuver and reconciliation. Nor was he as sure of himself on that ground as he was in the back files of *The Saturday Evening Post*. Struggling to keep his mark on *Three Comrades,* he appealed again and again to his past triumphs as an entertainer. After the collaborators' script was submitted, the producer Mankiewicz extensively rewrote it. Once more Fitzgerald's anger flared. "I guess all these years I've been kidding myself about being a good writer . . . ," he complained to Mankiewicz. "For nineteen years, with two years out for sickness, I've written best-selling entertainment, and my dialogue is supposedly right up at the top. But I learn from you that it isn't good dialogue and you can take a few hours off and do much better." [5]

Over Mankiewicz's head Fitzgerald appealed to Eddie Mannix, the studio's general manager, and Sam Katz, the administrative executive. "In writing over a hundred and fifty stories for George Lorimer, the great editor of *The Saturday Evening Post*, I found he made a sharp distinction between a sordid tragedy and a heroic tragedy—hating the former but accepting the latter as an essential and interesting part of life." [6] The tone was loftier but the implication was the same: Fitzgerald knew as much about good entertainment as they did, and because he was older and more experienced, perhaps more. Mankiewicz, Mannix, and Katz may not have known that Fitzgerald was exaggerating his own success—he had published more than sixty stories in the *Post,* a remarkable total in itself, even if less than half his claim. But they would not have doubted they knew more about movies than he did. *Three Comrades* was a popular film and the leading actress won an award for her performance. Fitzgerald received a screen credit on the picture, and if he were striving for success as a screenwriter, outwardly he had taken a big step toward his goal. But Fitzgerald did not gladly suffer the indignities he felt Paramore and Mankiewicz had inflicted upon him, and he was already in process of giving up his plans to forge a new career.

Fitzgerald's life and thoughts are more thoroughly recorded for his Hollywood years than for any other period in his career, yet one must feel that his state of mind is more closely veiled in these years than in any others. Living across the continent from his family and friends, he wrote more letters than ever before, and since he was dictating now to a secretary, the carbons have all been preserved. But there were good reasons why he should want to conceal his true feelings as he never had before. He had just gone through a physical and mental decline of serious proportions; he was in debt more than forty thousand dollars. Optimism was his watchword, then; any suggestion of discouragement and discontent could only have raised doubts in the East about his capacity to carry through his work and pay off his debts.

Moreover, the nature of his life in Hollywood reinforced his desire to appear cheerful, bland, and conventional. He knew that he had come out west on probation, and that sobriety and responsibility were basic conditions of his survival in Hollywood. The movie colony itself formed as isolated and inbred a community as a diplomatic enclave in a hostile foreign country. His desire for privacy in so public an atmosphere was intensified by his romance with Sheilah Graham, the Hollywood newspaper columnist. Consciously Fitzgerald did not try to dissimulate to anyone, yet in several ways the life he led took on the character of a double life—in no way more significantly than in his outward life as a screenwriter and his secret life as an artist planning to re-emerge some day as a butterfly from his cocoon.

At some point, not long after he arrived in Hollywood, Fitzgerald determined once more to write fiction. In his letters he was most straightforward in writing to a friend who shared neither his Eastern nor his Hollywood acquaintances. While he was working on *Three Comrades* he wrote her, "I feel something fermenting in me or the times that I can't express and I don't yet know what lights or how strong will be thrown on it. I don't know, even, whether I shall be the man to do it. Perhaps the talent, too long neglected, has passed its prime." [7] But what he considered his humiliation on *Three Comrades* gave new urgency to his own secret plans and hopes. "I am considered a success in Hollywood," he wrote to his friend again in March 1938, "because something which I did not write is going on under my name, and something which I did write has been quietly buried without any fuss or row—not even a squeak from me. The change from regarding this as a potential art to looking at it as a cynical business has begun." [8] That same day he told Maxwell Perkins, "I am filling a notebook with stuff that will be of more immediate interest to you, but please don't mention me ever as having any plans." [9]

M-G-M had renewed Fitzgerald's six-month contract for an additional year with a raise in pay. After *Three Comrades* Fitzgerald went to work on a script called "Infidelity," designed as a vehicle for the actress Joan Crawford. Since the film was based on a magazine story rather than a novel, Fitzgerald had far more freedom than he was allowed at any point on *Three Comrades,* and he approached more closely than ever the situation he had hoped for on his arrival. But because of censorship difficulties the script was put aside. Then the ironies of his new career took another twist. He was put to work on *The Women* with Donald Ogden Stewart, who had figured even more than Paramore in Fitzgerald's glamorous past. Stewart had written the first parody of Fitzgerald's popular fiction back in 1921. Now he, too, was a successful screenwriter, and Fitzgerald had little more to do on *The Women* than polish up Stewart's script. Thereafter he wrote a treatment and began a script for *Madame Curie,* but was dropped from the picture after disagreements on how it should be done. At the end of 1938 his M-G-M contract expired, and it was not renewed. The new career was over, with nothing for the moment more tangible to show than a lot of cancelled debts.

Fitzgerald could not have worked seriously on fiction while he was under contract to M-G-M; the movie work took up too much time and energy. Instead in his free time he carried on a project he had begun in North Carolina during the days of his crack-up, organizing and arranging his notebooks. He put in order his scattered notes and odd bits of manuscript by categories: anecdotes, ideas, moments, and more than a dozen others. In the selection from the notebooks Edmund Wilson printed in *The Crack-Up,* a large portion of the notes may be identified as passages from published short stories that Fitzgerald "stripped and permanently buried." A careful collation would probably find in the notebooks some snatch of dialogue or description from every story Fitzgerald chose not to reprint. The notebooks make clear that what Fitzgerald wanted to keep from his buried stories were primarily passages of sentimental romance—descriptions of beautiful heroines and of love-smitten heroes. Another major portion of the notebooks is made up of passages from discarded sections of the early *Tender Is the Night* manuscript, the story of Francis Melarky to which Fitzgerald gave the working titles *Our Type* and *The World's Fair*. It is unlikely that Fitzgerald organized the notebooks as a working device or sourcebook for future fiction; rather, he was emulating *The Notebooks of Samuel Butler*, a book he had admired from his youth, and may have had in mind their eventual publication.

The original part of Fitzgerald's notebooks lies in his brief section of notes and comments on literature. In the moments when he worked on the notebooks he may have been incapable of writing fiction, but his sense of his art and intellect came through with greater clarity than ever. Through his notebooks he made a private peace with Hemingway: "I talk with the authority of failure—Ernest with the authority of success. We could never sit across the same table again." Yet even as he referred to his personal failure, Fitzgerald knew that it was part of something greater than himself. "The two basic stories of all times are *Cinderella* and *Jack the Giant Killer*," he wrote, "—the charm of women and the courage of men. The Nineteenth Century glorified the merchant's cowardly son. Now a reaction." The merchant's cowardly son is not a precise description of the convention of the genteel romantic hero, who required, whether in Tom Sawyer or Penrod Schofield or one of Fitzgerald's own heroes, a basic daring and imagination; but it cuts through the surface of the convention and reveals that the bravery and cleverness of the genteel hero belong to a woman's world, a polite society world, rather than to a world of manly courage.

How strongly Fitzgerald joined in the reaction against the merchant's cowardly son he made clear in a sardonic note about Booth Tarkington, who still wrote sentimental genteel stories for the *Post* with undiminished vigor as he approached three-score and ten. "Tarkington: I have a horror of going into a personal debauch and coming out of it devitalized with no interest except an acute observation of the behavior of colored people, children, and dogs." Fitzgerald had gone into a personal debauch and come out of it devitalized and written thereafter several stories featuring children and colored people, and even one entirely about dogs. But they were not his only interests, as obviously he felt they were Tarkington's. Why he had come out differently from Tarkington he suggested in a note on D. H. Lawrence, with whom Fitzgerald had come to share an abhorrence of the merchant's cowardly son. "D. H. Lawrence's great effort to synthesize animal and emotional—things he left out. Essential pre-Marxian. Just as I am essentially Marxian." Fitzgerald was not saying he was a Marxist, only that he had learned—whether from social instinct or personal circumstances or intellectual development —to comprehend social classes and social mores in basically economic terms. His "essentially Marxian" outlook enabled him to understand his own failure in a wider context than the personal, just as he had come to understand the failure of a class and the weakness of its literary genre. "Show me a hero," Fitzgerald put down in his notebook, "and I will write you a tragedy." [10] The unequivocal conviction of that sentence amounted, in 1938, almost to a prophecy.

III

Fitzgerald's plans for a new novel were already taking shape by the spring of 1938. The notebook he mentioned as being of immediate interest to Maxwell Perkins in March could not have been a notebook filled mainly with snatches from *Our Type* and old *Post* stories, so it must have been a book of notes for something new. But for more than a year thereafter Fitzgerald could not have advanced with it very far. The burden of his motion-picture work was too great for serious creative effort; and after M-G-M dropped his contract in January 1939, he continued as a screenwriter on a free-lance basis. He worked for several weeks on the script of *Gone with the Wind* and then signed on as a writer for the movie *Winter Carnival*. His trip to Dartmouth for the filming turned into a personal disaster that served nearly to wipe out his career as a free-lance screenwriter and plunged him as well into serious illness. He worked briefly on one more movie, *Air Raid*, and suffered through another bout of illness before he was capable of creative work in midsummer 1939. By then his financial security had been wiped out, and to meet current expenses he had to try once more to write popular stories for the magazines.

But he had come to loathe that work, and he could bring it off no longer. The first story he wrote was turned down by the *Post* and then by *Collier's;* it may have been the story about Hollywood, "Discard," published posthumously by *Harper's Bazaar* in 1948, among the most inept and formless stories Fitzgerald ever wrote. *Collier's* did accept from Fitzgerald a Civil War story he had begun back in 1936; when it was printed nearly a year later Fitzgerald confessed to his wife and daughter that "it seemed terrible to me." [11] But if Fitzgerald had lost his touch as a writer of popular sentimental stories his talent as a short-story writer still had not completely deserted him. For *Esquire,* which Arnold Gingrich held open as always to him, Fitzgerald wrote two brief stories that were published late in 1939. "Design in Plaster" is a story similar to "Image on the Heart," about the conduct of a man who is jealous of his woman's interest in a Frenchman; "The Lost Decade" is the story of a man's reactions after returning to the world from a ten-year drunk.[12] Neither is an important story, but together they demonstrate a new hardness and a new worldliness in Fitzgerald's attitude toward his material. His inability to sell his sentimental stories released him from the evasive formulas which he had been able to overcome only in a handful of his popular stories. Thereafter he wrote two retrospective stories— "Three Hours Between Planes" and "News of Paris—Fifteen Years Ago," both published posthumously—which retained the old quality of romantic emotion, and yet treated the relations between men and women with an honesty, almost a toughness, rarely before attained in his short fiction.[13]

Yet it was hardly Fitzgerald's intention in the summer and fall of 1939 to let his best energies and perspectives, even if he could accommodate them as never before in his short stories, go to waste in the back pages of *Esquire.* Over the years his market had called for long stories, twice the length or more of what *Esquire* could use; and among his best short stories, "May Day," "The Diamond as Big as the Ritz," and "The Rich Boy" are the length of novellas. "News of Paris—Fifteen Years Ago," because it is an unfinished draft for a story, provides a useful insight into Fitzgerald's tactics as a writer. The relations among the characters are suggested rather than defined;

Fitzgerald's prose is as deep and as subtle as it is because the story is a fragment—because the scene is open-ended and sufficient to itself, as in a novel. Had Fitzgerald completed the story it seems likely that in giving it form and focus, a beginning, a climax, and an end, he would have reshaped his material into a tighter, more direct, more logical structure, thus sacrificing some of its depth and subtlety for the requirements of the short form as he had always practiced it. Contrary to the belief of some of Fitzgerald's interpreters that he was essentially a poet writing in alien forms, Fitzgerald rather developed his talent and fulfilled his creative intentions most completely in the novel. "I wish now I'd *never* relaxed or looked back," he wrote in 1940 to his daughter, "—but said at the end of *The Great Gatsby:* 'I've found my line—from now on this comes first. This is my immediate duty—without this I am nothing.'...." [14]

But his immediate financial needs still had to be met, and the only avenue open to him remained the short story. Instead of exchanging sentiment for seriousness, though, he had another plan in mind. "It isn't particularly likely that I'll write a great many more stories about young love...," he explained to Kenneth Littauer, fiction editor of *Collier's.* "Nevertheless, an overwhelming number of editors continue to associate me with an absorbing interest in young girls—an interest that at my age would probably land me behind the bars." In describing his new strategy, Fitzgerald's point of reference once more was his genteel predecessor, Booth Tarkington, perhaps because Tarkington continued so consistently as a successful magazine writer. "My hope is that, like Tarkington, if I can no longer write *M. Beaucaire* and *The Gentleman from Indiana,* I can make people laugh instead, as he did in *Seventeen,* which is completely objective and unromantic." [15] Now that his own daughter was seventeen, Fitzgerald once more could find amusement in Tarkington's oblivious adolescents, as he had in his own collegiate days.

From sentiment Fitzgerald turned, then, to satire. The shift came suddenly in September 1939, when the energy that produced the serious stories "Design in Plaster," "The Lost Decade," and "Three Hours Between Planes," gave out in the middle of an unfinished story. Yet literally he could not subsist unless he wrote and sold something. Hurriedly he wrote a story about a middle-aged failure, a drunk, a Hollywood hack screenwriter who had never made the transition from silent films to talkies. Within a week he had finished another, and ten days after that a third. The Pat Hobby stories so clearly met his need for a new subject, one that could draw on his most recent experience, one with continuity and the limitless possibilities of a series, and most of all one that would bring him immediate cash on acceptance—that he wrote ten in all before the year was out, and a total of seventeen.

But Fitzgerald never allowed himself to believe that in Pat Hobby he had come up with a middle-aged equivalent to Tarkington's genteel adolescents as a subject for satire. When he was half-way through the series he referred to it in a letter to Maxwell Perkins as "unprofitable hacking for *Esquire*," a comment hardly commensurate with a sincere satiric intention; and the fact that he followed many of the original submissions with revised manuscripts suggests that he was primarily interested in payment on acceptance, and only secondarily on the quality of his prose in print.[16] In any case the Pat Hobby stories hardly meet the requirements of satire: they are infrequently and then only briefly humorous. On the contrary their plots more often turn on pain and violence: a broken leg, a heart attack, even death. By the time he wrote these stories, Fitzgerald had read Nathanael West's novel about Hollywood, *The Day of the Locust*, where the scene of Harry Greener's death, even against the reader's will, is gruesomely funny.[17] Fitzgerald was not deeply concerned with attaining similar satiric effects. Rather, the Pat Hobby stories served him best—besides their primary purpose as a source of income —as a purgation, a clearing away of the debris of his aborted Hollywood career, a cleansing of whatever bitterness or self-reproach he felt for having tried and failed as a screenwriter. For Fitzgerald planned to put his Hollywood material to far more significant uses, and the Pat Hobby stories fulfilled a valuable enough purpose if they drained off his small vindictiveness and petty piques, leaving his mind clear and objective for the large task at hand, a new novel. Rushed by the possibilities of selling serial rights to the novel—thus relieving himself of the necessity to write more Hobby stories—Fitzgerald began the novel in October 1939, only a few weeks after the Hobby series was launched.

IV

From his first conception of the new novel, Fitzgerald intended to set it in Hollywood. The idea of writing a Hollywood novel, however, may have come to him even before he entered the motion-picture community as a screenwriter. In 1936, when he was laid up with his shoulder injury in North Carolina, he told Maxwell Perkins that he was thinking about another novel; and it may be that the possibility of a Hollywood novel was suggested to him then by the death of Irving Thalberg, the Metro-Goldwyn-Mayer producer, in September 1936.

One can hardly re-create Fitzgerald's frame of mind when he learned of Thalberg's death, but the circumstances were such as to be deeply affecting. Thalberg was two and a half years younger than Fitzgerald. When they first met in 1927—Fitzgerald age thirty, Thalberg twenty-seven—they presented curious parallels and contrasts to each other, contrasts that Fitzgerald, by later evidence, keenly felt. Both men came from distantly immigrant, respectable, middle-class backgrounds. Fitzgerald had been the first significant Irish Catholic American novelist, Thalberg one of many ambitious Jewish business and professional men who found large possibilities in motion pictures—like Joseph Black, born Bloeckman, the movie man Fitzgerald created with curiously mixed disdain and respect in his 1922 novel, *The Beautiful and Damned.* In 1927 Fitzgerald brought to Hollywood the artistry he had developed and the fame he had earned—and confronted in Thalberg a man who possessed neither artistry nor fame, who was rather a gifted entrepreneur, and a man who preferred anonymity. What Thalberg possessed was power, and with power, responsibility; and it was Thalberg's sense of power that fascinated Fitzgerald. In retrospect he came to feel that Thalberg indeed was an artist in his use and consciousness of power.

Fitzgerald worked on a film for Thalberg in 1932, but under circumstances of collaborative writing that could only make Fitzgerald chafe. In 1934, Fitzgerald believed it was Thalberg who turned down *Tender Is the Night* for M-G-M—and thus cut off Fitzgerald's only means of escape from the downward spiral into his crack-up. In his mood of melancholy, with his fortieth birthday a few days ahead, Fitzgerald's response to Thalberg's death could only have been complex and intense.[18]

But two full years passed before Fitzgerald began seriously to plan his novel about Hollywood, and by late 1938 his own experience of Hollywood, and the place itself, had changed enormously since Thalberg's death. During his year and a half under contract to M-G-M, Fitzgerald gained the intimate day-to-day knowledge of studio operations he had lacked when he previously knew Thalberg. When Fitzgerald worked for M-G-M, moreover, the studio was entering a period of crisis and change with which Thalberg had nothing to do. During Fitzgerald's tenure there the old order which Thalberg exemplified came under attack from three different sources—from minority stockholders, who accused executives of hoarding profits for themselves through excessively high salaries and bonuses; from unions, seeking to organize the studios; and from the federal government, which filed antitrust suits against film companies that owned studios and theaters together.[19]

Fitzgerald's own experience in Hollywood and the new economic developments of the late thirties formed the background for his Hollywood novel quite as much as his brief encounters with Thalberg or the legend Thalberg left behind him. Monroe Stahr in *The Last Tycoon* is no more a portrait of Irving Thalberg than Dick Diver in *Tender Is the Night* is a portrait of Gerald Murphy or Jay Gatsby a portrait of one or another gangster bootlegger Fitzgerald occasionally glimpsed on Long Island in the early twenties. What shapes the character of Monroe Stahr is not so much the persons, living or dead, on whom he may have been modeled, nor the setting on which Fitzgerald drew for plots and scenes, but rather Fitzgerald's literary motives and artistic skills; for *The Last Tycoon*, as for all other significant work he produced throughout his career, Fitzgerald was neither biographer nor autobiographer nor social reporter, but in all essential aspects a creative artist. The form and substance for Fitzgerald's portrait of a producer and an enterprise were provided partly by factual models but just as much by his own resources.

As he began to make plans for the novel in mid-1938, Fitzgerald regarded these resources of his with a certain sadness and uncertainty, and yet with urgent determination. By now his past was a remote, almost a historical, experience, and he felt himself a forgotten author, forgotten even by his publishers of twenty years' standing. To his daughter at school in the East, toward whom distance made him feel even more insistent and possessive, he wrote poignant letters warning her against his own mistakes, revealing his innermost feelings about his past. He told her he had made a mistake in marrying her mother. "I was a man divided—she wanted me to work too much for *her* and not enough for my dreams." He warned her too about how much she could rely on himself. "You don't realize that what I am doing here is the last tired effort of a man who once did something finer and better." But despite his sadness and uncertainty, perhaps because of them, he was not yet willing to give up the beliefs he developed and maintained as the bedrock of his literary career. "My generation of radicals and breakers-down," he told his daughter, "never found anything to take the place of the old virtues of work and courage and the old graces of courtesy and politeness." [20]

A woman wrote to him about her nervous breakdown, and Fitzgerald answered, "I can only say this: that if you are in any mess caused by conflict between old idealisms, religious or social, and the demands of the immediate present, you will probably have to make a decision between them." [21] Around the same time, on the inside back cover on his copy of James Joyce's *Dubliners*, he put down more succinctly than ever before his artistic perspective on the conflict between ideals and realities that formed so central a theme in his fiction. "I am interested in the individual," he wrote, "only in his relation to society. We have wandered in imaginary loneliness through imaginary woods for a hundred years—Too long." [22] For himself, the necessity of choice concerned him far less than the nature of the conflict itself. Once more in his art Fitzgerald felt capable with Keats "of being in uncertainties, Mysteries, doubts . . . of remaining content with half knowledge." [23] In his new novel he meant to dramatize, rather than resolve, the conflict between old idealisms and the demands of the immediate present—dramatize it in his portrait of a Hollywood producer enmeshed in the political and economic struggles of his day: the last tycoon.

In September 1939, encouraged by the interest of Kenneth Littauer at *Collier's*, Fitzgerald described his plans for the novel in a lengthy letter, and in October he began to write. A few weeks later he was able to show Littauer about six thousand words, in hope of arranging monthly advance payments for serial rights. But Littauer wanted to see more before making a definite decision, and temporarily he said no. The *Post* also read the manuscript, and was not ready to commit itself either. Presumably the section Fitzgerald gave them comprised the first scenes of the novel, on the transcontinental flight and at the Hermitage in Nashville, scenes which convey Fitzgerald's subject only obliquely, and with which he later grew dissatisfied. Failing to obtain his advance, Fitzgerald fell back on Pat Hobby stories for *Esquire* to meet expenses through the winter of 1940. In late spring a producer hired him to write a script from his short story, "Babylon Revisited." That job carried him through the summer, and another movie assignment took up his time through early fall. Between these tasks Fitzgerald moved ahead on the novel.[24]

He was living Hollywood intensely in his art now, and hardly living in the social and professional community of Hollywood at all. As the novel grew in length its daily life came to envelop his own. Released almost from the cares of time, his mind in spare moments slipped into retrospective moods: he thought often of the past. When an aunt died he cast his mind back over his family heritage, pondering the sources of the values he had inherited and put to such important uses in his art. "What a sense of honor and duty," he wrote of his father's generation, "—almost eighteenth century rather than Victorian. How lost they seemed in the changing world—my father and Aunt Elise struggling to keep their children in the haute bourgeoisie when their likes were sinking into obscure farm life or being lost in the dark boarding houses of Georgetown."[25] And there was more than simply historical pathos in Fitzgerald's feeling for his father's generation, for he, too, seemed lost in a changing world, struggling to keep his daughter in Vassar College as he faded into obscurity, like a Nathanael West character, in one of Hollywood's pink and mustard Moorish flats. "But to die, so completely and unjustly after having given so much!" he lamented to Maxwell Perkins, not for his physical death but the death of his reputation, the death in life of a writer whom no one any longer reads. "Even now there is little published in American fiction that doesn't slightly bear my stamp—in a *small* way I was an original."[26]

In a small way now he worked to regain the distinctive style and form that marked his greatest artistry. For his new novel he took

The Great Gatsby as the model. "It is a constructed novel like *Gatsby*," he wrote his wife, "with passages of poetic prose when it fits the action, but no ruminations or side-shows like *Tender*. Everything must contribute to the dramatic movement. . . . It is a novel *à la Flaubert* without 'ideas' but only people moved singly and in mass through what I hope are authentic moods." [27] By early December 1940, he had progressed far enough so that he could talk of completing the first draft in one month's time. But he had already suffered his first heart attack, and one month's time was not left to him. On December 20, 1940, he was struck by a second heart attack, and on the following day by a third, and fatal, one. With the last and most ambitious of his novels only half finished, F. Scott Fitzgerald died at the age of forty-four.

V

Fitzgerald's old friend Edmund Wilson edited the completed portion of *The Last Tycoon* and published it in 1941 with *The Great Gatsby* and several of the most important stories. In his notes Wilson made clear that Fitzgerald intended to revise the chapters he had written; and they comprise only a little more than half of Fitzgerald's projected outline for the story. *The Last Tycoon* remains then only a fragment—a fragment of great interest and of considerable accomplishment, but a fragment nonetheless, and not amenable therefore to criticism or interpretation in the same manner as Fitzgerald's earlier work. The social and economic themes which were to play so important a role had barely been alluded to in the chapters Fitzgerald wrote; nor had he fully resolved the problems of telling his story through the eyes of Cecilia Brady, a movie producer's daughter. For all the incomparable touches that show how well Fitzgerald had recovered his skill as a stylist, inevitably there are frequent inconsistencies and rough spots. With the example of *Gatsby* guiding him so closely, Fitzgerald surely would have placed great importance on the final polishing of the text. Even *Madame Bovary* had been brought to life only in Flaubert's last revisions, as Edmund Wilson some years later learned to his surprise.[28] Yet Fitzgerald completed enough of *The Last Tycoon*, and brought his themes sufficiently to focus, so that his intentions and his means for carrying them through may partly be described.

Fitzgerald's choice of Hollywood as his subject was dictated by far more than his predicament in being linked to it, more even than his interest in the character and genius of Irving Thalberg. He was drawn to write about Hollywood—as in his most idealistic moments he felt himself drawn to work in it—because of his fascination with the public arts, with popular modes of entertainment. Motion pictures now seemed to him the most glittering power among the popular arts. In Monroe Stahr's projection room, "Dreams hung in fragments at the far end of the room, suffered analysis, passed—to be dreamed in crowds, or else discarded" (56). Hollywood was now the spokesman for America's dreams, the motion-picture industry fulfilled the role Fitzgerald himself once aspired to—in a limited way indeed had attained. Hollywood not only spoke for the nation's dreams, it manufactured them—and to Fitzgerald this signified far more than simply the skills and popularity of a single art form. If the movies made the dreams America dreamed, then they were more than just an art form, they were a focal point of national culture, a molder of the nation's destiny.

Fitzgerald's concern with national destiny was revived in 1940 by a gift from Maxwell Perkins, J. F. C. Fuller's book, *Decisive Battles: Their Influence Upon History and Civilization.* Acknowledging the gift in a letter to Perkins, Fitzgerald recalled his own first encounter with Oswald Spengler's thought—though dating it incorrectly—and once again considered Spengler's ideas and influence.[29] Spengler himself went into *The Last Tycoon* with one of Fitzgerald's light and ironic touches: Kathleen, the woman Stahr loves, had been educated by a man "who wanted me to read Spengler—everything was for that. All the history and philosophy and harmony was all so I could read Spengler, and then I left him before we got to Spengler." Stahr asks about Spengler, and she laughs: "I tell you we didn't get to him" (91). But Fitzgerald had not forgotten what he had learned from Spengler, and writing at a time when Spengler's prophecies seemed partly coming true—at a time when German armies were over-running France—he took Spengler's concept of historical destiny more seriously than ever before. In *The Last Tycoon* he seemed ca-

334

pable of rendering it not through one single personality, as in *Tender Is the Night*, but over a far wider cultural and social scene.

The themes of national history and national destiny are introduced at the very start of *The Last Tycoon*. The flight carrying Cecilia Brady and the three movie men across the continent to Hollywood is grounded at Nashville by a storm. The writer Wylie White invites Cecilia on a drive outside the city to Andrew Jackson's homestead, The Hermitage. Manny Schwartz, the former studio executive down on his luck, goes along too. The modern, mechanical atmosphere of planes and airports with which the novel opens gives way suddenly to a pastoral mood—"real cows, with warm, fresh, silky flanks," mooing in the night (9)—and then as suddenly to a mock pastoral, Cecilia's memory of a flock of sheep on a studio back lot, and a man standing up in a car saying, "swell." The Hermitage itself seems impenetrable and formless in the night, a great grey hulk, a big white box, unequal to the weight of moral values that it bears. But Manny Schwartz has come to take his own life there, and Cecilia belatedly imagines why. "He had come a long way from some Ghetto to present himself at that raw shrine. Manny Schwartz and Andrew Jackson—it was hard to say them in the same sentence. It was doubtful if he knew who Andrew Jackson was as he wandered around, but perhaps he figured that if people had preserved his house Andrew Jackson must have been someone who was large and merciful, able to understand. At both ends of life man needed nourishment: a breast —a shrine. Something to lay himself beside when no one wanted him further, and shoot a bullet into his head" (13).

Manny Schwartz's act is extreme, yet the need Cecilia envisioned for him, his search for some connection with the past, concerns them all. Hollywood is a new world on the far frontier, a "mining town in lotus land" (11), peopled by immigrants—Irishmen like Cecilia's father and Jews like Schwartz and Marcus and Stahr. Hollywood itself grasps for a large and merciful past with which to associate, a past able to understand it. After the first scene at Nashville, however, the link with the past is pursued by analogy to a presidential figure even more imposing than Jackson and universally significant, Abraham Lincoln.

In the completed portion of *The Last Tycoon* Lincoln is viewed as a symbol of the past through three separate perspectives, gradually broadening out to a perception of the essential links between the present and the past. First Lincoln is brought down to the entertainment level of the movies, as nature seemed mocked and humiliated in Cecilia's recollection of the sheep on the studio back lot. Stahr explains to the English writer Boxley what a "routine" is. "It means an act ... George Jessel talks about 'Lincoln's Gettysburg routine'" (33). On its own terms Hollywood admires Lincoln as a clever entertainer.

The second vision of Lincoln's connection with the present comes from the visiting Danish nobleman Prince Agge. Passing through the studio commissary, Agge observes the extras dressed in the costumes of another century, Hollywood's appropriation of the past for its entertainment purposes.

> Then he saw Abraham Lincoln, and his whole feeling suddenly changed. He had been brought up in the dawn of Scandinavian socialism when Nicolay's biography was much read. He had been told Lincoln was a great man whom he should admire, and he hated him instead, because he was forced upon him. But now seeing him sitting here, his legs crossed, his kindly face fixed on a forty-cent dinner, including dessert, his shawl wrapped around him as if to protect himself from the erratic air-cooling—now Prince Agge, who was in America at last, stared as a tourist at the mummy of Lenin in the Kremlin. This, then, was Lincoln. Stahr had walked on far ahead of him, turned waiting for him—but still Agge stared.
> This, then, he thought, was what they all meant to be.
> Lincoln suddenly raised a triangle of pie and jammed it in his mouth, and, a little frightened, Prince Agge hurried to join Stahr. (48-9)

Rather than reducing the past to its own terms, Hollywood in Prince Agge's eyes seems able to make the past live again, to bring forth the best of the past as a standard for its aspirations. Yet what frightened him was the realization that the true past, the past of human lives and living moments, was dead, no less empty and inanimate than Andrew Jackson's mansion; and when they tried to bring it back to life they created nothing but themselves dressed up in old costumes. A vital link between Hollywood's values and the exemplary qualities of the nation's past could only be forged if Hollywood

336

produced, on its own, a figure who could rise to meet the standards of the past.

Through the subtle eyes of the English writer Boxley, in the third vision, Lincoln's symbolic value and his historical significance were brought to life again in the struggles and aspirations of Monroe Stahr. "He had been reading Lord Charnwood and he recognized that Stahr like Lincoln was a leader carrying on a long war on many fronts; almost single-handed he had moved pictures sharply forward through a decade, to a point where the content of the 'A productions' was wider and richer than that of the stage. Stahr was an artist only, as Mr. Lincoln was a general, perforce and as a layman" (106). Stahr himself, with his efforts and his values, alone makes the connection with the past a meaningful one, alone gives Hollywood its significant link with the national destiny. The gap between Stahr and his environment, between destiny grasped and destiny mocked, is brilliantly conveyed in the scene of Stahr's telephone call from the "President." Thinking it is President Roosevelt, with whom he has talked before, Stahr is impressed, formal, eager—then crestfallen. For the call in reality is from an agent or publicity man trying to interest Stahr in an orang-outang which resembles President McKinley.

Why is Stahr, though, the significant one among so many others outwardly like him? "He was a rationalist," Cecilia explains his indifference to Marxism, "who did his own reasoning without benefit of books—and he had just managed to climb out of a thousand years of Jewry into the late eighteenth century. He could not bear to see it melt away—he cherished the parvenu's passionate loyalty to an imaginary past" (118). Yet surely he was neither the only emancipated Jew nor the only parvenu on the studio lot. Earlier, in a lyrical flight of romantic imagination, Cecilia envisions him soaring high on strong wings. "And while he was up there he had looked on all the kingdoms, with the kind of eyes that can stare straight into the sun. Beating his wings tenaciously—finally frantically—and keeping on beating them, he had stayed up there longer than most of us, and then, remembering all he had seen from his great height of how things were, he had settled gradually to earth" (20). But Cecilia's fancy is hardly consistent with her unsentimental honesty and wry sense of ironies; nor does her image of Stahr's foresight

337

explain his particular capacity for leadership, why he was "a marker in industry like Edison and Lumière and Griffith and Chaplin" who "led pictures way up past the range and power of the theatre, reaching a sort of golden age, before the censorship" (28). "ACTION IS CHARACTER," Fitzgerald reminded himself in capital letters in his notes, and by showing Stahr's qualities of leadership in action Fitzgerald intended to demonstrate rather than simply proclaim his special nature.

Stahr was an artist, Boxley thought, only perforce and as a layman—an artist first in life, as a necessary condition for making his artistry effective among professionals. Significantly Stahr reveals the particular nature of his artistry in the scenes with the skeptical Englishman, who questions the value of movies themselves as an art. In the first scene Boxley comes in angry and disgusted at his collaborators, at the very nature of the form. Stahr begins to talk: "Suppose you're in your office. . . . A pretty stenographer that you've seen before comes into the room and you watch her—idly." Stahr describes her taking off her gloves, opening her purse and dumping out the contents. He stands up and throws his own keys on the table. The girl, he continues his story, puts her gloves in the stove and is about to light it. The telephone rings. She answers it, speaks, hangs up, goes back to the stove and lights the match. "You glance around very suddenly and see that there's another man in the office, watching every move the girl makes—" (32). Stahr puts his keys away. He has vividly conveyed a sense of dramatic action, and Boxley is won over.

In the second scene with Boxley, Stahr demonstrates his theatrical sense once more. He takes Boxley with him to a stalemated script conference. "He took some change out of his pocket, looked up at the suspended light and tossed up half a dollar, which clanked into the bowl. He looked at the coins in his hands and selected a quarter" (106). For half an hour four or five men pitch coins into the light fixture while Boxley works over the script. Suddenly Boxley speaks up with criticism and new ideas. "Pitching the coins had done it as much as Boxley. Stahr had re-created the proper atmosphere—never consenting to be a driver of the driven, but feeling like and acting like and even sometimes looking like a small boy getting up a show" (107). Action is character and Stahr acts with a subtle sense of dramatic movement, with a capacity for involving others in his schemes, like a small boy getting up a show: Stahr, like Gatsby and Dick Diver, like half a hundred characters in Fitzgerald's short stories, is the willful young man of clever imagination, the genteel romantic hero. But just before the note, "ACTION IS CHARAC-TER," Fitzgerald had warned himself, "Don't wake the Tarkington ghosts" (163). Monroe Stahr's character is drawn within the basic framework of genteel romantic heroism, but with Stahr more than with any other of his heroes Fitzgerald thrust away the formulas of Victorian sentiment and conservative evasion, and shaped the character by developed artistic and intellectual conceptions of his own.

As Fitzgerald conceived the character of Monroe Stahr he brought the special nature of his hero to its consummation. His genteel heroes in the past had been creative figures who constructed social settings out of their imaginations—Gatsby's orgiastic parties with their regenerative function, Dick Diver's manners which recognized each person's proud uniqueness, gave each one back his blurred and buried self. Yet in each case the hero regarded his creative role as mere entertainment, a brief expedient as substitute for, or means toward, fulfilling romantic dreams of love. Neither man took up the role, moreover, with a fully conscious commitment: Gatsby assumed it out of a vast romanticism and a grand naïveté, Dick Diver from force of circumstance and personal weakness. Each in his own way was shaped by the ghostly Tarkington qualities Fitzgerald now cautioned himself against, the qualities of the romantic young man convinced that society offered him love and wealth in return for his talents and his good behavior. Both *The Great Gatsby* and *Tender Is the Night* dramatize, in different ways, the tragic or pathetic consequences of this false belief. But not until Monroe Stahr in *The Last Tycoon* was Fitzgerald capable of creating a genteel romantic hero in complete command and fully committed to his special powers.

In *The Last Tycoon* the character of Monroe Stahr was not meant to be the sole support for the novel's central themes, but rather the means whereby Fitzgerald drew them together into a unified whole. Stahr is the genteel romantic hero raised to the status of a creative figure by the practical nature of his leadership in the motion-picture industry, an industry dedicated to entertainment on a grander and more ambitious scale than any other, ever, in history. He had begun his rise to power from the base where all Fitzgerald's significant genteel heroes started, the romantic dreams and social aspirations of the middle-class young man on the make; and it is his nature as a genteel romantic hero that gives meaning to Cecilia Brady's observation that "he cherished the parvenu's passionate loyalty to an imaginary past" (118). The past to which Stahr gave his loyalty—the past of Lincoln, the eighteenth-century values of honor and duty—may have been an imaginary past, but how could there be a connection at all with the past, a historical destiny for the nation, without someone to imagine it? When Stahr spoke, he made even so cynical and indifferent a man as Wylie White feel "a great purposefulness. The mixture of common sense, wise sensibility, theatrical ingenuity, and a certain half-naïve conception of the common weal which Stahr had just stated aloud, inspired him to do his part, to get his block of stone in place, even if the effort were foredoomed, the result as dull as a pyramid" (43). Common sense, wise sensibility, theatrical ingenuity, and a half-naïve conception of the common weal—in sum, the genteel romantic hero, brought to his full stature at last. "There's always some lousy condition...," Stahr says to Boxley. "Our condition is that we have to take people's own favorite folklore and dress it up and give it back to them. Anything beyond that is sugar. So won't you give us some sugar, Mr. Boxley?" (105).

Monroe Stahr is the perfect model of F. Scott Fitzgerald's genteel romantic hero, in the perfect position for his talents. If in the uncompleted portion of the novel Stahr was to be defeated by social and economic forces he could not control, it was not to be a sign of weakness in himself, but of his full participation in the movement of national history, his submersion in a social destiny larger than the self. Fitzgerald had come a long way with the stereotyped character he had inherited from the sentimental novels and boys' stories of the Gilded Age. From Amory Blaine forward he had tried to wrest the willful young man of creative imagination away from the conservative role in a stable social setting which genteel literature had established for him, to explore his traits and talents with the styles and techniques of modern literature, to state his plight in relevant post–World War social and economic terms. With *The Great Gatsby* he re-created the genteel hero as a grand and tragic figure, and wished then to turn to something else. But he had not said his last about the genteel hero, and in *Tender Is the Night* he extended his themes in a different way. Again he felt he was done with genteel heroism as a subject, and then again he changed his mind.

With *The Last Tycoon* Fitzgerald returned once more to the tradition in which he had worked throughout his career, reaffirming his connection with the literary past, unifying and confirming his effort to make past themes and values live again by stating them anew. How far he had come from the ghosts of Booth Tarkington and genteel American literature he made clear by his understanding that his father's sense of honor and duty belonged to the eighteenth century rather than the Victorian age, and by associating Monroe Stahr's vision of an imaginary past, his half-naïve conception of a common weal, with the eighteenth century, too. In a way Fitzgerald was making articulate for the first time in years his realization, back in the early twenties, of the difference between plutocrats and aristocrats, a distinction of central importance in his career, which cleared away the confusions of *The Beautiful and Damned* and made possible the subtle renderings of wealth and values in *The Great Gatsby*.

In his final conception of the genteel romantic hero, Fitzgerald demonstrated with greater clarity and depth than ever before why, in no small way, he was an original. In the genteel American literature of Fitzgerald's youth, the romantic hero devoted his talents to the plutocrats, to the class that ruled because of wealth. Fitzgerald tore this figure down and in his major novels re-created him. His romantic heroes, resembling the genteel stereotype in all outward aspects, gave their loyalties to an aristocratic sense of virtue that seemed once to have existed in an older America. They were visionaries of a moral order that the American past made available to them, even if an imaginary one; and the tragedy and pathos of their individual lives bound them essentially to the nation's destiny. Show me a hero, Fitzgerald had said, and I will write you a tragedy. Fitzgerald's genteel romantic heroes were real heroes, men with the audacity and imagination and skill to create their visions of felicity in a living social setting; and their defeats were not only tragedies of the self, but tragedies for the society that bore them and yet could not sustain them. Throughout his career Fitzgerald never rested content with his intellect and accomplished artistry, but struggled always in his novels toward a firmer understanding of the moral qualities and values he dramatized in conflict, toward a finer control over his art. In his generation of American novelists F. Scott Fitzgerald filled the role of Laocoön. He was the Last Laocoön; the last until another novelist succeeds him.

ACKNOWLEDGMENTS

A book is both a solitary and a communal enterprise. It is a pleasure to record the names of those who have personally or intellectually shared in making this one. With all other students of F. Scott Fitzgerald, I am indebted to the biographical researches of Arthur Mizener, Henry Dan Piper, and Andrew Turnbull; among earlier critical studies on Fitzgerald, I have been particularly aided by the work of James E. Miller, Jr., and Matthew J. Bruccoli. Alexander P. Clark, Curator of Manuscripts, greatly assisted me on several visits to the Fitzgerald collection at the Princeton University Library. I am also indebted to Mrs. Neda M. Westlake and Lyman W. Riley in using manuscript collections at the University of Pennsylvania Library, and to Richard Hart and Betty Adler for their help at the H. L. Mencken Room, Enoch Pratt Free Library, Baltimore.

Kenneth S. Lynn and Frank B. Freidel encouraged the project from an early stage and gave me valuable advice and criticism on the manuscript at many points. William W. Freehling and Sally Steinberg read portions of the manuscript, and their criticisms of style and conception have significantly helped me. Whitney Blake and Mary Ollmann of Oxford University Press made many valuable suggestions and improvements in the text. Penny Gottlieb assisted me greatly in the final work of preparing the manuscript, and Judith Reynolds in compiling the index. Mrs. Linda Marshall, Mrs. Dorothy Foster, and Mrs. Esther Rentschler typed the manuscript. A grant from the Graduate School of Arts and Sciences, Harvard University, enabled me to begin the project, and a grant from the Faculty Research Fund of the Horace H. Rackham School of Graduate Studies of The University of Michigan helped me to complete it. My wife, Kathryn Kish Sklar, has given this book on every page the imprint of her exceptional editorial skill and critical judgment.

For permission to quote from the writings of F. Scott Fitzgerald I am grateful to Charles Scribner's Sons and The Bodley Head, Ltd., for works published by them; New Directions for *The Crack-Up* by F. Scott Fitzgerald, copyright 1945 by New Directions, reprinted by permission of the publisher; Random House, Inc., for the preface to *The Great Gatsby*, Modern Library Edition, copyright 1934 by The Modern Library, Inc.; and Harold Ober Associates, Inc., for all other published and unpublished writings.

For permission to quote from copyrighted works of authors other than Fitzgerald I have to thank the following: Doubleday & Company, Inc., for *The Birth of Tragedy* and *The Genealogy of Morals* by Friedrich Nietzsche and *A Parody Outline of American History* by Donald Ogden Stewart; E. P. Dutton Co., Inc., for *The Ordeal of Mark Twain* by Van Wyck Brooks and *Salt* by Charles G. Norris; Harcourt, Brace & World, Inc., for *Dickens, Dali and Others* by George Orwell; Harper & Row, Publishers, Inc., for *Seventeen* by Booth Tarkington; The Belknap Press of Harvard University Press for *John Keats* by Walter Jackson Bate; Houghton Mifflin Company for *The Far Side of Paradise* by Arthur Mizener; Alfred A. Knopf, Inc., for *William Faulkner* by Irving Howe, *The Letters of H. L. Mencken* edited by Guy Forgue, *The Magic Mountain* by Thomas Mann, translator H. T. Lowe-Porter, and *The Decline of the West* by Oswald Spengler, translator Charles Francis Atkinson; J. B. Lippincott Company for *Booth Tarkington, Gentleman from Indiana* by James Woodress and *Hear Us O Lord from Heaven Thy Dwelling Place* by Malcolm Lowry; The Macmillan Company for *A Vision* by William Butler Yeats, copyright 1938; *The New Republic* for "This Side of Paradise" by R.V.A.S., reprinted by permission of *The New Republic*, 1920, Harrison-Blaine of N.J. Inc.; the *New York Post* for "Flappers and Philosophers" and "The Rag-Bag of the Soul" by Edmund Wilson, Jr., reprinted by permission of the *New York Post*,

NOTES

For the convenience of readers who may wish to refer to Fitzgerald's published writings, where possible the most recent and most readily available editions are cited. A complete list of Fitzgerald's published writing may be found in Henry Dan Piper, "F. Scott Fitzgerald: A Checklist," *The Princeton University Library Chronicle*, XII (Summer 1951), pp. 196-208, and a comprehensive list of criticism on Fitzgerald (through 1962) in Jackson R. Bryer, "F. Scott Fitzgerald and His Critics: A Bibliographical Record," *Bulletin of Bibliography*, XXIII (January-April 1962), pp. 155-8; (May-August 1962), pp. 180-83; (September-December 1962), pp. 201-8. The practice has been followed, in quoting in the text from Fitzgerald's published and unpublished writing, of silently correcting typographical and other minor errors, which, if allowed to remain, only distract attention from primary considerations.

CHAPTER ONE, pages 3-30

1. Malcolm Lowry, "Through the Panama," in *Hear Us O Lord from Heaven Thy Dwelling Place* (Philadelphia, 1961), p. 31.
2. Andrew Turnbull, *Scott Fitzgerald* (New York, 1962), p. 20.
3. James Thompson Bixby, *The Crisis in Morals: An Examination of Rational Ethics in the Light of Modern Science* (Boston, 1891); reprinted as *The Ethics of Evolution: The Crisis in Morals Occasioned by the Doctrine of Development* (Boston, 1900). A list of books by cultural spokesmen for the genteel tradition is provided by Howard Mumford Jones and Richard M. Ludwig, *Guide to American Literature and Its Background Since 1890*,

third edition, revised and enlarged (Cambridge, Mass., 1964), pp. 121-2.
4. Asa Don Dickinson, *Booth Tarkington* (New York, 1914), p. 2.
5. F. Scott Fitzgerald, "Who's Who—And Why," in *Afternoon of an Author*, ed. Arthur Mizener (Princeton, 1957), p. 84.
6. Christian Gauss, "Edmund Wilson, the Campus and the Nassau 'Lit'," *The Princeton University Library Chronicle*, V (February 1944), pp. 44-5.
7. Booth Tarkington, "An Appreciation," in Mark Twain, *The Adventures of Tom Sawyer*, Works, Stormfield Edition, 8 (New York, 1929), p. xiii.
8. F. Scott Fitzgerald, *"Penrod and Sam," The Nassau Literary Magazine*, LXXII (January 1917), p. 291.
9. Booth Tarkington, *Seventeen* (New York, 1916), pp. 26-7.
10. Quoted in James Woodress, *Booth Tarkington, Gentleman from Indiana* (Philadelphia, 1954), p. 191.
11. F. Scott Fitzgerald, "Echoes of the Jazz Age," in *The Crack-Up*, ed. Edmund Wilson (New York, 1945), p. 15.
12. Woodress, *Booth Tarkington*, p. 191.
13. Shane Leslie, "Scott Fitzgerald's First Novel," *The Times Literary Supplement* (November 6, 1959), p. 643, and "Some Memories of Scott Fitzgerald," *The Times Literary Supplement* (October 31, 1958), p. 632.
14. George N. Shuster, *The Catholic Spirit in Modern English Literature* (New York, 1922), pp. 211, 213, 217.
15. F. Scott Fitzgerald, "The Ordeal," in *The Apprentice Fiction of F. Scott Fitzgerald, 1909-1917*, ed. John Kuehl (New Brunswick, N.J., 1965), pp. 82, 84, 86-7.
16. Shane Leslie, *The Celt and the World* (New York, 1917), p. 224.
17. F. Scott Fitzgerald, *"The Celt and the World," The Nassau Literary Magazine*, LXXIII (May 1917), pp. 104-5.
18. Andrew Turnbull, ed., *The Letters of F. Scott Fitzgerald* (New York, 1963), to Mrs. Richard Taylor, p. 414; to Edmund Wilson, pp. 321, 324. Hereafter cited as *Letters*.
19. Shane Leslie, *The End of a Chapter* (New York, 1916), preface, quoted by Fitzgerald in *"The Celt and the World,"* p. 104. Father Fay's intellectual position is expressed in Sigourney W. Fay, "The Genesis of the Super-German," *The Dublin Review*, CLXII (April-June 1918), pp. 224-33, written in collaboration with Henry Adams. See also Ernest Samuels, *Henry Adams, The Major Phase* (Cambridge, Mass., 1964), pp. 580-82.
20. Irving Howe, *William Faulkner: A Critical Study*, second edition, revised (New York, 1952). Vintage Edition, p. 296.
21. Katherine Gauss Jackson and Hiram Haydn, eds., *The Papers of Christian Gauss* (New York, 1957), p. 140.
22. *Letters*, pp. 319-20.
23. *Papers of Christian Gauss*, p. 340.
24. Quoted in Turnbull, *Scott Fitzgerald*, p. 103.
25. Edmund Wilson, "Thoughts on Being Bibliographed," *The Princeton University Library Chronicle*, V (February 1944), p. 54; reprinted in

Edmund Wilson, *Classics and Commercials: A Literary Chronicle of the Forties* (New York, 1950), p. 110.

26. *Papers of Christian Gauss,* pp. 340-41.

27. Quoted in Leon Edel and Gordon N. Ray, eds., *Henry James and H. G. Wells: A Record of Their Friendship, Their Debate on the Art of Fiction, and Their Quarrel* (Urbana, Ill., 1958), p. 245. This collection presents the argument over novels of "saturation" or novels of "selection" in which Wells and James engaged, and which terms have been applied to Fitzgerald's development, notably in James E. Miller, Jr., *F. Scott Fitzgerald: His Art and Technique* (New York, 1964).

28. George Orwell, "Wells, Hitler, and the World State," in *Dickens, Dali and Others: Studies in Popular Culture* (New York, 1946), p. 121.

29. Van Wyck Brooks, *The World of H. G. Wells* (New York, 1915), pp. 91-2.

30. F. Scott Fitzgerald, "Babes in the Woods," in *The Apprentice Fiction,* pp. 133, 140.

31. F. Scott Fitzgerald, "The Debutante," in *The Apprentice Fiction,* pp. 94, 98.

32. F. Scott Fitzgerald, "The Pierian Springs and the Last Straw," in *The Apprentice Fiction,* pp. 165-7, 172-4.

33. F. Scott Fitzgerald, "Sentiment—and the Use of Rouge," in *The Apprentice Fiction,* pp. 145-6, 149-50, 154-5, 157.

34. F. Scott Fitzgerald, "Tarquin of Cheepside," in *The Apprentice Fiction,* p. 122.

35. "Who's Who—And Why," p. 84.

36. Quoted in Roger Burlingame, *Of Making Many Books* (New York, 1946), p. 48.

37. *Letters,* pp. 317-18.

38. *Letters,* p. 371.

39. "Who's Who—And Why," pp. 84-5.

40. *Letters,* p. 371.

41. *Letters,* p. 323.

42. Five chapters of "The Romantic Egotist" are in the F. Scott Fitzgerald Papers, Princeton University Library.

43. "The Romantic Egotist," pp. 32, 9, 16, 34; Ch. V, 22, 31; 32, 34.

44. Brooks, *The World of H. G. Wells,* pp. 91-2.

45. "The Romantic Egotist," pp. 33-4.

46. *Letters,* p. 453.

47. Burlingame, *Of Making Many Books,* p. 67.

CHAPTER TWO, pages 31-57

1. F. Scott Fitzgerald, *This Side of Paradise* (New York, 1920; reset, 1960), p. 209. Hereafter cited in the text.

2. Fitzgerald's inscription to Mencken is in a presentation copy of *This Side*

of Paradise in the H. L. Mencken Room, Enoch Pratt Free Library, Baltimore, Maryland.

3. *Letters*, p. 138.
4. [Edmund Wilson], "The Literary Spotlight, VI: F. Scott Fitzgerald," *The Bookman*, LV (March 1922), p. 24. Reprinted, in a greatly revised version, in Edmund Wilson, *The Shores of Light: A Literary Chronicle of the Twenties and Thirties* (New York, 1952), p. 33.
5. "Preface," typewritten manuscript in the Fitzgerald Papers.
6. Quoted in Arthur Mizener, *The Far Side of Paradise: A Biography of F. Scott Fitzgerald* (Boston, 1951), p. 87.
7. [Wilson], "The Literary Spotlight," p. 22, and *The Shores of Light*, p. 28.
8. "Preface."
9. *Letters*, p. 323.
10. Robert Langbaum, *The Poetry of Experience: The Dramatic Monologue in Modern Literary Tradition* (New York, 1957), Norton Edition, p. 146.
11. "The Romantic Egotist," p. 32.
12. "The Romantic Egotist," p. 34.
13. Quoted in Turnbull, *Scott Fitzgerald*, p. 103.
14. F. Scott Fitzgerald, "The Crack-Up," in *The Crack-Up*, p. 69.
15. Brooks, *The World of H. G. Wells*, pp. 91-2.
16. Langbaum, *The Poetry of Experience*, p. 146.

CHAPTER THREE, pages 58-78

1. *Letters*, pp. 456-7.
2. Charles G. Norris, *Salt, or the Education of Griffith Adams* (New York, 1918), p. 52.
3. Norris, *Salt*, p. 362.
4. F. Scott Fitzgerald, "Poor Old Marriage," *The Bookman*, LIV (November 1921), p. 253. A review of *Brass* by Charles G. Norris.
5. *Letters*, p. 144.
6. F. Scott Fitzgerald, "The Baltimore Anti-Christ," *The Bookman*, LIII (March 1921), pp. 79-81. A review of *Prejudices: Second Series*, by H. L. Mencken.
7. Both lists are given in the footnotes to John Kuehl, "Scott Fitzgerald's Reading," *The Princeton University Library Chronicle*, XXII (Winter 1961), pp. 87-8.
8. *Letters*, pp. 143-4.
9. *Letters*, p. 139.
10. *Letters*, p. 141.
11. *Letters*, p. 391.
12. Quoted in Mizener, *The Far Side of Paradise*, p. 326, footnote 61.
13. F. Scott Fitzgerald, "Dalrymple Goes Wrong," in *Flappers and Philosophers* (New York, new edition, 1959), p. 165. *Flappers and Philosophers*

also contains the following stories: "Benediction," "The Ice Palace," "The Cut-Glass Bowl," "The Four Fists," "Head and Shoulders," "Bernice Bobs Her Hair," and "The Offshore Pirate." Hereafter citations to stories from *Flappers and Philosophers* appear in the text.

14. Fitzgerald's inscription to Mencken is in a presentation copy of *Flappers and Philosophers* in the H. L. Mencken Room, Enoch Pratt Free Library.

15. F. Scott Fitzgerald, *Tales of the Jazz Age* (New York, 1922), p. vii. "The Camel's Back" is currently in print in *Six Tales of the Jazz Age and Other Stories* (New York, 1960).

16. *Letters,* p. 392.

17. *Letters,* p. 144.

18. Ibid.

19. *Letters,* p. 462.

20. See H. L. Mencken, *A Book of Prefaces* (New York, 1917), pp. 63, 88-9. Actually, Fitzgerald's statement to President Hibben is a direct quote from Hugh Walpole, whom Mencken twice quotes on Conrad.

21. Quoted by Charles G. Norris in his foreword to Frank Norris, *Vandover and the Brute* (New York, 1914), p. vii.

22. F. Scott Fitzgerald, "May Day," in *Babylon Revisited and Other Stories* (Scribner Library Edition, New York, 1960), p. 25. Hereafter cited in the text.

23. The Maxfield Parrish advertisement for "Edison Mazda" light bulbs has been reprinted in John Mason Brown, ed., *The Ladies' Home Journal Treasury* (New York, 1956), p. 30.

CHAPTER FOUR, pages 79-107

1. *Letters,* p. 144.

2. "Poor Old Marriage," p. 253.

3. *Letters,* p. 463.

4. F. Scott Fitzgerald to Burton Rascoe, December 7, 1920, in the Burton Rascoe Papers, University of Pennsylvania Library.

5. Burton Rascoe to James Branch Cabell, November 20, 1920, in Padraic Colum and Margaret Freeman Cabell, eds., *Between Friends, Letters of James Branch Cabell and Others* (New York, 1962), pp. 205-6.

6. Knopf advertisement quoted in *Letters,* p. 146.

7. *Letters,* p. 465.

8. James Branch Cabell, *Beyond Life* (New York, 1919), pp. 304-7.

9. *Letters,* p. 467.

10. *Letters,* p. 465.

11. *Letters,* p. 145.

12. *Letters,* p. 377.

13. *Letters,* to Leslie, p. 377; to the McQuillans, p. 466; to Cabell, p. 468.

14. H. L. Mencken, "Books More or Less Amusing," *The Smart Set*, LXII September 1920), p. 140.
15. Guy Forgue, ed., *The Letters of H. L. Mencken* (New York, 1962), p. 195.
16. H. L. Mencken, "Chiefly Americans," *The Smart Set*, LXIII (December 1920), p. 140.
17. *Letters*, p. 463.
18. Rascoe to Cabell, November 20, 1920, in Colum and Cabell, eds., *Between Friends*, p. 206.
19. Fitzgerald to Rascoe, December 7, 1920, in the Rascoe Papers.
20. *Letters*, p. 145.
21. F. Scott Fitzgerald, "The Jelly-Bean," in *Six Tales of the Jazz Age and Other Stories*, p. 27. Hereafter cited in the text.
22. F. Scott Fitzgerald, "The Lees of Happiness," in *Six Tales of the Jazz Age and Other Stories*, p. 127. Hereafter cited in the text.
23. F. Scott Fitzgerald, "O Russet Witch!" in *Six Tales of the Jazz Age and Other Stories*, p. 116. Hereafter cited in the text.
24. *Tales of the Jazz Age*, pp. vii-xi.
25. Data on sales to movies is in Fitzgerald's ledger, Fitzgerald Papers.
26. *Letters*, p. 376.
27. Mencken, "Chiefly Americans," p. 140.
28. *Letters*, p. 466.
29. *Letters*, p. 468.
30. *Letters*, pp. 326-7.
31. H. L. Mencken, "On Being an American," *Prejudices: Third Series* (New York, 1922), pp. 63-4.
32. F. Scott Fitzgerald, *The Beautiful and Damned* (New York, 1922), p. 369. Hereafter cited in text.
33. H. L. Mencken, "The Niagara of Novels," *The Smart Set*, LXVII (April 1922), pp. 140-41.
34. Mencken, "Books More or Less Amusing," p. 140.
35. H. L. Mencken, "The National Letters," *Prejudices: Second Series* (New York, 1920), pp. 65 ff.
36. [Wilson], "The Literary Spotlight," p. 24; *The Shores of Light*, p. 32.
37. F. Scott Fitzgerald, "The Author's Apology," in *Letters*, p. 459.

CHAPTER FIVE, pages 108-34

1. H. L. Mencken, "Taking Stock," *The Smart Set*, LXVII (March 1922), p. 139.
2. Newspaper clipping (N.P., n.d. [1917]), in "A Scrapbook Record . . . ," compiled by F. Scott Fitzgerald, in the Fitzgerald Papers.
3. "With College Men," *The New York Times Book Review*, May 9, 1920, p. 240.

4. *"This Side of Paradise," The Booklist*, XVI (June 1920), p. 312.
5. Advertisement in *Publisher's Weekly*, XCVII (April 10, 1920), pp. 1140-41.
6. R.S.L., "Ernest Poole and Booth Tarkington at Their Best," *Publisher's Weekly*, XCVII (April 17, 1920), p. 1289.
7. Margaret Emerson Bailey, "A Chronicle of Youth by Youth," *The Bookman*, LI (June 1920), pp. 471-2.
8. R.S.L., "Ernest Poole and Booth Tarkington at Their Best," p. 1289.
9. Quoted in "Our New Novelists of the 'Early' Twenties," *Current Opinion*, LXVIII (June 1920), pp. 824-5.
10. Ibid.
11. Ibid.
12. Ibid.
13. "Youth Will Be Served," *The Independent*, CIII (July 10, 1920), pp. 53-4.
14. Margaret Emerson Bailey, "A Chronicle of Youth by Youth," pp. 471-2.
15. H. W. Boynton, "New American Novels: The Individual Bobs Up," *The Review*, II (April 17, 1920), p. 393.
17. "Reforms and Beginnings," *The Nation*, CX (April 24, 1920), pp. 557-8.
18. R.V.A.S., "This Side of Paradise," *The New Republic*, XXII (May 12, 1920), p. 362. Reprinted in Alfred Kazin, ed., *F. Scott Fitzgerald, The Man and His Work* (Cleveland and New York, 1951), pp. 48-9.
19. Heywood Broun, "Paradise and Princeton," *New-York Tribune*, April 11, 1920. Reprinted in Kazin, *F. Scott Fitzgerald*, pp. 50-52.
20. "The Author's Apology," in *Letters*, p. 459.
21. F. Scott Fitzgerald, "An Interview with F. Scott Fitzgerald," *The Saturday Review*, XLIII (November 5, 1960), pp. 26, 56.
22. Mizener, *The Far Side of Paradise*, p. 117.
23. Mizener, *The Far Side of Paradise*, pp. 102, 120.
24. *Letters*, p. 376.
25. Mencken, "Books More or Less Amusing," p. 140.
26. "Sic Transit," *The Nation*, CXI (September 18, 1920), p. 330.
27. "Flappers and Philosophers," *The Literary Review* of the New York *Evening Post* (September 25, 1920), p. 9.
28. Mencken, "Chiefly Americans," p. 140.
29. "Flappers and Philosophers," *The Booklist*, XVII (October 1920), p. 31.
30. *Letters*, p. 378.
31. "Flappers and Philosophers," *The Catholic World*, CXII (November 1920), p. 268.
32. Figures on Fitzgerald's income come from his ledger, F. Scott Fitzgerald Papers, Princeton University Library.
33. Sidney Howard, "Flowers That Bloom in the Spring, (A Bouquet of Younger Writers)," *The Bookman*, LIII (April 1921), pp. 116, 122.
34. "The Gossip Shop," *The Bookman*, LIII (April 1921), p. 190.
35. "The Gossip Shop," *The Bookman*, LIII (August 1921), p. 576.
36. Donald Ogden Stewart, "An Outline of American History, III: The Courtship of Miles Standish, In the Manner of F. Scott Fitzgerald," *The Book-*

man, LIII (August 1921), pp. 505-10. Reprinted in Donald Ogden Stewart, *A Parody Outline of American History* (New York, 1921), pp. 87-103, and in Arthur Mizener, ed., *F. Scott Fitzgerald: A Collection of Critical Essays* (Englewood Cliffs, N.J., 1963), pp. 92-7.

37. *Letters,* pp. 465-6.
38. "The Baltimore Anti-Christ," pp. 79-81.
39. *Letters,* pp. 151, 152.
40. John Peale Bishop, "Three Brilliant Young Novelists," in *The Collected Essays of John Peale Bishop,* Edmund Wilson, ed. (New York, 1948), pp. 229-33.
41. [Wilson], "The Literary Spotlight," pp. 20-25; *The Shores of Light,* pp. 27-35.
42. *Letters,* pp. 330-31.
43. *Letters,* pp. 332-4.
44. [Wilson], "The Literary Spotlight," pp. 23, 25. These remarks were subsequently revised out of the article when it was later reprinted.
45. Louise Maunsell Field, "*The Beautiful and Damned,*" *The New York Times Book Review* (March 5, 1922), p. 16.
46. H. W. Boynton, "Flashlight and Flame," *The Independent,* CVIII (April 22, 1922), p. 397.
47. Henry Beston, "*The Beautiful and Damned,*" *The Atlantic Monthly,* CXXIX (June 1922), pp. 8, 10.
48. "A Dance of the Midges," *The Literary Digest,* LXXIV (July 15, 1922), pp. 51-3.
49. "*The Beautiful and Damned,*" *The Catholic World,* CXV (August 1922), pp. 699-700.
50. Edwin Francis Edgett, "*The Beautiful and Damned,*" *Boston Evening Transcript,* March 11, 1922, III, p. 10.
51. Zelda Sayre Fitzgerald, "*The Beautiful and Damned,*" *New-York Tribune,* April 2, 1922.
52. Quoted in *Current Opinion,* LXXII (May 1922), p. 694.
53. Robert Littell, "*The Beautiful and Damned,*" *The New Republic,* XXX (May 17, 1922), p. 348.
54. Vivian Shaw [Gilbert Seldes], "This Side of Innocence," *The Dial,* LXXII (April 1922), pp. 419-21.
55. Carl Van Doren, "The Roving Critic," *The Nation,* CXIV (March 15, 1922), p. 318.
56. Burton Rascoe, "Novels from the Younger Men," *The Bookman,* LV (May 1922), pp. 304-6.
57. Mencken, "The Niagara of Novels," pp. 140-41.
58. *Letters,* p. 328.
59. *Letters,* p. 329.
60. *Letters,* p. 332.
61. *Letters,* p. 471.
62. Quoted in Turnbull, *Scott Fitzgerald,* p. 341.

63. *Letters*, p. 161.
64. *Letters*, p. 353.
65. Quoted in Turnbull, *Scott Fitzgerald*, p. 113.
66. "The Gossip Shop," *The Bookman*, LV (May 1922), pp. 333-4.
67. Mencken, "Taking Stock," p. 139.
68. *Letters*, p. 159.
69. "Topics of the Times," *The New York Times* (June 27, 1922), p. 14.
70. "The Gossip Shop," *The Bookman*, LV (June 1922), pp. 445-6.
71. *Letters*, p. 158.
72. G.B.M., *"Tales of the Jazz Age," The New Republic*, XXXII (November 1, 1922), p. 257; *"Tales of the Jazz Age," The Dial*, LXXIV (March 1923), p. 311; H. L. Mencken, "Some New Books," *The Smart Set*, LXX (July 1923), p. 141.
73. *Tales of the Jazz Age*, p. viii.
74. *Tales of the Jazz Age*, p. xi.
75. *"Tales of the Jazz Age," The Dial*, p. 311.
76. "The Gossip Shop," *The Bookman*, LVII (May 1923), p. 374.
77. Christopher Ward, *The Triumph of the Nut and Other Parodies* (New York, 1923), pp. 105-18.
78. John Farrar, "To See or Not To See," *The Bookman*, LVIII (September 1923), pp. 57-8; see also *"The Vegetable," The New York Times Book Review*, May 13, 1923, pp. 17, 22.
79. F. Scott Fitzgerald, "Does a Moment of Revolt Come Sometime to Every Married Man?" *McCall's*, LI (March 1924), p. 21. Figures on earnings are from Fitzgerald's ledger, Fitzgerald Papers.
80. Edward J. O'Brien, ed., *The Best Stories of 1924 and the Yearbook of the American Short Story* (Boston, 1925), and *The Best Short Stories of 1925 and the Yearbook of the American Short Story* (Boston, 1926). Of the eleven stories, O'Brien gave two stars to "Our Own Movie Queen" and "Pusher-in-the-Face," and one star to "John Jackson's Arcady," "The Unspeakable Egg," "The Baby Party," and "One of My Oldest Friends." (Three stars was his highest rating, which Fitzgerald up to then had won for "Two for a Cent" and "Absolution.") Fitzgerald himself considered "Our Own Movie Queen," "The Unspeakable Egg," and "John Jackson's Arcady" in the category of stories he "stripped and permanently buried." See ledger in the Fitzgerald Papers. Besides "The Baby Party," he reprinted from those eleven " 'The Sensible Thing,' " "Rags Martin-Jones and the Pr-nce of W-les," and "Gretchen's Forty Winks."
81. Edmund Wilson, Jr., "Imaginary Conversations, II: Mr. Van Wyck Brooks and Mr. Scott Fitzgerald," *The New Republic*, XXXVIII (April 30, 1924), pp. 249-54. A revised version appears in Wilson, *The Shores of Light*, pp. 141-55.
82. Ernest Boyd, *Portraits: Real and Imaginary* (London, 1924), p. 220; Paul Rosenfeld, *Men Seen: Twenty-Four Modern Authors* (New York, 1925), reprinted in *The Crack-Up*, pp. 317-22.

83. Wilson, "Imaginary Conversations, II," p. 249.

84. "The Gossip Shop," *The Bookman*, LIX (August 1924), pp. 767-8.

CHAPTER SIX, pages 135-62

1. Robert W. Stallman, "Gatsby and the Hole in Time," *Modern Fiction Studies*, I (November 1955), pp. 2-16, quoting Fitzgerald's remark in *Letters*, p. 289. Fitzgerald owned an English edition of *The Decline of the West* published in 1927, "F. Scott Fitzgerald Books Returned to Mrs. Lanahan," in the Fitzgerald Papers. Kenneth Burke's translation of the preface to *The Decline of the West* began its run in *The Dial* in November 1924, but that was still too late for *The Great Gatsby*. See Oswald Spengler, "The Downfall of Western Civilization," trans. Kenneth Burke, *The Dial*, LXXVII (November 1924), pp. 361-78; (December 1924), pp. 482-504; LXXVIII (January 1925), pp. 9-26.

2. The best general comparison of Fitzgerald's technique with Conrad's is in Miller, *F. Scott Fitzgerald, His Art and Technique*. For a list of critical studies of *The Great Gatsby* see Maurice Beebe and Jackson R. Bryer, "Criticism of F. Scott Fitzgerald: A Selected Checklist," *Modern Fiction Studies*, VII (Spring 1961), pp. 82-94.

3. See *Letters*, p. 472.

4. *Letters*, pp. 146-7.

5. *Letters*, p. 148.

6. *Letters*, p. 470.

7. *Letters*, pp. 327-8.

8. Quoted by Miller, *F. Scott Fitzgerald, His Art and Technique*, p. 49.

9. Bishop, "Three Brilliant Young Novelists," pp. 229-33.

10. *Letters*, p. 328.

11. *Letters*, pp. 149-51.

12. *Editor to Author*, p. 30.

13. *Letters*, p. 328.

14. *Tales of the Jazz Age*, p. ix. "The Curious Case of Benjamin Button" is currently in print in *Six Tales of the Jazz Age and Other Stories*, pp. 60-83. "Two for a Cent," which appeared originally in *The Metropolitan Magazine*, LV (April 1922) p. 23, was reprinted in Edward J. O'Brien, ed., *The Best Short Stories of 1922 and the Yearbook of the American Short Story* (Boston, 1923), pp. 115-31.

15. *Tales of the Jazz Age*, p. viii.

16. *Letters*, p. 471.

17. Ibid.

18. Van Wyck Brooks, *The Ordeal of Mark Twain* (New York, 1920). Meridian Edition, pp. 217, 236.

19. Wilson, "Imaginary Conversations, II: Mr. Van Wyck Brooks and Mr.

Scott Fitzgerald," pp. 249-54; *The Shores of Light,* pp. 141-55. By "racial ideal" Brooks of course meant "national ideal."

20. Brooks, *The Ordeal,* p. 19; "The Diamond as Big as the Ritz," is in *Babylon Revisited and Other Stories,* p. 75. Hereafter citations to "The Diamond as Big as the Ritz" will be found in the text.
21. Brooks, *The Ordeal,* p. 67.
22. Brooks, *The Ordeal,* p. 66. Mark Twain's novel was *The Gilded Age, A Tale of To-Day* (Hartford, 1873), written in collaboration with Charles Dudley Warner.
23. [Wilson], "The Literary Spotlight," pp. 20-25; *The Shores of Light,* pp. 27-35.
24. Brooks, *The Ordeal,* p. 182.
25. Brooks, *The Ordeal,* p. 39.
26. Brooks, *The Ordeal,* p. 174.
27. Upton Sinclair, *The Brass Check, A Study of American Journalism* (Pasadena, Calif., [1917]); James Harvey Robinson, *The Mind in the Making: The Relation of Intelligence to Social Reform* (New York, 1921).
28. *Letters,* p. 154.
29. Ibid.
30. *Editor to Author,* pp. 30-31.
31. Quoted in Kuehl, "Scott Fitzgerald's Reading," p. 87.
32. *Letters,* p. 159.
33. For *Chance,* see Miller, *F. Scott Fitzgerald, His Art and Technique,* p. 107; for *Lord Jim* and "Heart of Darkness," see Robert W. Stallman, "Conrad and *The Great Gatsby," Twentieth Century Literature,* I (April 1955), pp. 5-12, and Jerome Thale, "The Narrator as Hero," *Twentieth Century Literature,* III (July 1957), pp. 69-73.
34. Friedrich Nietzsche, *The Birth of Tragedy* and *The Genealogy of Morals,* trans. Francis Golffing (Anchor edition, New York, 1956), p. 235.
35. *Letters,* p. 339.
36. Kuehl, "Scott Fitzgerald's Reading," p. 87.
37. Joseph Conrad, "Youth," in *The Portable Conrad,* Morton Dauwen Zabel, ed. (New York, 1957), p. 106.
38. Conrad, "Youth," p. 148; F. Scott Fitzgerald, "Under Fire," *The Literary Review* of the New York *Evening Post,* III (May 26, 1923), p. 715, a review of *Through the Wheat,* by Thomas Boyd. In the quotation as printed in Fitzgerald's review there were several minor errors which have been silently corrected.
39. Joseph Conrad, *Nostromo, A Tale of the Seaboard* (New York, 1921), pp. 300, 319.
40. *Letters,* p. 339.
41. *Letters,* p. 335.
42. *Letters,* p. 337.
43. *This Side of Paradise,* p. 25.
44. *This Side of Paradise,* p. 210.

45. *This Side of Paradise,* p. 209.
46. *Letters,* p. 141.
47. Wilson, "Thoughts on Being Bibliographed," p. 57; *Classics and Commercials,* p. 114.
48. See Edmund Wilson, Jr., "The Poetry of Drought," *The Dial,* LXXIII (December 1922), pp. 611-16.
49. *Letters,* p. 337.
50. Edmund Wilson, Jr., "Ulysses," *The New Republic,* XXXI (July 5, 1922), pp. 164-6.
51. *Letters,* p. 337.
52. *Letters,* p. 339.
53. Wilson, "Ulysses," p. 165.
54. *Letters,* p. 339.
55. Wilson, "Ulysses," p. 166.
56. Edmund Wilson, Jr., "The Rag-Bag of the Soul," *The Literary Review* of the New York *Evening Post,* III (November 25, 1922), pp. 237-8.
57. F. Scott Fitzgerald, "Minnesota's Capital in the Role of Main Street," *The Literary Digest International Book Review,* I (March 1923), pp. 35-6, a review of *Being Respectable* by Grace Flandrau.
58. F. Scott Fitzgerald, "Winter Dreams," in *Babylon Revisited and Other Stories,* p. 123. Hereafter citations to "Winter Dreams" will be found in the text.
59. F. Scott Fitzgerald, "Absolution," in *Babylon Revisited and Other Stories,* p. 144.
60. Wilson, "The Rag-Bag of the Soul," p. 238; "Absolution," p. 141.
61. "Absolution," p. 150.
62. *Letters,* p. 473.
63. F. Scott Fitzgerald, " 'The Sensible Thing,' " in *All the Sad Young Men* (New York, 1926), p. 234.
64. F. Scott Fitzgerald, "Rags Martin-Jones and the Pr-nce of W-les," in *All the Sad Young Men,* pp. 133-60.
65. F. Scott Fitzgerald, "The Third Casket," *The Saturday Evening Post,* CXCVI (May 31, 1924), p. 9.
66. F. Scott Fitzgerald, "The Unspeakable Egg," *The Saturday Evening Post,* CXCVII (July 12, 1924), p. 12.
67. F. Scott Fitzgerald, "John Jackson's Arcady," *The Saturday Evening Post,* CXCVII (July 26, 1924), p. 102.

CHAPTER SEVEN, pages 163-96

1. Fitzgerald's copy of André Malraux's *Man's Hope* (New York, 1938), in which he made his notations on *The Great Gatsby* is in the Fitzgerald Papers.
2. Mencken's warning about Fitzgerald's "dangerous versatility" appears most

prominently in his review of *Tales of the Jazz Age*, Mencken, "Some New Books," p. 141.

3. *This Side of Paradise*, p. 77.
4. *This Side of Paradise*, p. 131.
5. See Mencken, "The National Letters," pp. 65 ff., and Nietzsche, *The Genealogy of Morals*.
6. *The Beautiful and Damned*, especially p. 4.
7. "The Offshore Pirate," pp. 37, 39, 46.
8. "The Ice Palace," pp. 58, 54.
9. *Tales of the Jazz Age*, p. viii.
10. Quoted in Walter Jackson Bate, *John Keats* (Cambridge, Mass., 1963), p. 243.
11. Quoted in Bate, *John Keats*, p. 249.
12. *Letters*, p. 163.
13. *Letters*, p. 164.
14. *Letters*, p. 172. See also Turnbull, *Scott Fitzgerald*, p. 144.
15. *Letters*, pp. 169, 170. William Arrowsmith, trans., *The Satyricon of Petronius* (Ann Arbor, Mich., 1959).
16. *Letters*, to Perkins, p. 168; to Edmund Wilson, p. 340.
17. Perkins to Fitzgerald, in *Editor to Author*, p. 39; Fitzgerald to Perkins, *Letters*, p. 173.
18. Thomas Mann, "The Making of the Magic Mountain," in *The Magic Mountain* (New York, 1961), p. 727.
19. F. Scott Fitzgerald, *The Great Gatsby* (New York, 1925; Scribner Library Edition), p. 36. Hereafter cited in text.
20. This story is told in the standard nineteenth-century English biography, William Wallace, *Kant* (Edinburgh & London, 1882), p. 41. The parallel between Nick's lawn and the symbolism of primitive rites is suggested by the discussion of "archaic ontology" in Mircea Eliade, *Cosmos and History: The Myth of the Eternal Return* (New York, 1954).
21. *Letters*, p. 169.
22. *Editor to Author*, p. 39.
23. H. L. Mencken, "*The Great Gatsby*," in Kazin, *F. Scott Fitzgerald*, p. 89.

CHAPTER EIGHT, pages 197-221

1. *Letters*, p. 166.
2. *Letters*, p. 341.
3. *Letters*, p. 171. Perkins's response to the manuscript of *Gatsby* is in *Editor to Author*, pp. 38-41.
4. *Letters*, p. 355.
5. *Letters*, p. 357. Bishop's review, slighting Fitzgerald and praising Dos Passos as a genius, was Bishop, "Three Brilliant Young Novelists," pp. 229-33.

6. *Letters,* pp. 172, 175.
7. *Letters,* p. 355.
8. *Letters,* p. 168.
9. *Letters,* p. 341.
10. *Letters,* pp. 178-9.
11. *Letters,* p. 357; "The Gossip Shop," *The Bookman,* LIX (August 1924), pp. 767-8.
12. *Letters,* p. 151.
13. William Rose Benét, "An Admirable Novel," *The Saturday Review of Literature,* I (May 9, 1925), pp. 739-40; Carl Van Vechten, "Fitzgerald on the March," *The Nation,* CXX (May 20, 1925), pp. 575-6.
14. "New Books in Brief," *The Independent,* CXIV (May 2, 1925), p. 507.
15. "The Editor Recommends—," *The Bookman,* LXI (June 1925), pp. 469-70.
16. Van Vechten, "Fitzgerald on the March," p. 576.
17. John M. Kenny, Jr., "The Great Gatsby," *The Commonweal,* II (June 3, 1925), p. 110.
18. Benét, "An Admirable Novel," p. 740.
19. Thomas Caldecot Chubb, "Baghdad-on-Subway," *The Forum,* LXXIV (August 1925), pp. 310-11.
20. H. L. Mencken, "The Great Gatsby," Baltimore *Evening Sun,* May 2, 1925, p. 9, reprinted in Kazin, *F. Scott Fitzgerald,* pp. 88-92; see also H. L. Mencken, "New Fiction," *The American Mercury,* V (July 1925), pp. 382-3.
21. Ernest Hemingway, *A Moveable Feast* (New York, 1964), pp. 154-76: The text of Maxwell Perkins's cable to Fitzgerald is in Turnbull, *Scott Fitzgerald,* p. 149.
22. *Letters,* pp. 180-81.
23. *Letters,* p. 181.
24. *Letters,* p. 179. This letter has been misdated by the editor. It properly belongs after the letter dated May 1, 1925.
25. *Letters,* p. 342; Fitzgerald's reference to "boob critics" is in *Letters,* p. 181; his diatribe against Thomas Boyd and naturalistic novels in *Letters,* pp. 183-90.
26. *Letters,* pp. 480-81.
27. F. Scott Fitzgerald, "Love in the Night," *The Saturday Evening Post,* CXCVII (March 14, 1925), p. 18.
28. F. Scott Fitzgerald, "The Adjuster," in *All the Sad Young Men,* pp. 189-90.
29. F. Scott Fitzgerald, "Not in the Guidebook," *Woman's Home Companion,* LII (November 1925), p. 9.
30. Gertrude Stein's and Edith Wharton's letters are reprinted in *The Crack-Up,* pp. 308-9.
31. Louis Bromfield, "The New Yorker," *The Bookman,* LXI (August 1925), pp. 683-5. Fitzgerald's reference to "cheap reviewers" is from a letter to Maxwell Perkins, *Letters,* p. 185.

32. Gilbert Seldes, "Spring Flight," *The Dial*, LXXIX (August 1925), pp. 162-4.
33. Gilbert Seldes, "New York Chronicle," *The New Criterion*, IV (June 1926), p. 171.
34. Eliot's letter is printed in *The Crack-Up*, p. 310.
35. Miss Stein's letter is in *The Crack-Up*, p. 308.
36. *Letters*, to Perkins, p. 182; to Seldes, p. 485.
37. Fitzgerald wrote an account of this incident in an article, unpublished during his lifetime, "The High Cost of Macaroni," *Interim*, IV, Nos. 1 and 2 (1954), pp. 6-15.
38. *Letters*, p. 486.
39. Hemingway, *A Moveable Feast;* Morley Callaghan, *That Summer in Paris* (New York, 1963).
40. *Letters*, pp. 166, 167, 169.
41. *Letters*, p. 484.
42. Tarkington to Julian Street, March 7, 1932, quoted in Woodress, *Booth Tarkington*, p. 265.
43. F. Scott Fitzgerald, "How To Waste Material: A Note on My Generation," in *Afternoon of an Author*, pp. 117, 119, 120.
44. F. Scott Fitzgerald, "The Rich Boy," in *Babylon Revisited and Other Stories*, p. 152. Hereafter citations to "The Rich Boy" will be found in the text.
45. *This Side of Paradise*, p. 104.
46. F. Scott Fitzgerald, "A Penny Spent," *The Saturday Evening Post*, CXCVII (October 10, 1925), p. 8.
47. *Letters*, p. 182.
48. A close study of the development of the novel is Matthew J. Bruccoli, *The Composition of "Tender Is the Night": A Study of the Manuscripts* (Pittsburgh, 1963).
49. William Rose Benét, "Art's Bread and Butter," *The Saturday Review of Literature*, II (April 3, 1926), p. 682.
50. "The Editor Recommends—," *The Bookman*, LXIII (May 1926), pp. 348-9.
51. "All the Sad Young Men," *The Dial*, LXXX (June 1926), p. 521; "All the Sad Young Men," *The Outlook*, CXLIII (May 5, 1926), p. 33.
52. *Letters*, p. 200.
53. F. Scott Fitzgerald, "Presumption," *The Saturday Evening Post*, CXCVIII (January 9, 1926), p. 234.
54. F. Scott Fitzgerald, "The Adolescent Marriage," *The Saturday Evening Post*, CXCVIII (March 6, 1926), p. 233.
55. F. Scott Fitzgerald, "The Dance," in Lillie Ryttenberg and Beatrice Lang, *Samples: A Collection of Short Stories* (New York, 1927), p. 222.
56. *Letters*, p. 392; F. Scott Fitzgerald, "Your Way and Mine," *The Woman's Home Companion*, LIV (May 1927), p. 7.
57. *Letters*, p. 306.
58. *Letters*, p. 495.

59. *Letters,* p. 395.
60. *Letters,* pp. 221-2.
61. F. Scott Fitzgerald, "On Schedule," *The Saturday Evening Post,* CCV (March 18, 1933), p. 16.
62. Gorham Munson, "Our Post-War Novel," *The Bookman,* LXXIV (October 1931), p. 142.
63. Lawrence Leighton, "An Autopsy and a Prescription," *Hound & Horn,* V (July-September 1932), pp. 519-39. Fitzgerald remarked on the Munson and Leighton articles in a letter to Mrs. Bayard Turnbull, *Letters,* p. 433. See also Hemingway's reply to Leighton in *Hound & Horn,* VI (October-December 1932), p. 135.
64. *This Side of Paradise,* pp. 17-18.

CHAPTER NINE, pages 222-48

1. Perkins to Fitzgerald, April 27, 1926, in *Editor to Author,* p. 47. Fitzgerald owned a copy of *The Decline of the West,* Vol. 1, bearing the date 1927, "F. Scott Fitzgerald Books Returned to Mrs. Lanahan," in the Fitzgerald Papers.
2. Harry Salpeter, "Fitzgerald, Spenglerian," New York *World,* April 3, 1927, p. 12 M.
3. *The Great Gatsby,* p. 99.
4. "The Rich Boy," p. 152.
5. Oswald Spengler, *The Decline of the West, I: Form and Actuality,* tr. Charles Francis Atkinson (New York, 1926), pp. 5, 8-9, 25. Spengler's life and thought are discussed in H. Stuart Hughes, *Oswald Spengler* (New York, 1952; Scribner Library Edition, revised, 1962).
6. Spengler, *Decline of the West,* I, 3, 31, 32, 34.
7. Spengler, *Decline of the West,* I, 45-6.
8. "Stripped and permanently buried" are terms Fitzgerald used in his ledger, in the Fitzgerald Papers.
9. Keats quoted in Bate, *John Keats,* p. 249. Fitzgerald discussed the placing of "Crazy Sunday" in a letter to his agent, Harold Ober, in *Letters,* p. 403.
10. "The Gossip Shop," *The Bookman,* LXV (April 1927), p. 234.
11. F. Scott Fitzgerald, "Jacob's Ladder," *The Saturday Evening Post,* CC (August 20, 1927), pp. 4, 5, 64.
12. F. Scott Fitzgerald, "The Love Boat," *The Saturday Evening Post,* CC (October 8, 1927), p. 8.
13. F. Scott Fitzgerald, "A Short Trip Home," in *Taps at Reveille* (New York, 1935; reset, 1960), p. 273.
14. F. Scott Fitzgerald, "The Bowl," *The Saturday Evening Post,* CC (January 21, 1928), p. 100.
15. F. Scott Fitzgerald, "Magnetism," in *The Stories of F. Scott Fitzgerald,* ed. Malcolm Cowley (New York, 1951), pp. 235, 239.

16. Van Vechten, "Fitzgerald on the March," pp. 575-6. *This Side of Paradise* was compared to Tarkington's work in R.S.S., "Ernest Poole and Booth Tarkington at Their Best," *Publisher's Weekly*, XCVII (April 17, 1920), p. 1289.
17. *Letters*, p. 494.
18. Quoted in Woodress, *Booth Tarkington*, p. 191.
19. *Letters*, pp. 494-5. Eight Basil Duke Lee stories were publishing in *The Saturday Evening Post* from April 28, 1928, to April 27, 1929. They are at present in print as follows: "The Scandal Detectives," "The Freshest Boy," "He Thinks He's Wonderful," "The Captured Shadow," and "The Perfect Life" in *Taps at Reveille*, pp. 3-113: "A Night at the Fair," "Forging Ahead," and "Basil and Cleopatra," in *Afternoon of an Author*, pp. 15-69. A ninth story, "That Kind of Party," unpublished in Fitzgerald's lifetime, was printed in *The Princeton University Library Chronicle*, XII (Summer 1951).
20. F. Scott Fitzgerald, "The Last of the Belles," in *Taps at Reveille*, p. 216.
21. "The Rough Crossing" is regarded as directly autobiographical by Mizener, *The Far Side of Paradise*, p. 211.
22. F. Scott Fitzgerald, "The Rough Crossing," in *The Stories of F. Scott Fitzgerald*, pp. 270, 254.
23. F. Scott Fitzgerald, "Majesty," in *Taps at Reveille*, p. 233.
24. F. Scott Fitzgerald, "At Your Age," *The Saturday Evening Post*, CCII (August 17, 1929), pp. 6, 80.
25. F. Scott Fitzgerald, "The Swimmers," *The Saturday Evening Post*, CCII (October 19, 1929), pp. 13, 150, 152, 154.
26. F. Scott Fitzgerald, "Two Wrongs," in *Taps at Reveille*, p. 200.
27. F. Scott Fitzgerald, "First Blood," in *Taps at Reveille*, p. 115.
28. F. Scott Fitzgerald, "A Snobbish Story," *The Saturday Evening Post*, CCIII (November 29, 1930), p. 42.
29. F. Scott Fitzgerald, "Emotional Bankruptcy," *The Saturday Evening Post*, CCIV (August 15, 1931), pp. 8-9, 60, 65. The other two Josephine stories, "A Nice Quiet Place" and "A Woman with a Past," are in *Taps at Reveille*, pp. 132-71.
30. F. Scott Fitzgerald, "The Bridal Party," in *The Stories of F. Scott Fitzgerald*, p. 286.
31. F. Scott Fitzgerald, "One Trip Abroad," in *Afternoon of an Author*, pp. 148, 163.
32. F. Scott Fitzgerald, "The Hotel Child," *The Saturday Evening Post*, CCIII (January 31, 1931), p. 8.
33. F. Scott Fitzgerald, "Babylon Revisited," in *Babylon Revisited and Other Stories*, pp. 210, 214, 215, 229, 230.
34. The stories by F. Scott Fitzgerald referred to in the text appeared as follows: "Indecision," *The Saturday Evening Post*, CCIII (May 16, 1931), p. 12; the remainder in *The Saturday Evening Post*, CCIV: "A New Leaf," July 4, 1931, p. 12; "Flight and Pursuit," May 14, 1932, p. 16; "Between

Three and Four," September 5, 1931, p. 8; "A Change of Class," September 26, 1931, p. 6.

35. F. Scott Fitzgerald, "Six of One—," *Redbook*, LVIII (February 1932), pp. 22, 88.

36. *Letters*, p. 229. The stories by F. Scott Fitzgerald referred to in the text may be located as follows: "Crazy Sunday" in *Babylon Revisited and Other Stories*, p. 231; *The Saturday Evening Post*, CCIV: "A Freeze-Out," December 19, 1931, p. 6, and "Diagnosis," February 20, 1932, p. 18; *The Saturday Evening Post*, CCV: "What a Handsome Pair!" August 27, 1932, p. 16, and "The Rubber Check," August 6, 1932, p. 6.

CHAPTER TEN, pages 249-92

1. The "General Plan" for *Tender Is the Night* is in Mizener, *The Far Side of Paradise*, pp. 307-14, and Bruccoli, *The Composition of "Tender Is the Night,"* pp. 76-82. Bruccoli makes clear that Fitzgerald found his inspiration for the "General Plan" in Matthew Josephson's *Zola and His Time*. See Bruccoli, *The Composition*, pp. 86-8.
2. *Letters*, p. 182.
3. F. Scott Fitzgerald, "One Hundred False Starts," in *Afternoon of an Author*, p. 132.
4. "General Plan," Mizener, *The Far Side of Paradise*, pp. 307-8.
5. "The Rich Boy," p. 152.
6. The most complete study of the early manuscripts of *Tender Is the Night* may be found in Bruccoli, *The Composition of "Tender Is the Night."*
7. Quoted in Arthur Mizener, "A Note on 'The World's Fair,'" *The Kenyon Review*, X (Autumn 1948), p. 701.
8. Quoted in Bruccoli, *The Composition of "Tender Is the Night,"* p. 27. An *American Tragedy*'s critical and popular reception is described in W. A. Swanberg, *Dreiser* (New York, 1965), pp. 302-3.
9. T. S. Eliot's comment on *The Great Gatsby* is printed in *The Crack-Up*, p. 310.
10. Mizener, "A Note on 'The World's Fair,'" p. 701.
11. F. Scott Fitzgerald, "The World's Fair," *The Kenyon Review*, X (Autumn 1948), pp. 569-70. "The World's Fair" is a section from the early manuscript of the novel, when its central character was Francis Melarky.
12. Quoted in Mizener, "A Note on 'The World's Fair,'" p. 703.
13. "Six of One—," p. 88.
14. *Letters*, p. 222.
15. Alex Munthe, *The Story of San Michele* (New York, 1929).
16. *Letters*, pp. 361-2.
17. See *Letters*, pp. 194, 480.
18. *Letters*, p. 179.

19. D. H. Lawrence, *Fantasia of the Unconscious*, in *Psychoanalysis and the Unconscious* and *Fantasia of the Unconscious* (Compass Edition, New York, 1960), pp. 60, 214-15.
20. Lawrence, *Fantasia of the Unconscious*, pp. 132-4, 145.
21. Information on Fitzgerald's ownership of Jung's books is in "F. Scott Fitzgerald Books Returned to Mrs. Lanahan," Fitzgerald Papers.
22. C. G. Jung, *Psychological Types, or the Psychology of Individuation*, tr. H. Godwin Baynes (New York, 1923), p. 421.
23. *Letters*, p. 433.
24. "General Plan," Mizener, *The Far Side of Paradise*, p. 308.
25. Zelda Fitzgerald to John Peale Bishop, n.d., in the John Peale Bishop Papers, Princeton University Library.
26. Fitzgerald's copy of *The Communist Manifesto* is in the Fitzgerald Papers.
27. W. B. Yeats, *A Vision* (New York, 1961), p. 134.
28. Lionel Trilling, *Beyond Culture* (New York, 1965), p. 67.
29. F. Scott Fitzgerald, *Tender Is the Night* (Scribner Library edition, New York, 1961), p. 3. Hereafter citations to *Tender Is the Night* will be found in the text.
30. "Mrs. Burnett's vicious tracts" refers to the works of Mrs. Frances Hodgson Burnett (1849-1924), author of several score sentimental children's stories and novels, among them *Little Lord Fauntleroy* and *A Little Princess*. Mrs. Burnett is studied in the context of her genre in Marghanita Laski, *Mrs. Ewing, Mrs. Molesworth, and Mrs. Hodgson Burnett* (New York, 1951).
31. Lawrence, *Fantasia of the Unconscious*, p. 122.
32. "Basil and Cleopatra," in *Afternoon of an Author*, pp. 58-9.
33. The revised version was prepared by Malcolm Cowley from "the author's final revisions" and published in F. Scott Fitzgerald, *Three Novels* (Modern Standard Authors edition, New York, 1953).
34. *Letters*, p. 182.

CHAPTER ELEVEN, pages 293-315

1. *Letters*, p. 363.
2. *Letters*, pp. 435-6.
3. *Letters*, to Andrew Turnbull, pp. 504-5; to Frances Scott Fitzgerald, p. 3. The *Post* story was "On Schedule," p. 17.
4. *Letters*, p. 247.
5. F. Scott Fitzgerald, "More Than Just a Home," *The Saturday Evening Post*, CCV (June 24, 1933), p. 34. The other stories Fitzgerald wrote while working on *Tender Is the Night* were "One Interne," in *Taps at Reveille*, pp. 294-313; "On Schedule"; "I Got Shoes," *The Saturday Evening Post*, CCVI (September 23, 1933), p. 14; and "The Family Bus," *The Saturday Evening Post*, CCVI (November 4, 1933), p. 8.
6. *Letters*, pp. 237, 241.

7. *Letters*, p. 239. Fitzgerald's revisions for *Tender Is the Night* are discussed thoroughly in Bruccoli, *The Composition of "Tender Is the Night."*
8. *Letters*, p. 241.
9. *Letters*, p. 240.
10. Mary M. Colum, "The Psychopathic Novel," *The Forum*, XCI (April 1934), pp. 220, 223; J. D. A. [J. Donald Adams], "Scott Fitzgerald's Return to the Novel," *The New York Times Book Review*, April 15, 1934, p. 7; John Chamberlain, "*Tender Is the Night*," *The New York Times*, April 13, 1934, p. 17, April 16, 1934, p. 15, reprinted in Kazin, *F. Scott Fitzgerald*, pp. 95-9; Horace Gregory, "A Generation Riding to Romantic Death," New York *Herald Tribune Books*, April 15, 1934, p. 5. Henry Seidel Canby's review was "In the Second Era of Demoralization," *The Saturday Review of Literature*, XXXIV (April 14, 1934), pp. 630-31.
11. C. Hartley Grattan, in "The Literary Caravan," *The Modern Monthly*, VIII (July 1934), pp. 375-7; reprinted as "*Tender Is the Night*" in Kazin, *F. Scott Fitzgerald*, pp. 104-7.
12. William Troy, "The Worm i' the Bud," *The Nation*, CXXXVIII (May 9, 1934), p. 540.
13. *Letters*, p. 512.
14. *Letters*, p. 510.
15. *Letters*, p. 234.
16. *Letters*, p. 237.
17. *Letters*, p. 256.
18. Fitzgerald's four medieval stories appeared in *Redbook* as follows: "In the Darkest Hour," LXIII (October 1934), p. 15; "Count of Darkness," LXV (June 1935), p. 20; "The Kingdom in the Dark," LXV (August 1935), p. 58; "Gods of Darkness," LXXVIII (November 1941), p. 30.
19. F. Scott Fitzgerald, "New Types," *The Saturday Evening Post*, CCVII (September 22, 1934), p. 81; "No Flowers," *The Saturday Evening Post*, CCVII (July 21, 1934), p. 10. The third story was "Her Last Case," *The Saturday Evening Post*, CCVII (November 3, 1934), p. 10.
20. "Show Mr. and Mrs. F to Number—" and "Auction—Model 1934" are reprinted in *The Crack-Up*, pp. 41-62. "The Fiend" is reprinted in *Taps at Reveille*, pp. 314-20, and "The Night Before Chancellorsville" is also in *Taps at Reveille*, pp. 211-15, where in the most recent edition it is called "The Night of Chancellorsville" in the table of contents and "The Night at Chancellorsville" on p. 211.
21. *Letters*, p. 249.
22. *Letters*, p. 252. Citations for the stories mentioned in the text may be found in the notes to Chapter Nine.
23. F. Scott Fitzgerald, *The Great Gatsby* (Modern Library edition, New York, 1934), pp. viii-x. "How To Waste Material: A Note on My Generation" is in *Afternoon of an Author*, pp. 117-22. Frank Norris's "The True Reward of a Novelist" is quoted by Charles G. Norris in his foreword to Norris, *Vandover and the Brute*, p. vii. Fitzgerald's reading of Norris is discussed in Chapter Three above.

24. *Letters*, p. 308. Hemingway's letter to Fitzgerald is quoted in Turnbull, *Scott Fitzgerald*, pp. 244-5. Hemingway's personal reminiscences about Fitzgerald at an earlier period, in the twenties, were published posthumously in *A Moveable Feast*, pp. 149-93.

25. *Letters*, p. 347. Wilson published six installments of *To the Finland Station* in *The New Republic* in the fall of 1934, although the book itself was not published until 1940.

26. *Letters*, p. 417.

27. An undated, unidentified clipping refers to Fitzgerald's speech in Baltimore, a clipping from the *New York World-Telegram*, October 3, 1935, tells about the radio program, both in clipping folders in the Fitzgerald Papers. Fitzgerald's radio drama may have been the anti-war satire published posthumously as "The Broadcast We Almost Heard Last September," *Furioso*, III (Fall, 1947), pp. 8-10.

28. The quotations are taken from undated, unidentified clippings in the Fitzgerald Papers. The decline in Fitzgerald's reputation, when others carried the flapper manner to excesses he did not share, is described above in Chapter Five.

29. Anthony Buttitta, "Fitzgerald's Six Generations," *The News and Observer* (Raleigh, N.C.), September 1, 1935, p. 3.

30. William Troy, "The Perfect Life," *The Nation*, CXV (April 17, 1935), pp. 454-6.

31. F. Scott Fitzgerald, "The Intimate Strangers," *McCall's*, LXII (June 1935), p. 12.

32. *Letters*, p. 261.

33. *Letters*, p. 263.

34. *Letters*, p. 526.

35. F. Scott Fitzgerald, "One Hundred False Starts," *Afternoon of an Author*, p. 132.

36. *Letters*, pp. 528-9.

37. F. Scott Fitzgerald, "Image on the Heart," *McCall's*, LXIII (April 1936), p. 62.

38. F. Scott Fitzgerald, "The Crack-Up," in *The Crack-Up*, p. 72. The three essays appear in *The Crack-Up*, pp. 69-84, but the titles of the second and third are incorrectly transposed. Fitzgerald's reference to the essays as "biography" was in his ledger, Fitzgerald Papers. Further citations from the three essays will be found in the text.

39. F. Scott Fitzgerald, "Too Cute for Words," *The Saturday Evening Post*, CCVIII (April 18, 1936), p. 16; "Inside the House," (June 13, 1936), p. 18.

40. F. Scott Fitzgerald, "Three Acts of Music," in *The Armchair Esquire*, Arnold Gingrich and L. Rust Hills, eds., (London, 1959), p. 87.

41. F. Scott Fitzgerald, "Author's House," in *Afternoon of an Author*, p. 189.

42. F. Scott Fitzgerald, "Afternoon of an Author," in *Afternoon of an Author*, p. 181.

43. "Afternoon of an Author," p. 178.
44. Ernest Hemingway, "The Snows of Kilimanjaro," *Esquire*, VI (August 1936), pp. 27, 194-201. In subsequent printings of the story the name was changed to "Julian."
45. Michael Mok, "The Other Side of Paradise," *The New York Post*, September 25, 1936; *Time*, XXVIII (October 5, 1936), p. 54. Fitzgerald described the person who was his artistic conscience in "Pasting It Together" (incorrectly titled "Handle with Care"), *The Crack-Up*, p. 79. The person is not named, but Fitzgerald's remarks make it clear that it was Hemingway.
46. *Letters*, p. 543.
47. *Letters*, p. 269.
48. F. Scott Fitzgerald, "Early Success," in *The Crack-Up*, p. 90.

CHAPTER TWELVE, pages 316-42

1. This note, found among papers marked "Literary Notebooks" in the Fitzgerald Papers, was not printed with the notebooks but in the notes for *The Last Tycoon*, F. Scott Fitzgerald, *The Last Tycoon, An Unfinished Novel*, ed. Edmund Wilson, in *Three Novels*, p. 163. References to *The Last Tycoon* will appear hereafter in the text.
2. *Letters*, pp. 16-17.
3. "Pasting It Together" (incorrectly titled "Handle With Care"), in *The Crack-Up*, p. 78.
4. *Letters*, p. 560. Fitzgerald's friendship with Paramore in the early twenties is indicated in letters to Edmund Wilson from that period, *Letters*, pp. 328, 332. Neither reference to Paramore is listed under Paramore's name in the index, *Letters*, p. 613. "Fred Paramore" in *The Beautiful and Damned* is a patriot, Puritan, and teetotaler, pp. 261-76. Background information on Metro-Goldwyn-Mayer during Fitzgerald's tenure there is provided by Bosley Crowther's history of the company, *The Lion's Share: The Story of an Entertainment Empire* (New York, 1957).
5. *Letters*, p. 563.
6. *Letters*, p. 565.
7. Letter to Beatrice Dance, [1937], Fitzgerald Papers.
8. Letter to Beatrice Dance, March 4, 1938, Fitzgerald Papers.
9. *Letters*, p. 276.
10. Edmund Wilson's selection from "The Note-Books" comprise a large portion of *The Crack-Up*, pp. 93-242. Quoted passages may be found, respectively, on pp. 181, 180, 179, 178, and 122. Fitzgerald's dog story was "Shaggy's Morning," *Esquire*, III (May 1935), p. 26; Fitzgerald read one of Booth Tarkington's sentimental genteel stories, "Sinful Dadda Little," *The Saturday Evening Post*, CCXII (July 22, 1939), p. 8, with "complete disgust." His comment is in *Letters*, p. 58.

11. *Letters*, p. 81. The Civil War story was "The End of Hate," *Collier's*, CV (June 22, 1940), p. 9; "Discard," *Harper's Bazaar*, LXXXII (January 1948), p. 103.
12. F. Scott Fitzgerald, "Design in Plaster," in *Afternoon of an Author*, pp. 190-95; "The Lost Decade," in *The Stories of F. Scott Fitzgerald*, pp. 470-73.
13. F. Scott Fitzgerald, "Three Hours Between Planes," in *The Stories of F. Scott Fitzgerald*, pp. 464-9; "News of Paris—Fifteen Years Ago," in *Afternoon of an Author*, pp. 221-6.
14. *Letters*, p. 79.
15. *Letters*, p. 588.
16. *Letters*, p. 286. All the Pat Hobby stories were collected in F. Scott Fitzgerald, *The Pat Hobby Stories* (New York, 1962). Arnold Gingrich's introduction to the stories, and a revised manuscript he prints as an appendix, provide evidence about Fitzgerald's motives and his desire to improve his hastily written manuscripts once he had been paid for them.
17. Nathanael West, *The Day of the Locust*, in *The Complete Works of Nathanael West* (New York, 1957), pp. 339-43.
18. The possibility of a new novel is mentioned in *Letters*, p. 269. Thalberg's life and career are discussed extensively in Crowther, *The Lion's Share*, especially pp. 74-8 for his background and pp. 236-8 for the circumstances of his death.
19. Crowther, *The Lion's Share*, pp. 251-2.
20. *Letters*, pp. 32-3, 36.
21. *Letters*, p. 590.
22. Fitzgerald's copy of *Dubliners* is in the Fitzgerald Papers. From other marginal notations and handwritten items in the Fitzgerald Papers it seems clear that Fitzgerald wrote these words during his years in Hollywood.
23. Keats quoted in Bate, *John Keats*, p. 249.
24. Fitzgerald's letter to Littauer, September 29, 1938, is printed with *The Last Tycoon*, pp. 138-41. The primary source of information and insights into Fitzgerald's state of mind, his work, and his plans during his Hollywood years is Sheilah Graham's memoir, Sheilah Graham and Gerold Frank, *Beloved Infidel: The Education of a Woman* (New York, 1958), pp. 173 ff.
25. *Letters*, pp. 419-20. Several years after Fitzgerald's death, Edmund Wilson, writing to Christian Gauss about Princeton's effect upon himself, John Peale Bishop, and Fitzgerald, remarked that the college gave them all "a sort of eighteenth-century humanism." The full comment is quoted in Chapter One above.
26. *Letters*, p. 288.
27. *Letters*, pp. 128, 131.
28. Wilson mentioned his discovery of Flaubert's final revisions in a letter to Christian Gauss, April 27, 1950, in *The Papers of Christian Gauss*, pp. 348-9.
29. *Letters*, pp. 289-90.

INDEX

Murphy, Gerald, 250, 253, 330
Murphy, Sara (Mrs. Gerald), 250, 253

Nassau Literary Magazine, The, 8, 14,
18, 20, 21-4, 26, 32, 51, 65, 87, 121
Nathan, George Jean, 60, 61, 79, 80, 117,
127-8
Nathan, Robert, 121
Nation, The, 111, 113, 115, 116, 126,
200, 297
New Republic, The, 111, 113, 115, 125,
130, 154, 200, 304
New York Post, 314
New York Times, The, 111, 123, 129, 296
Newman, John Henry, 29
Newman School, 11
Nietzsche, Friedrich Wilhelm, 12, 50, 61,
86, 99, 103, 104, 119, 143, 153, 166,
208, 223, 269; The Birth of Tragedy,
153; The Genealogy of Morals, 62, 151
Norris, Charles G., 60, 72; Brass, 80, 138;
Salt, or the Education of Griffith Adams,
58-60, 62, 63-4, 81, 174
Norris, Frank, 60, 61, 71, 72, 73, 82, 83,
84-5, 91, 93-4, 95, 223; McTeague:
A Story of San Francisco, 63, 72, 76;
"The True Reward of the Novelist,"
72-3, 304; Vandover and the Brute, 33,
63, 72, 74-5, 82, 94, 96
Nye, Gerald P., 305

Ober, Harold, 63, 64, 71, 132, 217, 219,
233, 313
O'Brien, Edward J., 132
O'Neill, Eugene, 152
Oppenheim, E. Phillips, 108, 294
Orwell, George, 19

Paine, Albert B., Mark Twain, a Biog-
raphy, 137, 138
Paramore, Ted, 320, 321, 323
Parrish, Maxfield, 77-8
Perkins, Maxwell, 30, 31, 33, 35, 61, 62-
3, 71, 72, 79, 86, 115, 120, 128, 129,
136, 137-8, 148, 149, 150, 151, 173-4,
191, 197, 199, 201-2, 206-7, 208, 209,
215, 218, 219, 222, 248, 252, 253, 258-
9, 294, 295, 296, 298, 299, 301, 302,
307, 315, 323, 325, 328, 329, 332, 334
Petronius, The Satyricon, 174, 189
Phillips, David Graham, 6, 80; Susan
Lenox, 63
Philoctetes, myth of, 23, 189, 280-81
Plato, 18, 54
Poe, Edgar Allan, 53, 252
Poet Lore, 25
Poole, Ernest, 6, 111
Porter, Eleanor H., 108
Pound, Ezra, 207
Princeton University, 5, 6-7, 8, 11, 12,
15-20, 26, 27, 28, 32, 40, 44, 45, 48, 49,

54, 66, 71, 72, 79, 109, 113, 128, 129,
223, 305, 310, 311
Prometheus myth, 146, 155, 160, 172
Proust, Marcel, 154
Public Enemy (movie), 300
Pyne, M. T., 17

Rascoe, Burton, 79-81, 86, 126, 128-9,
202; "Fanfare," 80, 86
Redbook, 198, 217, 245, 299, 300, 304,
307
Remarque, Erich Maria, Three Comrades,
320
Reynolds, Paul, 86
Richmond, Grace S., 108
Rimbaud, Arthur, 298
Robeson, Paul, 305
Robinson, James Harvey, The Mind in
the Making, 148-9
Roman Catholic religion, 10-12, 14, 44,
45, 116, 154-5, 157, 160, 169-70
Rosenfeld, Paul, 132-3, 220
Rousseau, Jean Jacques, 16

St. Francis of Assisi, 311
St. Paul Academy, 5
St. Paul Daily News, 137
Santayana, George, 3
Saturday Evening Post, The, 7, 25, 62,
64, 71, 72, 84, 109-10, 111, 115, 116,
120, 127, 132, 162, 198, 203, 217, 219,
227-8, 234, 239, 245, 293, 294, 295,
298, 300, 304, 311, 313, 315, 317, 319,
321, 324, 325, 326, 332
Schopenhauer, Arthur, 19, 34
Scribner, Charles, II, 82
Scribner's, see Charles Scribner's Sons
Scribner's Magazine, 62, 64, 71, 129, 154,
295
Seldes, Gilbert, 125-6, 204-5, 206, 207,
297-8; The Seven Lively Arts, 204
Shakespeare, William, 24, 78, 107; The
Rape of Lucrece, 24
Shaw, George Bernard, 12, 18, 21, 33,
105, 122, 137, 148-9, 311; Fabian
Essays, 18
Shaw, Vivian (pseud.), see Seldes, Gil-
bert
Shelley, Percy Bysshe, 174
Shuster, George N., The Catholic Spirit
in Modern English Literature, 12
Sinclair, Upton, The Brass Check, a Study
of American Journalism, 148, 149
Smart Set, The, 13, 32, 33, 60, 61, 62, 64,
71, 72, 84, 85, 109, 115, 116, 117, 124,
126, 127
Spencer, Herbert, 237
Spengler, Oswald, The Decline of the
West, 135, 222-6, 236-7, 238, 257-8,
263, 264, 334-5
Stallman, R. W., 135

375